The Religious

BLACKWELL READINGS IN CONTINENTAL PHILOSOPHY

Series Editor: Simon Critchley, University of Essex

Each volume in this superb new series provides a detailed introduction to and overview of a central philosophical topic in the Continental tradition. In contrast to the author-based model that has hitherto dominated the reception of the Continental philosophical tradition in the English-speaking world, this series presents the central issues of that tradition, topics that should be of interest to anyone concerned with philosophy. Cutting across the stagnant ideological boundaries that mark the analytic/Continental divide, the series will initiate discussions that reflect the growing dissatisfaction with the organization of the English-speaking philosophical world. Edited by a distinguished international forum of philosophers, each volume provides a critical overview of a distinct topic in Continental philosophy through a mix of both classic and newly commissioned essays from both philosophical traditions.

The Body: Classic and Contemporary Readings
Edited and introduced by Donn Welton

Race
Edited by Robert Bernasconi

The Religious
Edited by John D. Caputo

The Political
Edited by David Ingram

The Religious

Edited by

John D. Caputo

BLACKWELL
Publishers

Copyright © Blackwell Publishers Ltd 2002

First published 2002

2 4 6 8 10 9 7 5 3 1

Blackwell Publishers Inc.
350 Main Street
Malden, Massachusetts 02148
USA

Blackwell Publishers Ltd
108 Cowley Road
Oxford OX4 1JF
UK

Library of Congress Cataloging-in-Publication Data

The religious / edited by John D. Caputo.
    p. cm.—(Blackwell readings in Continental philosopy)
Includes bibliographical references and index.
ISBN 0–631–21168–3 (alk. paper)—ISBN 0–631–21169–1 (pb.: alk. paper)
1. Religion—Philosophy 2. Philosophical theology. I. Caputo, John D.   II. Series

BL51.R3517   2001
210—dc21   00-069787

British Library Cataloguing in Publication Data
A CIP catalogue record for this book is available from the British Library.

Typeset in Bembo on 10.5/12.5pt
by Kolam Information Services Pvt. Ltd., Pondicherry, India
Printed in Great Britain by MPG Books Ltd, Bodmin Cornwall

This book is printed on acid-free paper.

In Memoriam

David R. Cook (1933–1998)

Friend and Benefactor

CONTENTS

CONTRIBUTORS

Ellen T. Armour is Associate Professor and Chair of Religious Studies at Rhodes College in Memphis, Tennessee. She is the author of *Deconstruction, Feminist Theology, and the Problem of Difference: Subverting the Race/Gender Divide* (University of Chicago, 1999). Her current research mines deconstruction in search of resources for thinking the sacred that can sustain attention to racial and sexual differences.

Kevin Hart is Professor of English and Comparative Literature at Monash University in Melbourne, Australia. He is the author of *The Trespass of the Sign* (expanded edition, Fordham University Press, 2000), *A. D. Hope* (Oxford University Press), *Samuel Johnson and the Culture of Property* (Cambridge University Press), and is the editor of *The Oxford Book of Australian Religious Verse*. He is currently completing a study entitled *The Dark Gaze: Maurice Blanchot and Friends* and has started another book entitled *The Experience of God*.

Dominique Janicaud is Professor of Philosophy at the University of Nice. He is the author of *Le tournant théologique de la Phénoménologie française*, an English translation of which was published by Fordham University Press (2000), and *La Phénoménologie éclatée*, which expands the argument of that book; he is also the author of *Powers of the Rational* (1995) and numerous works in French, including *Hegel et le destin de la Grèce*.

Grace M. Jantzen is John Rylands Professorial Research Fellow and Co-Director of the Centre for Religion, Culture and Gender in the Department of Religions and Theology at the University of Manchester. Her most recent books include *Power, Gender and Christian Mysticism* (Cambridge University Press, 1995) and *Becoming Divine: Towards a Feminist Philosophy of Religion* (Manchester University Press and Indiana University Press, 1998).

Richard Kearney is a professor of philosophy at Boston College and University College Dublin. He has written many books on contemporary European philosophy, including *The Wake of Imagination, States of Mind, Poetics of Imagining,* and *Poetics of Modernity.* He has also published a political study entitled *Postnationalist Ireland,* two novels, *Sam's Fall, Walking at Sea-level,* and a book of poetry, *Angel of Patrick's Hill.*

Walter Lowe, Professor of Systematic Theology at the Candler School of Theology and the Graduate Division of Religion, Emory University, is the author of *Evil and the Unconscious* and *Theology and Difference: The Wound of Reason.* Professor Lowe is currently at work on a constructive Christian theology.

Jean-Luc Marion is professor of philosophy at the Sorbonne and the University of Chicago. His major works include *God without Being: Hors-texte* (Chicago, 1991), *Reduction and Givenness: Investigations of Husserl, Heidegger, and Phenomenology* (Northwestern University Press, 1998), *Cartesian Questions* (Chicago, 1999), and *Idol and Distance* (Fordham, 2000). English translations of *Etant donné, Prolégomènes à la charité* and *De Surcroît* are currently in preparation.

John Milbank is Frances Myers Ball Professor of Philosophical Theology at the University of Virginia. Previously he was Reader in Philosophical Theology at the University of Cambridge and a Fellow of Peterhouse. He is the author, amongst other works, of *Theology and Social Theory: Beyond Secular Reason, The World made Strange: Theology, Language and Culture,* and *Truth in Aquinas* (with Catherine Pickstock). He is a co-editor (with Graham Ward and Catherine Pickstock) of *Radical Orthodoxy.*

Mark I. Wallace is Associate Professor and Chair of Religion, Swarthmore College. He is the author of *Fragments of the Spirit: Nature, Violence, and the Renewal of Creation* and *The Second Naiveté: Barth, Ricoeur, and the New Yale Theology,* editor of Paul Ricoeur's *Figuring the Sacred: Religion, Narrative, Imagination,* and co-editor of *Curing Violence: Religion and the Thought of René Girard.* He is a member of the Constructive Theology Workgroup, active in the environmental justice movement in the Philadelphia area, and recently received an ACLS Contemplative Practice Fellowship to redesign his course offerings along eco-friendly lines.

Sharon Welch is Professor of Religious Studies and Women's Studies at the University of Missouri–Columbia. She is the author of *Communities of Resistance and Solidarity: A Feminist Theology of Liberation* (Orbis, 1985), *A Feminist Ethic of Risk* (Fortress Press, 1990, and Revised Edition, 2000), and *Sweet Dreams in America: Making Ethics and Spirituality Work* (Routledge, 1999). Professor Welch has been on the faculties of Rhodes College and Harvard Divinity School, and has been a visiting professor at Uppsala University and the University of Amsterdam.

Merold Westphal is Distinguished Professor of Philosophy at Fordham University. He has recently edited *Postmodern Philosophy and Christian Thought.* Among his many books are *History and Truth in Hegel's Phenomenology; God, Guilt, and Death* and *Suspicion and Faith.* His recent research has been on Lévinas and on the relation of postmodern philosophy and Christian faith. He has been President of the Hegel Society of America, the Kierkegaard Society, and Executive Co-Director of the Society for Phenomenology and Existential Philosophy, and he edits the Indiana University Press Series in the Philosophy of Religion.

Charles E. Winquist is the Thomas J. Watson Professor of Religion at Syracuse University. He is the author and editor of numerous books including, most recently, *Epiphanies of Darkness: Deconstruction in Theology* (1986, 1998) and *Desiring Theology* (1995).

ACKNOWLEDGMENTS

The authors and publishers gratefully acknowledge the following for permission to reproduce copyright material:

Kierkegaard's Writings, Vol. VII, *Philosophical Fragments*. Copyright 1985 by Princeton University Press. Reprinted by permission of Princeton University Press;

Kierkegaard's Writings, Vol. VIII, *The Concept of Anxiety*. Copyright 1980 by Princeton University Press. Reprinted by permission of Princeton University Press;

Kierkegaard's Writings, Vol. XX, *Practice in Christianity*. Copyright 1991 by Princeton University Press. Reprinted by permission of Princeton University Press;

Martin Heidegger, "Phenomenology and Theology," trans. James G. Hart, John Maraldo, and William McNeil, in *Pathmarks*, ed. William McNeill (Cambridge: Cambridge University Press, 1998), pp. 39–62. Originally from *The Piety of Thinking: Essays by Martin Heidegger*, trans. and ed. James G. Hart and John Maraldo (Bloomington: Indiana University Press, 1976). Copyright James G. Hart;

"The Onto-theo-logical Constitution of Metaphysics" in Martin Heidegger, *Identity and Difference*. Copyright © 1969 by Harper & Row, Publishers Inc. Reprinted by permission of HarperCollins Publishers, Inc.;

"Diachrony and Representation," Emmanuel Lévinas, *Entre-Nous: On Thinking of the Other*. Copyright Columbia University Press, 1998. Reprinted with permission of the publisher;

Jacques Derrida, "Circumfession," from Geoffrey Bennington and Jacques Derrida, *Jacques Derrida*. Copyright University of Chicago Press, 1993. Reprinted with permission of the publisher;

"Belief Itself" from Luce Irigaray, *Sexes and Genealogies*. Copyright Columbia University Press, 1993. Reprinted with permission of the publisher;

Jean-Luc Marion, "The Final Appeal of the Subject," from Jean-Luc Marion, "L'interloqué, in *Who Comes After the Subject*, ed. Eduardo Cadava, Peter Conner, and Jean-Luc Nancy. Reproduced by permission of Taylor and Francis/Routledge. Revised translation by Simon Critchley, "The Final Appeal of the Subject," *Deconstructive Subjectivities*, ed. Simon Critchley and Peter Dews (Albany: SUNY, 1996), published by permission of Simon Critchley;

Dominique Janicaud, "Veerings," from *The Theological Turn of French Phenomenology* as found in *Phenomenology and the "Theological Turn:" The French Debate*, ed. Jean-François Courtine et al. Copyright Fordham University Press, 2000. Reprinted with permission of publisher. Translated by Bernard Prusak.

The publishers apologize for any errors or omissions in the above list and would be grateful to be notified of any corrections that should be incorporated in the next edition or reprint of this book.

INTRODUCTION: WHO COMES AFTER THE GOD OF METAPHYSICS?

John D. Caputo

I   Landmarks

When Hegel said that in his philosophy the "pictorial" thinking that goes on in Christianity at last clears its head and achieves crisp conceptual form, Kierkegaard groaned in pain. When Hegel said that with the advent of his "Philosophy of Spirit," the Absolute finally achieves self-consciousness, Kierkegaard quipped that the Almighty Creator of heaven and earth did not come into the world and assume the form of a servant in order to consult with German metaphysicians about the nature of the divine being. The bite that Kierkegaard took out of the hide of Hegelian metaphysics is for me the beginning of the "end of metaphysics." It is at least the most recent beginning of the end of metaphysics, since the religious project of keeping the nose of the philosophical camel from nuzzling under the tent of faith is as old as the scolding that St. Paul (who seemed to set off a riot wherever he visited) gave to the Corinthians for their misguided attempts to speculate God into the highest heavens instead of trembling before the living God.

After Kierkegaard, Nietzsche would follow and launch a merciless "attack upon Christendom" of his own, for strictly irreligious purposes, of course, or (depending on how you want to look at it) for the purposes of a religion of the earth centered on the god Dionysus. Nietzsche could not think of things mean enough to say about Paul (or Augustine), who were Kierkegaard's heroes. But Nietzsche would have agreed with Kierkegaard that the pale bloodless speculations of the nineteenth-century metaphysicians, and the pale bloodless lives of the nineteenth-century Christian European bourgeoisie, represented a singularly sick substitute and pallid imitation of a robust and passionate "life." If Nietzsche located the passionate life in ancient Greek tragedy and bloodthirsty Roman conquerors, Kierkegaard located it in the early apostolic age when Christians had the fortitude to face the Romans' lions and to make an Abrahamic leap of faith in fear and trembling.

After Kierkegaard and Nietzsche, no major philosopher (there are always local revivals and minor outbreaks) has had the nerve to try metaphysics again, not in the classical manner, and not in such a way as to really catch on. After them, all that was left to do was to pick up the pieces, figure out what had happened, and write the story of the "destruction of the history of ontology"[1] or of the "end of metaphysics."[2] That is the role that fell to Heidegger, the great chronicler and part time undertaker of metaphysics. Heidegger told the tale of how metaphysics had spun itself out, having never been up to its self-appointed task to think the meaning or truth of Being. The latter was a mantle that he, in all humility, felt called upon to assume up by way of a new alliance with the very poets whom Plato, the first metaphysician, tried to run out of town. For better or for worse, Heidegger has described the scene of contemporary continental philosophy within which everyone works, including those who concern themselves with God and religious faith.

Thus, in organizing the present volume, I have taken my lead from Jean-Luc Nancy, who, when guest-editing a volume of the journal *Topoi* some years ago, posed the question, "Who comes after the subject?"[3] What is the state of human subjectivity, Nancy asked his contributors, after the "death" or delimitation of the subject in Freud, Nietzsche, Heidegger, structuralism, and post-structuralism? I have posed an analogous question to our contributors, "Who comes after the God of metaphysics?" or "What comes after onto-theo-logic?" What becomes of God and of religious faith after the onto-theo-logical "first cause" has been sent packing?

For it is clearly not God who is dead, an illusion entertained mostly by academics, but metaphysics's God, the God of metaphysical theology; it is speculative ruminations on God's nature and causal arguments demonstrating God's existence whose health has been recently declining. Thus, in the place of the "first cause," or the "unmoved mover," we have heard of the God (or gods) before whom I can sing and dance (Heidegger), the God beyond Being (Lévinas), and most recently the God without Being (Marion). Even contemporary French philosophers like Jacques Derrida, who writes of "my religion," and Luce Irigaray, who writes of "becoming divine," thinkers who would be counted out as cold hard-hearted atheists by conventional confessional standards cannot stop talking about God.[4]

The talk about God and religion in contemporary continental philosophy bears almost no resemblance to what passes for traditional "philosophy of religion." The latter has typically concerned itself with offering proofs for the immortality of the soul and for the existence of God, and with identifying and analyzing the divine attributes. This tradition, which goes back to the scholastic debates of the high middle ages, is largely perpetuated today in the works of contemporary Anglo-American philosophers, who offer the old wine of metaphysical theology in the new bottles of analytic philosophy. Richard Swinburne alone can fill a blackboard with the symbolic logic of his proofs. All over Anglo-America, logicians and epistemologists, from the Dutch Reformed to the Roman Catholic confessions, hasten to stretch a net of argumentation under faith in the divine being, lest the leap of faith end up falling to the floor in a great crash.[5]

We on the continental side of this divide have sworn off that sort of thing and taken our stand with the equally traditional objection to the ontotheological tradition, voiced in a prophetic counter-tradition that stretches from Paul to Pascal and Luther, and from Kierkegaard to the present, with honorary headquarters in a Jerusalem that is constitutionally wary of visitors from Athens. The objectifying tendencies, the preoccupation with cognitive certainty, the confusion of religious life with assenting to certain propositions, prove to be almost completely irrelevant to anyone with the least experience of religious matters, which beg to be treated differently and on their own terms. The God of the traditional philosophy of religion is a philosopher's God explicating a philosopher's faith, to be found, if anywhere, only on the pages of philosophy journals, not in the hearts of believers or the practice of faith. This philosopher's God is a creature of scholastic, modernist, and Enlightenment modes of thinking that deserve nothing so much as a decent burial.

So who, or what, comes next? After the funeral? The answer, or the beginnings of the answer, lie in Husserl's ground-breaking investigations into the "phenomenological" method, whose "principle of all principles" is to approach things in the terms in which they themselves are given, rather than on the terms which we (read: philosophers) have decided in advance is what they deserve.[6] Let us leave the guns of metaphysics at the door and let God and religious faith feel free to speak for themselves. As the great German mystic-preacher Meister Eckhart said, God desires nothing more of us than that we let go of our creaturely mode of existing and let God be God in us.[7] Let faith, or religious life, or the divine life among us, be what they are, without cutting them down to fit the presuppositions of western metaphysics or theology, which, as Johannes de Silentio once quipped, sits in the window all rouged waiting for the philosophers to come walking by.

It was Heidegger who got this project off the ground. His own earliest work in the "first Freiburg" period (1919–23) was inspired precisely by the task of retrieving the unique and "pre-philosophical" character of concrete life as it was embedded in the earliest New Testament communities, "before" the philosophers had laid hands upon it, a project that eventually resulted in *Being and Time*, arguably the most important work of continental philosophy written in the twentieth century. Later on, after his repudiation of Christianity during his Nazi years, this project was completely inverted: to get back to the primordial Greek experience of Being before it was contaminated by Christianity. But the whole "table" not of "categories" but of "existentialia" in *Being and Time* can be traced back to two crucial lecture courses delivered by Heidegger in 1920–1: (1) an interpretation of the "factical" experience of time in Paul's letters to the Thessalonians; (2) a close commentary on the Tenth Book of the *Confessions* in which Heidegger sketched the structure of "Care" on the basis of a gloss on the very Pauline struggle that Augustine daily waged with himself, which Augustine called the *bellum quotidianum*.[8] While Heidegger always had a healthy, even Pauline respect for the distance that the life of faith keeps from philosophy, for which it must always appear "foolish," he also held, inconsistently I think, that "fundamental ontology" (or later the "thought of Being") was the ultimate "corrective" to theology that in the end enclosed the experience of faith within its borders. That is the basic objection that both Lévinas and Marion would have against Heidegger, whatever their respective debts to Heidegger may be: Heidegger thinks that it is the office of philosophy or "thought" to set down the conditions under which it is possible to speak of the living God. In "Phenomenology and Theology," reprinted here, a work that belongs to the end of the *Being and Time* period (1928), a text that may be taken as Heidegger's final adieu to Christian theology, he argues for the primacy of the formal ontological and existential structures of fundamental ontology over its ontic and existentiell instantiations, among which he includes theology as the "positive" science (it "posits" an existent), not of

God, but of "Christianness" (*Christlichkeit*), faith in the Crucified, which reflected the young Heidegger's interest in Luther's *theologia crucis*. Still, while faith in the Crucified may come "after" the scholastic ontology of objective presence (*Vorhandensein*), it must always remain enclosed with "fundamental ontology" so as not to lose its bearings.

In his later writings, especially in "The Onto-theo-logical Constitution of Metaphysics," which is excerpted below, Heidegger argued that the God who had made his way into philosophy was, as he famously said, not the God before whom one can pray and sacrifice, or sing and dance. God's entrée into philosophy, Heidegger said, was by way of the "onto-theo-logical" project. By this Heidegger meant the ontological project of sorting out the common properties of being as such (*to on he on*), of which God, as the Supreme being (*primum ens*) was the supreme instance and exemplification, on the one hand, and the theological project of establishing God (*theos*) as the first cause (*prima causa*) of all (other) beings, on the other hand. Just as being provides the horizon for thinking of God as the supreme instance of being, God returns the favor to being by providing the cause of beings. This project, whose first form is Aristotle's *Metaphysics*, where "first philosophy" has both an ontological and a theological moment, stretches through the great medieval Christian syntheses of Greek metaphysics with the biblical God, an idea that goes back to Philo Judaeus, and comes to a head in the metaphysical systems of "modernity," of Enlightenment scholasticism, whose illegitimate trespass beyond the limits of experience was criticized by Kant under the name of "ontotheologic." If Kant sought to put an end to ontotheological speculation and to replace it with ethics, Heidegger wanted to open the door, not to a new round of speculation, to be sure, but to a new meditation upon God after, or at the limits of, onto-theo-logic, a God who would emerge from a meditative experience of the upsurge of Being as emergence into unconcealment (*aletheia*), where "mortals" dwell upon the "earth" under the "skies" and before the "gods."

Heidegger had clearly abandoned his interest in retrieving the primitive Christian experience of God and he had in mind instead a very Greco-Hölderlinian and poetic experience, which Levinas rightly declared was "pagan" (although pagans have their place, too). But Heidegger's point about a non-metaphysical God was well made and it applied no less to the God before whom the Jewish psalmist had also sung and danced, even if Heidegger never had an interest in Jews and had lost all his interest in Christianity.[9] Nonetheless, what Heidegger said about the God before whom one dances and sings had a genuinely biblical ring to it, which is where he himself first learned it to begin with. To see the biblical punch this expression packs, we must turn to Kierkegaard and Lévinas, arguably the two greatest biblical or religious philosophers of the last two centuries.

That is why I have launched this volume with a deep draft from the Kierkegaardian well. For it is with Kierkegaard that the contemporary delimitation of metaphysics is set in motion, and for motives that are deeply religious (while following Nietzsche, magnificent critic as he is of ethics and religion at their worst, tends to lead in another direction, which is also useful but not our concern in this collection). To Hegel's outrageous claim that the Absolute reached crisp conceptual clarity in the realm of Hegelian "absolute knowledge," the pseudonym Johannes Climacus rejoined that the Absolute is an "absolute paradox," thank you very much, totally and "*absolutely other*" to thought, the occasion of thinking's highest "potentiation" and deepest passion, which is its passion to think what cannot be thought. A thinker without a paradox is like a lover without a passion, Climacus quips viz., a mediocre fellow (see "The Absolute Paradox"). To Hegel's outrageous claim that "Spirit" is the happy reconciliation and speculative unity of the divine and the human, Kierkegaard posed the category of the "essential offense," of the living contradiction of "true God, true man," and hence insisted on the impossibility that Christ could "directly communicate" his divinity. If we walked beside him on the streets of Galilee his divinity would not only be concealed from our gaze by the "incognito" of his humanity, but we would even be repelled at the thought that here was the God man. The only way this could be communicated at all is "indirectly," which at bottom means by *faith*. Finally, it was Kierkegaard who introduced a completely new way a thinking about time, or rather a very old and biblical way of thinking about time, that was news to the philosophers, which profoundly shaped the work of Heidegger in *Being and Time*. As a Christian "category," time is not the steady beat of now (chronological) time, but the irruptive disturbance of the "*Moment*" ("kairological" time) in which time intersects with eternity and everything hangs in the balance of a decision, a once and for all leap, which we also must "repeat" from day to day, putting our hands to the plow without looking back (Lk. 9:62), in a "forward repetition."

Lévinas had a lot in common with Kierkegaard, although he complained that Kierkegaard was too interested in being eternally happy and it is also obvious that anybody who wants to "suspend ethics" made Lévinas nervous.[10] Lévinas also owed a lot to Heidegger but he never forgave him for his infamous support of National Socialism and he always thought that the "paganism" of the later Heidegger's "divinities" was directly related to his politics and his turn away from the biblical God. So Lévinas redefined Kierkegaard's and Heidegger's projects and reversed their gears, so to speak. Lévinas's idea is to rethink the religious in terms of our obligation to the other, not in terms of becoming happy, and to rethink God, not by way of a renewed experience of the truth of Being, but by getting beyond the anonymity of Being and experiencing the God whose withdrawal from the world leaves a divine trace on the face of the stranger. Lévinas sought to liberate God from the horizon of Being altogether, for Being – from Parmenides to Heidegger – is a creature of the philosophers, an "ontological" straightjacket that philosophers have used to bind up the living God. Lévinas was perfectly prepared to describe what is "beyond Being" or "otherwise than Being" as "metaphysical," rather than as coming "after metaphysics," by which he meant what is genuinely transcendent, thoroughly and utterly "other" (*tout autre*) than our conscious life. He meant an "infinite" that utterly outstrips the limits of our "comprehension," which in the form of the Hegelian "*Begriff*" would seize hold of everything ("totality"). So by "metaphysics" Lévinas meant the *tout autre*, which everybody else nowadays thinks comes after metaphysics, while Lévinas saved the word "ontology" for what everybody else calls metaphysics now, viz., the philosophical discipline which houses the conceptions and preconceptions, the horizons of understanding, that the philosophers want to impose upon things.

By metaphysical transcendence, Lévinas meant something thoroughly *ethical*, which suggests Kant's idea that the genuine content of religion is the Moral Law and that behind visible appearance lies the invisible sphere of morality. For Lévinas, the name of God is not a gigantic semantic event whose unpacking keeps the tenured philosophers employed for a lifetime, but an ethical command to serve the widow, the orphan, and the stranger. The name of God is not something to "comprehend" but a name that demands a response, the biblical "here I am" (*hineni, me voici*), and its whole power lies in the responsibility it awakens in us to serve the neighbor and the stranger. So for Lévinas the sphere of "being" and "ontology" meant the visible and "phenomenal" realm of things as they present themselves to us in a primarily cognitive experience, by which even "phenomenology" itself remains trapped, while the movement "beyond being" has to do with responding to the invisible power of the "other" (*autrui*) who commands us from on high, who solicits our service while all along eluding our comprehension.[11]

In "Diachrony and Representation," which is reprinted below, Lévinas argues that knowledge, vision and cognition ("representation") always come "too late" (diachrony) to encounter the other, that the other has "always already" laid claim to us "before" we are able to catch our breath or catch up with the other. Knowledge is never "contemporaneous" with the other (synchrony), never able to comprehend the other and get the other within its grasp. We are instead laid siege to by the other whose ethical claim upon us belongs to an immemorial past that was never present to us (like the moment of creation itself). Lévinas means that we did not have to be consulted nor was our consent required for this responsibility to the other to obtain. We are always already responsible; we are not asked to "assume" responsibility. This also means that the transcendence of the other is not delivered by an extraordinary mystical experience but is contained in the most commonplace everyday encounter, e.g., in a simple "hello" or "goodbye," in which there is nothing "said" (no propositional or cognitive content) but only the bottomless simplicity of "saying" (living speech, sociality). "Goodbye," "God-be-with-you," "*adieu*" – these are the first words of metaphysics for Lévinas. At the end of this powerful essay, Lévinas says that the name of God comes into our vocabulary in a primordial way, not as the thematic object of theological investigation, but as the name of our always already being ordered to God (*à Dieu*), to the other in the name of God, which lends a metaphysical depth to this commonplace greeting.

Together, Kierkegaard and Lévinas, who constitute something of Jewish and Christian counterparts to each other, have submitted continental philosophy to a salutary shock of something different. They have held the feet of Greco-ontotheological thinking to the fire of a rush of biblical categories – like the uncontainable "thought" of the "wholly other," the category of "singularity," and new ideas of time thought not in terms of the smooth flow of nows but in terms that reflect the discontinuity of creation, as something requiring renewal from moment to moment. In so doing they have renewed contemporary continental thought, leaving buried within it deep deposits of biblical thinking, traces of which show up in the oddest places.

That is why I have concluded the selection of "landmark" texts on "the religious" by drawing upon the works of Jacques Derrida and Luce Irigaray, two thinkers who by the standards of the local pastor or rabbi, not to mention the next annual meeting of the Southern Baptist Convention in Nashville, are officially "atheists." Irigaray could make her own what Derrida says in his ever tantalizing way that he can "rightly pass for an atheist."[12] But if so, Derrida and Irigaray are not garden variety atheists, because the language of religion, God, and divinity is deeply significant for both of them.

Indeed, their atheism, far from posing an impediment to their being religious, is in fact a condition of its possibility, a condition of what Derrida calls – and once again I think that Irigaray can join in – a "religion without religion,"[13] which for them is the best kind. (For one thing, one is spared a good many tiresome sermons, which are heard in their entirety only by insomniacs.)

I have reproduced here a selection from Derrida's hauntingly beautiful, enigmatic, and formidably difficult *Circumfession*, an autobiographical piece in fifty-nine "periphrases" or aphoristic diary entries, that Derrida wrote in 1989, his fifty-ninth year, while his mother was dying a slow death in Nice. Upon the body of this stunning text are grafted numerous passages from Augustine's *Confessions*, in Latin, so that the text evokes the image of a Derrida as a slightly atheistic Jewish Augustine, a "little black and Arab Jew," growing up on the *rue Saint Augustin* in the Franco-Christian colony of Algeria which is the historical homeland of Augustine (Thagaste is about a hundred miles from Algiers). To hear Augustine's Latin is to hear the language in which the Vichy government issued an official declaration limiting the number of Jews in public school which sent Derrida home from the Lycée during the war. Now, like Augustine, having crossed the Mediterranean for the mother country (France/Rome), as his mother (Georgette/Monica) lies dying in Nice/Ostia, he, the son of these tears, inscribes his *circumfessions*, the confessions of a circumcised Jew in "Christian Latin French." It is in this context that we hear the startling confession of "my religion about which nobody understands anything, any more than does my mother who asked other people ... if I still believed in God ... but she must have known that the constancy of God in my life is called by other names" (#30). The failure to take heed of his religion, Derrida says, has caused him to be read "less and less well over almost twenty years." What religion? What God? What a surprise! We knew nothing of this! Derrida's religion is, to summarize a subtle point all too brutally, his passion for the impossible, his praying and weeping, in imitation of the prayers and tears of St. Augustine, over the justice to come, or the hospitality to come, or the gift, or even the "messianic" future. Derrida at prayer, asking "what do I love when I love my God?," Derrida's religion – that is the radical novelty of this text which is, for our purposes, the central text in any possible attempt to think about God "after metaphysics," the God "*Ja*-weh," to follow the pun of Angelus Silesius, the God of yes (*Ja*), of the "come, *oui, oui*," to the future, which, like the end of the Book of Revelation, is Derrida's most fundamental prayer.[14]

Pursuing a different but complementary direction Luce Irigaray has also made a place for a God before whom we can dance and sing. "But can a mortal still sing?," she asks towards the end of "Belief Itself," which is reproduced below. Have mortals saved the breath to sing before the god, or to mingle their voice with the "divine breath"? Do they dare breathe a song to the breath of life, to life's holy spirit? Can living things, beings of flesh and blood, find a divine element, a divine air or "sacred ether" in which to sing and breathe? Or has all this been forgotten in their awful pursuit of safety and shelter? In order to break out into the open of this air of divinity, the open air of the divine milieu, Irigaray seeks nothing less than to reshape our "imaginary," to displace the phallic imaginary to which Freud erected a great and tall monolith, whether by this we mean the imaginary of God the Father of traditional monotheism, or of the father as God, Freud's psychoanalytic critique of religion, which turns on the same patriarchal axis as the religion it critiques. In its place Irigaray describes a feminine imaginary that goes back to our "natality," to the womb of life, to the great, encompassing, liquid sea from which we emerge by a traumatic and painful separation. To this end, Irigaray takes several clues from Heidegger. (1) If each "epoch" is assigned its own unique question, our fundamental question today is that of sexual difference. (2) If the violence of control and manipulation, the "*Gestell,*" is always the problem, and if the *Gestell* is always the issue of an "oblivion," Irigaray identifies an oblivion with which Heidegger himself is complicitous, and Lévinas too, and mainstream male philosophers from Plato to the present. They have forgotten their natality, their flesh, the first gasp of air they drew at the moment of birth, which they continue to forget with every breath they take. They have to a man forgotten that they are born of woman, flesh of flesh. They forget and repress her, the mother, except to reappropriate her in the service of their project, their projection, their erection, in order to assert their auto-erect autarchy, to make themselves as safe and sheltered as they once were but can never be again. But like all repression this ultimately issues in more violence. What our times require is a recollective thinking, but one that would recall the pain of this initial separation, that would "confess" our natality, our limits and the humility of our fleshly condition, in order to learn to mingle one's song with the divine breath. In a commentary that reads Heidegger against Heidegger, Irigaray goes back to the exquisite verse from Angelus Silesius, "the rose is without why," which is the subject of a very remarkable commentary by Heidegger in *The Principle of Reason*.[15] Irigaray insists upon the *flesh* of the rose as a dimension that Heidegger omits.

"Belief Itself," which is Irigaray's contribution to a 1980 colloquium at Cerisy-la-Salle on Jacques Derrida, and also the point of departure for her *The Forgetting of Air in Martin Heidegger* (1983), takes its lead from Derrida's discussion in the *Post Card* of the *fort-da* story in Freud. When Derrida notices that Ernst is not throwing the reel from the bed but into the bed (the bed is *fort*) through the curtains surrounding the bed, this opens up for Irigaray a reinterpretation of this scene in terms of the womb, placental veil, and umbilical cord, which leads us to the lyrical conclusion on mingling one's song with the divine breath. The essay is nicely analyzed for us in the studies done by Ellen Armour and Grace Jantzen below, who take it as their point of departure.

II   The Contemporary Essays

The ancient demand of the religious heart that is voiced by Meister Eckhart – to give up our own will and let God be God in us – and taken up again variously by Kierkegaard, Heidegger, Lévinas, Derrida, and Irigaray, each in their own way, has been made today in a sharp and incisive way by Jean-Luc Marion. So I begin the contemporary essays with a study by Marion, the most important religious thinker in current continental philosophy and the architect of a radically new and controversial version of phenomenology.

Marion contends that phenomenology cannot be what it is, cannot honor its first and primary obligation to "givenness" (*donation, Gegebenheit*), unless it takes into account "unconditional" givenness, the phenomenon par excellence that he calls variously as a phenomenologist the "saturated phenomenon"[16] or the "gift" and that his religious faith teaches him to call God. Thus when Marion responds to Nancy's question, "who comes after the subject?.," in the essay we have reproduced below, "The Final Appeal of the Subject," by answering, the one who is laid claim to by the gift of an unconditional call, he is also responding to *our* question, "who comes after the God of metaphysics?" Marion argues that Dasein in *Being and Time* is not the true successor to the subject because there is something subjective still about Dasein's anticipatory resoluteness. This constitutes the radical "autarky" (*autarcie*) of an autonomous Self, standing alone before death, which overcomes the epistemological subject only by reinstating another, more radical, existential subject. The very success and power of this figure of the autarchic Self lies in the fact that Dasein completes the circuit of its Being by being both the caller and the called. This blocks the way to Being, since Dasein cannot, as such, appeal to anything other than itself, while Being, if there is any, would break into and break up this circuit. If, in his later writings, Heidegger lets Dasein be claimed by Being (*Anspruch des Seins*), that is at the cost of this autarky, which is perhaps why these later writings speak of "human beings" (*Mensch*) rather than of Dasein, which is the very name of autarky. This *Mensch*, which comes after the autarchic Self, which comes after the epistemological subject, which "succeed[s] the subject without still inheriting subjecti(vi)ty", is called by Heidegger *der Angesprochene*, which Marion translates "*l'interloqué*," the one who is "interpellated" or "interlocuted," the one upon whom claim is made.

In Marion's "interlocuted" one can also hear echos of Lévinas's "accused" or "persecuted" because when the subject is claimed, its proper response is not "I" but Lévinas's "me," *me voici*, see me here, ready to respond, being laid claim to and orphaned of transcendental agency. The interlocuted is divested of autarky, surprised from the ground up, summoned as before a judge. But then who or what is the agency that claims the interlocuted? Is it conscience (Kant)? The Other One (*autrui*) (Lévinas)? Being (Heidegger)? God? But as soon as this question is answered, or even posed, as soon as the caller is determined, the interlocuted reassumes control of its destiny, becomes synchronous with the caller, and the subject has been reinstated. However, "according to the order of phenomenological description," I can at least say that I know myself as claimed by something I-know-not-what. The very "confusion" and "indeterminacy" of this "anonymous a priori" do not weaken the claim but rather testify to it and assure that it comes as a surprise, as the first wound of the subject.

In *Reduction and Givenness* Marion develops his position in terms of three successive, more radical "phenomenological reductions" which turn on the maxim: "so much reduction, so much givenness," the stricter and more rigorous a reduction is made of the subject and subjective conditions, the more ample and unconditional the field of givenness.[17] By minimizing the subjective contribution and maximizing givenness, we reach a point of unconditional givenness where the subject has disappeared as a subject and been displaced by the "interlocuted." (1) In the "transcendental" reduction, adumbrated by Descartes and Kant but brought to perfection by Husserl, a reduction is made to the intentional subject, to the pure noetic stream of subjective processes, in which intentional "objects" of experience are formed or "constituted." Everything transcendent and metaphysical is excluded in order to let the experienced object be "given" as such. (2) But this first reduction leaves standing the vast armature of transcendental subjectivity, of a primarily cognitive "consciousness" looking on a world of standing "objects." In *Being and Time* Heidegger exposed the presuppositions of intentional consciousness and proposed in its place what Marion calls the "existential reduction," which is outlined in "The Final Appeal of the Subject," in which the radically engaged structure of Dasein as being-in-the-world and "care" emerges in the place of Husserl's abstract epistemological and intentional subject and the thin or "flat" "objects" of transcendental philosophy.

(3) But the second reduction leaves standing the upright "autarkical" existential subject itself, resolute and self-possessed Dasein who answers to its own inner call of conscience, and this blocks the flow of givenness and maintains the world within the measure of the fore-structures of Dasein's understanding. Thus a third and still more radical "reduction" is required in which both the transcendental and existential subject are reduced, in order to let what gives itself be unconditionally given, be what it is, or more than it "is," in all its uncontainable and saturating profusion. Such a "subject" then is nothing subjective, neither constituting nor resolute, no longer marching to the beat of its own inner call, but now entirely and radically responsive to the call of unconditional givenness, of what gives itself to us unconditionally. This call cannot be identified – as the Father or Yahweh – but comes as the pure form of calling itself, without further determination or constriction. If the first reduction is made to the transcendental subject, and the second to the existential subject, the third is made to what comes after the subject, to something purely "interlocuted," to a pure auditor called up by and laid claim to by the pure form of the call. If the first reduction releases the appearance of "objectivity," and the second the phenomenon of Being, the third reduction lead us back beyond Being to the "gift" of "unconditioned givenness" itself in the figure of the pure form of the call. With the absolute and unconditional "givenness" of what is given at this point, we reach the limits of "phenomenology." The eyes and ears of phenomenology are bedazzled and confused by an uncontainable and saturating phenomenon; to take a step further requires faith and theology, whose office is it to clarify that we are here addressed by the gift of a giving God, the giver of all good gifts, and the one who calls Israel to hear (Deut. 6:4). Marion thus holds to a correlational method of his own, one in which the results of a phenomenology more radically pursued but still remaining within its own methodological boundaries are correlative to what theology and faith calls God or the address of God to his people, which can then name what leaves phenomenology speechless.

All this is just too much to bear for Dominique Janicaud. Rather than a "corre-lation" Janicaud sees a "hi-jacking" of recent French phenomenology by Marion, but first of all by Lévinas, after having been dominated early on by very un-theological figures like Jean-Paul Sartre. Instead of a phenomenology that remains rigorously loyal to what presents itself just insofar as and strictly within the methodological limits of what presents itself, phenomenology is now being led by the nose of transparently theological presuppositions which set out from the start to turn phenomenological givenness into the gift of God's own self-giving, as Marion's life long interest in mystical theology testifies. Just so, Husserl must have flipped in his grave when Lévinas proposed the idea of an infinity that traumatizes the subject, exceeds the limits of appearance and overwhelms the correlative subjective acts that are requisite for the appearance of any phenomenon. Whoever the God may be who comes after metaphysics, he has no business showing up at phenomenology's door. Janicaud published this argument in a polemical essay entitled *The Theological Turn of French Phenomenology*, which tracks this theological seizure of phenomenology from Lévinas through Marion, Jean-Louis Chrétien, and Michel Henry. Janicaud is careful to grant that phenomenology must come to grips with a certain alterity and excess of experience, a certain "invisibility."[18] But he insists that this invisibility must always be woven into experience itself, as Merleau-Ponty's work on the "intertwining" of the visible and the invisible shows: "not an absolute invisible . . . but an invisible *of* this world."[19] Merleau-Ponty's caution stands in stark contrast to the audacity of Lévinas, for whom the invisible assumes the form of metaphysical transcendence and is the issue of a patently theological desire for the biblical God.

In the excerpt that follows, which is the chapter that discusses Marion, Janicaud contests the methodological and disciplinary rigor of Marion's "pure form of the call" in *Reduction and Givenness* which flatly contradicts the rightful and cautious exclusion of such pure transcendence by Husserl in *Ideas I*. It is too simple to say that phenomenology, either in Hegel or in the "transcendental reduction" of Husserl, represents a simple exit out of metaphysics, Janicaud argues, even as one must question whether what the later Heidegger calls "thinking" (not "phenomenology") is properly understood in terms of a deepening of phenomenology's "reductions" rather than as simply moving past any use of "reduction." Thus it is a questionable trajectory that leads up to the third and still more questionable "pseudo-reduction" whose outcome is a completely attenuated phenomenality, a "dry mystical night," an empty and vacuous non-phenomenon that takes leave not only of phenomenology but also of common sense, a structure that Marion himself describes as given in and as a state of "confusion." The incoherence of this phenomenon that is "not yet manifest" is not disguised, Janicaud contends, by invoking the cover of a "phenomenology of the unapparent," an expression borrowed by Marion from Heidegger[20] to describe the new phenomenology. For Janicaud it is used as an "alibi" for incoherence: a givenness that cannot be given, a phenomenon that cannot appear, a structure stripped down to the nakedness of a pure and empty form.

This interesting debate raises at least two questions. (1) Janicaud has no antipathy to theology and he does not insist on a "strict observance" Husserlianism; phenomenology, he rightly says, does not belong to Husserl or to anyone else. Furthermore, he admits that phenomenology is not the whole of philosophy, that it has its limits, and that there is room for the separate demands of faith and theology, so long as they are not allowed to dictate the agenda of phenomenology itself. How far removed is he then from Marion's own position when Marion concedes that with the saturated phenomenology we reach the limits of phenomenology and experience the need for faith in order to take another step forward and give words to our experience? (2) That leads to another and closely related question: while Janicaud and Marion agree that this experience is one of "confusion," is its confusion a function of profusion, which invites a theological "clarification" (Marion), or of vacuity, which does not (Janicaud)? How would we set about deciding that? Or is the "undecidability" final?

The next three essays variously take their point of departure from Derrida whose delimitation of metaphysical conceptuality is essential to their attempts to push beyond the God of metaphysics. In a very rich essay that includes illuminating discussions of

Heidegger, Lévinas, Barth, Rahner, and Jungel, Kevin Hart approaches this question in terms of what he calls an "experience" of God, where experience has not the subjectivistic sense of a private *Erlebnis* but the more robust sense of an encounter (*Erfahrung*) with something other. Experience for Hart is not modeled after Marion's saturated phenomenon but is closely to what he calls, following Derrida, an "interruption," that is, something that breaches our settled horizons. An "experience" for Hart does not confirm us in our sense of presence but disconfirms our expectations and exposes us to something that is withdrawn, which is why he says that the experience of God is also something of a non-experience. I am interrupted by a "call" that ought not to be reduced to ethics, however much we have to learn from Lévinas, but includes an experience of the natural world as God's handiwork, a solicitation by the natural world which addresses us, like Augustine's creatures singing in chorus "he made us." Taking his lead in this essay from Karl Rahner, Hart envisages an experience of God that includes both a horizontal dimension, a world-horizon of experience, and a certain vertical breaching of these horizons by something that disturbs them and that solicits us from afar. Does this breach of horizon also "saturate" them? – Marion would want to know.

Like the Australian Hart, Irish philosopher Richard Kearney is also interested in the experience of interruption. Using a phrase of Derrida's that they both can embrace, to experience God is to experience the possibility of the impossible. In "Eschatology of the Possible God," Kearney searches for a post-metaphysical God of whom the best thing we may say is not that God "is," but rather that God "may be." Like Heidegger, who said in *Being and Time* that possibility is higher than actuality,[21] who also did not think that phenomenology was Husserl's private property, Kearney seeks an "eschatological" understanding of possibility that paves the way to a new understanding of God in terms of "the possible." This expression is freed from the traditional metaphysical idea of the possible as something lower or imperfect that requires actualization, a "potency" that is always excluded from God. Kearney first reviews the sense of potency in Husserl (the goal of possible fulfillment of an ideal limit or telos), Bloch (the dialectical principle of hope, the magnet that draws us toward the dream of peace and justice that animates all great art and religion), and Heidegger's notion of the quiet power of the possible, a text from *Being and Time* that Heidegger takes up in *A Letter on Humanism*, where it is taken to mean the loving-giving of Being itself, which plays on "loving" or liking (*mögen*) and being able to (*vermögen*). Kearney's argument comes to a head when he takes up a recent piece by Derrida entitled "*Comme si c'était possible*, 'within such limits,'" and in so doing Kearney comes closer to Derrida than in any previous writing of his. The "perhaps" is the necessary condition of possibility of every experience, which arises from the unpredictable otherness of the future, of the possible as the impossible. The "im-" of "impossible" does not mean denial or negation but something that *im*pels beyond our own possibilities *into* the possibility of the impossible or what Kearney calls the "more than impossible."

Mark Wallace also makes use of the work of Derrida to move beyond the God of onto-theo-logic but in a quite different direction, viz., to expose what he calls "the green face of God" or the "Earth God." By this Wallace means an eco-theology which turns on rethinking the pure or absolute "Spirit" of onto-theo-logic, and rereading the biblical texts in terms of the elements of fire, air, earth, and water, an undertaking that would of course be very congenial to Irigaray as well. The ontotheological tradition pits spirit against matter, soul against body, in a series of binary oppositions whose most inglorious moment – *pace* the Augustinians whose papers appear later on – is Augustine's famous argument that sexual desire is a sign that the entire physical world groans under God's judgment. Derrida has loosened theology's tongue in this regard, inspiring it with a salutary distrust of the metaphysical names of God and opening up the possibility of a faith or even a religion purged of its desire for metaphysical security. Far removed from the unfeeling unmoved mover of ontotheology, the Earth God is the subject of the Bible's "green pneumatology," a healing life force and life-giving breath who animates all things. The spirit is the air that animates things, the water that refreshes us, the fire that ignites our spirit, and various earthen things like a dove or an olive tree. The Spirit on Wallace's account is always underfoot as the earth that sustains us. These are not symbols of Spirit, but the way the Spirit is enfleshed and dwells among us.

The next three essays take their point of departure for thinking about God and religion after ontotheologic from the work of Luce Irigaray, and the essay by Winquist that follows them belongs to her ambiance. What would happen to religion, what sort of religion would emerge, each of these thinkers asks, if instead of forgetting and repressing the pain of the primal separation from the maternal flesh, which lies at the heart of classical ontotheologic, according to Irigaray, we were to acknowledge and confront our loss?

Taking her lead from Irigaray's "Belief Itself," the essay we have reproduced in this collection, Ellen Armour argues that there is a complicity among phallocentrism, logocentrism, and ontotheologic, so that no attempt to circumvent ontotheologic can succeed if it still remains in the grips of phallocentrism. So even if we grant the claim made by Jean-Luc Marion that the "death of God" is the death of philosophy's God which opens the way to the truly Christian God, preeminently realized, according to *God without Being*, in the Eucharist (the Eucharist is also important for the "radical orthodoxists"), it remains the case, Armour contends with Irigaray, that the Christian and specifically Eucharistic God is phallocentrically conceived and as such is still inscribed within the economy of onto-theologic. This claim is based on Irigaray's contention that a central, perhaps the central figure of the western cultural imaginary is the unmourned and unacknowledged sacrifice of the maternal body which is masked under the Eucharistic sacrifice of the son. The work of "belief itself" is to maintain this mask and obscure the feminine body it conceals. This interpretation rests on a complex analysis offered by Irigaray which compares Freud's analysis of the *fort/da* game with a female analysand who presented to Irigaray with the symptom of bleeding at the consecration of the Eucharist, as if it were her body and blood being sacrificed, and this even if she were not attending mass. But if we expose the masking operation performed by belief and acknowledge our mourning for the maternal body, we will recover religion, not as a system of beliefs but in its material practices. That is the role that Derrida's *Circumfession* plays for Armour, where the loss of the maternal body is not obscured but thematized as the source of his writing, where this body is not mastered but acknowledged in Derrida's moving discourse on the open sores and wounded body of his dying mother. Thus instead of a religion that turns on a masculine subject, whose strong belief in his transcendence over death arises from his personal relationship to God, man to man, Armour invokes "another sacrality" where loss is acknowledged, where our only companions are angels and roses, without the consolations of "belief," where we are invited to put ourselves at risk in order to encounter the other.

Grace Jantzen's essay, "'Barely by a breath…': Irigaray on Rethinking Religion," takes up "Belief Itself," in terms of the dialogue not with Derrida but with Heidegger, whose "recalling of Being" subsists in a "forgetting of air." By privileging the solid earth, Heidegger's thought turns on a classical ontotheological idea of transcendence as standing erect on the earth that forgets birth, mother, body, and blood, in short, sexual difference. Dasein's "thrownness" is, in French, a *déréliction*, a being abandoned to the world in a painful separation that man will not let himself recall. Much as he wills not to will, much as he wants to let the earth be earth, and to let the rose be without why, Heidegger will not let himself be immersed in the primal flood of more liquid flowing elements like air and water that signify the primal sea in which all flesh is born and all life takes its origin. So Jantzen proposes to rethink religion not by thinking divinity away but by thinking our way through to "becoming divine."[22] What would happen, she also asks, if we let ourselves recall this birth? Then instead of repression, we would have a genuine *Gelassenheit* and openness that acknowledges the loss that constitutes the defining moment of our life on earth, the painful parting or parturition of our birth. Then instead of erecting the discourses of mastery, the armatures of belief systems that men devise to control life and death and to keep this pain at bay, the word would be free at last to become flesh and the divine would be enfleshed among us, between us, lovers face to face. Divine love would then be the medium that sweeps the lovers up into each other's arms. This divine become flesh is our becoming divine, which means we can meet each other in the medium, the light and air and ambiance, of mercy and respect. Then we can live like the rose, without why, flourishing in earth and water and air, in unadorned beauty, living from out of the inner wealth and overflowing spirit, *pneuma*, of life itself.

Walter Lowe's effort to think God after metaphysics is directed at securing a post-metaphysical conception of "transcendence," one that comes after the classical metaphysical notion of an "ascent" to the "infinite," which devalues life in the finite here below. Lowe seeks a transcendence in and to the finite itself – where "infinite" would mean not "non-finite" but "in-the-finite" – not unlike the early Heidegger's notion of transcendence into finite Being, transcendence into the Nothing. But it is not Heidegger that Lowe ultimately has on his mind but Irigaray and her notion of the "sensible transcendental," of the finite ecstasy afforded by the sensible world, of returning to the elements. The paradigm for Lowe's second thoughts about transcendence is Irigaray's critical interpretation of the allegory of the cave, the *locus classicus* of the classical account of transcendence, as the womb from which male philosophers have been trying to escape so that transcendence for them expresses a disdain for being born of flesh. This new idea of transcendence turns on a new and positive idea of the finite, not as confining limit, as in Kant's example of the dove that thinks it is confined by the air that sustains it (Jonathan Livingston Seagull, who wants to soar to pure freedom). No soaring airless freedom of the soul from the body for this Irigarayan transcendence, Lowe embraces transcendence as life in the elements, in the enveloping medium in which soul and body "marry." What then is God's transcendence? Who is the God who comes after metaphysics? Not a God of infinite distance from earth and flesh, but the infinite freedom to make Godself immanent, in-the-finite, incarnate.

Charles Winquist reframes the question about ontotheologic as a question about "materiality." For him, classical ontotheologic moves about in a certain innocence of the materiality of thought and language, which means that the movement beyond ontotheologic must take the form of making materiality an object of express theoretical reflection. That would mean that the God who comes after ontotheologic assumes a more material form, a notion also found in Irigaray's idea of a "sensible transcendental," and reflects a sharper sensitivity to the multiplicity of sacred places. To this end, Winquist distinguishes the visible materiality of physical objects, like stones and cities, from the hidden and invisible materiality of "discourse" which thickens the texture of our thought and language and deprives them of transparency. When the great masters of suspicion began to rethink Kant's pure epistemological subject, they launched this project for us. Marx exposed the economic motives that shape abstract thought; Nietzsche expounded truth as a certain species of lying; Freud shocked everyone by arguing that conscious life is shaped by an unconscious sexuality, a project that has been radicalized in our own day by Lacan and Kristeva. Derrida, too, when he redescribes *différance* in the more graphic terms of a place, *khora,* a notion also used by Kristeva, points to the material matrix of thinking. What then of religion? Winquist's point is not to explain religion away but to realize and materialize it, to humanize, situate, and concretize it, and to treat these several materializations as so many gifts. Religion expresses our ultimate orientation to reality, an orientation that shifts from place to place, that varies with the materiality and the "heterogeneous singularities" it holds sacred, and that gives words and practices to our deepest desires. Like love – as Winquist's opening citation from Marguerite Duras indicates. That is why I have "situated" this essay within the ambiance of Irigaray and her divine milieu, the divine mid-place of love.

Merold Westphal and John Milbank think that it is St. Augustine who provides the way back to the future of the God who comes after metaphysics. While Westphal is a more sensitive and sympathetic reader of Heidegger, Derrida, and Lévinas than the "radical orthodoxists," he shares with them a conviction that the classical theology of St. Augustine, forged at the onset of the tradition of metaphysical theology, holds the key to a post-metaphysical way of thinking about God. If Westphal follows the line that leads from Augustine to Kierkegaard, and hence to contemporary continental thought, Milbank follows the line from Augustine into the high middle ages and medieval metaphysics and is antagonistic to Kierkegaard[23] and subsequent post-structuralist continental thought. Indeed, in their contributions to this volume Grace Jantzen remarks that "radical orthodoxy" (Milbank, Ward, Pickstock) is an *Ersatz* version of a "medieval or pre-modern religion of certainties and securities," while Ellen Armour says that Derrida and Lévinas are straw men whom Pickstock in particular has criticized in an "unconscionable and irresponsible" manner. Westphal's orthodoxy, on the other hand, is more liberal or dialogical. Westphal thinks that the substance of the ontotheological tradition is true enough *in itself,* but the tradition from Kierkegaard to

Derrida has shown that *we* poor existing individuals just don't have proofs for all those things. Reality is a system for God, Climacus said, but not for us. Milbank on the other hand thinks that ontotheologic does very well for itself, thank you very much, but it just needs to be restored to its premodern glory, from Augustine to Aquinas, undistorted by Scotus and modernity, failing which we will be abandoned to modernity and its "empty heart."

With characteristic wit, order, and clarity Westphal argues that the terms for the search for the God who comes after metaphysics have been set for us by Heidegger, who warned us that before the *causa sui* we can neither sing nor dance, Lévinas, who warned us not to cut the alterity of God down to fit the limits of our ontological comprehension, and Marion, who warned us about the threat that is posed when the concepts of metaphysics become idols in which we behold our own visage. Where can we find a God who exceeds these limits, who comes after these attempts to contain and constrain the divine excess? By leaping far ahead into the future of Augustine's *Confessions*, a magnificent premodern text that offers postmoderns a view of what is to come. For there, Westphal argues, we find God as the mystery that exceeds the wisdom of the Greek onto-theologic (Heidegger), as the voice that exceeds vision so as to establish a relation irreducible to comprehension (Lévinas), and as the gift of love who exceeds the concepts with which we aim at God (Marion).

For John Milbank, what comes after ontotheology, which is a term of abuse arising from the line of thought stretching from Kant to Heidegger, is ontotheology properly understood, set free from the distortions and misrepresentations of it perpetrated by modernism and postmodernism, the latter being for Milbank but a later stage of modernism. The case in point in this essay is the problem of evil, where the ontotheological account is the Augustinian theory that evil is a privation, which is in fact being defended by Hannah Arendt in her account of the banality of evil, while the "postmodern Kantians" (Nancy, Žižek) hold that the malevolence of the Holocaust requires a theory of "radical evil," of a positive lust for evil pursued for its own sake. The postmodern Kantians object that privation theory provides an ontological excuse for evils like Auschwitz: we can always plead that our finitude made us do it. Were we perfectly plugged into being and the good, which is impossible for a finite being, we would never fall for evil, which is a lack of being and the good. Thus for them, only a will perversely capable of willing evil as a part of its structural make up, rather than as a result of a contingent fall (original sin), can account for such malevolence. But Milbank wants to turn the tables on the postmoderns. By arguing that it is part of the ontological structure of the will to be inherently capable of evil, we can always plead that our radical ontological freedom made us do it, which is one more ontological excuse. For Christian theology (Augustine), finitude is no excuse, because finite being is good, a finite good, not a defect; the defect arises when it is distorted by original sin, which is healed by grace. Indeed, privation theory does not "explain" evil, but finds it inexplicable, and so it does not offer any excuses. The will of itself wills the good, and it is baffling why the will would in Adam before the fall have willed otherwise, even as why we descendants of Adam after the fall should refuse the grace that heals our sinful tendency is just as baffling as Adam's original sin. That is why Augustine says that the origin of evil must be passed over as darkness and silence. The political upshot of this debate, Milbank argues, is to flag an unnerving slide of liberalism into totalitarianism.

When Arendt pointed out that Eichmann had a Kantian respect for duty, she added that it was a parody of Kant. But Milbank argues that, with a purely formal idea of the good, the only practical way to know our will is good is to obey the law of the state, and hence that "Eichmann had it more right than he knew." Liberalism has an empty heart and it is vulnerable to being besieged by irrational cults of race, science, or belief.

I place Sharon Welch's essay last because she refused to take my bait. Instead of answering my question, she puts my question into question, and thus provides this volume with a salutary adieu (if I may say so). She does not want to be drawn into a war between the Ontotheologicians and the Overcomers over what is an idol (ontotheological) and what is truly divine. She will not be tempted into the game of outflanking and outsmarting her predecessors, of showing how the ontotheological still clings to all *their* projects while she alone has found the way to drive a stake into the heart of ontotheologic. She does not believe in any master *coup*, like Barth's Protestant principle, or Derrida's messianic affirmation of justice, or Irigaray's maternal flesh, or Lévinas's *tout autre*, or Marion's *Dieu sans l'être*, or the Augustinian God of the Radical Orthodoxists. All these structures can be used for good or ill, even as justice can be explained in completely opposite terms (justice has just as much to do the "here and now" as with the *tout autre*). Although she admires Grace Jantzen's project, she does not desire God or even want to become divine; it would be enough to become human, "vibrantly imperfect." Her passion is not for the impossible, like the Derrideans, but for the possible and realizable. She does not believe in God, or in the impossible, but in "alchemy," by which she means the power to take something that can serve good or ill and turn it to the ends of justice. The "religious" for her, then, is not a specific content, a body of beliefs, which Jantzen and Armour, following Irigaray, have also argued, but a power of conjuring that transforms quotidian things, a power of wondering at the everyday. Taking her lead from womanist and native American spirituality, she argues that the passion for justice is neither an achievement of ours nor a duty sent from on high, but a legacy handed down like a gift from the generations that formed us. The religious is an ensemble of energies and encounters that, intrinsically amoral in themselves, we try to turn to good. To be sure, this too is one more story, Welch concedes, that is no more likely to lead to justice than any another, one that is fraught with its own perils of complacency, of settling for too little, even as the generations that formed us can also smother us. But it gets us past prophetic denunciations and identifying ourselves with a righteous vanguard that alone knows the way. Instead of overcoming metaphysics Welch wants, in the words of Laura Bohannen, to "return to laughter," which is religious enough. One might say of this "laughter" what Johannes de Silentio says of the Hegelians on faith: they think that they have surpassed it with something serious, while one can spend a lifetime trying to get that far.

Notes

1   See Martin Heidegger, *Being and Time*, trans. John Macquarrie and Edward Robinson (New York: Harper & Row, 1962), §6.

2   See Martin Heidegger, *Basic Writings*, ed. D. F. Krell, 2nd edn. (New York: Harper & Row, 1993), pp. 431ff.

3   An expanded American version of this issue was published as *Who Comes After the Subject?*, ed. E. Cadava, P. O'Connor, Jean-Luc Nancy (New York: Routledge, 1991).

4   To a lesser extent this is also true of Jean-François Lyotard who was working on a book on Augustine at the time of his death, *La Confession d'Augustin* (Paris: Galilée, 1998); English translation, *The Confession of Augustine*, trans. Richard Beardsworth (Stanford: Stanford University Press, 2000) see also his *The Hyphen: Between Judaism and Christianity* (New York: Prometheus Books, 2000).

5   See Richard Swinburne, *Is There a God?* (Oxford: Oxford University Press, 1996).

6   Edmund Husserl, *Ideas toward a Pure Phenomenology and a Phenomenological Psychology*, trans. Fred Kersten (The Hague: M. Nijhoff, 1982), §24.

7   *Meister Eckhart*, trans. Robert Blakney (New York: Harper & Row, 1941), p. 127.

8   See Martin Heidegger, *Gesamtausgabe*, vol. 60, *Phänomenologie des religiösen Lebens*, (1) "Einführung in die Phänomenologie der Religion" (Wintersemester 1920/21), Ed. Matthias Jung and Thomas Regehly; (2) "Augustinus und der Neuplatonismus" (Sommersemester 1921); (3) "Ausarbeitungen und Entwürfe," ed. Claudius Strube (Frankfurt/Main: Klostermann, 1995). For excellent commentaries on these lectures see Theodore Kisiel, *The Genesis of Heidegger's Being and Time* (Berkeley: University of California Press, 1993) and John van Buren, *The Young Heidegger: Rumor of the Hidden King* (Bloomington: Indiana University Press, 1994).

9   For a survey of Heidegger's evolving attitudes toward the Christian faith see John D. Caputo, *Demythologizing Heidegger* (Bloomington: Indiana University Press, 1993), ch. 9, "Heidegger's Gods."

10 See Emmanuel Levinas, *Proper Names*, trans. Michael Smith (Stanford: Stanford University Press, 1996), pp. 66–79. See the interesting attempt of Jacques Derrida to bring Levinas and Kierkegaard into closer proximity in *The Gift of Death*, trans. David Wills (Chicago: University of Chicago Press, 1995), pp. 83–4.

11 Levinas's major works are *Totality and Infinity: Essay on Exteriority*, trans. Alphonso Lingis (Pittsburgh: Duquesne University Press, 1969) and *Otherwise than Being or Beyond Essence*, trans. Alphonso. Lingis (The Hague: Nijhoff, 1981). See also his "God and Philosophy" in *Emmanuel Levinas: Basic Philosophical Writings*, ed. Adriaan Peperzak, Simon Critchley, and Robert Bernasconi (Bloomington: Indiana University Press, 1996), pp. 129–48, and for a commentary Bettina Bergo, "A Reading of Emmanuel Levinas's 'Dieu et la philosophie,'" *Graduate Faculty Philosophy Journal*, 16, 1 (Spring, 1993): 134–6.

12 See below, Derrida, "Circumfession," sec. 30.

13 Derrida, *The Gift of Death*, p. 49.

14 For more on Derrida's "religion" see John D. Caputo, *The Prayers and Tears of Jacques Derrida: Religion without Religion* (Bloomington: Indiana University Press, 1997) and *Deconstruction in a Nutshell: A Conversation with Jacques Derrida*, edited with a commentary (New York: Fordham University Press, 1997); and Hent de Vries, *Philosophy and the Turn to Religion* (Baltimore: Johns Hopkins University Press, 1999).

15 *The Principle of Reason*, trans. Reginald Lilly (Bloomington: Indiana University Press, 1991). For a commentary, see John D. Caputo *The Mystical Element in Heidegger's Thought* rev. edn. (New York: Fordham University Press, 1986).

16 See Jean-Luc Marion, "The Saturated Phenomenon," trans. Thomas Carlson in *Philosophy Today*, 40, 1 (Spring, 1996): 103–24. This essay, which originally appeared as "*Le Phénomène saturé*," in *Phénoménologie et Théologie*, ed. Jean-François Courtine (Paris: Criterion, 1992), pp. 79–128, appears in a combined volume entitled *Phenomenology and the Theological Turn: The French Debate*, ed. Jean-François Courtine et al. from Fordham

University Press (2000), which contains the English translations both of *Phénoménologie et Théologie* and Janicaud's *The Theological Turn of French Phenomenology*, from which we have excerpted chapter 3 below.

17 Jean-Luc Marion, *Reduction and Givenness: Investigations of Husserl, Heidegger, and Phenomenology*, trans. Thomas Carlson (Evanston: Northwestern University Press, 1998), pp. 203–5.

18 For the points of view of Chrétien, Henry and Marion, see *Phenomenology and the Theological Turn: The French Debate* (above). Janicaud has elaborated his views in a fuller form in *La Phénoménologie éclatée* (Paris: L'éclat, 1998). For a comparable debate, see the exchange between Marion and Derrida entitled "On the Gift," in *God, the Gift and Postmodernism*, ed. John D. Caputo and Michael J. Scanlon (Bloomington: Indiana University Press, 1999), pp. 54–78, and my commentary "Apostles of the Impossible: Derrida and Marion," in *God, the Gift and Postmodernism*, pp. 185–222.

19 Maurice Merleau-Ponty, *Visible and Invisible*, trans. Alphonso Lingis (Evanston: Northwestern University Press, 1968), p. 151.

20 Heidegger, "Zähringen Seminar" in *Vier Seminare*, Gesamtausgabe vol. 15 (Frankfurt: Klostermann, 1986), p. 377: the appearance of a being, a book, say, depends upon the non-appearance of the horizon which makes it possible (its Being).

21 Heidegger, *Being and Time*, §7c, p. 63.

22 Luce Irigaray, *Sexes and Genealogies*, p. 68.

23 See the critical appreciation of Kierkegaard in John Milbank, "The Sublime in Kierkegaard," in *Post-Secular Philosophy*, ed. Philip Blond (London: Routledge, 1998), pp. 131–56.

PART I

LANDMARKS

1

THE MOMENT: SELECTIONS FROM *THE CONCEPT OF ANXIETY*

Vigilius Haufniensis

Anxiety as the Consequence of that Sin which Is Absence of the Consciousness of Sin

In the two previous chapters, it was maintained continually that man is a synthesis of psyche and body that is constituted and sustained by spirit. In the individual life, anxiety is the moment – to use a new expression that says the same as was said in the previous discussion, but that also points toward that which follows.

In recent philosophy there is a category that is continually used in logical no less than in historical-philosophical inquiries. It is the category of transition. However, no further explanation is given. The term is freely used without any ado, and while Hegel and the Hegelian school startled the world with the great insight of the presuppositionless beginning of philosophy, or the thought that before philosophy there must be nothing but the most complete absence of presuppositions, there is no embarrassment at all over the use in Hegelian thought of the terms "transition," "negation," "mediation," i.e., the principles of motion, in such a way that they do not find their place in the systematic progression. If this is not a presupposition, I do not know what a presupposition is. For to use something that is nowhere explained is indeed to presuppose it. The system is supposed to have such marvelous transparency and inner vision that in the manner of the *omphalopsychoi* [navel souls] it would gaze immovably at the central nothing until at last everything would explain itself and its whole content would come into being by itself. Such introverted openness to the public was to characterize the system. Nevertheless, this is not the case, because systematic thought seems to pay homage to secretiveness with respect to its innermost movements. Negation, transition, mediation are three disguised, suspicious, and secret agents (*agentia* [main springs]) that bring about all movements. Hegel would hardly call them presumptuous, because it is with his gracious permission that they carry on their ploy so unembarrassedly that even logic uses terms and phrases borrowed from transition in time: "thereupon," "when," "as being it is this," "as becoming it is this," etc.

Let this be as it may. Let logic take care to help itself. The term "transition" is and remains a clever turn in logic. Transition belongs in the sphere of historical freedom, for transition is a *state* and it is actual. Plato fully recognized the difficulty of placing transition in the realm of the purely metaphysical, and for that reason the category of *the moment* cost him so much effort. To ignore the difficulty certainly is not to "go further" than Plato. To ignore it, and thus piously to deceive thought in order to get speculation afloat and the movement in logic going, is to treat speculation as a rather finite affair. However, I remember once having heard a speculator say that one must not give undue thought to the difficulties beforehand, because then one never arrives at the point where he can speculate. If the important thing is to get to the point where one can begin to speculate, and not that one's speculation in fact becomes true speculation, it is indeed resolutely said that the important thing is to get the point of speculating, just as it is praiseworthy for a man who has no means of riding to Deer Park in his own carriage to say: One must not trouble himself about such things, because he can just as well ride a coffee grinder. This, of course, is the case. Both riders hope to arrive at Deer Park. On the other hand, the man who firmly resolves not to trouble himself about the means of conveyance, just as long as he can get to the point where he can speculate, will hardly reach speculation.

In the sphere of historical freedom, transition is a state. However, in order to understand this correctly, one must not forget that the new is brought about through the leap. If this is not maintained, the transition will have a quantitative preponderance over the elasticity of the leap.

Man, then, is a synthesis of psyche and body, but he is also a *synthesis of the temporal and the eternal*. That this often has been stated, I do not object to at all, for it is not my wish to discover something new, but rather it is my joy and dearest occupation to ponder over that which is quite simple.

As for the latter synthesis, it is immediately striking that it is formed differently from the former. In the former, the two factors are psyche and body, and spirit is the third, yet in such a way that one can speak of a synthesis only when spirit is posited. The latter synthesis has only two factors, the temporal and the eternal. Where is the third factor? And if there is no third factor, there really is no synthesis, for a synthesis that is a contradiction cannot be completed as a synthesis without a third factor, because the fact that the synthesis is a contradiction asserts that it is not. What, then, is the temporal?

If time is correctly defined as an infinite succession, it most likely is also defined as the present, the past, and the future. This distinction, however, is incorrect if it is considered to be implicit in time itself, because the distinction appears only through the relation of time to eternity and through the reflection of eternity in time. If in the infinite succession of time a foothold could be found, i.e., a present, which was the dividing point, the division would be quite correct. However, precisely because every moment, as well as the sum of the moments, is a process (a passing by), no moment is a present, and accordingly there is in time neither present, nor past, nor future. If it is claimed that this division can be maintained, it is because the moment is *spatialized*, but thereby the infinite succession comes to a halt, it is because representation is introduced that allows time to be represented instead of being thought. Even so, this is not correct procedure, for even as representation, the infinite succession of time is an infinitely contentless present (this is the parody of the eternal). The Hindus speak of a line of kings that has ruled for 70,000 years. Nothing is known about the kings, not even their names (this I assume). If we take this as an example of time, the 70,000 years are for thought an infinite vanishing; in representation it is expanded and is spatialized into an illusionary view of an infinite, contentless nothing. As soon as the one is regarded as succeeding the other, the present is posited.

The present, however, is not a concept of time, except precisely as something infinitely contentless, which again is the infinite vanishing. If this is not kept in mind, no matter how quickly it may disappear, the present is posited, and being posited it again appears in the categories: the past and the future.

The eternal, on the contrary, is the present. For thought, the eternal is the present in terms of an annulled succession (time is the succession that passes by). For representation, it is a going forth that nevertheless does not get off the spot, because the eternal is for representation the infinitely contentful present. So also in the eternal there is no division into the past and the future, because the present is posited as the annulled succession.

Time is, then, infinite succession; the life that is in time and is only of time has no present. In order to define the sensuous life, it is usually said that it is in the moment and only in the moment. By the moment, then, is understood that abstraction from the eternal that, if it is to be the present, is a parody of it. The present is the eternal, or rather, the eternal is the present, and the present is full. In this sense the Latin said of the deity that he is *praesens* (*praesentes dii* [the presence of the gods]), by which expression, when used about the deity, he also signified the powerful assistance of the deity.

The moment signifies the present as that which has no past and no future, and precisely in this lies the imperfection of the sensuous life. The eternal also signifies the present as that which has no past and no future, and this is the perfection of the eternal.

If at this point one wants to use the moment to define time and let the moment signify the purely abstract exclusion of the past and the future and as such the present, then the moment is precisely not the present, because the intermediary between the past and the future, purely abstractly conceived, is not at all. Thus it is seen that the moment is not a determination of time, because the determination of time is that it "passes by." For this reason time, if it is to be defined by any of the determinations revealed in time itself, is time past. If, on the contrary, time and eternity touch each other, then it must be in time, and now we have come to the moment.

"The moment" is a figurative expression, and therefore it is not easy to deal with. However, it is a beautiful word to consider. Nothing is as swift as a blink of the eye, and yet it is commensurable with the content of the eternal. Thus when Ingeborg looks out over the sea after Frithiof, this is a picture of what is expressed in the figurative word. An outburst of her emotion, a sigh or a word, already has as a sound more of the determination of time and is more present as something that is vanishing and does not have in it so much of the presence of the eternal. For this reason a sigh, a word, etc. have power to relieve the soul of the burdensome weight, precisely because the burden, when merely expressed, already begins to become something of the past. A blink is therefore a designation of time, but mark well, of time in the fateful conflict when it is touched by eternity. What we call the moment, Plato calls τὸ ἐξαίφνης [the sudden]. Whatever its etymological explanation, it is related to the category of the invisible, because time and eternity were conceived equally abstractly, because the concept of temporality was lacking, and this again was due to the lack of the concept of spirit. The Latin term is *momentum* (from *movere* [to move]), which by derivation expresses the merely vanishing.

Thus understood, the moment is not properly an atom of time but an atom of eternity. It is the first reflection of eternity in time, its first attempt, as it were, at stopping time. For this reason, Greek culture did not comprehend the moment, and even if it had comprehended the atom of eternity, it did not comprehend that it was the moment, did not define it with a forward direction but with a backward direction. Because for Greek culture the atom of eternity was essentially eternity, neither time nor eternity received what was properly its due.

The synthesis of the temporal and the eternal is not another synthesis but is the expression for the first synthesis, according to which man is a synthesis of psyche and body that is sustained by spirit. As soon as the spirit is posited, the moment is present. Therefore one may rightly say reproachfully of man that he lives only in the moment, because that comes to pass by an arbitrary abstraction. Nature does not lie in the moment.

It is with temporality as it is with sensuousness, for temporality seems still more imperfect and the moment still more insignificant than nature's apparently secure endurance in time. However, the contrary is the case. Nature's security has its source in the fact that time has no significance at all for nature. Only with the moment does history begin. By sin, man's sensuousness is posited as sinfulness and is therefore lower than that of the beast, and yet this is because it is here that the higher begins, for at this point spirit begins.

The moment is that ambiguity in which time and eternity touch each other, and with this the concept of *temporality* is posited, whereby time constantly intersects eternity and eternity constantly pervades time. As a result, the above-mentioned division acquires its significance: the present time, the past time, the future time.

By this division, attention is immediately drawn to the fact that the future in a certain sense signifies more than the present and the past, because in a certain sense the future is the whole of which the past is a part, and the future can in a certain sense signify the whole. This is because the eternal first signifies the future or because the future is the incognito in which the eternal, even though it is incommensurable with time, nevertheless preserves its association with time. Linguistic usage at times also takes the future as identical with the eternal (the future life – the eternal life). In a deeper sense, the Greeks did not have the concept of the eternal; so neither did they have the concept of the future. Therefore Greek life cannot be reproached for being lost in the moment, or more correctly, it cannot even be said that it was lost, for temporality was conceived by the Greeks just as naively as sensuousness, because they lacked the category of spirit.

The moment and the future in turn posit the past. If Greek life in any way denotes any qualification of time, it is past time. However, past time is not defined in its relation to the present and the future but as a qualification of time in general, as a passing by. Here the significance of the Platonic "recollection" is obvious. For the Greeks, the eternal lies behind as the past that can only be entered backwards. However, the eternal thought of as the past is an altogether abstract concept, whether

the eternal is further defined philosophically (a philosophical dying away) or historically.

On the whole, in defining the concepts of the past, the future, and the eternal, it can
be seen how the moment is defined. If there is no moment, the eternal appears behind
as the past. It is as when I imagine a man walking along a road but do not posit the
step, and so the road appears behind him as the distance covered. If the moment is
posited but merely as a *discrimen* [division], then the future is the eternal. If the moment
is posited, so is the eternal, but also the future, which reappears as the past. This is
clearly seen in the Greek, the Jewish, and the Christian views. The pivotal concept in
Christianity, that which made all things new, is the fullness of time, but the fullness of
time is the moment as the eternal, and yet this eternal is also the future and the past. If
attention is not paid to this, not a single concept can be saved from a heretical and
treasonable admixture that annihilates the concept. One does not get the past by itself
but in a simple continuity with the future (with this the concepts of conversion,
atonement, and redemption are lost in the world-historical significance and lost in the
individual historical development). The future is not by itself but in a simple continuity
with the present (thereby the concepts of resurrection and judgment are destroyed).

Let us now consider Adam and also remember that every subsequent individual
begins in the very same way, but within the quantitative difference that is the
consequence of the relationship of generation and the historical relationship. Thus
the moment is there for Adam as well as for every subsequent individual. The synthesis
of the psychical and the physical is to be posited by spirit; but spirit is eternal, and the
synthesis is, therefore, only when spirit posits the first synthesis along with the second
synthesis of the temporal and the eternal. As long as the eternal is not introduced, the
moment is not, or is only a *discrimen* [boundary]. Because in innocence spirit is
qualified only as dreaming spirit, the eternal appears as the future, for this is, as has
been said, the first expression of the eternal, and its incognito. Just as (in the previous
chapter) the spirit, when it is about to be posited in the synthesis, or, more correctly,
when it is about to posit the synthesis as the spirit's (freedom's) possibility in the
individuality, expresses itself as anxiety, so here the future in turn is the eternal's
(freedom's) possibility in the individuality expressed as anxiety. As freedom's possibility
manifests itself for freedom, freedom succumbs, and temporality emerges in the same
way as sensuousness in its significance as sinfulness. Here again I repeat that this is only
the final psychological expression for the final psychological approximation to the
qualitative leap. The difference between Adam and the subsequent individual is that for
the latter the future is reflected more than for Adam. Psychologically speaking, this
more may signify what is appalling, but in terms of the qualitative leap it signifies the
nonessential. The highest difference in relation to Adam is that the future seems to be
anticipated by the past or by the anxiety that the possibility is lost before it has been.

The possible corresponds exactly to the future. For freedom, the possible is the
future, and the future is for time the possible. To both of these corresponds anxiety in
the individual life. An accurate and correct linguistic usage therefore associates anxiety
and the future. When it is sometimes said that one is anxious about the past, this seems
to be a contradiction of this usage. However, to a more careful examination, it appears
that this is only a manner of speaking and that the future in one way or another
manifests itself. The past about which I am supposed to be anxious must stand in a

relation of possibility to me. If I am anxious about a past misfortune, then this is not because it is in the past but because it may be repeated, i.e., become future. If I am anxious because of a past offense, it is because I have not placed it in an essential relation to myself as past and have in some deceitful way or another prevented it from being past. If indeed it is actually past, then I cannot be anxious but only repentant. If I do not repent, I have allowed myself to make my relation to the offense dialectical, and by this the offense itself has become a possibility and not something past. If I am anxious about the punishment, it is only because this has been placed in a dialectical relation to the offense (otherwise I suffer my punishment), and then I am anxious for the possible and the future.

Thus we have returned to where we were in Chapter I. Anxiety is the psychological state that precedes sin. It approaches sin as closely as possible, as anxiously as possible, but without explaining sin, which breaks forth only in the qualitative leap.

The moment sin is posited, temporality is sinfulness. We do not say that temporality is sinfulness any more than that sensuousness is sinfulness, but rather that when sin is posited, temporality signifies sinfulness. Therefore he sins who lives only in the moment as abstracted from the eternal. But to speak foolishly and by way of accommodation, had Adam not sinned, he would in the same moment have passed over into eternity. On the other hand, as soon as sin is posited, it is of no help to wish to abstract from the temporal any more than from the sensuous.

2

THE WHOLLY OTHER: SELECTIONS FROM *PHILOSOPHICAL FRAGMENTS*

Johannes Climacus

The Absolute Paradox (A Metaphysical Caprice)

Although Socrates did his very best to gain knowledge of human nature and to know himself – yes, even though he has been eulogized for centuries as the person who certainly knew man best – he nevertheless admitted that the reason he was disinclined to ponder the nature of such creatures as Pegasus and the Gorgons was that he still was not quite clear about himself, whether he (a connoisseur of human nature) was a more curious monster than Typhon or a friendlier and simpler being, by nature sharing something divine (see *Phaedrus*, 229 e). This seems to be a paradox. But one must not think ill of the paradox, for the paradox is the passion of thought, and the thinker without the paradox is like the lover without passion: a mediocre fellow. But the ultimate potentiation of every passion is always to will its own downfall, and so it is also the ultimate passion of the understanding [*Forstand*] to will the collision, although in one way or another the collision must become its downfall. This, then, is the ultimate paradox of thought: to want to discover something that thought itself cannot think. This passion of thought is fundamentally present everywhere in thought, also in the single individual's thought insofar as he, thinking, is not merely himself. But because of habit we do not discover this. Similarly, the human act of walking, so the natural scientists inform us, is a continuous falling, but a good steady citizen who walks to his office mornings and home at midday probably considers this an exaggeration, because his progress, after all, is a matter of mediation – how could it occur to him that he is continually falling, he who unswervingly follows his nose.

But in order to get started, let us state a bold proposition: let us assume that we know what a human being is. In this we do indeed have the criterion of truth, which all Greek philosophy *sought*, or *doubted*, or *postulated*, or *brought to fruition*. And is it not noteworthy that the Greeks were like this? Is this not, so to speak, a brief summary of the meaning of the Greek mentality, an epigram it has written about itself and by which it is better served than by the sometimes prolix works written about it? Thus the proposition is worth assuming, and for another reason as well, since we have already explained it in the two previous chapters, whereas anyone desiring to give an explanation of Socrates different from ours must see to it that he does not fall into the snares of the earlier or later Greek skepticism. If the Socratic theory of recollection and of every human being as universal man is not maintained, then Sextus Empiricus stands there ready to make the transition implied in "to learn" not merely difficult but impossible, and Protagoras begins where he left off, with everything as the measure of man, in the sense that he is the measure for others, but by no means in the Socratic sense that the single individual is for himself the measure, no more and no less.

We know, then, what man is, and this wisdom, the worth of which I, least of all, will denigrate, can continually become richer and more meaningful, and hence the truth also. But then the understanding stands still, as did Socrates, for now the understanding's paradoxical passion that wills the collision awakens and, without really understanding itself, wills its own downfall. It is the same with the paradox of erotic love. A person lives undisturbed in himself, and then awakens the paradox of self-love as love for another, for one missing. (Self-love is the ground or goes to the ground in all love, which is why any religion of love [Kjærlighed] we might conceive would presuppose, just as epigrammatically as truly, one condition only and assume it as given: to love oneself in order to command loving the neighbor as oneself.) Just as the lover is changed by this paradox of love so that he almost does not recognize himself any more (the poets, the spokesmen of erotic love, testify to this, as do the lovers themselves, since they allow the poets to take only the words from them, not their state), so also that intimated paradox of the understanding reacts upon a person and upon his self-knowledge in such a way that he who believed that he knew himself now no longer is sure whether he perhaps is a more curiously complex animal than Typhon or whether he has in his being a gentler and diviner part (σκοπῶ οὐ ταῦτα, ἀλλ' ἐμαυτόν, εἴτε τι θηρίον ὂν τυγχάνω Τυφῶνος πολυπλοκώτερον καὶ μᾶλλον ἐπιτεθ- υμμένον, εἴτε ἡμερώτερόν τε καὶ ἁπλούστερον ζῷον, θείας τινὸς καὶ- ἀτύφου μοίρας φύσει μετχόν. *Phaedrus* 230 a).

But what is this unknown against which the understanding in its paradoxical passion collides and which even disturbs man and his self-knowledge? It is the unknown. But it is not a human being, insofar as he knows man, or anything else that he knows. Therefore, let us call this unknown *the god*. It is only a name we give to it. It hardly occurs to the understanding to want to demonstrate that this unknown (the god) exists. If, namely, the god does not exist, then of course it is impossible to demonstrate it. But if he does exist, then it is foolishness to want to demonstrate it, since I, in the very moment the demonstration commences, would presuppose it not as doubtful – which a presupposition cannot be, inasmuch as it is a presupposition – but as decided, because otherwise I would not begin, easily perceiving that the whole thing would be impossible if he did not exist. If, however, I interpret the expression "to demonstrate the existence [Tilværelse] of the god" to mean that I want to demonstrate that the unknown, which exists, is the god, then I do not express myself very felicitously, for then I demonstrate nothing, least of all an existence, but I develop the definition of a concept. It is generally a difficult matter to want to demonstrate that something exists – worse still, for the brave souls who venture to do it, the difficulty is of such a kind that fame by no means awaits those who are preoccupied with it. The whole process of demonstration continually becomes something entirely different, becomes an expanded concluding development of what I conclude from having presupposed that the object of investigation exists. Therefore, whether I am moving in the world of sensate palpability or in the world of thought, I never reason in conclusion to existence, but I reason in conclusion from existence. For example, I do not demonstrate that a stone exists but that something which exists is a stone. The court of law does not demonstrate that a criminal exists but that the accused, who does indeed exist, is a criminal. Whether one wants to call existence an *accessorium* [addition] or the eternal *prius* [presupposition], it can never be demonstrated. We shall take our time; after all, there is no reason for us to rush as there is for those who, out of concern for themselves, or for the god, or for something else, must rush to get proof that something exists. In that case, there is good reason to make haste, especially if the one involved has in all honesty made an accounting of the danger that he himself or the object being investigated does not exist until he proves it and does not dishonestly harbor the secret thought that essentially it exists whether he demonstrates it or not.

If one wanted to demonstrate Napoleon's existence from Napoleon's works, would it not be most curious, since his existence certainly explains the works but the works do not demonstrate *his* existence unless I have already in advance interpreted the word "his" in such a way as to have assumed that he exists. But Napoleon is only an individual, and to that extent there is no absolute relation between him and his works – thus someone else could have done the same works. Perhaps that is why I cannot reason from the works to existence. If I call the works Napoleon's works, then the demonstration is superfluous, since I have already mentioned his name. If I ignore this, I can never demonstrate from the works that they are Napoleon's but demonstrate (purely ideally) that such works are the works of a great general etc. However, between the god and his works there is an absolute relation. God is not a name but a concept, and perhaps because of that his *essentia involvit existentiam* [essence involves existence].

God's works, therefore, only the god can do. Quite correct. But, then, what are the god's works? The works from which I want to demonstrate his existence do not immediately and directly exist, not at all. Or are the wisdom in nature and the goodness or wisdom in Governance right in front of our noses? Do we not encounter the most terrible spiritual trials here, and is it ever possible to be finished with all these trials? But I still do not demonstrate God's existence from such an order of things, and even if I began, I would never finish and also would be obliged continually to live *in suspenso* lest something so terrible happen that my fragment of demonstration would be ruined. Therefore, from what works do I demonstrate it? From the works regarded ideally – that is, as they do not appear directly and immediately. But then I do not demonstrate it from the works, after all, but only develop the ideality I have presupposed; trusting in *that*, I even dare to defy all objections, even those that have not yet arisen. By beginning, then, I have presupposed the ideality, have presupposed that I will succeed in accomplishing it, but what else is that but presupposing that the god exists and actually beginning with trust in him.

And how does the existence of the god emerge from the demonstration? Does it happen straightway? Is it not here as it is with the Cartesian dolls? As soon as I let go of the doll, it stands on its head. As soon as I let go of it – consequently, I have to let go of it. So also with the demonstration – so long as I am holding on to the demonstration (that is, continue to be one who is demonstrating), the existence does not emerge, if for no other reason than that I am in the process of demonstrating it, but when I let go of the demonstration, the existence is there. Yet this letting go, even that is surely something; it is, after all, *meine Zuthat* [my contribution]. Does it not have to be taken into account, this diminutive moment, however brief it is – it does not have to be long, because it is a *leap*. However diminutive this moment, even if it is this very instant, this very instant must be taken into account. If someone wants to have it forgotten, I will take the occasion to tell a little anecdote in order to show that it does indeed exist. Chrysippus was trying to determine a qualitative limit in the progressive or retrogressive operation of a sorites. Carneades could not grasp the point at which the quality actually made its appearance. Chrysippus told him that one could pause for a moment in the reckoning, and then, then – then one could understand it better. But Carneades replied: Please, do not let me disturb you; you may not only pause but may even lie down and go to sleep – it will not make any difference. When you wake up, we shall begin again where you stopped. And that, of course, is how it really is; trying to get rid of something by sleeping is just as useless as trying to obtain something by sleeping.

Therefore, anyone who wants to demonstrate the existence of God (in any other sense than elucidating the God-concept and without the *reservatio finalis* [ultimate reservation] that we have pointed out – that the existence itself emerges from the demonstration by a leap) proves something else instead, at times something that perhaps did not even need demonstrating, and in any case never anything better. For the fool says in his heart that there is no God, but he who says in his heart or to others: Just wait a little and I shall demonstrate it – ah, what a rare wise man he is! If, at the moment he is supposed to begin the demonstration, it is not totally undecided whether the god exists or not, then, of course, he does not demonstrate it, and if that is the situation in the beginning, then he never does make a beginning – partly for fear that he will not succeed because the god may not exist, and partly because he has nothing with which to begin. – In ancient times, such a thing would have been of hardly any concern. At least Socrates, who did indeed advance what is called the physico-teleological demonstration for the existence of God, did not conduct himself in this way. He constantly presupposes that the god exists, and on this presupposition he seeks to infuse nature with the idea of fitness and purposiveness. If he had been asked why he conducted himself in this manner, he presumably would have explained that he lacked the kind of courage needed to dare to embark on such a voyage of discovery without having behind him the assurance that the god exists. At the god's request, he casts out his net, so to speak, to catch the idea of fitness and purposiveness, for nature itself comes up with many terrifying devices and many subterfuges in order to disturb.

The paradoxical passion of the understanding is, then, continually colliding with this unknown, which certainly does exist but is also unknown and to that extent does not exist. The understanding does not go beyond this; yet in its paradoxicality the under-standing cannot stop reaching it and being engaged with it, because wanting to express its relation to it by saying that this unknown does not exist will not do, since just saying that involves a relation. But what, then, is this unknown, for does not its being the god merely signify to us that it is the unknown? To declare that it is the unknown because we cannot know it, and that even if we could know it we could not express it, does not satisfy the passion, although it has correctly perceived the unknown as frontier. But a frontier is expressly the passion's torment, even though it is also its incentive. And yet it can go no further, whether it risks a sortie through *via negationis* [the way of negation] or *via eminentiae* [the way of idealization].

What, then, is the unknown? It is the frontier that is continually arrived at, and therefore when the category of motion is replaced by the category of rest it is the different, the absolutely different. But it is the absolutely different in which there is no distinguishing mark. Defined as the absolutely different, it seems to be at the point of being disclosed, but not so, because the understanding cannot even think the absolutely different; it cannot absolutely negate itself but uses itself for that purpose and consequently thinks the difference in itself, which it thinks by itself. It cannot absolutely transcend itself and therefore thinks as above itself only the sublimity that it thinks by itself. If the unknown (the god) is not solely the frontier, then the one idea about the different is confused with the many ideas about the different. The unknown is then in διασπορά [dispersion], and the understanding has an attractive selection from among what is available and what fantasy can think of (the prodigious, the ridiculous, etc.).

But this difference cannot be grasped securely. Every time this happens, it is basically an arbitrariness, and at the very bottom of devoutness there madly lurks the capricious arbitrariness that knows it itself has produced the god. If the difference cannot be grasped securely because there is no distinguishing mark, then, as with all such dialectical opposites, so it is with the difference and the likeness — they are identical. Adhering to the understanding, the difference has so confused the understanding that it does not know itself and quite consistently confuses itself with the difference. In the realm of fantastical fabrication, paganism has been adequately luxuriant. With respect to the assumption just advanced, which is the self-ironizing of the understanding, I shall merely trace it in a few lines without reference to whether it was historical or not. There exists [*existere*], then, a certain person who looks just like any other human being, grows up as do other human beings, marries, has a job, takes tomorrow's livelihood into account as a man should. It may be very beautiful to want to live as the birds of the air live, but it is not permissible, and one can indeed end up in the saddest of plights, either dying of hunger – if one has the endurance for that – or living on the goods of others. This human being is also the god. How do I know that? Well, I cannot know it, for in that case I would have to know the god and the difference, and I do not know the difference, inasmuch as the understanding has made it like unto that from which it differs. Thus the god has become the most terrible deceiver through the understanding's deception of itself. The understanding has the god as close as possible and yet just as far away.

Someone may now be saying, "I know full well that you are a capricemonger, but you certainly do not believe that it would occur to me to be concerned about a caprice so curious or so ludicrous that it probably has never occurred to anyone and, above all, is so unreasonable that I would have to lock everything out of my consciousness in order to think of it." That is exactly what you have to do, but then is it justifiable to want to keep all the presuppositions *you* have in your consciousness and still presume to think about your consciousness without any presuppositions? Most likely you do not deny the consistency of what has been developed – that in defining the unknown as the different the understanding ultimately goes astray and confuses the difference with likeness? But this seems to imply something different, namely, that if a human being is to come truly to know something about the unknown (the god), he must first come to know that it is different from him, absolutely different from him. The understanding cannot come to know this by itself (since, as we have seen, it is a contradiction); if it is going to come to know this, it must come to know this from the god, and if it does come to know this, it cannot understand this and consequently cannot come to know this, for how could it understand the absolutely different? If this is not immediately clear, then it will become more clear from the corollary, for if the god is absolutely different from a human being, then a human being is absolutely different from the god – but how is the understanding to grasp this? At this point we seem to stand at a paradox. Just to come to know that the god is the different, man needs the god and then comes to know that the god is absolutely different from him. But if the god is to be absolutely different from a human being, this can have its basis not in that which man owes to the god (for to that extent they are akin) but in that which he owes to himself or in that which he himself has committed. What, then, is the difference? Indeed, what else but sin, since the difference, the absolute difference, must have been caused by the individual himself. We stated this in the foregoing by saying that the individual is untruth and is this through his own fault, and we jestingly, yet earnestly, agreed that it is too much to ask him to find this out for himself. Now we have come to the same point again. The connoisseur of human nature became almost bewildered about himself when he came up against the different; he no longer knew whether he was a more curious monster than Typhon or whether there was something divine in him. What did he lack, then? The consciousness of sin, which he could no more teach to any other person than any other person could teach it to him. Only the god could teach it – if he wanted to be teacher. But this he did indeed want to be, as we have composed the story, and in order to be that he wanted to be on the basis of equality with the single individual so that he could completely understand him. Thus the paradox becomes even more terrible, or the same paradox has the duplexity by which it manifests itself as the absolute – negatively, by bringing into prominence the absolute difference of sin and, positively, by wanting to annul this absolute difference in the absolute equality.

But is a paradox such as this conceivable? We shall not be in a hurry; whenever the contention is over a reply to a question and the contending is not like that on the race track, it is not speed that wins but correctness. The understanding certainly cannot think it, cannot hit upon it on its own, and if it is proclaimed, the understanding cannot understand it and merely detects that it will likely be its downfall. To that extent, the understanding has strong objections to it; and yet, on the other hand, in its paradoxical passion the understanding does indeed will its own downfall. But the paradox, too, wills this downfall of the understanding, and thus the two have a mutual understanding, but this understanding is present only in the moment of passion. Let us consider the condition of erotic love [*Elskov*], even though it is an imperfect metaphor. Self-love lies at the basis of love [*Kjærlighed*], but at its peak its paradoxical passion wills its own downfall. Erotic love also wills this, and therefore these two forces are in mutual understanding in the moment of passion, and this passion is precisely erotic love. Why, then, should the lover not be able to think this, even though the person who in self-love shrinks from erotic love can neither comprehend it nor dare to venture it, since it is indeed his downfall. So it is with the passion of erotic love. To be sure, self-love has foundered, but nevertheless it is not annihilated but is taken captive and is erotic love's *spolia opima* [spoils of war]. But it can come to life again, and this becomes erotic love's spiritual trial. So also with the paradox's relation to the understanding, except that this passion has another name, or, rather, we must simply try to find a name for it.

3

FAITH: SELECTIONS FROM *PRACTICE IN CHRISTIANITY*

By Anti-Climacus

§ 1
The God-man is a Sign

What is meant by a *sign*? A sign is the denied immediacy or the second being that is different from the first being. This is not to say that the sign is not immediately something but that it is a sign, and it is not immediately that which it is as a sign or as a sign is not the immediate that it is. A navigation mark is a sign. Immediately it certainly is something, a post, a lamp, etc., but a sign it is not immediately; that it is a sign is something different from what it immediately is. – This underlies all the mystification by means of signs, for the sign is only for the one who knows that it is a sign and in the strictest sense only for the one who knows what it means; for everyone else the sign is that which it immediately is. – Even if it were not so, that there is someone who has made this or that into a sign and there is no agreement with anyone that this is supposed to be a sign, if I see something striking and call it a sign, this involves a term based on reflection. The striking thing is the immediate, but my regarding it as a sign (which is a reflection, something I in a certain sense take from myself) indeed expresses that I think that it is supposed to mean something. But that it is supposed to *mean* something is its being something different from what it immediately is. Consequently, I do not deny its immediacy in regarding it as a sign, although I do not know definitely either that it is a sign or what it is supposed to mean.

A *sign of contradiction* is a sign that intrinsically contains a contradiction in itself. There is no contradiction in its being immediately this or that and also a sign, for there must certainly be an immediate entity for it to be a sign; a literal nothing is not a sign either. A sign of contradiction, however, is a sign that contains a contradiction in its composition. To justify the name of "sign," there must be something by which it draws attention to itself or to the contradiction. But the contradictory parts must not annual each other in such a way that the sign comes to mean nothing or in such a way that it becomes the opposite of a sign, an unconditional concealment. – A communication that is the unity of jest and earnestness is thus a sign of contradiction. It is no direct communication; it is impossible for the recipient to say *directly* which is which, simply because the one communicating does not *directly* communicate either jest or earnestness. Therefore the earnestness in this communication lies in another place, or somewhere else, lies in making the recipient self-active — from the purely dialectical point of view, the highest earnestness with regard to communication. But such a communication must secure for itself a something by which it draws attention to itself, by which it occasions and invites a heeding of the communication; and on the other hand the combination of jest and earnestness must not be lunacy either, because then there is no communication; whereas, if jest or earnestness completely dominates, it is direct communication.

A sign is not what it is in its immediacy, because in its immediacy no sign *is*, inasmuch as "sign" is a term based on reflection. A sign of contradiction is that which draws attention to itself and, once attention is directed to it, shows itself to contain a contradiction.

In Scripture the God-man is called a sign of contradiction — but what contradiction, if any, could there be at all in the speculative unity of God and man? No, there is no contradiction in that, but the contradiction — and it is as great as possible, is the qualitative contradiction — is between being God and being an individual human being. In addition to being what one is immediately, to be a sign is to be a something else also. To be a sign of contradiction is to be a something else that stands in contrast to what one immediately is. So it is with the God-man. Immediately, he is an individual human being, just like others, a lowly, unimpressive human being, but now comes the contradiction — that he is God.

But lest this contradiction become a contradiction that exists for no one or does not exist for anyone — somewhat like a mystification that is so extraordinarily successful that its effect is nil — there must be something that draws attention to it. The miracle essentially serves this purpose, and a single direct statement about being God. Yet neither the miracle nor the single direct statement is absolutely direct communication; for in that case the contradiction is *eo ipso* canceled. As far as the miracle, which is the object of *faith*, is concerned, this is certainly easy to see; as for the second, that the single direct statement is nevertheless not direct communication, this will be shown later.

The God-man is the sign of contradiction, and why? Because, replies Scripture, because he was to disclose the thoughts of hearts. Does all the modern thought about the speculative unity of God and man, all this that regards Christianity only as a teaching, does this have the remotest resemblance to the essentially Christian? No, in the modern approach everything is made as direct as putting one's foot in a sock — and the Christian approach is the sign of contradiction that discloses the thoughts of hearts. The God-man is an individual human being — not a fantastic unity that has never existed except *sub specie aeterni* [under the aspect of eternity], and he is anything but an assistant professor who teaches directly to parroters or dictates paragraphs for shorthand writers — he does exactly the very opposite, he discloses the thoughts of hearts. Ah, it is so cozy to be listeners and transcribers when everything is so completely direct. Gentlemen listeners and transcribers must watch out — it is the thoughts of *their* hearts that are to be disclosed.

And only the sign of contradiction can do this: it draws attention to itself and then it presents a contradiction. There is a something that makes it impossible not to look —

and look, as one is looking one sees as in a mirror, one comes to see oneself, or he who is the sign of contradiction looks straight into one's heart while one is staring into the contradiction. A contradiction placed squarely in front of a person – if one can get him to look at it – is a mirror; as he is forming a judgment, what dwells within him must be disclosed. It is a riddle, but as he is guessing the riddle, what dwells within him is disclosed by the way he guesses. The contradiction confronts him with a choice, and as he is choosing, together with what he chooses, he himself is disclosed.

Note. We see that direct communication is an impossibility for the God-man, for inasmuch as he is the sign of contradiction he cannot communicate himself directly; to be a sign is already a term based on reflection, to say nothing of being the sign of contradiction. One also perceives that the modern confusion has managed to make all Christianity into direct communication only by leaving out the communicator, the God-man. As soon as the communicator is not thoughtlessly taken away or the communication is taken and the communicator left out, as soon as the communicator is taken into account and the communicator is the God-man, a sign, a sign of contradiction, then direct communication is impossible, as it was in the situation of contemporaneity. But nowadays we have managed to have it done in another way. It is eighteen hundred years since Christ lived; then he is forgotten – only his teaching lasts – yes, that is, Christianity has been abolished.

§ 2
The Form of a Servant is Unrecognizability (The Incognito)

What is unrecognizability? Unrecognizability is not to be in the character of what one essentially is – for example, when a policeman is in plain clothes.

And thus it is unrecognizability, the absolute unrecognizability, when one is God, then to be an individual human being. To be the individual human being or an individual human being (in a certain sense it is a matter of indifference whether he is a high-ranking or a low-ranking person) is the greatest possible distance, the infinitely qualitative distance, from being God, and therefore it is the most profound incognito.

But the modern age has abolished Christ, has either thrown him out completely and taken his teaching or has made him fantastical and has fantastically imputed to him direct communication. Not so in the situation of contemporaneity; remember, too, that Christ willed to be incognito expressly because he wanted to be the sign of contradiction. But these eighteen hundred years, what supposedly has been learned from them, and on the other hand, the total ignorance and inexperience of most people with regard to what it means to want to be incognito, an ignorance and inexperience due to the rampant didacticizing, whereas what it means to exist is completely forgotten – this has confused the conception of the God-man.

The majority of people living in Christendom today no doubt live in the illusion that if they had been contemporary with Christ they would have recognized him immediately despite his unrecognizability. They utterly fail to see how they betray that they do not know themselves; it totally escapes them that this conviction they have, whereby they presumably think to glorify Christ, is blasphemy, contained in the nonsensical-undialectical climax of clerical roaring: *to such a degree* was Christ God that one could immediately and directly perceive it, instead of: he was true God, and therefore *to such a degree* God that he was unrecognizable – thus it was not flesh and blood but the opposite of flesh and blood that inspired Peter to recognize him.

Essentially, Christ is remodeled. He is made into a man who himself was aware of being the extraordinary – but whom his contemporaries failed to notice. This may still be true. But the fabricating does not stop there; we fabricate that Christ really would have liked to be *directly* recognizable as the extraordinary he was, but that the blind infatuation of his contemporaries iniquitously refused to understand him. In other words, we betray that we utterly fail to understand what it means to be an incognito. It was Christ's free resolve from eternity to want to be incognito. Thus to think that we honor him by saying or thinking: If I had lived contemporary with him, I certainly would have recognized him directly – we insult him, and since it is Christ we are insulting, this means that we are blasphemous.

But the majority of people do not exist [*existere*] at all in the more profound sense. They have never made themselves existentially familiar with – that is, they have never ventured in action – the idea of wanting to be incognito. Let us take a simple human situation. When I want to be incognito (omitting here the reason and whether I have a right to be that), is it then a compliment if someone comes up to me and says: I knew you right away; it is the very opposite, it is a satire on me. But perhaps the satire was justified and my incognito poor. But now let us imagine a person who managed to maintain an incognito: he *wants* to be incognito; he presumably wants to be recognized but not *directly*. That he is not recognized directly for what he is cannot be something that simply happens to him, for it is indeed his own free decision. But here is the real secret, most people have no intimation of this superiority over oneself, and this superiority over oneself of wanting to be incognito in such a way that one seems much lowlier than one is – of this they have no intimation whatsoever. Or if an intimation did dawn upon them, they would no doubt think: What lunacy, suppose the incognito succeeded so well that one was actually taken to be what one pretended to be! Most people come scarcely any further than that, if they come that far. They discover here a self-contradiction, which in the service of the good is genuine self-denial: the good man does his very best to maintain his incognito, and his incognito is that he is something far lowlier than he is. Thus someone chooses an incognito that shows him far lowlier than he is; he perhaps thinks of the Socratic principle: In order truly to will the good, one must avoid even the appearance of doing it. The incognito is his free decision. Using all his inventiveness and intrepidity, he exerts himself to the utmost of his powers to maintain the incognito. Either he succeeds or he fails. If he succeeds – well, then he has, humanly speaking, done himself harm: he has made all people think the least of him. What self-denial! On the other hand, what an enormous exertion, for at every moment he has had it in his power to show his true character. What self-denial, for what is self-denial without freedom. What supreme self-denial if the incognito is so successful that, even if he were to speak directly, no one would believe him.

But that such a superiority exists or could exist, of this people have no conception at all. How far removed one is from it would be learned if one were to attempt to obtain a direct communication from such a superior person, or if he himself were to begin any such thing and gave it – one would learn it when he assumed the incognito again. So let us imagine, for example, a noble, sympathetic person who as a precaution or for any other reason whatsoever found an incognito to be necessary. For that he chooses, for example, to appear to be an egotist. Now he discloses himself to someone, shows him his true character, and the other person believes it, is gripped by it. So they understand each other. The other person is perhaps also of the opinion that he understands the incognito – he does not perceive that it was indeed removed, that he understood it with the aid of *direct* communication, that is, with the help of the person who *was* incognito but was not incognito as long as he communicated the understanding to him. Let us now imagine that for some reason or other the superior person has the notion or finds it necessary to reassume the incognito between the two who, as they say, understood each other – what then? Then it will be settled whether the other person is as great a dialectician as the first, or whether the other has faith in the possibility of this kind of self-denial. In other words, it will be settled whether the other person is capable of penetrating an incognito, or of steadfastly maintaining the understanding in the face of it, or of understanding it by himself. The moment the superior person assumes the incognito, he naturally does everything to maintain it and does not help the other person at all; on the contrary, he devises the strategy best calculated to deceive him – that is, to maintain his incognito. Now if he is essentially the superior one, he succeeds. The other person at first resists a little by way of direct communication, "This is a deception; you are not that way." But the incognito is maintained; no direct communication follows, and the other person once again believes that this person is an egotist and perhaps says, "For a moment I believed in him, but now even I see that he is an egotist." The point is that he cannot really hold to the idea that the unrecognizable person does not prefer to be recognized as the good man he is; the point is that he can understand an incognito only as long as the unrecognizable person shows him by direct communication that it is an incognito, that it is so and how – that is, as long as there is no incognito, or at least as long as the unrecognizable person is not in the character of being unrecognizable, gathering all his mental powers to maintain the unrecognizability and leaving the other person to himself. As long as the first person helps him with direct communication about the unrecognizability, he can understand it and – the self-denial, for then there really is none. But when there is, he cannot understand him. In other words, the other person really does not believe in the possibility that there could be self-denial such as that. – Whether a person has the right to mystify in this way, whether a person is capable of doing it, whether, if he could, his defense that he was maieutically developing the other person was adequate, or, from another point of view, whether it is not specifically his duty, assuming that it is self-denial and not pride – this I do not decide. Please regard this as merely an imaginary construction in thought that nevertheless does provide illumination regarding "unrecognizability."

And now the God-man! He is God but chooses to become this individual human being. This, as said before, is the most profound incognito or the most impenetrable unrecognizability that is possible, because the contradiction between being God and being an individual human being is the greatest possible, the infinitely qualitative contradiction. But it is his will, his free decision, and therefore it is an omnipotently maintained incognito. Indeed, by allowing himself to be born he has in a certain sense bound himself once and for all; his unrecognizability is so omnipotently maintained that in a way he himself is in the power of his own incognito, in which lies the literal *actuality* of his purely human suffering, that this is not merely appearance but in a certain sense is the assumed incognito's upper hand over him. Only in this way is there in the profoundest sense earnestness concerning his becoming true man; this is also why he suffers through the utmost suffering of feeling himself abandoned by God. He is not, therefore, at any moment beyond suffering but is actually in suffering, and this purely human experience befalls him, that the actuality proves to be even more terrible than the possibility, that he who freely assumed unrecognizability yet actually suffers as if he were trapped or had trapped himself in unrecognizability. It is a strange kind of dialectic: that he, omnipotent, binds himself and does it so omnipotently that he actually feels bound, suffers under the consequence of his loving and free decision to become an individual human being – to that degree there was earnestness in his becoming an actual human being. But so it had to be if he was to be the sign of contradiction that discloses the thoughts of the heart. – The imperfection in any human being's unrecognizability is the very arbitrariness with which he can annihilate it at any moment; the more he is able to prevent this and make it less possible, the more perfectly in earnest is the unrecognizability. But the God-man's unrecognizability is an omnipotently maintained incognito, and the divine earnestness is precisely this – that it was maintained to such an extent that he himself suffered purely humanly under the unrecognizability.

Note. It is easily seen that direct communication is an impossibility when one is so kind as to take the communicator into account and is not so absentminded about Christianity as to forget Christ. In relation to unrecognizability or for someone in unrecognizability, direct communication is an impossibility, because the direct communication does indeed directly state what one essentially is – but unrecognizability means not to be in the character of what one essentially is. Thus there is a contradiction that nevertheless makes direct communication indirect, that is, makes direct communication impossible. If there is to be a direct communication that remains a direct communication, one must step out of the incognito; otherwise that which in the first is direct communication (the direct statement) still does not become direct communication through the second (the incognito of the communicator).

§ 3
The Impossibility of Direct Communication

The opposite of direct communication is indirect communication. The latter can be produced in two ways.

Indirect communication can be an art of communication in redoubling the communication; the art consists in making oneself, the communicator, into a nobody, purely objective, and then continually placing the qualitative opposites in a unity. This is what some pseudonymous writers are accustomed to calling the double-reflection of the communication. For example, it is indirect communication to place jest and earnestness together in such a way that the composite is a dialectical knot – and then to be a nobody oneself. If anyone wants to have anything to do with this kind of communication, he will have to untie the knot himself. Or, to bring attack and defense into a unity in such a way that no one can directly say whether one is attacking or defending, so that the most zealous supporter of the cause and its most vicious foe can both seem to see in one an ally – and then to be nobody oneself, an absentee, an objective something, a nonperson. If, for example, at a given time faith seems to have vanished from the world, something one must advertise for in the Lost-and-Found columns, it perhaps can be beneficial in dialectically luring forth faith – yet I do not decide whether it can be beneficial. But here is an example of indirect communication or communication in double-reflection. One presents faith in the eminent sense and represents it in such a way that the most orthodox sees it as a defense of the faith and the atheist sees it as an attack, while the communicator is a zero, a nonperson, an objective something – yet he perhaps is an ingenious secret agent who with the aid of this communication finds out which is which, who is the believer, who the atheist; because this is disclosed when they form a judgment about what is presented, which is neither attack nor defense.

But indirect communication can also appear in another way, through the relation between the communication and the communicator. The communicator is present here, whereas in the first instance he was left out, yet, please note, by way of a negative reflection. But our age actually knows no other kind of communication than that mediocre method of didacticizing. What it means to exist has been completely forgotten. Any communication concerning existing requires a communicator; in other words, the communicator is the reduplication of the communication; to exist in what one understands is to reduplicate.

But this communication still cannot be called indirect communication just because there is a communicator who himself exists in what he communicates. If, however, the communicator himself is dialectically defined and his own being is based on reflection, then all direct communication is impossible.

So it is with the God-man. He is a sign, the sign of contradiction; he is unrecognizable – therefore any direct communication is impossible. In other words, if the communication by a communicator is to be direct, then not only the communication must be direct, but the communicator himself must be directly defined. If not, then even the most direct statement by such a communicator still does not – because of the communicator, because of what the communicator is – become direct communication.

If someone says directly: I am God; the Father and I are one, this is direct communication. But if the person who says it, the communicator, is this individual human being, an individual human being just like others, then this communication is not quite entirely direct, because it is not entirely direct that an individual human being should be God – whereas what he says is entirely direct. Because of the communicator the communication contains a contradiction, it becomes indirect communication; it confronts you with a choice: whether you will believe him or not.

One could very well weep when one reflects on the state of Christianity in Christendom with regard to what is used in sermon presentation again and again and with the greatest self-importance, as if one were saying something really striking and convincing. They say that Christ himself has directly said that he was God, the only begotten Son of the Father. They reject with horror any concealment as unworthy of Christ, as vanity and conceit in connection with so earnest a matter, the most earnest of all matters, the salvation of mankind. They maintain that Christ has given us a direct answer to a direct question. Alas, such pastors do not know at all whereof they speak; it is as if it were hidden from their eyes that they are abolishing Christianity. He who was an offense to the Jews, foolishness to the Greeks, the mystery by whom everything was revealed, but in the mystery – him they humanly make over into a kind of earnest public figure, almost as earnest as the pastor. If one will only take the trouble to say to such a person with a direct and cozy joviality, "Tell me now in all earnestness," then without any fear and trembling before the Deity, without the death throes that are the birth pangs of faith, without the shudder that is the beginning of worship, without the horror of the possibility of offense, one immediately and directly comes to know what cannot be known directly.

Yes, indeed, Christ himself did very directly say that he was the Father's only begotten Son, that is, the *sign of contradiction* – has *very directly* said it. What does that mean? See, here we are again. If he is the sign of contradiction, then he cannot give a direct communication – that is, the statement can be entirely direct, but the fact that he is involved, that he, the sign of contradiction, says it, makes it indirect communication. Yes, indeed, Christ did say: Believe in me, and it is an entirely direct statement. But if the one who says it is the sign of contradiction, what then? Then this direct statement in his mouth specifically expresses that to believe is not something so entirely direct or that even his call to believe is indirect communication.

And now with regard to *earnestness*, such pastors on the whole understand earnestness just about as well as they understand Christianity. The earnestness is precisely this – that Christ cannot give a direct communication, that the single direct statement, like the miracle, can serve only to make aware in order that the person who has been made aware, facing the offense of the contradiction, can choose whether he will believe or not.

But the essentially Christian is confused in every way. Christ is made into the speculative unity of God and man, or Christ is thrown out altogether and his teaching is taken, or Christ is really made into an idol. Spirit is the denial of direct immediacy. If Christ is true God, then he also must be unrecognizable, attired in unrecognizability, which is the denial of all straightforwardness. Direct recognizability is specifically characteristic of the idol. But this is what people make Christ into, and this is supposed to be earnestness. They take the direct statement and fantastically form a character corresponding to it (preferably sentimental, with the gentle look, the friendly eye, or whatever else such a foolish pastor can hit upon), and then it is *directly* altogether certain that Christ is God.

What abominable, sentimental frivolity! No, one does not manage to become a Christian at such a cheap price! He is the sign of contradiction, and by the direct statement he attaches himself to you only so that you must face the offense of the contradiction, and the thoughts of your heart are disclosed as you choose whether you will believe or not.

§ 4
In Christ the Secret of Sufferings is the Impossibility of Direct Communication

Christ's sufferings, how he was mocked, scourged, and crucified, have been much and often discussed, especially in earlier times. But in all this, an entirely different kind of suffering seems to be forgotten, the suffering of inwardness, suffering of soul, or what might be called the secret of the sufferings that were inseparable from his life in unrecognizability from the time he appeared until the very last.

It is always painful to have to conceal an inwardness and have to seem to be other than one is — so it is in a merely human situation. It is the most grievous human suffering, and the person who suffers in this way, alas, in one day he often has greater suffering than from all physical tortures combined. I do not presume to decide whether there actually are such collisions or whether a person when he experiences such a collision does not also sin every moment he remains in it — I am speaking only of the suffering. The collision is this, out of love for another person to have to conceal an inwardness and seem to be other than one is. The pains are purely psychical and are as compounded as possible. But it is not good for a pain to be compounded; with each new compounding it acquires one sting more. First there is the painfulness of one's own suffering, for if it is blissful to belong to another person in the mutual under-standing of love, of friendship, then it is painful to have to keep this inwardness to oneself. In the next place, there is the suffering on behalf of the other person. That which is love's solicitude, a love that would do everything, sacrifice its life for the other, here finds its expression in something that has a likeness to the most extreme kind of cruelty — alas, and yet it is love. Finally, the painfulness is the suffering of responsibility. Thus it is out of love to annihilate, immediately and directly, one's own love, yet preserving it, out of love to be cruel to the beloved, out of love to take upon oneself this enormous responsibility.

But now the God-man! The true God *cannot* become directly recognizable, but direct recognizability is what the purely human, what the human beings to whom he came, would plead and implore him for as an indescribable alleviation. And out of love he becomes man! He is love, and yet at every moment he exists he must crucify, so to speak, all human compassion and solicitude — for he can become only the object of faith. But everything called purely human compassion is related to direct recogniz-ability. Yet if he does not become the object of *faith*, he is not true God; and if he is not true God, then he does not save people either. Therefore, by the step he takes out of love he at the same time plunges that person, mankind, into the most horrible decision. Indeed, it is as if one heard a cry from human compassion: Oh, why are you doing this! And yet he does it out of love; he does it to save people. But out there in the horror of this decision he must keep them at a distance if, saved in faith, they are to belong to him at all — and he is love. Out of love he wants to do everything for people; he stakes his life for them, he suffers ignominious death for them — and for them he suffers this life — in divine love and compassion and mercy (compared with which all human compassion counts as nothing) to have to be, humanly speaking, so severe. His whole life is a suffering of inwardness. And then the last part of his life begins with the nocturnal betrayal, then he suffers physical pain and mistreatment; then he endures the suffering of being betrayed by a friend, of standing alone, ridiculed, mocked, spat upon, wearing a crown of thorns and dressed in purple, alone with his, humanly speaking, lost cause — see, what a man, alone among his infuriated enemies — what a dreadful setting, deserted by all his friends — what frightful loneliness! Yet a human being can also suffer in this way, suffer the same mistreatment, suffer even the desertion of his best friend, but then no more. If this is surmounted, then for a human being the cup of suffering is emptied. Here, however, the cup of suffering is filled again, the most bitter of all – he suffers so that this, his suffering, can become and does become an offense to the few believers. It is true that he suffers only once, but unlike a human being he does not escape with the first time of suffering – he suffers through the most grievous suffering the second time, in his concern and grief that his suffering is an occasion for offense.

No human being can comprehend this suffering; to want to comprehend it is presumption.

As far as I who am attempting to describe this am concerned, I perhaps owe a little explanation here. I may at times betray such an acquaintance with concealed inwardness, the suffering of real self-denial, that someone could perhaps have the notion that I, even though an ordinary human being, nevertheless am such a person, one of those rare noble human beings. Far from it. In a strange manner, and not exactly on account of my virtues but rather on account of my sins, I have purely formally become aware of the secrets of existence and the secretiveness of existence in a way in which these and this presumably do not exist for many people. I do not pride myself on this, for it is not on account of my virtues. But I make an honest effort to use this knowledge to illuminate what is humanly true and what is humanly the true good. And this I use in turn to prompt, if possible, an awareness of the holy – about which I always add that no human being can comprehend this and that in regard to this the beginning and ending is worship. Even if one comprehended, fully comprehended, the purely human, this understanding is still a misunderstanding in regard to the God-man. – What responsibility I bear, no one understands as I do. Let no one take the trouble to terrify me on this account, for to him who can terrify me in a totally different way I relate myself in fear and trembling. But then, too, not very many understand as I do that Christianity has been abolished in Christendom.

§ 5
The Possibility of Offense is to Deny Direct Communication

The possibility of offense, as we have tried to show, is present at every moment, confirming at every moment the chasmic abyss between the single individual and the God-man over which faith and faith alone reaches. Thus it is not, to repeat again and again, an accidental relation, so that some perceive the possibility of offense and others not; no, the possibility of offense is the stumbling block for all, whether they choose to believe or they are offended.

Therefore the communication begins with a repulsion. But to begin with a repulsion is to deny direct communication. This is easy to perceive; it presents itself almost physically for perception. Anything that presents itself directly cannot be said to repulse first of all, but anything that presents itself in such a way that it first of all repulses cannot be said to present itself directly. On the other hand, it cannot be said to repulse only, because it presents itself, but in such a way that it first repulses.

But take away the possibility of offense, as has been done in Christendom, and all Christianity becomes direct communication, and then Christianity is abolished, has become something easy, a superficial something that neither wounds nor heals deeply enough; it has become the false invention of purely human compassion that forgets the infinite qualitative difference between God and man.

§ 6
To Deny Direct Communication is to Require Faith

The possibility of offense, the relation in which it begins, is in the most profound sense the expression for "making aware" or expresses that the greatest possible attention is required on the part of a human being (indeed, on a scale that is anything but the purely human, for it is on a divine scale) with respect to the decision to become a believer. Direct communication perhaps also seeks as well as it can to make the recipient aware: it pleads and implores him, it lays the importance of the cause right on his heart; it admonishes, threatens, etc. – this is all direct communication again, and therefore there is neither sufficient earnestness with regard to the supreme decision nor is sufficient awareness gained.

No, the way to begin is to deny direct communication – that is earnestness. The possibility of offense is frightful, and yet, just like the Law in relation to the Gospel, it is rigorousness that is part of the earnestness. There is no direct communication and no direct reception: there is a choice. It does not take place, as in direct communication, with coaxing and threatening and admonishing – and then, then, quite imperceptibly, little by little comes the transition, the transition to accepting it more or less, to keeping oneself convinced of it, to being of the opinion etc. No, a very specific kind of reception is required – that of faith. And faith itself is a dialectical qualification. Faith is a choice, certainly not direct reception – and the recipient is the one who is disclosed, whether he will believe or be offended.

But the whole of modern philosophy has done everything to delude us into thinking that faith is an immediate qualification, that it is the immediate – which in turn is linked up with having abolished the possibility of offense, having made Christianity into a teaching, having abolished the God-man and the situation of contemporaneity. What modern philosophy understands by faith is really what is called having an opinion or what in everyday language some people call "to believe." Christianity is made into a teaching; this teaching is then proclaimed to a person, and he believes that it is as this teaching says. Then the next stage is to "comprehend" this teaching, and this philosophy does. All of this would be entirely proper if Christianity were a teaching, but since it is not, all this is totally wrong. Faith in a significant sense is related to the God-man. But the God-man, the sign of contradiction, denies direct communication – and calls for faith.

That to deny direct communication is to require faith can be simply pointed out in purely human situations if it is kept in mind that faith in its most eminent sense is related to the God-man. Let us examine this and to that end take the relationship between two lovers. I first assume this situation: in the most ardent terms, the lover assures the beloved of his love, and his entire bearing corresponds to this assurance, almost sheer adoration. He now asks the beloved, "Do you *believe* that I love you?" The beloved answers, "Yes, I *do believe* it." This is how we do indeed talk. But let us now suppose that the lover has the idea of wanting to test the beloved to see whether she does believe him. What does he do? He cuts off all direct communication, changes himself into a duplexity; as a possibility it looks deceptive, as if he possibly could be just as much a deceiver as the faithful lover. This is making oneself into a riddle, but what is a riddle? A riddle is a question, and what does the question ask about? It asks whether she loves him. − Now, I do not decide whether he has the right to do this; I merely follow the thought-categories, and in any case it must be kept in mind that a maieutic teacher to a certain extent does the same thing, poses the dialectical duplexity, but with the directly opposite intention, just to turn the other person away from him, to turn him inward in order to make him free, not in order to draw him to himself. − The difference in the lover's conduct is easy to see. In the first instance he asks directly: Do you believe me? In the second instance he makes himself into a question: whether she believes him. He perhaps bitterly comes to regret that he allowed himself to do such a thing − I have nothing to do with that; I merely follow the thought-categories. From a dialectical point of view, it is positively certain that the latter method is a far more basic way in which to require faith. The purpose of the latter method is to make the beloved disclose herself in a choice; that is, out of this duplexity she must choose which character she believes is the true one. If she chooses the good character, it is disclosed that she believes him. It is disclosed, since he does not help her at all; on the contrary, by means of the duplexity he has placed her entirely alone without any assistance whatsoever. He is a duplexity, and now the question is what she judges about him, but he understands it differently, for he sees that it is not he who is being judged but it is she who is disclosed in how she judges. Whether he is allowed to do this, I do not decide − I merely pursue the thought-categories. His method, which as long as it lasts may cause him indescribable suffering in unrest and concern, is simultaneously an almost chilling, inhuman indifference, and yet again the most intense passion. But he requires faith. Dialectically he is right, that to believe when one receives direct communication is altogether too direct.

Christianity has never understood by faith anything like this. The God-man must require faith and in order to require faith must deny direct communication. In a certain sense he cannot do otherwise, and he does not want it otherwise. As the God-man he is qualitatively different from any man, and therefore he must deny direct communication; he must *require* faith and require that he become the *object of faith*.

In the relation between individuals, one person must and shall be content with the other's assurance that he believes him; no one has the right to make himself into an object of faith for the other person. If one person is to use dialectical redoubling [*Fordoblelse*] in relation to another, he must in exactly the opposite way use it maieutically in order to avoid becoming an object of faith or an approximation thereof for another. The dialectical duplexity [*Dobbelthed*] is provisional; the next stage unconditionally brings falseness if, instead of using the dialectical duplexity for parrying, a person allows himself the presumption of becoming an object of faith for another person. But even with respect to the maieutic I do not decide to what extent, Christianly speaking, it is to be approved.

But only the God-man cannot do otherwise and, as qualitatively different from man, must insist upon being the object of faith. If he does not become this, he becomes an idol − and therefore he must deny direct communication because he must require faith.

§ 7

The Object of Faith is the God-man Precisely Because the God-man is the Possibility of Offense

So inseparable is the possibility of offense from faith that if the God-man were not the possibility of offense he could not be the object of faith, either. Thus the possibility of offense is taken up into faith, is assimilated by faith, is the negative mark of the God-man. For if there were no possibility of offense, there would be direct recognizability, and then the God-man would be an idol; then direct recognizability is paganism.

One sees how little the gratitude of Christianity has been earned through the abolition of the possibility of offense, how it has been made into a pleasant, a sentimental paganism.

For this is the law: the person who abolishes faith abolishes the possibility of offense, such as when speculation substitutes comprehending for having faith; and the person who abolishes the possibility of offense abolishes faith, such as when the sentimental sermon presentation falsely attributes direct recognizability to Christ. But whether faith is abolished or whether the possibility of offense is abolished, something else is also abolished: the God-man. And if the God-man is abolished, Christianity is abolished.

And in truth, the eighteen hundred years have not contributed a jot to demonstrating the truth of Christianity; on the contrary, with steadily increasing power they have contributed to abolishing Christianity. It is not at all the case, either, as one might logically assume when the demonstration [*Bevis*] of the eighteen hundred years is applauded, that now in the nineteenth century one is convinced [*overbeviist*] of the truth of Christianity in a way totally different from the way the people were in the first and second generations – it is indeed rather the case (and this really sounds somewhat satirical on the worshipers and adorers of that demonstration) that in proportion as the demonstration increased in power – fewer and fewer were convinced. But this is what happens when once and for all the crucial point in something is missed: frightful confusions can result that increase from generation to generation. Now, since it has been *demonstrated*, and on an enormous scale, that Christianity is the truth, now there is no one, almost no one, who is willing to make any sacrifice for its sake. When one – shall I say when one "only" believed its truth – then one sacrificed life and blood. What a frightful delusion! If only, as that pagan who burned the libraries, one could push aside those eighteen hundred years – if one cannot do that, then Christianity is indeed abolished. If only it could be made evident to all those orators who demonstrate the truth of Christianity by the eighteen hundred years and win people, if only it could be made evident to them, frightful as it is, that they are betraying, denying, abolishing Christianity – if that cannot be done, then Christianity is abolished.

4

PHENOMENOLOGY AND THEOLOGY

Martin Heidegger

Preface

This little book contains a lecture and a letter.

The lecture "Phenomenology and Theology" was given on March 9, 1927, in Tübingen and was again delivered on February 14, 1928, in Marburg. The text presented here forms the content of the immediately reworked and improved second part of the Marburg lecture: "The Positivity of Theology and Its Relation to Phenomenology." In the Introduction to Being and Time *(1927) §7, pp. 27ff., one finds a discussion of the notion of phenomenology (as well as its relation to the positive sciences) that guides the presentation here.*

The letter of March 11, 1964, gives some pointers to major aspects for a theological discussion concerning "The Problem of a Nonobjectifying Thinking and Speaking in Today's Theology." The discussion took place at Drew University in Madison, New Jersey, on April 9–11, 1964.

These texts were published for the first time in Archives de Philosophie, *vol. 32 (1969), pp. 356ff., with an accompanying French translation.*

This little book might perhaps be able to occasion repeated reflection on the extent to which the Christianness of Christianity and its theology merit questioning; but also on the extent to which philosophy, in particular that presented here, merits questioning.

Almost one hundred years ago there appeared simultaneously (1873) two writings of two friends: the "first piece" of the Thoughts Out of Season *of Friedrich Nietzsche, wherein "the glorious Hölderlin" is mentioned; and the "little book"* On the Christianness of Today's Theology *of Franz Overbeck, who established the world-denying expectation of the end as the basic characteristic of what is primordially Christian.*

To say both writings are unseasonable also in today's changed world means: For the few who think among the countless who reckon, these writings intend and point toward that which itself perseveres before the inaccessible through speaking, questioning, and creating.

For a discussion of the wider realm of investigation of both writings, see Martin Heidegger, "Nietzsche's Word: 'God Is Dead,'" in Holzwege *(1950), pp. 193ff.; and "European Nihilism" and "The Determination of Nihilism in the History of Being" in* Nietzsche, *vol. II, pp. 7–232 and 233–96. Both texts were published separately in 1967.*

Freiburg im Breisgau, August 27, 1970

The popular understanding of the relationship between theology and philosophy is fond of opposing faith and knowledge, revelation and reason. Philosophy is that interpretation of the world and of life that is removed from revelation and free from faith. Theology, on the other hand, is the expression of the credal understanding of the world and of life – in our case a Christian understanding. Taken as such, philosophy and theology give expression to a tension and a struggle between two worldviews. This relationship is decided not by scientific argument but by the manner, the extent, and the strength of the conviction and the proclamation of the worldview.

We, however, see the problem of the relationship *differently* from the very start. It is for us rather a question about the *relationship of two sciences*.

But this question needs a more precise formulation. It is not a case of comparing the factical circumstances of two historically given sciences. And even if it were, it would be difficult to describe a unified state of affairs regarding the two sciences today in the midst of their divergent directions. To proceed on a course of comparison with respect to their factical relationship would yield no *fundamental* insight as to how Christian theology and philosophy are related to one another.

Thus what is needed as a basis for a fundamental discussion of the problem is an ideal construction of the ideas behind the two sciences. One can decide their possible relationship to one another from the possibilities they both have as sciences.

Posing the question like this, however, presupposes that we have established the idea of science in general, as well as how to characterize the modifications of this idea that are possible in principle. (We cannot enter into this problem here; it would have to be taken up in the prolegomena to our discussion.) We offer only as a guide the following formal definition of science: science is the founding disclosure, for the sheer sake of disclosure, of a self-contained region of beings, or of being. Every region of objects, according to its subject matter and the mode of being of its objects, has its own mode of possible disclosure, evidence, founding, and its own conceptual formation of the knowledge thus arising. It is evident from the idea of science as such – insofar as it is understood as a possibility of Dasein – that there are two basic possibilities of science: sciences of beings, of whatever is, or ontic sciences; and *the* science of being, the ontological science, philosophy.

Ontic sciences in each case thematize a given being that in a certain manner is always already disclosed *prior* to scientific disclosure. We call the sciences of beings as given – of a *positum* – positive sciences. Their characteristic feature lies in the fact that the objectification of whatever it is that they thematize is oriented directly toward beings, as a continuation of an already existing prescientific attitude toward such beings. Ontology, or the science of being, on the other hand, demands a fundamental shift of view: from beings to being. And this shift nevertheless keeps beings in view, but for a modified attitude. We shall not go into the question of the method of this shift here.

Within the circle of actual or possible sciences of beings – the positive sciences – there is between any two only a relative difference, based on the different relations that in each case orient a science to a specific region of beings. On the other hand, every positive science is *absolutely*, not relatively, different from philosophy. Our thesis, then, is that *theology is a positive science, and as such, therefore, is absolutely different from philosophy*.

Hence one must ask how theology is related to philosophy in the light of this absolute difference. It is immediately clear from the thesis that theology, as a positive science, is in principle closer to chemistry and mathematics than to philosophy. Put in this way, we have the most extreme formulation of the relationship between theology and philosophy – one that runs counter to the popular view. According to this popular view, each of the sciences [philosophy and theology], to a certain extent, has as its theme the same area: human life and the world. But they are guided by different points of view. The one proceeds from the principle of *faith*, the other from the principle of *reason*. However, our thesis is: Theology is a positive science and as such is absolutely different from philosophy.

The task of our discussion will be to characterize theology as a positive science and, on the basis of this characterization, to clarify its possible relationship to philosophy, which is absolutely different from it.

Note that we are considering theology here in the sense of Christian theology. This is not to say that Christian theology is the only theology. The most central question is whether, indeed, theology in general is a science. This question is deferred here, not because we wish to evade the problem, but only because that question cannot be asked meaningfully until the idea of theology has been clarified to a certain extent.

Before turning to the discussion proper, we wish to submit the following considerations. In accordance with our thesis, we are considering a positive science, and evidently one of a particular kind. Therefore a few remarks are in order about what constitutes the positive character of a science as such.

Proper to the positive character of a science is: first, that a being that in some way is already disclosed is to a certain extent come upon as a possible theme of theoretical objectification and inquiry; second, that this given *positum* is come upon in a definite prescientific manner of approaching and proceeding with that being. In this manner of procedure, the specific content of this region and the mode of being of the particular entity show themselves. That is, this disclosure is prior to any theoretical apprehending, although it is perhaps implicit and not thematically known. Third, it is proper to the positive character of a science that this prescientific comportment toward whatever is given (nature, history, economy, space, number) is also already illuminated and guided by an understanding of being – even if it be nonconceptual. The positive character can vary according to the substantive content of the entity, its mode of being, the manner in which it is prescientifically disclosed, and the manner in which this disclosedness belongs to it.

The question thus arises: Of what sort is the positive character of theology? Evidently this question must be answered before we can be in a position to determine its relation to philosophy. But setting down the positive character of theology will not yet sufficiently clarify its status as a science. We have not yet arrived at the full concept of theology as a science, but only at what is proper to it as a positive science. If thematizing is supposed to adjust the direction of inquiry, the manner of investigation, and the conceptuality to the particular *positum* in each case, it is more to the point here to identify the specific scientific character belonging to the specific positive character of theology. Therefore, only by identifying the positive *and* the scientific character of theology do we approach this discipline as a positive science and acquire the basis for characterizing its possible relationship to philosophy.

Thus our consideration obtains a threefold division:
A. the positive character of theology;
B. the scientific character of theology;
C. the possible relation of theology, as a positive science, to philosophy.

A. The Positive Character of Theology

A positive science is the founding disclosure of a being that is given and in some way
already disclosed. The question arises: What is already given for theology? One might
say: What is given for Christian theology is Christianity as something that has come
about historically, witnessed by the history of religion and spirit and presently visible
through its institutions, cults, communities, and groups as a widespread phenomenon
in world history. Christianity: the given *positum*; and hence theology: the science of
Christianity. That would evidently be an erroneous characterization of theology, for
theology itself belongs to Christianity. Theology itself is something that everywhere in
world history gives testimony to its intimate connection with Christianity itself as a
whole. Evidently, then, theology cannot be the science of Christianity as something that
has come about in world history, because it is a science that itself belongs to the history of
Christianity, is carried along by that history, and in turn influences that history.

Is theology therefore a science that itself belongs to the history of Christianity in the
way that every historical [*historische*] discipline is itself a historical [*geschichtliche*] appearance, namely, by representing the historical development of its consciousness of
history? If this were the case, then we could characterize theology as the self-
consciousness of Christianity as it appears in world history. However, theology does
not belong to Christianity merely because, as something historical, the latter has a place
in the general manifestations of culture. Rather, theology is a knowledge of that which
initially makes possible something like Christianity as an event in world history.
Theology is a conceptual knowing of that which first of all allows Christianity to
become an originarily historical event, a knowing of that which we call Christianness
pure and simple. Thus we maintain that *what is given for theology (its positum) is
Christianness*. The latter decides the form theology will take as the positive science
that thematizes it. The question arises: what does "Christianness" mean?

We call faith Christian. The essence of faith can formally be sketched as a way of
existence of human Dasein that, according to its own testimony – itself belonging to
this way of existence – arises *not from* Dasein or spontaneously *through* Dasein, but
rather from that which is revealed in and with this way of existence, from what is
believed. For the "Christian" faith, that being which is primarily revealed to faith, and
only to it, and which, as revelation, first gives rise to faith, is Christ, the crucified God.
The relationship of faith to the cross, determined in this way by Christ, is a Christian
one. The crucifixion, however, and all that belongs to it is a historical event, and
indeed this event gives testimony to itself as such in its specifically historical character
only for faith in the scriptures. One "knows" about this fact only *in believing*.

That which is thus revealed in faith is, in accordance with its specific "sacrificial"
character, imparted specifically to individual human beings factically existing historic-

ally (whether contemporaneous or not), or to the community of these individuals existing as a community. The imparting of this revelation is not a conveyance of information about present, past, or imminent happenings; rather, this imparting lets one "part-take" of the event that is revelation (= what is revealed therein) itself. But the part-*taking* of faith, which is realized only in existing, is *given* as such always only through faith. Furthermore, this "part-taking" and "having part in" the event of the crucifixion places one's entire existence [*Dasein*] – as a Christian existence, i.e., one bound to the cross – before God. And thereby the existence struck by this revelation is revealed to itself in its forgetfulness of God. Thus – and again I speak only of an ideal construction of the idea – being placed before God means that existence is reoriented in and through the mercy of God grasped in faith. Thus faith understands itself only in believing. In any case, the believer does not come to know anything about his specific existence, for instance, by way of a theoretical confirmation of his inner experiences. Rather, he can only "believe" this possibility of existence as one which the Dasein concerned does not independently master, in which it becomes a slave, is brought before God, and is thus born *again*. Accordingly, the proper existentiell meaning of faith is: *faith = rebirth*. And rebirth does not mean a momentary outfitting with some quality or other, but a way in which a factical, believing Dasein historically exists in *that* history which begins with the occurrence of revelation; in *that* history which, in accord with the very meaning of the revelation, has a definite uttermost end. The occurrence of revelation, which is passed down to faith and which accordingly occurs in faithfulness itself, discloses itself only to faith.

Luther said, "Faith is permitting ourselves to be seized by the things we do not see" (*Werke* [Erlangen Ausgabe], vol. 46, p. 287). Yet faith is not something that merely reveals that the occurring of salvation is something happening; it is not some more or less modified type of knowing. Rather, faith is an appropriation of revelation that co-constitutes the Christian occurrence, that is, the mode of existence that specifies a factical Dasein's Christianness as a particular form of destiny. *Faith is the believing-understanding mode of existing in the history revealed, i.e., occurring, with the Crucified.*

The totality of this being that is disclosed by faith – in such a way, indeed, that faith itself belongs to the context of its disclosure – constitutes the character of the *positum* that theology finds before it. *Presupposing* that theology is enjoined on faith, out of faith, and for faith, and *presupposing* that science is a *freely* performed, conceptual disclosure and objectification, theology is constituted in thematizing faith and that which is disclosed through faith, that which is "revealed." It is worthy of note that faith is not just the manner in which the *positum* objectified by theology is already disclosed and presented; faith itself is a theme for theology. And not only that. Insofar as theology is enjoined upon faith, it can find sufficient motivation for itself only in faith. If faith would totally oppose a conceptual interpretation, then theology would be a thoroughly *inappropriate* means of grasping its object, faith. It would lack something so essential that without this it could never become a science in the first place. The necessity of theology, therefore, can never be deduced from a purely rationally constructed system of sciences. Furthermore, faith not only motivates the intervention of an interpretive science of Christianness; at the same time, faith, as rebirth, is *that* history to whose occurrence theology itself, for its part, is supposed to contribute.

Theology has a meaning and a legitimacy only if it functions as an ingredient of faith, of this particular kind of historical occurrence.

By attempting to elucidate this connection [between theology and faith], we are likewise showing how, through the specific positive character of theology, i.e., through the Christian occurrence disclosed in faith as faith, the scientific character of the science of faith is prefigured.

B. The Scientific Character of Theology

Theology is the science of faith.

This says several things:

(1) Theology is the science of that which is disclosed in faith, of that which is believed. That which is believed in this case is not some coherent order of propositions about facts or occurrences which we simply agree to – which, although theoretically not self-evident, can be appropriated because we agree to them.

(2) Theology is accordingly the science of the very comportment of believing, of faithfulness – in each case a revealed faithfulness, which cannot possibly be any other way. This means that faith, as the comportment of believing, is itself believed, itself belongs to that which is believed.

(3) Theology, furthermore, is the science of faith, not only insofar as it makes faith and that which is believed its object, but because it itself arises out of faith. It is the science that faith of itself motivates and justifies.

(4) Theology, finally, is the science of faith insofar as it not only makes faith its object and is motivated by faith, but because this objectification of faith itself, in accordance with what is objectified here, has no other purpose than to help cultivate faithfulness itself for its part.

Formally considered, then, faith as the existing relation to the Crucified is a mode of historical Dasein, of human existence, of historically being in a history that discloses itself only in and for faith. Therefore theology, as the science of faith, that is, of an intrinsically *historical* [geschichtlichen] mode of being, is to the very core a *historical* [historische] science. And indeed it is a unique sort of historical science in accord with the unique historicity involved in faith, i.e., with "the occurrence of revelation."

As conceptual interpretation of itself on the part of faithful existence, that is, as historical knowledge, theology aims solely at that transparency of the Christian occurrence that is revealed in, and delimited by, faithfulness itself. Thus the goal of this historical science is concrete Christian existence itself. Its goal is never a valid system of theological propositions about general states of affairs within one region of being that is present at hand among others. The transparency of faithful existence is an understanding of existence and as such can relate only to existing itself. Every theological statement and concept addresses itself in its very content to the faithful existence of the individual in the community; it does *not* do so subsequently, on the basis of some practical "*application.*" The specific content of the object of theology demands that the appropriate theological knowledge never take the form of some free-floating knowledge of arbitrary states of affairs. Likewise, the theological transparency and conceptual interpretation of faith cannot found and secure faith in its legitimacy, nor can it in any way make it easier to accept faith and remain constant in faith. Theology can only render faith more difficult, that is, render it more certain that faithfulness cannot be gained through the science of theology, but solely through faith. Hence theology can permit the serious character of faithfulness as a "graciously bestowed" mode of existence to become a matter of conscience. Theology "can" perform this; i.e., it is capable of this, but it is *only possibly* that it may have this effect.

In summary, then, theology is a *historical science*, in accordance with the character of the *positum* objectified by it. It would seem that with this thesis we are denying the possibility and the necessity of a *systematic* as well as a *practical* theology. However, one should note that we did not say that there is only "historical theology," to the exclusion of "systematic" and "practical" theology. Rather our thesis is: Theology as such is historical as a science, regardless of how it may be divided into various disciplines. And it is precisely this characterization that enables one to understand why and how theology originally divided into a systematic, a historical (in the narrower sense), and a practical discipline – not in addition, but in keeping with the specific unity of its theme. The philosophical understanding of a science is, after all, not achieved by merely latching on to its factical and contingent, pregiven structure and simply accepting the technical division of labor in order then to join the various disciplines together externally and subsume them under a "general" concept. Rather, a philosophical understanding requires that we question beyond the factically existing structure and ascertain *whether* and *why* this structure is demanded by the essence of the science in question and to what extent the factical organization corresponds to the idea of the science as determined by the character of its *positum*.

In reference to theology it thus becomes evident that, because it is a conceptual interpretation of Christian existence, the content of all its concepts is essentially related to the Christian occurrence as such. *To grasp the substantive content and the specific mode of being of the Christian occurrence, and to grasp it solely as it is testified to in faith and for faith, is the task of systematic theology.* If indeed faithfulness is testified to in the *scriptures*, systematic theology is in its essence *New Testament theology*. In other words, theology is not systematic in that it first breaks up the totality of the content of faith into a series of *loci*, in order then to reintegrate them within the framework of a system and subsequently to prove the validity of the system. It is systematic not by constructing a system, but on the contrary by *avoiding* a system, in the sense that it seeks solely to bring clearly to light the intrinsic ο ὐστημα of the Christian occurrence as such, that is, to place the believer who understands conceptually into the history of revelation. The more historical theology is and the more immediately it brings to word and concept the historicity of faith, the more is it "systematic" and the less likely is it to become the slave of a system. The radicality with which one knows of this task and its methodological exigencies is the criterion for the scientific level of a systematic theology. Such a task will be more certainly and purely accomplished the more directly theology permits its concepts and conceptual schemes to be determined by the mode of being and the specific substantive content of *that* entity which it objectifies. The more unequivocally theology disburdens itself of the application of some philosophy and its system, the more *philosophical* is its own radical scientific character.

On the other hand, the more systematic theology is in the way we have designated, the more immediately does it found the *necessity of historical theology in the narrower sense* of exegesis, church history, and history of dogma. If these disciplines are to be genuine *theology* and not special areas of the general, profane historical sciences, then they *must* permit themselves to be guided in the choice of their object by systematic theology correctly understood.

The Christian occurrence's interpretation of itself as a historical occurrence also implies, however, that its own specific historicity is appropriated ever anew, along with an understanding, arising from that historicity, of the possibilities of a faithful existence [*Dasein*]. Now because theology, as a systematic as well as a historical discipline, has for its primary object the Christian occurrence in its Christianness and its historicity, and because this occurrence specifies itself as a mode of existence of the believer, and existing is action, πρᾶξις, *theology in its essence has the character of a practical science*. As the science of the action of God on human beings who act in faith it is already "innately" homiletical. And for this reason alone is it possible for theology itself to constitute itself in its factical organization as practical theology, as homiletics and catechetics, and not on account of contingent requirements that demand, say, that it apply its theoretical propositions to a practical sphere. *Theology is systematic only when it is historical and practical. It is historical only when it is systematic and practical. And it is practical only when it is systematic and historical.*

All of these characteristics essentially hang together. The contemporary controversies in theology can turn into a genuine exchange and fruitful communication only if the problem of theology as a science is followed back to the central question that derives from considering *theology as a positive science*: What is the ground of the specific unity and necessary plurality of the systematic, historical, and practical disciplines of theology?

We can add a few clarifications to this sketchy outline of the character of theology by showing what theology is *not*.

Etymologically regarded, theo-logy means: science of God. But God is in no way the object of investigation in theology, as, for example, animals are the theme of zoology. Theology is not speculative knowledge of God. And we hit upon the concept of theology no better when we expand the theme and say: The object of theology is the all-inclusive relationship of God to man and of man to God. In that case theology would be the philosophy or the history of religion, in short, *Religionswissenschaft*. Even less is it the psychology of religion, i.e., the science of man and his religious states and experiences, the analysis of which is supposed to lead ultimately to the discovery of God in man. One could, however, admit that theology does not coincide in general with speculative knowledge of God, the scientific study of religion, or the psychology of religion – and still want to stress that theology represents a special case of the philosophy and history of religion, etc., namely, the philosophical, historical, and psychological science of the Christian religion.

Yet it is clear from what we have said that systematic theology is not a form of the philosophy of religion applied to the Christian religion. Nor is church history a history of religion limited to the Christian religion. In all such interpretations of theology the idea of this science is abandoned from the very beginning. That is, it is *not* conceived with regard to the specific positive character of theology, but rather is arrived at by way of a deduction and specialization of nontheological sciences – philosophy, history, and psychology – sciences that, indeed, are quite heterogeneous to one another. Of course, to determine where the limits of the scientific character of theology lie, i.e., to determine how far the specific exigencies of faithfulness itself can and do press for conceptual transparency and still remain faithful, is both a difficult and a central problem. It is tied most closely to the question about the original ground of the unity of the three disciplines of theology.

In no case may we delimit the scientific character of theology by using an *other* science as the guiding standard of evidence for its mode of proof or as the measure of rigor of its conceptuality. In accord with the *positum* of theology (which is essentially disclosed only in faith), not only is the access to its object unique, but the evidence for the demonstration of its propositions is quite special. The conceptuality proper to theology can grow only out of theology itself. There is certainly no need for it to borrow from other sciences in order to augment and secure its proofs. Nor indeed can it attempt to substantiate or justify the evidence of faith by drawing on knowledge gained from other sciences. *Rather, theology itself is founded primarily by faith*, even though its statements and procedures of proof formally derive from free operations of reason.

Likewise, the shortcomings of the nontheological science with respect to what faith reveals is no proof of the legitimacy of faith. One can allow "faithless" science to run up against and be shattered by faith only if one already faithfully holds fast to the truth of faith. But faith misconceives itself if it then thinks that it is first proven right or even thereby fortified when the other sciences shatter against it. The substantive legitimacy of all theological knowledge is grounded in faith itself, originates out of faith, and leaps back into faith.

On the grounds of its specific positive character and the form of knowing which this determines, we can now say that theology is a fully autonomous ontic science. The question now arises: How is this positive science, with its specific positive and scientific character, related to philosophy?

C. The Relation of Theology, as a Positive Science, to Philosophy

If faith does not need philosophy, the *science* of faith as a *positive* science does. And here again we must distinguish: The positive science of faith does not need philosophy for the founding and primary disclosure of its *positum*, Christianness, which founds itself in its own manner. The positive science of faith needs philosophy only in regard to its scientific character, and even then only in a uniquely restricted, though basic, way.

As a science theology places itself under the claim that its concepts show and are appropriate to the being that it has undertaken to interpret. But is it not the case that that which is to be interpreted in theological concepts is precisely that which is disclosed only through, for, and in faith? Is not that which is supposed to be grasped conceptually here something essentially inconceivable, and consequently something whose content is not to be fathomed, and whose legitimacy is not to be founded, by purely rational means?

Nevertheless, something can very well be inconceivable and never primarily disclosable through reason without thereby excluding a conceptual grasp of itself. On the contrary: if its inconceivability as such is indeed to be disclosed properly, it can only be by way of the appropriate conceptual interpretation – and that means pushing such interpretation to its very limits. Otherwise the inconceivability remains, as it were, mute. Yet this interpretation of faithful existence is the task of theology. And so, why philosophy? Whatever is discloses itself only on the grounds of a preliminary (although not explicitly known), preconceptual understanding of what and how such a being is. Every ontic interpretation operates on the basis, at first and for the most part concealed, of an ontology. But can such things as the cross, sin, etc., which manifestly belong to the ontological context of Christianness, be understood specifically as to what they are and how they are, except through faith? How does one ontologically disclose the what (the essence) and the how (the mode of being) underlying these fundamental concepts that are constitutive of Christianness? Is faith to become the criterion of knowledge for an ontological-philosophical explication? Are not the basic theological concepts completely withdrawn from philosophical-ontological reflection?

Of course one should not lose sight here of something essential: the explication of basic concepts, insofar as it proceeds correctly, is never accomplished by explicating and defining isolated concepts with reference to themselves alone and then operating with them here and there as if they were playing chips. Rather, all such explication must take pains to envision and hold constantly in view in its original totality the primary, self-contained ontological context to which all the basic concepts refer. What does this mean for the explication of basic theological concepts?

We characterized faith as the essential constitutive element of Christianness: faith is rebirth. Though faith does not bring itself about, and though what is revealed in faith can never be founded by way of a rational knowing as exercised by autonomously functioning reason, nevertheless the sense of the Christian occurrence as rebirth is that Dasein's prefaithful, i.e., unbelieving, existence is sublated [*aufgehoben*] therein. Sublated does not mean done away with, but raised up, kept, and preserved in the new creation. One's pre-Christian existence is indeed existentielly, ontically, overcome in faith. But this existentiell overcoming of one's pre-Christian existence (which belongs to faith as rebirth) means precisely that one's overcome pre-Christian Dasein is existentially, ontologically included within faithful existence. To overcome does not mean to dispose of, but to have at one's disposition in a new way. Hence we can say that precisely because all basic theological concepts, considered in their full regional context, include a content that is indeed existentielly powerless, i.e., *ontically* sublated, they are *ontologically* determined by a content that is pre-Christian and that can thus be grasped purely rationally. All theological concepts necessarily contain *that* understanding of being that is constitutive of human Dasein as such, insofar as it exists at all.[2] Thus, for example, sin is manifest only in faith, and only the believer can factically exist as a sinner. But if sin, which is the counterphenomenon to faith as rebirth and hence a phenomenon of existence, is to be interpreted in theological concepts, then the *content* of the concept *itself*, and not just any philosophical preference of the theologian, calls for a return to the concept of guilt. But guilt is an original ontological determination of the existence of Dasein.[3] The more originally and appropriately the basic constitution of Dasein is brought to light in a genuine ontological manner and the more originally, for example, the concept of guilt is grasped, the more clearly it can function as a guide for the theological explication of sin.

But if one takes the ontological concept of guilt as a guide, then it seems that it is primarily philosophy that decides about theological concepts. And, then, is not theology being led on the leash by philosophy? Not at all. For sin, in its essence, is not to be deduced rationally from the concept of guilt. Even less so should or can the basic fact of sin be rationally demonstrated, in whatever manner, by way of this orientation to the ontological concept of guilt. Not even the factical possibility of sin is in the least bit evidenced in this way. Only one thing is accomplished by this orientation; but that one thing is indispensable for theology as a science: The theological concept of sin as a concept of existence acquires that correction (i.e., co-direction) that is necessary for it insofar as the concept of existence has pre-Christian content. But the primary direction (derivation), the source of its Christian content, is given only by faith. *Therefore ontology functions only as a corrective to the ontic, and in particular pre-Christian, content of basic theological concepts.*

Here one must note, however, that this correction does not found anything, in the way, for example, that the basic concepts of physics acquire from an ontology of nature their original foundation, the demonstration of all their inner possibilities, and hence their higher truth. Rather, this correction is only formally indicative; that is to say, the ontological concept of guilt as such is never a theme of theology. Also the concept of sin is not simply built up upon the ontological concept of guilt. Nevertheless, the latter is determinative in one respect, in that it formally indicates the ontological character of *that* region of being in which the concept of sin *as a concept of existence* must necessarily maintain itself.

In thus formally indicating the ontological region, there lies the directive not to calculate philosophically the specific theological content of the concept but rather to allow it to arise out of, and to present itself within, the specific existential dimension of faith thereby indicated. Thus, formally indicating the ontological concept does not serve to bind but, on the contrary, to release and point to the specific, i.e., credal source of the disclosure of theological concepts. The function of ontology here is not to direct, but only, in "co-directing," to correct.

> Philosophy is the formally indicative ontological corrective of the ontic and, in particular, of the pre-Christian content of basic theological concepts.

But it is not of the essence of philosophy, and it can never be established by philosophy itself or for its own purpose, that it must have such a corrective function for theology. On the other hand, it can be shown that philosophy, as the free questioning of purely self-reliant Dasein, does of its essence have the task of directing all other nontheological, positive sciences with respect to their ontological foundation. As ontology, philosophy does provide the *possibility* of being employed by theology as a corrective, in the sense we have discussed, if indeed theology is to be factical with respect to the facticity of faith. The demand, however, that it *must* be so employed is not made by philosophy as such but rather by theology, insofar as it understands itself to be a science. In summary, then, the precise formulation is:

> Philosophy is the possible, formally indicative ontological corrective of the ontic and, in particular, of the pre-Christian content of basic theological

concepts. But philosophy can be what it is without functioning factically as this corrective.

This peculiar relationship does not exclude but rather includes the fact that *faith*, as a specific possibility of existence, is in its innermost core the mortal enemy of the *form of existence* that is an essential part of *philosophy* and that is factically ever-changing.[4] Faith is so absolutely the mortal enemy that philosophy does not even begin to want in any way to do battle with it. This *existentiell opposition* between faithfulness and the free appropriation of one's whole Dasein is not first brought about by the sciences of theology and philosophy but is *prior* to them. Furthermore, it is precisely this *opposition* that must bear the *possibility of a community of the sciences* of theology and philosophy, if indeed they are to communicate in a genuine way, free from illusions and weak attempts at mediation. Accordingly, there is no such thing as a Christian philosophy; that is an absolute "square circle." On the other hand, there is likewise no such thing as a neo-Kantian, or axiological, or phenomenological theology, just as there is no phenomenological mathematics. Phenomenology is always only the name for the procedure of ontology, a procedure that essentially distinguishes itself from that of all other, positive sciences.

It is true that someone engaged in research can master, in addition to his own positive science, phenomenology as well, or at least follow its steps and investigations. But philosophical knowledge can become genuinely relevant and fertile for his own positive science *only when*, within the problematic that stems from such positive deliberation on the ontic correlations in his field, he comes upon the basic concepts of his science and, furthermore, questions the suitability of traditional fundamental concepts with respect to those beings that are the theme of his science. Then, proceeding from the demands of his science and from the horizon of his own scientific inquiry, which lies, so to speak, on the frontiers of his basic concepts, he can search back for the original ontological constitution of those beings that are to remain and *become* anew the object of his science. The questions that arise in this way methodically thrust beyond themselves insofar as that *about which* they are asking is accessible and determinable only ontologically. To be sure, scientific communication between researchers in the positive sciences and philosophy cannot be tied down to definite rules, especially since the clarity, certainty, and originality of critiques by scientists of the foundations of their own positive sciences change as often and are as varied as the stage reached and maintained by philosophy at any point in clarifying its own essence. This communication becomes and remains genuine, lively, and fruitful only when the respective positive-ontic and transcendental-ontological inquiries are guided by an instinct for the issues and by the certainty of scientific good sense, and when all the questions about dominance, pre-eminence, and validity of the sciences recede behind the inner necessities of the scientific problem itself.

Appendix

The Theological Discussion of "The Problem of a Nonobjectifying Thinking and Speaking in Today's Theology" – Some Pointers to Its Major Aspects

Freiburg im Breisgau, March 11, 1964

What is it that is worth questioning in this problem? As far as I see, there are *three themes* that must be thought through.

(1) Above all else one must determine *what* theology, as a mode of thinking and speaking, is to place in discussion. That is the Christian faith, and what is believed therein. Only if this is kept clearly in view can one inquire how thinking and speaking are to be formulated so that together they correspond to the proper sense and claim of faith and thus avoid projecting into faith ideas that are alien to it.

(2) *Prior* to a discussion of *non*objectifying thinking and speaking, it is ineluctable that one state what is intended by *objectifying* thinking and speaking. Here the question arises whether or not all thinking and speaking are objectifying by their very nature.

Should it prove evident that thinking and speaking are by no means in themselves already objectifying, then this leads to a third theme.

(3) One must decide to what extent the problem of a nonobjectifying thinking and speaking is a genuine problem at all, whether one is not inquiring here about something in such a way that only circumvents the matter, diverts from the theme of theology and unnecessarily confounds it. In this case the convened theological dialogue would have the task of clearly seeing that it was on a path leading nowhere with its problem. This would – so it seems – be a merely negative result of the dialogue. But it only seems that way. For in truth this would necessitate that theology once and for all get clear about the requisite of its major task not to borrow the categories of its thinking and the form of its speech from philosophy or the sciences, but to think and speak out of faith for faith with fidelity to its subject matter. If this faith by the power of its own conviction concerns the human being as human being in his very nature, then genuine theological thinking and speaking have no need of any special preparation in order to reach people and find a hearing among them.

These three themes have to be placed in discussion in more detail. I for my part, proceeding from philosophy, can give some pointers only with regard to the second topic. For it is the task of theology to place in discussion the first theme, which necessarily underlies the entire dialogue if it is not to remain up in the air.

The third theme comprises the theological consequences of the first and second, when they are treated sufficiently.

I shall now attempt to give some pointers for treating the *second* theme but this again only in the form of a few questions. One should avoid the impression that dogmatic theses are being stated in terms of a Heideggerian philosophy, when there is no such thing.

Some pointers with regard to the second theme

Prior to placing in discussion the question of a *non*objectifying thinking and speaking in theology, it is necessary to reflect on what one understands by an *objectifying* thinking and speaking, as this problem has been put to the theological dialogue. This reflection necessitates that we ask:

Is objectifying thinking and speaking a particular kind of thinking and speaking, or does all thinking as thinking, all speaking as speaking, necessarily have to be objectifying?

This question can be decided only if beforehand the following questions are clarified and answered:

(a) What does objectifying mean?
(b) What does thinking mean?
(c) What does speaking mean?
(d) Is all thinking in itself a speaking, and all speaking in itself a thinking?
(e) In what sense are thinking and speaking objectifying, and in what sense are they not?

It is of the nature of the matter that these questions interpenetrate when we place them in discussion. The entire weight of these questions, however, lies at the basis of the problem of your theological dialogue. Moreover, these same questions – when more or less clearly and adequately unfolded – form the still hidden center of those endeavors toward which the "philosophy" of our day, from its most extreme counterpositions (Carnap → Heidegger), tends. One calls these positions today: the technical-scientist view of language and the speculative-hermeneutical experience of language.

Both positions are determined by tasks profoundly different from one another. The first position desires to subjugate all thinking and speaking, including that of philosophy, to a sign-system that can be constructed logically or technically, that is, to secure them as an instrument of science. The other position has arisen from the question: what is it that is to be experienced as the proper matter of philosophical thinking, and how is this matter (being as being) to be said?

Hence neither position is concerned with a philosophy of language as a separate province (in the way we have a philosophy of nature or of art). Rather, both positions recognize language as the realm within which the thinking of philosophy and every kind of thinking and saying move and reside. Insofar as the Western tradition has tended to determine the essence of man as that living being that "has language," as ζῶ.ον λόγον ἔχον (even man as an acting being is such only as one that "has language"), the debate between the two positions has nothing less at stake than the question of human existence and its determination.

It is up to theology to decide in what manner and to what extent it can and should enter into this debate.

We preface the following brief elucidation of questions (a) to (e) with an observation that presumably led to the occasion for proposing the "problem of a nonobjectifying thinking and speaking in today's theology." I mean the widespread, uncritically accepted opinion that all thinking, as representing, and all speaking, as vocalization, are already "objectifying." It is not possible here to trace this opinion in detail back to its origins. The determining factor has been the distinction, set forth in an unclarified manner long ago, between the rational and the irrational. This distinction in turn is brought to bear in the jurisdiction of a reasonable but itself unclarified thinking.

Recently, however, the teaching of Nietzsche, Bergson, and the life-philosophers set the standard for this claim concerning the objectifying character of all thinking and speaking. To the extent that, in speaking,[1] we say "is" everywhere, whether expressly or not, yet being means presence, which in modern times has been interpreted as objectivity – to that extent thinking as re-presenting and speaking as vocalization have inevitably entailed a solidifying of the intrinsic flow of the "life-stream," and thus a falsifying thereof. On the other hand, such a consolidation of what is permanent, even though it falsifies, is indispensable for the preservation and continuance of human life. The following text from Nietzsche's *Will to Power*, no. 715 (1887/88), may suffice to document this variously modified opinion: "The means of expression in language cannot be used to express 'becoming'; to posit continually a more crude world of what is permanent, of things, etc. [i.e., of objects] is part of our *irredeemable need for preservation*."

The following pointers[2] to questions (a) through (e) are themselves to be understood and thought through as questions. For the phenomenon most worthy of thought and questioning remains the mystery of language – wherein our entire reflection has to gather itself – above all when it dawns on us that language is not a work of human beings: language speaks. Humans speak only insofar as they co-respond to language. These statements are not the offspring of some fantastic "mysticism." Language is a primal phenomenon which, in what is proper to it, is not amenable to factual proof but can be caught sight of only in an unprejudiced experience of language. Humans may be able to invent artificial speech constructions and signs, but they are able to do so only in reference to and from out of an already spoken language. Thinking remains critical also with respect to primal phenomena. For to think critically means to distinguish (χρίνειν) constantly between that which requires proof for its justification and that which, to confirm its truth, demands a simple catching sight of and taking in. It is invariably easier to set forth a proof in a given case than, in a differently presented case, to venture into catching sight of and holding in view.

(a) What does it mean to objectify? To make an object of something, to posit it as object and represent it only as such. And what does object mean? In the Middle Ages *obiectum* signified that which is thrown before, held over and against our perceiving, imagination, judging, wishing, and intuiting. *Subiectum*, on the other hand, signified the ὑποχείμενον, that which lies present before us from out of itself (not brought before us by representation), whatever is present, e.g., things. The signification of the words *subiectum* and *obiectum* is precisely the reverse of what subject and object usually mean today: *subiectum* is what exists independently (objectively), and *obiectum* is what is merely (subjectively) represented.

As a consequence of Descartes's reformulation of the concept of *subiectum* (cf. *Holzwege*, pp. 98ff.), the concept of object [*Objekt*] also ends up with a changed signification. For Kant object means what exists as standing over against [*Gegenstand*] the experience of the natural sciences. Every object stands over against, but not everything standing over against (e.g., the thing-in-itself) is a possible object. The categorical imperative, moral obligation, and duty are not objects of natural-scientific experience. When they are thought about, when they are intended in our actions, they are not thereby objectified.

Our everyday experience of things, in the wider sense of the word, is neither objectifying nor a placing over against. When, for example, we sit in the garden and take delight in a blossoming rose, we do not make an object of the rose, nor do we even make it something standing over against us in the sense of something represented thematically. When in tacit saying [*Sagen*] we are enthralled with the lucid red of the rose and muse on the redness of the rose, then this redness is neither an object nor a thing nor something standing over against us like the blossoming rose. The rose stands in the garden, perhaps sways to and fro in the wind. But the redness of the rose neither stands in the garden nor can it sway to and fro in the wind. All the same we think it and tell of it by naming it. There is accordingly a thinking and saying that in no manner objectifies or places things over against us.

The statue of Apollo in the museum at Olympia we can indeed regard as an object of natural-scientific representation; we can calculate the physical weight of the marble; we can investigate its chemical composition. But this objectifying thinking and speaking does not catch sight of the Apollo who shows forth his beauty and so appears as the visage of the god.

(b) What does it mean to think? If we heed what has just been set forth, it will be clear that thinking and speaking are not exhausted by theoretical and natural-scientific representation and statement. Thinking rather is that comportment that lets itself be given, by whatever shows itself in whatever way it shows itself, what it has to say of that which appears. Thinking is not necessarily a representing of something as an object. Only the thinking and speaking of the natural sciences is objectifying. If all thinking as such were objectifying, then it would be meaningless to fashion works of art, for they could never show themselves to anyone: one would immediately make an object of that which appears and thus would prevent the artwork from appearing.

The assertion that all thinking as thinking is objectifying is without foundation. It rests on a disregard of phenomena and belies a lack of critique.

(c) What does it mean to speak? Does language consist only in converting what is thought into vocables, which one then perceives only as tones and sounds that can be identified objectively? Or is the vocalization of speech (in a dialogue) something entirely different from a series of acoustically objectifiable sounds furnished with a signification by means of which objects are spoken about? Is not speaking, in what is most proper to it, a saying, a manifold showing of that which hearing, i.e., an obedient heeding of what appears, lets be said? Can one, if we keep only this carefully in view, still assert uncritically that speaking, as speaking, is always already objectifying? When we speak condolence to a sick person and speak to him heart to heart, do we make an object of this person? Is language only an instrument that we employ to manipulate objects? Is language at all within the human being's power of disposal? Is language only a work of humans? Is the human being that being that has language in its possession? Or is it language that "has" human beings, insofar as they belong to, pay heed to language, which first opens up the world to them and at the same time thereby their dwelling in the world?

(d) Is all thinking a form of speaking and all speaking a form of thinking?

The questions placed in discussion up to now direct us to surmise that thinking and speaking belong together (form an identity). This identity was testified to long ago, insofar as λόγος and λέγειν simultaneously signify talking and thinking. But this identity has still not been adequately placed in discussion and commensurately experienced. One principal hindrance is concealed in the fact that the Greek explication of language, that is to say the grammatical interpretation, is oriented to stating something about things. Later, modern metaphysics reinterpreted things to mean objects. This suggested the erroneous opinion that thinking and speaking refer to objects and only to objects.

If, on the other hand, we keep in view the decisive matter at stake, namely, that thinking is in each case a letting be said of what shows itself, and accordingly a co-responding (saying) to that which shows itself, then it will become evident to what extent poetizing too is a pensive saying. And the proper nature of this saying, it will be admitted, cannot be determined by means of the traditional logic of statements about objects.

It is this insight into the interrelation of thinking and saying that lets us see that the thesis that thinking and speaking as such necessarily objectify is untenable and arbitrary.

(e) In what sense do thinking and speaking objectify, and in what sense do they not? Thinking and speaking objectify, i.e., posit as an object something given, in the field of natural-scientific and technical representation. Here they are of necessity objectifying, because scientific-technological knowing must establish its theme in advance as a calculable, causally explicable *Gegenstand*, i.e., as an object as Kant defined the word. Outside this field thinking and speaking are by no means objectifying.

But today there is a growing danger that the scientific-technological manner of thinking will spread to all realms of life. And this magnifies the deceptive appearance that makes all thinking and speaking seem objectifying. The thesis that asserts this dogmatically and without foundation promotes and supports for its part a portentous tendency: to represent everything henceforth only technologically-scientifically as an object of possible control and manipulation. This process of unrestrained technological objectification naturally also affects language itself and its determination. Language is deformed into an instrument of reportage and calculable information. It is treated like a manipulable object, to which our manner of thinking must conform. And yet the saying of language is not necessarily an expressing of propositions *about* objects. Language, in what is most proper to it, is a saying *of* that which reveals itself to human beings in manifold ways and which addresses itself to human beings insofar as they do not, under the dominion of objectifying thinking, confine themselves to the latter and close themselves off from what shows itself.

That thinking and speaking are objectifying only in a derivative and limited sense can never be deduced by way of scientific proof. Insight into the proper nature of thinking and saying comes only by holding phenomena in view without prejudice.

Hence it just might be erroneous to suppose that only that which can be objectively calculated and proven technically and scientifically as an object is capable of being.

This erroneous opinion is oblivious of something said long ago that Aristotle wrote down: ἔστι γὰρ ἀπαιδευσία τὸ μὴ γιγνώσχειν τίνων δεῖ ζητεῖν ἀπόδειξιν χαὶ τίνων οὐ δεῖ. "It is the mark of not being properly brought up, not to see in relationship to what it is necessary to seek proofs and when this is not necessary" (*Metaphysics*, 1006 a6ff.).

Now that we have given these pointers we may turn to the third theme – the decision whether and to what extent the theme of the dialogue is a genuine problem – and say the following:

On the basis of our deliberations on the *second* theme, the problem put by the dialogue must be expressed less equivocally. It must, in a purposely pointed formulation, read: "the problem of a nontechnological, non-natural-scientific thinking and speaking in today's theology." From this more commensurate reformulation, it is very clear that the problem as stated is not a genuine problem insofar as it is geared to a presupposition whose nonsense is evident to anyone. Theology is not a natural science.

Yet the problem as stated conceals the positive task for theology. That task is for theology to place in discussion, within its own realm of the Christian faith and out of the proper nature of that faith, what theology has to think and how it has to speak. This task also includes the question whether theology can still be a science – because presumably it should not be a science at all.

Addition to the pointers

An example of an outstanding nonobjectifying thinking and speaking is poetry.

In the third of the *Sonnets to Orpheus*, Rilke says in poetic speech by what means poetic thinking and saying is determined. "Gesang ist Dasein" – "Song is existence" (cf. *Holzwege*, pp. 292ff.). Song, the singing saying of the poet, is "not coveting," "not soliciting" that which is ultimately accomplished by humans as an effect.

Poetic saying is "Dasein," existence. This word, "Dasein," is used here in the traditional metaphysical sense. It signifies: presence.

Poetic thinking is being in the presence of . . . and for the god. Presence means: simple willingness that wills nothing, counts on no successful outcome. Being in the presence of . . . : purely letting the god's presence be said.

Such saying does not posit and represent anything as standing over against us or as object. There is nothing here that could be placed before a grasping or comprehending representation.

"A breath for nothing." "Breath" stands for a breathing in and out, for a letting be said that responds to the word given us. There is no need for an extensive discussion in order to show that underlying the question of a thinking and saying commensurate to the matter at stake is the question of the being of whatever is and shows itself in each instance.

Being as presence can show itself in various modes of presence. What is present does not have to stand over against us; what stands over against us does not have to be empirically perceived as an object. (Cf. Heidegger, *Nietzsche*, vol. II, sections VIII and IX.)

Notes

1   First edition, 1970: Inadequate; instead: as those who dwell (i.e., interpret our abode in the world).
2   First edition, 1970: The pointers deliberately leave the ontological difference unheeded.

5

THE ONTO-THEO-LOGICAL
CONSTITUTION OF METAPHYSICS

In order to gain perspective in the seminar on the whole of Hegelian metaphysics, we chose as a temporary expedient an interpretation of the section which opens the first book of the *Science of Logic*, "The doctrine of Being." The section title alone gives us in each of its words enough to think about. It reads: "*With what must the beginning of science be made?*" Hegel's answer to this question consists in the demonstration that the beginning is "of a speculative nature." This means: the beginning is neither something immediate nor something mediated. We tried to express this nature of the beginning in a speculative sentence: "The beginning is the result." In accordance with the dialectical plurality of meanings of the "is," this means several things. It means for one thing: the beginning – taking *resultare* in its literal meaning[1] – is the rebound of thinking thinking itself out of the completion of the dialectical movement. The completion of this movement, the absolute Idea, is the totality developed within itself, the fullness of Being. The rebound from this fullness results in the emptiness of Being. In science (the absolute, self-knowing knowledge) the beginning must be made with this emptiness. The beginning and the end of the movement, and before them the movement itself, always remains Being. It has its being as the movement, revolving within itself, from fullness into the most extreme self-externalization and again from there into self-completing fullness. The matter of thinking thus is for Hegel thinking thinking itself as Being revolving within itself. In an inversion which is not only legitimate but necessary, the speculative sentence concerning the beginning runs: "The result is the beginning." The beginning must really be made with the result, since the beginning results from that result.

This says the same as the remark which Hegel adds in an aside and in parentheses, near the end of the section about the beginning: "(and *God* would have the uncontested right to have the beginning made with him)" (Lasson edition, vol. I, 63). According to the question that is the title of the section, we are now dealing with the "beginning of science." If science must begin with God, then it is the science of God: theology. This name is taken here in its later meaning of theo-logy as statements of representational thinking about God. θεόλογος, θεολογία mean at this point the mythopoetic utterance about the gods, with no reference to any creed or ecclesiastical doctrine.

Why is "science" – which since Fichte is the name for metaphysics – why is science theology? Answer: because science is the systematic development of knowledge, the Being of beings knows itself as this knowledge, and thus it is in truth. The schoolmen's name which during the transition from the medieval to the modern period emerges for the science of Being, that is, for the science of beings as such in general, is ontosophy or ontology. Western metaphysics, however, since its beginning with the Greeks has eminently been both ontology and theology, still without being tied to these rubrics. For this reason my inaugural lecture *What is Metaphysics?* (1929) defines metaphysics as the question about beings as such *and* as a whole. The wholeness of this whole is the unity of all beings that unifies as the generative ground. To those who can read, this means: metaphysics is onto-theo-logy. Someone who has experienced theology in his own roots, both the theology of the Christian faith and that of philosophy, would today rather remain silent about God when he is speaking in the realm of thinking. For the onto-theological character of metaphysics has become questionable for thinking, not because of any kind of atheism, but from the experience of a thinking which has discerned in onto-theo-logy the still *unthought* unity of the essential nature of meta-physics. This nature of metaphysics, however, still remains what is most worthy of thought for thinking, as long as thinking does not break off the conversation with its tradition, permeated by destiny, in an arbitrary manner thus unrelated to destiny.

In the fifth (1949) edition of *What is Metaphysics?*, a new introduction explicitly refers to the onto-theological nature of metaphysics. But it would be rash to assert that metaphysics is theology because it is ontology. One would say first: Metaphysics is theology, a statement about God, because the deity enters into philosophy. Thus the question about the onto-theological character of metaphysics is sharpened to the question: How does the deity enter into philosophy, not just modern philosophy, but philosophy as such? This question can be answered only after it has first been sufficiently developed as a question.

We can properly think through the question, How does the deity enter into philosophy?, only when that *to which* the deity is to come has become sufficiently clear: that is, philosophy itself. As long as we search through the history of philosophy merely historically, we shall find everywhere that the deity has entered into it. But assuming that philosophy, as thinking, is the free and spontaneous self-involvement with beings as such, then the deity can come into philosophy only insofar as philoso-phy, of its own accord and by its own nature, requires and determines that and how the deity enters into it. The question, How does the deity enter into philosophy?, leads back to the question, What is the origin of the onto-theological essential constitution of metaphysics? To accept this kind of question means to accomplish the step back.

In this step, we turn our thought to the essential origin of the onto-theological structure of all metaphysics. We ask: How does the deity, and therewith accordingly theology, and with theology the onto-theological character, enter into metaphysics? We raise this question in the context of a conversation with the whole of the history of philosophy. But we are questioning at the same time with a particular regard to Hegel. Here we are prompted to give thought first to a curious fact.

Hegel thinks of Being in its most empty emptiness, that is, in its most general aspect. At the same time, he thinks of Being in its fully completed fullness. Still, he does not call speculative philosophy, that is, philosophy proper, onto-theo-logy but rather

"Science of Logic." By giving it this name, Hegel brings to light something decisive. It would be easy, of course, to explain the designation of metaphysics as "logic" by pointing out that for Hegel the matter of thinking is "the idea," understanding that word as a *singulare tantum*. The idea, thinking, is obviously and by ancient custom the theme of logic. Certainly. But it is just as incontestable that Hegel, faithful to tradition, sees the matter of thinking in beings as such and as a whole, in the movement of Being from its emptiness to its developed fullness.

But how can "Being" ever come to present itself as "thought"? How else than by the fact that Being is previously marked as ground, while thinking – since it belongs together with Being – gathers itself toward Being as its ground, in the manner of giving ground and accounting for the ground.[2] Being manifests itself as thought. This means: the Being of beings reveals itself as the ground that gives itself ground and accounts for itself. The ground, the *ratio* by their essential origin are the Λόγος, in the sense of the gathering of beings and letting them be. They are the Ἐν Πάντα. Thus "science," that is, metaphysics, is in truth "logic" for Hegel not because the theme of science is thinking, but because *Being* remains the matter of thinking; while Being, ever since the early days when it became unconcealed in the character of Λόγος, the ground that grounds, claims thinking – the accounting of the ground – for itself.

Metaphysics thinks of beings as such, that is, in general. Metaphysics thinks of beings as such, as a whole. Metaphysics thinks of the Being of beings both in the ground-giving unity of what is most general, what is indifferently valid everywhere, and also in the unity of the all that accounts for the ground, that is, of the All-Highest. The Being of beings is thus thought of in advance as the grounding ground. Therefore all metaphysics is at bottom, and from the ground up, what grounds, what gives account of the ground, what is called to account by the ground, and finally what calls the ground to account.

Why do we mention this? So that we may experience the shopworn terms ontology, theology, onto-theology in their true gravity. At first and commonly, the terms ontology and theology do, of course, look like other familiar terms: psychology, biology, cosmology, archeology. The last syllable, -logy, means broadly and usually that we are dealing with the science of the soul, of living things, of the cosmos, of ancient things. But -logy hides more than just the logical in the sense of what is consistent and generally in the nature of a statement, what structures, moves, secures, and communicates all scientific knowledge. In each case, the -Logia is the totality of a nexus of grounds accounted for, within which nexus the objects of the sciences are represented in respect of their ground, that is, are conceived. Ontology, however, and theology are "Logics" inasmuch as they provide the ground of beings as such and account for them within the whole. They account for Being as the ground of beings. They account to the Λόγος, and are in an essential sense in accord with the Λόγος-, that is they are the logic of the Λόγος. Thus they are more precisely called onto-logic and theo-logic. More rigorously and clearly thought out, metaphysics is: onto-theo-logic.

We now understand the name "logic" in the essential sense which includes also the title used by Hegel, and only thus explains it: as the name for that kind of thinking which everywhere provides and accounts for the ground of beings as such within the whole in terms of Being as the ground (Λόγος). The fundamental character of metaphysics is onto-theo-logic. We should now be in a position to explain how the deity enters into philosophy.

To what extent is an explanation successful? To the extent that we take heed of the following: the matter of thinking is beings as such, that is, Being. Being shows itself in the nature of the ground. Accordingly, the matter of thinking, Being as the ground, is thought out fully only when the ground is represented as the first ground, πρώτη ἀρχή. The original matter of thinking presents itself as the first cause, the *causa prima* that corresponds to the reason-giving path back to the *ultima ratio*, the final accounting. The Being of beings is represented fundamentally, in the sense of the ground, only as *causa sui*. This is the metaphysical concept of God. Metaphysics must think in the direction of the deity because the matter of thinking is Being; but Being is in being as ground in diverse ways: as Λόγος, as ὑποκείμενον, as substance, as subject.

This explanation, though it supposedly touches upon something that is correct, is quite inadequate for the interpretation of the essential nature of metaphysics, because metaphysics is not only theo-logic but also onto-logic. Metaphysics, first of all, is neither only the one nor the other *also*. Rather, metaphysics is theo-logic because it is onto-logic. It is onto-logic because it is theo-logic. The onto-theological essential constitution of metaphysics cannot be explained in terms of either theologic or ontologic, even if an explanation could ever do justice here to what remains to be thought out.

For it still remains unthought by what unity ontologic and theo-logic belong together, what the origin of this unity is, and what the difference of the differentiated which this unity unifies. All of this still remains unthought. The problem here is obviously not a union of two independent disciplines of metaphysics, but the unity of *what* is in question, and in thought, in ontologic and theologic: beings as such in the universal and primal *at one with* beings as such in the highest and ultimate. The unity of this One is of such a kind that the ultimate in its own way accounts for the primal, and the primal in its own way accounts for the ultimate. The difference between the two ways of accounting belongs to the still-unthought difference we mentioned.

The essential constitution of metaphysics is based on the unity of beings as such in the universal and that which is highest.

Our task here is to deal with the question about the onto-theo-logical nature of metaphysics first of all simply as a question. Only the matter itself can direct us to the point with which the question about the onto-theological constitution of metaphysics deals. It can do so in this way, that we attempt to think of the matter of thinking in a more rigorous manner. The matter of thinking has been handed down to Western thinking under the name "Being." If we think of this matter just a bit more rigorously, if we take more heed of what is in contest in the matter, we see that *Being* means always and everywhere: the Being of *beings*. The genitive in this phrase is to be taken as a *genitivus objectivus*. *Beings* means always and everywhere the beings *of Being*; here the genitive is to be taken as a *genitivus subjectivus*. It is, however, with certain reservations that we speak of a genitive in respect to object and subject, because these terms, subject and object, in their turn stem from a particular character of Being. Only this much is clear, that when we deal with the Being of beings and with the beings of Being, we deal in each case with a difference.

Thus we think of Being rigorously only when we think of it in its difference with beings, and of beings in their difference with Being. The difference thus comes specifically into view. If we try to form a representational idea of it, we will at once be misled into conceiving of difference as a relation which our representing has added to Being and to beings. Thus the difference is reduced to a distinction, something made up by our understanding (*Verstand*).

But if we assume that the difference is a contribution made by our representational thinking, the question arises: a contribution to what? One answers: to beings. Good. But what does that mean: "beings"? What else could it mean than: something that *is*? Thus we give to the supposed contribution, the representational idea of difference, a place within Being. But "Being" itself says: Being which is *beings*. Whenever we come to the place to which we were supposedly first bringing difference along as an alleged contribution, we always find that Being and beings in their difference are already there. It is as in Grimm's fairytale *The Hedgehog and the Hare*: "I'm here already." Now it would be possible to deal with this strange state of affairs – that Being and beings are always found to be already there by virtue of and within the difference – in a crude manner and explain it as follows: our representational thinking just happens to be so structured and constituted that it will always, so to speak over its own head and out of its own head, insert the difference ahead of time between beings and Being. Much might be said, and much more might be asked, about this seemingly convincing but also rashly given explanation – and first of all, we might ask: where does the "between" come from, into which the difference is, so to speak, to be inserted?

We shall discard all views and explanations, and instead note the following: this thing that is called difference, we encounter it everywhere and always in the matter of thinking, in beings as such – encounter it so unquestioningly that we do not even notice this encounter itself. Nor does anything compel us to notice it. Our thinking is free either to pass over the difference without a thought or to think of it specifically as such. But this freedom does not apply in every case. Unexpectedly it may happen that thinking finds itself called upon to ask: what does it say, this Being that is mentioned so often? If Being here shows itself concurrently as the Being of . . . , thus in the genitive of the difference, then the preceding question is more properly: what do you make of the difference if Being as well as beings appear *by virtue of the difference*, each in its own way? To do justice to this question, we must first assume a proper position face to face with the difference. Such a confrontation becomes manifest to us once we accomplish the step back. Only as this step gains for us greater distance does what is near give itself as such, does nearness achieve its first radiance. By the step back, we set the matter of thinking, Being as difference, free to enter a position face to face, which may well remain wholly without an object.

While we are facing the difference, though by the step back we are already releasing it into that which gives thought, we can say: the Being of beings means Being which is beings. The "is" here speaks transitively, in transition. Being here becomes present in the manner of a transition to beings. But Being does not leave its own place and go over to beings, as though beings were first without Being and could be approached by Being subsequently. Being transits (that), comes unconcealingly over (that) which arrives as something of itself unconcealed only by that coming-over.[3] Arrival means: to keep concealed in unconcealedness – to abide present in this keeping – to be a being.

Being shows itself as the unconcealing overwhelming. Beings as such appear in the manner of the arrival that keeps itself concealed in unconcealedness.

Being in the sense of unconcealing overwhelming, and beings as such in the sense of arrival that keeps itself concealed, are present, and thus differentiated, by virtue of the Same, the differentiation. That differentiation alone grants and holds apart the "between," in which the overwhelming and the arrival are held toward one another, are borne away from and toward each other. The difference of Being and beings, as the differentiation of overwhelming and arrival, is the perdurance (*Austrag*) of the two in *unconcealing keeping in concealment*. Within this perdurance there prevails a clearing of what veils and closes itself off – and this its prevalence bestows the being apart, and the being toward each other, of overwhelming and arrival.

In our attempt to think of the difference as such, we do not make it disappear; rather, we follow it to its essential origin. On our way there we think of the perdurance of overwhelming and arrival. This is the matter of thinking, thought closer to rigorous thinking – closer by the distance of one step back: Being thought in terms of the difference.

We here need to insert a remark, however, concerning what we said about the matter of thinking – a remark that again and again calls for our attention. When we say "Being," we use the word in its widest and least definite general meaning. But even when we speak merely of a general meaning, we have thought of Being in an inappropriate way. We represent Being in a way in which It, Being, never gives itself. The manner in which the matter of thinking – Being – comports itself, remains a unique state of affairs. Initially, our customary ways of thinking are never able to clarify it more than inadequately. This we shall try to show by an example, bearing in mind from the start that nowhere in beings is there an example for the active nature of Being, because the nature of Being is itself the unprecedented exemplar.

Hegel at one point mentions the following case to characterize the generality of what is general: Someone wants to buy fruit in a store. He asks for fruit. He is offered apples and pears, he is offered peaches, cherries, grapes. But he rejects all that is offered. He absolutely wants to have fruit. What was offered to him in every instance *is* fruit and yet, it turns out, fruit cannot be bought.

It is still infinitely more impossible to represent "Being" as the general characteristic of particular beings. There is Being only in this or that particular historic character: Φύσις, Λόγος, Ἕν, Ἰδέα, Ἐνέργεια, Substantiality, Objectivity, Subjectivity, the Will, the Will to Power, the Will to Will. But these historic forms cannot be found in rows, like apples, pears, peaches, lined up on the counter of historical representational thinking.

And yet, did we not hear of Being in the historical order and sequence of the dialectical process that is in Hegel's thought? Certainly. But here, too, Being gives itself only in the light that cleared itself for Hegel's thinking. That is to say: the manner in which it, Being, gives itself, is itself determined by the way in which it clears itself. This way, however, is a historic, always epochal character which has being for us as such only when we release it into its own native past. We attain to the nearness of the historic only in that sudden moment of a recall in thinking. The same also holds true for the experience of the given character of that difference of Being and beings to which corresponds a given interpretation of beings as such. What has been said holds true above all also for our attempt in the step back out of the oblivion of the difference as such, to think this difference as the perdurance of unconcealing overcoming and of self-keeping arrival. If we listen more closely, we shall realize, of course, that in this discussion about perdurance we have already allowed the essential past to speak inasmuch as we are thinking of unconcealing and keeping concealed, of transition (transcendence), and of arrival (presence). In fact, it may be that this discussion, which assigns the difference of Being and beings to perdurance as the approach to their essence, even brings to light something all-pervading which pervades Being's destiny from its beginning to its completion. Yet it remains difficult to say how this all-pervasiveness is to be thought, if it is neither something universal, valid in all cases, nor a law guaranteeing the necessity of a process in the sense of the dialectical.

The only thing that now matters for our task is an insight into a possibility of thinking of the difference as a perdurance so as to clarify to what extent the onto-theological constitution of metaphysics has its essential origin in the perdurance that begins the history of metaphysics, governs all of its epochs, and yet remains everywhere concealed *as* perdurance, and thus forgotten in an oblivion which even escapes itself.

In order to facilitate that insight, let us think of Being, and in Being of the difference, and in the difference of perdurance in terms of that character of Being through which Being has cleared itself as Λόγος, as the ground. Being shows itself in the un-concealing overwhelming as that which allows whatever arrives to lie before us, as the grounding in the manifold ways in which beings are brought about before us. Beings as such, the arrival that keeps itself concealed in unconcealedness, is what is grounded; so grounded and so generated, it in turn grounds in its own way, that is, it effects, it causes. The perdurance of that which grounds and that which is grounded, as such, not only holds the two apart, it holds them facing each other. What is held apart is held in the tension of perdurance in such a way that not only does Being ground beings as their ground, but beings in their turn ground, cause Being in their way. Beings can do so only insofar as they "are" the fullness of Being: they are what *is* most of all.

Here our reflections reach an exciting juncture. Being becomes present as Λόγος in the sense of ground, of allowing to let lie before us. The same Λόγος, as the gathering of what unifies, is the Ἕν. This Ἕν, however, is twofold. For one thing, it is the unifying One in the sense of what is everywhere primal and thus most universal; and at the same time it is the unifying One in the sense of the All-Highest (Zeus). The Λόγος grounds and gathers everything into the universal, and accounts for and gathers everything in terms of the unique. It may be noted in passing that the same Λόγος also contains within itself the essential origin of the character of all language, and thus determines the way of utterance as a logical way in the broader sense.

Inasmuch as Being becomes present as the Being of beings, as the difference, as perduration, the separateness and mutual relatedness of grounding and of accounting for endures, Being grounds beings, and beings, as what *is* most of all, account for Being. One comes over the other, one arrives in the other. Overwhelming and arrival appear in each other in reciprocal reflection. Speaking in terms of the difference, this means: perdurance is a circling, the circling of Being and beings around each other. Grounding itself appears within the clearing of perdurance as something that *is*, thus itself as a being that requires the corresponding accounting for through a being, that is, causation, and indeed causation by the highest cause.

One of the classic examples in the history of metaphysics of this situation is found in a generally neglected text of Leibniz, which we shall call for short "The 24 Theses of Metaphysics" (Gerh. Phil. VII, 289 ff.; cf. M. Heidegger, *Der Satz vom Grund*, 1957, 51 ff.).

Metaphysics responds to Being as Λόγος, and is accordingly in its basic character-istics everywhere logic, but a logic that thinks of the Being of beings, and thus the logic which is determined by what differs in the difference: onto-theo-logic.

Since metaphysics thinks of beings as such as a whole, it represents beings in respect of what differs in the difference, and without heeding the difference as difference.

What differs shows itself as the Being of beings in general, and as the Being of beings in the Highest.

Because Being appears as ground, beings are what is grounded; the highest being, however, is what accounts in the sense of giving the first cause. When metaphysics thinks of beings with respect to the ground that is common to all beings as such, then it is logic as onto-logic. When metaphysics thinks of beings as such as a whole, that is, with respect to the highest being which accounts for everything, then it is logic as theo-logic.

Because the thinking of metaphysics remains involved in the difference which as such is unthought, metaphysics is both ontology and theology in a unified way, by virtue of the unifying unity of perdurance.

The onto-theological constitution of metaphysics stems from the prevalence of that difference which keeps Being as the ground, and beings as what is grounded and what gives account, apart from and related to each other; and by this keeping, perdurance is achieved.

That which bears such a name directs our thinking to the realm which the key words of metaphysics – Being and beings, the ground and what is grounded – are no longer adequate to utter. For what these words name, what the manner of thinking that is guided by them represents, originates as that which differs by virtue of the difference. The origin of the difference can no longer be thought of within the scope of metaphysics.

The insight into the onto-theological constitution of metaphysics shows a possible way to answer the question, "How does the deity enter into philosophy?," in terms of the essence of metaphysics.

The deity enters into philosophy through the perdurance of which we think at first as the approach to the active nature of the difference between Being and beings. The difference constitutes the ground plan in the structure of the essence of metaphysics. The perdurance results in and gives Being as the generative ground. This ground itself needs to be properly accounted for by that for which it accounts, that is, by the causation through the supremely original matter – and that is the cause as *causa sui*. This is the right name for the god of philosophy. Man can neither pray nor sacrifice to this god. Before the *causa sui*, man can neither fall to his knees in awe nor can he play music and dance before this god.

The god-less thinking which must abandon the god of philosophy, god as *causa sui*, is thus perhaps closer to the divine God. Here this means only: god-less thinking is more open to Him than onto-theo-logic would like to admit.

This remark may throw a little light on the path to which thinking is on its way, that thinking which accomplishes the step back, back out of metaphysics into the active essence of metaphysics, back out of the oblivion of the difference as such into the destiny of the withdrawing concealment of perdurance.

No one can know whether and when and where and how this step of thinking will develop into a proper (needed in appropriation) path and way and road-building. Instead, the rule of metaphysics may rather entrench itself, in the shape of modern technology with its developments rushing along boundlessly. Or, everything that results by way of the step back may merely be exploited and absorbed by metaphysics in its own way, as the result of representational thinking.

Thus the step back would itself remain unaccomplished, and the path which it opens and points out would remain untrod.

Such reflections impose themselves easily, but they carry no weight compared with an entirely different difficulty through which the step back must pass.

That difficulty lies in language. Our Western languages are languages of metaphysical thinking, each in its own way. It must remain an open question whether the nature of Western languages is in itself marked with the exclusive brand of metaphysics, and thus marked permanently by onto-theo-logic, or whether these languages offer other possibilities of utterance – and that means at the same time of a telling silence. The difficulty to which thoughtful utterance is subject has appeared often enough in the course of this seminar. The little word "is," which speaks everywhere in our language, and tells of Being even where It does not appear expressly, contains the whole destiny of Being – from the ἔστιν γὰρ εἶναι of Parmenides to the "is" of Hegel's speculative sentence, and to the dissolution of the "is" in the positing of the Will to Power with Nietzsche.

Our facing this difficulty that stems from language should keep us from hastily recasting the language of the thinking here attempted into the coin of a terminology, and from speaking right away about perdurance, instead of devoting all our efforts to thinking through what has been said. For what was said, was said in a seminar. A seminar, as the word implies, is a place and an opportunity to sow a seed here and there, a seed of thinking which some time or other may bloom in its own way and bring forth fruit.

Notes

1 *resultare* – to leap back, to rebound.
2 There are three closely related terms in the German text: "*begründen*" (to account for), "*ergründen*" (to give the ground), and "*gründen*" (to ground). In a consultation Heidegger clarified the relation of these terms as follows: "*Begründen*" has to do with beings and is ontic. "*Ergründen*" belongs to Being and is ontological. "*Gründen*" is the relationship of "*begründen*" and "*ergründen*" and encompasses both. (Trans.).
3 *Überkommnis*, coming-over, overwhelming (Trans.).

6

DIACHRONY AND REPRESENTATION

Emmanuel Lévinas

The sphere of intelligibility – of the meaningful – in which everyday life as well as the tradition of our philosophic and scientific thought maintains itself, is characterized by vision. The structure of a *seeing* having the *seen* for its object or theme – the so-called intentional structure – is found in all the modes of sensibility having access to things. It is found in the *intellectual* accession to states of affairs or the relationships between things; and also, apparently, in the way human beings interact, between beings who speak to each other, and who are said to see each other. Hence the priory of *knowing*, in which all that we call thought, intelligence, mind, or simply the psyche, is formed.

Knowledge and Presence

Thought, intelligence, mind, and psyche would appear to be *consciousness*, or on the threshold of consciousness. Human consciousness would be their perfected modality: the consciousness of an *I identical* in its *I think*, aiming at and embracing, or perceiving, all alterity under its thematizing gaze. This aiming of thought is called intentionality. This is a remarkable word, which first indicates the thematization of a *seeing* and, after a fashion, the contemplative character of the psyche, its being-at-a-distance from what is contemplated, which one easily takes as a model of dis-interestedness. But intentionality also indicates aspiration, finality, and desire, a moment of egotism or egoism and, at all events, of "egology." It is a moment that surely includes what have been called "drives," however little the latter are differentiated from a purely kinetic phenomenon in the physicist's object. In this sense, consciousness, of which the unconscious is itself a deficient mode, remains truly the dominant characteristic of our interpretation of mind. The *other*, "intentionally" aimed at, and invested and assembled by the apperception of the *I think*, comes – through that which is *thought* qua thought, through the noema – to fulfill, fill, or satisfy the aim, desire, or aspiration of the *I think* or its *noesis*. The other is thus present to the *I*. And this "being-present," or this *presence* of the "I think" to the *I*, is equivalent to *being*.

This presence or being is also a temporal modality. But it thus concretely signifies an ex-position of the other to the *I*, and thus precisely an *offering of itself, a giving of itself, a Gegebenheit*. It is a giving of alterity within presence, not only in the metaphorical sense of the term, but as a giving that signifies within a concrete horizon of a *taking*, already in reference to a "taking in hand." The presence of the present as temporality, an essential "at-handness" [*main-tenance*] so to speak, is the promise of something graspable, solid. This is probably the very promotion of the *thing*, the "something," the configuration of a *being* [*étant*] in being [*être*], to presence. And this prototypical trait of the knowledge of things is the necessary forerunner of the abstractions of understanding's idealized knowledge, as we have learned from Husserl's *Krisis*, or already, in theory at least, from his *Logical Investigations*.

Hence the technological potentialities of knowledge and vision contrast less sharply with the alleged theoretical purity and the alleged contemplative serenity of truth and the time of pure presence and pure representation; these potentialities and technological temptations are their horizon. They clash much less with the alleged dis-interestedness of theory than is thought by the critics of industrial modernity, denounced as deviation and corruption. Seeing or knowing, and taking in hand, are linked in the structure of intentionality, which remains the intrigue of a kind of thought that recognizes itself in consciousness: the "at-handness" [*main-tenance*] of the present emphasizes its immanence as the characteristic virtue of this sort of thought.

But once that step is taken, intelligibility and intelligence – being situated in thought understood as vision and knowledge, and being interpreted on the basis of intentionality – consist in privileging, in the temporality of thought itself, the present in relation to the past and the future. To comprehend the alteration of presence in the past and future would be a matter of reducing and bringing back the past and future to presence – that is, of re-presenting them. And, similarly, it would be a matter of understanding all alterity, which is brought together, received, and synchronized in presence within the *I think*, and which then is taken up in the identity of the *I* – it is a matter of understanding this alterity that has been taken up by the thought of the identical as *one's own* and, in so doing, of reducing one's *other* to the *same*. The other becomes the *I*'s very own in knowledge, which secures the marvel of immanence. Intentionality, in the aiming at and thematizing of being – that is, in presence – is a return to self as much as an issuing forth from self.

In thought understood as vision, knowledge, and intentionality, intelligibility thus signifies the reduction of the Other to the Same, synchrony as *being* in its egological gathering. The *known* expresses the unity of the transcendental apperception of the *cogito* or of the Kantian *I think*, the egology of presence affirmed from Descartes to Husserl, and even in Heidegger, where, in Section 9 of *Being and Time*, *Dasein*'s "to be" [*à-être*] is the source of *Jemeinigkeit* and thus of the *I*.

Does not the "seeing one another" between humans – that is, obviously, language – in turn revert to a seeing, and thus to this egological significance of intentionality, the egology of synthesis, the gathering of all alterity into presence, and the synchrony of representation? This is the usual way in which language is understood. It is true that, in speaking, knowledge and seeing have recourse to signs and are communicated in verbal signs to other people – which would go beyond the pure egological gathering of the signified into thematized presence. And it is true that the problem remains as to the motive for this communication. Why do we give an account to the other? Because we have something to say. But why is this known or represented something something to say? And, at the same time, the recourse to signs does not necessarily presuppose this communication. It can be justified by the necessity the *I* feels – in its solitary synthesis of apperception – of giving signs to itself, before speaking to anyone else. In its egological work of gathering the diverse into presence or into representation, it can, beyond immediate presence, search for the presence of what is already past or has not yet come about, and then recall them, foresee them, or name them, by signs.

One can, accordingly, even write for oneself. The fact that one cannot have thought without language, without recourse to verbal signs, would not then attest to any definitive rupture in the egological order of presence. It would only indicate the necessity of inner discourse. Finite thought divides in order to question and answer itself, but the thread is retied. Thought reflects on itself in interrupting its continuity of synthetic apperception, but still proceeds from the same "I think" or returns to it. It can even, in this gathering, pass from one term to another term apparently exclusive of the first, but that, owing to its very exclusion, would be announced and already recuperated. The dialectic that tears the *I* apart ends up with a synthesis and system whereby the tear is no longer seen. Dialectic is not a dialogue with the Other, or at least it remains a "dialogue of the soul with itself, proceeding by questions and answers." That is precisely how Plato defined thought. According to the traditional interpretation of discourse that goes back to this definition, the mind in speaking its thought remains no less one and unitary, the same in presence, a synchrony despite its to and fro movement in which the *I* could stand opposed to itself.

This unity and this presence are maintained in the empirical reality of inter-human speaking. For each of the interlocutors, speaking would consist in entering *into* the thought of the other, in fitting into it. This coincidence is Reason and interiority. Here the thinking subjects are multiple dark points, empirically antagonistic, in whom light is produced when they see each other, speak to each other, and coincide. The exchange of ideas will produce presence or representation in the unity of an utterance or an account naming or displaying a field of knowledge. It would fit within a single consciousness, within a *cogito* that remains Reason: universal Reason and egological interiority.

Language can be construed as internal discourse and can always be equated with the gathering of alterity into the unity of presence by the *I* of the intentional *I think*. Even if the other enters into this language – which is indeed possible – linkage to the egological work of representation is not interrupted by this entry. It would not be interrupted even when presence, beyond the re-presentation accomplished in memory and imagination, is confirmed by the work of the historian and the futurologist, or when, in a cultivated humanity, writing gathers the past and future into the presence of a book – a thing between two covers – or that of a library enclosed within a bookcase. This is the gathering of a historical narrative into the presence of a thing, the gathering of the being of beings into a being! It is the key moment of re-presentation and vision as the essence of thought! And this despite all the time that the reading of a book may take, during which this gathering together, or this texture of presence, returns to duration. And especially despite the past that had neither been present nor re-presented by anyone – the immemorial or an-archic past – and despite the inspired future, which no one anticipates. Such a past and future begin to signify time on the basis of the hermeneutic of the biblical "verses" of the text, without prior chronological reference to the metaphor of flux, nor to the still spatial images of the "hither" and "beyond."

Has time *thus* shown its incompressible intrigue? As it has already shown it in certain chiaroscuros of the phenomenology of time whose masterful example Husserl has already given us, in which the intentionality of re-tention and pro-tention would have, on the one hand, reduced the time of consciousness understood as the consciousness of time to the re-presentation of the living present – that is, still as the re-presentation of presence: "the being of beings," which it signifies – but in which, on the other hand, the *retaining* of re-tention differs from the protending of pro-tention only through the comprehension of time already given and pre-supposed in this very constitution – that is, as a time that slips by like a flux. This metaphor of "flux" lives off a temporality borrowed from the *being* [*étant*] that is a liquid whose particles are in movement, a movement already unfolding in time.

It is necessary, then, to ask if even the discourse that is called interior, which thus remains egological and on the scale of representation, despite its scission into questions and answers addressed by the *I* to itself, in which the association of several individuals is possible on condition that "each enter into the thought of the others" – one must ask if this very discourse, despite its allegedly interior scissions, does not already rest on a prior sociality with the other in which the interlocutors are distinct. It is necessary to ask if this effective, forgotten sociality is not nonetheless presupposed by the rupture, however provisional, between self and self, for the interior dialogue still to deserve the name dialogue. This sociality is irreducible to the im-manence of representation, is other than the sociality that would be reduced to the knowledge one can acquire about the other person as a known object, and would already support the immanence of an *I* having an experience of world. Does not the interior dialogue presuppose, beyond the *representation* of the other, a relationship to the other person as other, and not initially a relationship to the *other* already apperceived as the *same* through a reason that is universal from the start?

The moment has come to ask whether this entry of each into the representation of the others, whether this agreement between thoughts in the synchrony of the given, is the unique, original, and ultimate rationality of thought and discourse. One must ask whether this gathering of time into presence by intentionality – and thus whether the reduction of time to the essance of being, its reducibility to presence and representation – is the primordial intrigue of time. And one must ask whether the manifestation of presence, whether appearing, is equivalent to rationality. Is language meaningful only in its *said*, in its propositions in the indicative, everywhere at least latent, in the theoretical content of affirmed or virtual judgments, in pure communication of information – in its *said*, in all that can be written? Is it not meaningful in the sociality of *saying* [*dire*], in responsibility with regard to the other person who commands the questions and answers of the saying, and through the "non-presence" or the "appresentation" of the interlocutor, which thus contrasts strongly with the presence of things according to the underlying simultaneity of the given universe? From me to this interlocutor there is a temporality other than the one that allows itself to be assembled into the presence of the *said* and the *written*, a temporality that is concrete in this "from-me-to-the-other," but that immediately congeals into the abstraction of the synchronous in the synthesis of the "I think" that grasps it thematically.

Must we grant an unconditional priority in the signifying of meaning to this thematizing and theoretical grasp and to the order that is its *noematic* correlation, the order of presence, being as being, and objectivity? Is that where meaning arises? Should not knowledge interrogate itself about itself and its justification? And does not justi-fication – in its semantic context of rightness and justice – thus go back to the responsibility for the other, that is, to the proximity of the neighbor – as to the very domain of intelligibility or original rationality where, on this side of every theoretical explanation, in the human, the being that until then is justified in its natural unfolding as being, and as giving itself out to be the beginning of all rationalization, is brusquely put into question in me and seeks for itself a pre-initial rightness?

I have tried to show elsewhere that the judgments of true knowledge and thematic thought are summoned – or invented – on the basis of or apropos of certain exigencies that depend on the ethical significance of the other, inscribed in his or her face; imperatives in the face of the other who is incomparable to me and is unique; certain exigencies that make justice concrete. The fact that justice is thus found to be the source of the objectivity of logical judgment, and that it has to support the entire level of theoretical thought, amounts to denouncing neither rationality nor the structure of intentional thought, nor the synchronization of the diverse that it implies, nor the thematization of being by synthetic thought, nor the problematic of ontology. But I also think that the latter constitute the rationality of an already derived order, that responsibility for the other signifies an original and concrete temporality, and that the universalization of presence presupposes it. I also think that the sociality in which responsibility is made concrete in justice calls for and founds the objectivity of theoretical language, which "gathers" the diachrony of time into presence and repre-sentation through accounts and histories, and – *up to a certain point* – makes reason understandable (in view of justice itself) by *comparing* in knowledge/thought "incom-parable and unique" persons; comparing them as *beings [étants]* – that is, as individuals of a genus. I also think that institutions, courts, and thus the state, must concretely appear in this derived order of rationality.

But if it is not a matter, setting out from this analysis, of denouncing the intentional structure of thought as alienation, by showing its development from out of the "proximity of the neighbor" and "responsibility for the other," it is nevertheless important to lay stress on this development. The state, institutions, and even the courts that they support, expose themselves essentially to an eventually inhuman but char-acteristic determinism – politics. Hence it is important to be able to control this determinism in going back to its motivation in justice and a foundational inter-humanity. We have just taken some steps in this direction.

Alterity and Diachrony

Let us begin by inquiring as to whether, for an *I*, the alterity of the other initially signifies a logical alterity; the sort of alterity in which parts of a whole are marked off in opposition to one another, in which, in a purely formal way one, this one, is other to that one, and that one is, by the same token, other to this one. Between the persons included in this reciprocity, language would be but a reciprocal exchange of information or anecdotes, intended and gathered into the statements of each partner. Or whether, as I am inclined to think, the alterity of the other man to the *I* is first – and I dare say, is "positively" – the face of the other obligating the *I*, which, from the first – without deliberation – is responsive to the other. *From the first*: that is, the self answers "gratuitously," without worrying about reciprocity. This is the gratuitousness of the *for-the-other*, the response of responsibility that already lies dormant in a salutation, in the *hello*, in the *goodbye*. Such a language is prior to the statements of propositions communicating information and narrative. The *for-the-other* responsive to the neighbor, in the proximity of the neighbor, is a responsibility that signifies – or commands; precisely the face in its alterity and its ineffaceable and unassumable authority of *confronting* [*faire face*]. (Whom does one confront? Whence the authority? Questions not to be lost sight of!) But the *for-the-other* in the approach to the face – a for-the-other older than *consciousness of* . . . – precedes, in its obedience, all *grasping*, and remains prior to the intentionality of the *I*-subject in its being-in-the-world, which presents itself and gives itself a synthesized and synchronous world. The *for-the-other* arises in the *I* as a commandment understood by the *I* in its very obedience, as if obedience were its very accession to hearing the prescription, as if the *I* obeyed before having heard, as if the intrigue of alterity were woven prior to knowledge.

But now the simplicity of this primary obedience is upset by the third person emerging next to the other; the third person is himself also a neighbor, and also falls within the purview of the *I*'s responsibility. Here, beginning with this third person, is the proximity of a human plurality. Who, in this plurality, comes first? This is the time and place of the birth of the question: of a demand for justice! This is the obligation to compare unique and incomparable others; this is the moment of *knowledge* and, henceforth, of an objectivity beyond or on the hither side of the nakedness of the face; this is the moment of consciousness and intentionality. An objectivity born of justice and founded on justice, and thus required by the *for-the-other*, which, in the alterity of the face, commands the *I*. This is the call to re-presentation that ceaselessly covers over the nakedness of the face, giving it content and composure in a world. The objectivity of justice – whence its rigor – offending the alterity of the face that originally signifies or commands outside the context of the world, and keeps on, in its enigma or ambiguity, tearing itself away from, and being an exception to, the plastic forms of the presence and objectivity that it nonetheless calls forth in demanding justice.

Extra-ordinary exteriority of the face. Extra-ordinary, for order is justice: extra-ordinary or absolute in the etymological sense of that adjective, by virtue of its always being separable from every relation and synthesis, extricating itself from the very justice in which that exteriority is involved. The absolute – an abusive word – could probably take place concretely and have meaning only in the phenomenology, or in the rupture of phenomenology, to which the face of the other gives rise.

Face of the other – *underlying* all the particular forms of expression in which he or she, already right "in character," plays a role – is no less *pure expression*, extradition with neither defense nor cover, precisely the extreme rectitude of a *facing*, which in this nakedness is an exposure unto death: nakedness, destitution, passivity, and pure vulnerability. Face as the very *mortality* of the other human being.

But through this mortality, also, an assigned task and obligation that concern the *I* – that "concern me" – a coming face to face with authority, as if the invisible death to which the face of the other is exposed were, for the *I* that approaches it, his business, implicating him before his guilt or innocence, or at least without his intentional guilt. The *I* as hostage to the other human being is precisely called to answer for this death. Responsibility for the other in the *I*, independent of every engagement ever taken by this *I* and of all that would have ever been accessible to its initiative and its freedom, independent of everything that in the other could have "regarded" this *I*. But here, through the face of the other, through his mortality, everything that in the other does not regard me, "regards me." Responsibility for the other – the face signifying to me "thou shalt not kill," and consequently also "you are responsible for the life of this absolutely other other" – is responsibility for the one and only. The "one and only" means the *loved one*, love being the condition of the very possibility of uniqueness.

The condition or (noncondition) of the hostage is accentuated in the *I* approaching the neighbor. But so too is his *election*, the uniqueness of he who does not allow himself to be replaced. Such a one is no longer the "individual within a genus," called *I*, not "a particular case" of the "*I* in general." It is the I who speaks in the first person, like the one Dostoyevsky has say "I am the most guilty of all," in the obligation of each for each, as the most obligated – the one and only. Such is the one whose obligation with regard to the other is also infinite, who, without wondering about reciprocity, without asking questions about the other at the approach of his face, is never done with the neighbor.

The "relationship" from me to the other is thus asymmetrical, without noematic correlation of any thematizable presence. An awakening to the other man, which is not knowledge. Precisely the approach to the other man – the first one to come along in his *proximity* as fellowman – irreducible to knowledge, thought it may eventually call for knowledge, faced with others in the plural, a knowledge required by justice. Thought that is not an adequation to the other, for whom I can no longer be the measure, and who precisely in his uniqueness is refractory to every measure, but nonetheless a non-indifference to the other, love breaking the equilibrium of the equanimous soul. A putting into question within me of the natural position of the subject, of the perseverance of the *I* – of its morally serene perseverance – in its being; a putting into question of its *conatus essendi*, of its existential insistence. Here is indiscreet (or "unjust") presence, which was perhaps already at issue in "The Anaximander Fragment" as Heidegger interprets it in *Holzwege*. A putting into question of that "positivity" of the *esse* in its *presence*, signifying – brusquely – encroachment and usurpation! Did not Heidegger, despite all he wants to teach about the priority of the "thought of being" – here run up against the original significance of ethics? The offense done to others by the "good conscience" of being is already an offense to the stranger, the widow, and the orphan, who, from the faces of others, look at/regard the *I*.

Time and Sociality

I have attempted a "phenomenology" of sociality, taking as my point of departure the face of the other, proximity, by hearing – before all mimicry, in its facial straightforwardness, before all verbal expression, in its mortality, from the depths of that weakness – a voice that commands: an order addressed to me, not to remain indifferent to that death, not to let the other die alone; that is, an order to answer for the life of the other man, at the risk of becoming an accomplice to that death. The look with which the other faces the world, in its rectitude, means both his frailty and an authority not present in a simply logical *alterity*, which, as the counterpart of the identity of facts and concepts, distinguishes one from another, or reciprocally opposes the notions of them, by contradiction or contrariety. The alterity of the other is the extreme point of the "thou shalt not kill" and, in me, the fear of all the violence and usurpation that my existing, despite the innocence of its intentions, risks committing. The risk of occupying – from the moment of the *Da* of my *Dasein* – the place of an other and thus, on the concrete level, of exiling him, of condemning him to a miserable condition in some "third" or "fourth" world, of bringing him death. Thus an unlimited responsibility emerges in this fear for the other, a responsibility with which one is never done, which does not cease with the neighbor's utmost extremity – despite the merciless and realistic expression of the doctor, "condemning" a patient – even if the responsibility comes to nothing more at that time – as we powerlessly face the death of the other – than saying "here I am," or – in the shame of surviving – than pondering the memory of one's wrongdoings. Despite all the modern denunciations of the inefficacy and facileness of a "bad conscience"! It is a responsibility that, without doubt, contains the secret of sociality, whose total gratuitousness – thought it be of no avail at the limit – is called "love of one's neighbor" – that is, the very possibility of the uniqueness of the one and only (beyond the particularity of the individual in a genus). It is a love without concupiscence, but as irrefrangible as death.

A sociality not to be confused with some hypothetical lapse or privation supposed to have taken place within the unity of the One, in which "perfection" and the unity of coincidence, having fallen into separation, would aspire to their reunion. From the depths of the natural perseverance in being of a being assured of its *right to be* (to the point of being unaware of the concept and problem) – from the heart of a logically indiscernible identity (because it rests on itself and dispenses with every distinctive sign that would be necessary for identification) – from the depths of the identity of the *I*, precisely, and in opposition to that perseverance of good conscience, and calling into question that restful identity – there arises, awakened by the silent and imperative language spoken by the face of the other (thought it does not have the coercive power of the visible), the solicitude of a responsibility I do not have to make up my mind to take on, no more than I have to identify my own identity. A responsibility prior to deliberation and to which I was therefore exposed and dedicated before being dedicated to myself. A vow or a votive offering?

Immemorial Past

A responsibility anterior to all the logical deliberation required by the reasoned decision. Deliberation, i.e., already the reduction of the face of the other to a representation, to the objectivity of the visible, to its coercive power, which is of the world. The anteriority of responsibility is not that of an a priori idea interpreted on the basis of reminiscence – that is, referred to perception and the glimpsed intemporal presence based on the ideality of the idea or the eternity of a presence that does not pass, and whose duration or dia-chrony of time would be only a dissimulation, decline, deformation, or privation, in finite human consciousness.

Here we have, in the ethical anteriority of responsibility (for-the-other, in its priority over deliberation), a past irreducible to a hypothetical present that it once was. A past without reference to an identity naively (or naturally) assured of its right to a presence, in which everything supposedly began. Here I am in this responsibility, thrown back toward something that was never my fault or of my own doing, something that was never within my power or my freedom, something that never was my presence and never came to me through memory. There is an ethical significance in that responsibility – without the remembered present of any past commitment – in that an-archic responsibility. It is the significance of a past that concerns me, that "regards me" and is "my business," beyond all reminiscence, re-tention, re-presentation, reference to a remembered present. The significance, based on responsibility for the other man, of an immemorial past, which has come into the heteronomy of an order. My *nonintentional* participation in the history of humanity, in the past of the others, who "regard/look at me." In the depths of the concreteness of the time that is that of my responsibility for the other, there is the dia-chrony of a past that cannot be gathered into re-presentation.

Responsibility for the other does not amount to a thought going back to an *a priori* idea, previously given to the "I think" and rediscovered by the "I think." The natural *conatus essendi* of a sovereign *I* is put into question by the death or the mortality of the other, in the ethical vigilance through which the sovereignty of the *I* can see itself as "hateful," and see its "place in the sun" as the "image and beginning of the usurpation of the whole world." The responsibility for the other, signified as an order in the face of my neighbor is not, in me, a simple modality of "transcendental apperception." The order concerns me without it being possible for me to go back to the thematic presence of a being that would be the cause or the willing of this commandment. As I have said, it is not even a question here of receiving an order by first perceiving it and then subjecting oneself to it in a decision taken after having deliberated about it. In the proximity of the face, the subjection precedes the reasoned decision to assume the order that it bears. The passivity of this subjection is not like the receptivity of the intellectual operation that turns back into the act of assuming – into the spontaneity of receiving and grasping. Here there is absolute foreignness of an unassumable alterity, refractory to its assimilation into presence, alien to the apperception of the "I think" that always assumes what strikes it by re-presenting it. Unequaled dia-chrony of the past. Subjection preceding the understanding of the order – which attests to or measures an infinite authority. And without the future's being already given in the "to come" [*à-venir*], in which the grasp of anticipation – or protention – would offend the dia-chrony of time, brought on by the authority of an imperative.

A past that is articulated – or "thought" – without recourse to memory, without a return to "living presents," and that is not made up of representations. A past signifying on the basis of an irrecusable responsibility, which devolves on the *I* and is signified to it as a commandment, without, however, reverting back to an engagement that it would supposedly have made in some forgotten present. Past in the meaning of an inveterate obligation, older than any commitment, taking on its full meaning in the imperative that, in the guise of the face of the other, commands the *I*. A categorical imperative: without regard – so to speak – for any freely taken decision that would "justify" the responsibility; without regard for any *alibi*. An immemorial past, signified without ever having been present, signified on the basis of responsibility "for the other," in which obedience is the mode proper for listening to the commandment. Harkening to a commandment that is therefore not the recall of some prior generous dispositions toward the other man, which, forgotten or secret, belong to the constitution of the *ego*, and are awakened as an *a priori* by the face of the other. This hearing of a commandment as already obedience is not a decision emerging from a deliberation – be it dialectical – disclosing itself in the face of the other, the prescription deriving its necessity from a theoretical conclusion. A commandment whose power no longer signifies a force greater than mine. The commandment here does not proceed from a force. It comes – in the guise of the face of the other – as the renunciation of coercion, as the renunciation of its force and of all omnipotence. Its authority is not submissive to the determinism of formal and ontological structures. Its heteronomy does not inevitably signify enslavement. It is the heteronomy of an irrecusable authority – despite the necessities of being and its imperturbable routine, concerned with its own being. This is precisely the whole novelty of an ethics whose disobedience and transgression do not refute authority and goodness, and which, impotent but sovereign, returns in bad conscience. The latter does not attest to an incomplete thought, manifest in its generous nonviolence, nor to the immaturity of a childish reason. It signifies – beyond the contributions of memory, deliberation, and violent force – an exceptional sonority which, in its irreducibility, suggests the eventuality of a word of God.

Pure Future

The significance of an authority signifying *after and despite my death*, signifying to the finite *I*, to the *I* doomed to death, a meaningful order signifying beyond this death. Not, to be sure, any sort of promise of resurrection, but an obligation that death does not absolve and a future contrasting strongly with the synchronizable time of re-presentation, with a time offered to intentionality, in which the *I think* would keep the last word, investing what is imposed upon its powers of assuming.

Responsibility for the other to the point of dying for the other! This is how the alterity of the other – distant and near – affects, through my responsibility as an *I*, the utmost present, which, for the identity of my *I think*, still gathers itself together, as does all my duration, into presence or representation, but which is also the end of all egological attribution of meaning by intentional thought, an end to which, in my "being-for-death," this attribution of meaning would already be doomed, and which is anticipated in the seamless immanence of its conscious existing. In the paroxysm of the proximity of my neighbor, the face of the other man – which one was therefore right not to interpret as a representation – keeps its own way (imperative) of signifying a meaning to a mortal me, through the eventual exhaustion of its egological *Sinngebung* and the anticipated collapse of all meaning proceeding from this *Sinngebung*. Behold, in the other, a meaning and an obligation that oblige me beyond my death! The futuration of the future does not reach me as a to-come [à-venir], as the horizon of my anticipations or pro-tentions. Must one not, in this *imperative* meaning of the future that concerns me as a non-in-difference to the other, as my responsibility for the stranger – must one not, in this rupture of the natural order of being, understand what is improperly called super-natural? Is it not to hear an order that would be the word of God or, still more exactly, the very coming of God to the idea and its insertion into a vocabulary – whence the "recognizing" and naming of God in every possible Revelation? The futuration of the future – not as "proof of God's existence," but as "the fall of God into meaning." This is the singular intrigue of the duration of time, beyond its meaning as presence or its reducibility to presence, as in Saint Augustine himself – time as the to-God [à-Dieu] of theology!

Responsibility for the other man, being answerable for the death of the other, devotes itself to an alterity that is no longer within the province of re-presentation. This way of being devoted – or this devotion – is time. It remains a relationship to the other as other, and not a reduction of the other to the same. It is transcendence. In the finitude of time that the "being-toward-death" of *Sein und Zeit* sketches out – despite all the renewals of the received philosophy that this brilliant book brings us – the meaningful remains enclosed within the immanence of the *Jemeinigkeit* of the *Dasein* that *has to be [a à être]* and that thus – in spite of the denunciation of being as presence – still belongs to a philosophy of presence. Does not responsibility for the other's death – the fear for the other that no longer enters into the Heideggerian phenomenology of emotion, *Befindlichkeit* – consist in perceiving, in the finite being of the mortal *I* arrived at from the other's face, the meaning of a *future* beyond what happens to me, beyond what, for an *I*, is to come [à-venir]? Thus we have not gone to the end of thought and meaningfulness in dying! The meaningful continues beyond my death. Should we continue designating this non-in-difference of responsibility for the other by the word *relationship* even though the terms of every relationship are already, or still, within the ideality of the system, simultaneous? And does not dia-chrony (more formal than transcendence, but also more significant) prove to be irreducible to any noetic/noematic correlation, by the concreteness of the responsibility of one for the death of the other?

To-God [*A-Dieu*]

Subjection to the order that orders man, the *I*, to answer for the other is, perhaps, the harsh name of love. Love that is no longer what this compromised word of our literature and our hypocrisies expresses, but the very fact of the approach to the unique, and, consequently, to the absolutely *other*, piercing what merely *shows* itself – that is, what remains the "individual of a genus." Love here implies the whole order, or the whole disorder, of the psychic or the subjective, which would no longer be the abyss of the arbitrary in which the meaning of the ontological is lost, but the very place that is indispensable to the promotion of the *logical* category of *unicity*, beyond the hierarchy of genres, species and individuals, or, if you will, beyond the distinction between the universal and the individual.

Subjection to an absolute order, to authority par excellence, or to the authority of excellence or of the Good. Is it not the very occasion, or the "circumstances," in which, contrasting sharply with the perseverance of a *being* in its being, authority takes on its full sense? It brings neither promise nor relief, but the absolute of a requirement. It is the Word of God, perhaps, provided we only name God on the basis of that authority in which he merely comes to the idea. The "unknown" God does not take shape in a theme, and is exposed – because of that very transcendence, that very nonpresence – to atheism's denials. But is it certain that thematization is appropriate to the Infinite, that vision is the supreme excellence of the spirit, and that through the egoism and egology of being, the Infinite accedes to that original modality, thought?

The idea of the Infinite, in which thought thinks more than it can contain and, according to Descartes' Third Meditation, God is thought in man – is It not like a noesis without a noema? And is the concreteness of responsibility, in its extra-ordinary future of the uncontainable, not ordered by His Word in the face of the Other?

A subjection that precedes deliberation about the imperativeness of an order – which gives the measure of, if you will, or attests to, an infinite authority – but also an extreme refusal of coerciveness, a nonviolence turning away from the use of force, turning away with all the withdrawal of transcendence, with all its Infinity! Retreat of transcendence and indeclinable authority; already the dia-chrony of time? An infinite and indeclinable authority that does not prevent disobedience, that leaves time – which is to say, freedom. Such is the ambiguity of authority and nonviolence. The human, *qua* bad conscience, is the Gordian knot of this ambiguity of the idea of the Infinite, of the Infinite as idea. A bad conscience that is not just the sign of an incomplete reason and already the appeasement and the precipitate justification of sin and already all the good conscience of hypocrisy, but also a chance for holiness in a society of just men without good conscience, and, in the inextinguishable concern for justice, consent to the rigor of human justice.

Deformalization of Time

This meaning of a past that has not been my present and does not concern my reminiscence, and of a future that commands me in mortality or in the face of the other – beyond my powers, my finitude, and my being-doomed-to-death, no longer articulate the representable time of immanence and its historical present. Its dia-chrony, the "difference" of diachrony, does not signify pure rupture, but also non-in-difference and concordance that are no longer founded on the unity of transcendental appercep- tion, the most formal of forms, which, through reminiscence and hope, joins time up again in re-presenting it, but betrays it. I am not going to speak, however, about these concordances of dia-chrony, about the to-God of time, or about its pro-phecy, whose ultimate concreteness is time itself in its patience. Its "adventure" or "intrigue," which I have especially tried to distinguish from the presence of being, and which I have approached from the angle of the ethical in the human, can neither be constituted nor better said starting from any category or "existential." All the figures and words that try to express it – such as "transcendence" or "beyond" – are already derived from it. The *to-God* is neither the thematization of theologies, nor a finality, which goes toward an end point and not to the Infinite, nor eschatology, preoccupied with ultimate ends or promises rather than obligations toward men. The prepositions themselves, including the *to* and the *pro*, are already only metaphors of time, and cannot serve in its constitution.

It was important to me above all to speak in this study of how, in the human intrigue, past, future, and present are tied together in time, without this being the result of a simple degradation that the unity of the One may somehow (I know not how) have undergone, dispersing itself in *movement*, which since (or according to) Aristotle supposedly lead us to time in its diachrony. On such a view, the unity of time would lose itself in the flow of instants, and find itself again – without truly finding itself – in re-presentation, where the past gathers together instants by way of the memory's images, and the future by way of installments and promises. But I have sought time as the deformalization of the most formal form there is – the unity of the *I think*. Deformalization is that with which Bergson, Rosenzweig, and Heidegger, each in his own way, have opened the problematic of modern thought, by setting out from a concreteness "older" than the pure form of time: the freedom of invention and novelty (despite the persistence of the kinetic image of *running*) in Bergson; the biblical conjunction of "Creation, Revelation, and Redemption" in Rosenzweig; and the "nearness to things," *Geworfenheit*, and *Sein-zum-Tode* (despite the still kinetic *ex* of the *ecstases* [*exstases*] in Heidegger). Is it forbidden to also recall that in *The Two Sources of Morality and Religion*, the "durée" of *Time and Free Will* and *Matter and Memory*, which is conceived of as "élan vital" in *Creative Evolution*, means love of my neighbor and what I have called "to-God"? But does one have the right to avoid this comparison, in spite of all the lessons of the half century that separates us from the publication of *The Two Sources of Morality and Religion*?

What seems in fact to transpire – after the attempts to think time starting from the face of the Other, in which "God comes to our minds," as an authority that there commands indeclinably, but also refuses to compel and commands while renouncing omnipotence – is the necessity to think time in the devotion of a theology without theodicy. To be sure, this religion is impossible to propose to others, and consequently is impossible to preach. Contrary to a religion that feeds on representations, it does not begin in promise. Should we recognize in it the difficult piety – all the certainties and personal risks – of the twentieth century, after the horrors of its genocides and its Holocaust?

To be sure, one may wonder whether the time of promises ever stands at the beginning elsewhere than in pedagogy, and whether service without promises is not the only one to merit – and even to accomplish – promises. But these two questions seem already suspect of preaching.

7

"MY RELIGION": SELECTIONS FROM *CIRCUMFESSION*

Jacques Derrida

1   The crude word, fight with him in this way over what's crude, as though first of all I liked to raise the stakes, and the expression "raise the stakes" belongs only to my mother, as though I were attached to him so as to look for a fight over what talking crude means, as though I were trying relentlessly, to the point of bloodshed, to remind him, for he knows it, *cur confitemur Deo scienti*,[1] of what is demanded of us by what's crude, doing so thus in my tongue, the other one, the one that has always been running after me, turning in circles around me, a circumference licking me with a flame and that I try in turn to circumvent, having never loved anything but the impossible, the crudeness I don't believe in, and the crude word lets flow into him through the channel of the ear, another vein, faith, profession of faith or confession, belief, credulity, as though I were attached to him just to look for a quarrel by opposing a naive, credulous piece of writing which by some immediate transfusion calls on the reader's belief as much as my own, from this dream in me, since always, of another language, an entirely crude language, of a half-fluid name too, there, like blood, and I hear them snigger, poor old man, doesn't look likely, not going to happen tomorrow, you'll never know, superabundance of a flood after which a dike becomes beautiful like the ruin it will always have walled up inside it, cruelty above all, blood again, *cruor, confiteor*, what blood will have been for me, I wonder if Geoff knows it, how could he know that that morning, a November 29, 1988, a sentence came, from further away than I could ever say, but only one sentence, scarcely a sentence, the plural word of a desire toward which all the others since always seemed, confluence itself, to hurry, an order suspended on three words, *find the vein*, what a nurse might murmur, syringe in hand, needle upward, before *taking blood*, when for example in my childhood, and I remember that laboratory in the rue d'Alger, the fear and vagueness of a glorious appeasement both took hold of me, took me blind in their arms at the precise moment at which by the point of the syringe there was established an invisible passage, always invisible, for the continuous flowing of blood, absolute, absolved in the sense that nothing seemed to come between the source and the mouth, the quite complicated apparatus of the syringe being introduced in that place only to allow the passage and to disappear as instrument, but continuous in that other sense

that, without the now brutal intervention of the other who, deciding to interrupt the flow once the syringe, still upright, was withdrawn from the body, quickly folded my arm upward and pressed the swab inside the elbow, the blood could still have flooded, not indefinitely but continuously to the point of exhausting me, thus aspirating toward it what I called: the glorious appeasement.

2   From the invisible inside, where I could neither see nor want the very thing that I have always been scared to have revealed on the scanner, by *analysis* – radiology, echography, endocrinology, hematology – a crural vein expelled my blood outside that I thought beautiful once stored in that bottle under a label that I doubted could avoid confusion or misappropriation of the vintage, leaving me nothing more to do, the inside of my life exhibiting itself outside, *expressing* itself before my eyes, absolved without a gesture, dare I say of writing if I compare the pen to a syringe, and I always dream of a pen that would be a syringe, a suction point rather than that very hard weapon ... what can be got around or not which comes back to me without ever having taken place, I call it circumcision, see the blood but also what comes, cauterization, coagulation or not, strictly contain the outpouring of circumcision, one circumcision, mine, the only one, rather than circumnavigation or circumference, although the unforgettable circumcision has carried me to the place I had to go to, and circumfession if I want to say and do something of an avowal without truth turning around itself, an avowal without "hymn" (hymnology) and without "virtue" (aretalogy), without managing to close itself on its possibility, unsealing abandoning the circle open, wandering on the periphery, taking the pulse of an encircling phrase, the pulsion of the paragraph which never circumpletes itself, as long as the blood, what I call thus and thus call, continues its venue in its vein.

3   If I let myself be loved by the lucky vein of this word, this is not for the *alea* or the mine it's enough to exploit by hacking out writing on the machine, nor for the blood, but for everything that all along this word vein lets or makes come the chance of events on which no program, no logical or textual machine will ever close, since always in truth has operated only by not overcoming the flow of raw happenings, not even the theologic program elaborated by Geoff who remains very close to God, for he knows everything about the "logic" of what I might have written in the past but also of what I might think or write in the future, on any subject at all, so that he can rightly do without quoting any singular sentences that may have come to me and which that "logic" or "alogic" would suffice to account for, transcendental deduction of me, so that I should have nothing left to say that might surprise him still and bring something about for him, who you would be tempted to compare to Augustine's God when he asks whether there is any sense in confessing anything to him when He knows everything in advance, which did not stop my compatriot from going beyond this *Cur confitemur Deo scienti*, not toward a verity, a severity of avowal which never amounts merely to speaking the truth, to making anything known or to presenting oneself naked in one's truth, as though Augustine still wanted, by force of love, to bring it about that in *arriving* at God, something should happen to God, and *someone* happen to him who would transform the science of God into a learned ignorance, he says he has to do so in *writing*, precisely, after the death of his mother, over whom he

does not deplore the fact of not having wept, not that I dare link what he says about confession with the deaths of our respective mothers, I am not writing about Saint Georgette, the name of my mother, whom her brother sometimes used to call Geo, nor about Saint Esther, her sacred name, the one not to be used, the letters of a name I have used so much so that it might remain, for my mother was not a saint, not a Catholic one in any case, but what these two women had in common is the fact that Santa Monica, the name of the place in California near to which I am writing, also ended her days, as my mother will too, on the other side of the Mediterranean, far from her land, in her case in the cemetery in Nice which was profaned in 1984, and the son reports her wishes, i.e., that *nos concurrimus, sed cito reddita est sensui et aspexit astantes me et fratrem meum et ait nobis quasi quaerenti similis: "ubi eram?" deinde nos intuens maerore attonitos: "pontis hic" inquit "matrem uestram." ego silebam et fletum frena-bam,*[2] sentences I quote in Latin, I have taught a lot about these subjects, and if I must not continue doing so here, I owe it to autobiography to say that I have spent my life teaching so as to return in the end to what mixes prayer and tears with blood, *salus non erat in sanguine.*

6   Salvation being at this price, which has no other future alas than the name without literature, people will say that I'm giving G. a jealous scene, G. whom I love and admire, as will rapidly have been understood, whom I prefer, oh yes, and I could never have accepted, jealous as I am, to write a book, a book about me, with anybody else, fighting with him over the right to deprive me of my events, i.e. to embrace the generative grammar of me and behave as though it was capable, by exhibiting it, of appropriating the law which presides over everything that can happen to me through writing, what I can write, what I have written or ever could write, for it is true that if I succeed in surprising him and surprising his reader, this success, success itself, will be valid not only for the future but also for the past for by showing that every writing to come cannot be engendered, anticipated, preconstructed from this matrix, I would signify to him in return that something in the past might have been withdrawn, if not in its content at least in the sap of the idiom, from the effusion of the signature, what I was calling a moment ago by the name of name and that I would be trying, against him, that would be my rule here, my law for the duration of these few pages, to reinscribe, reinvent, obliging the other, and first of all G., to recognize it, to pronounce it, no more than that, to call me finally beyond the owner's tour he has just done, forgetting me on the pretext of understanding me, and it is as if I were trying to oblige him to recognize me and come out of this amnesia of me which resembles my mother while I say to myself when I read this matrix there's the survivress signing in my place and if it is right, and it is, faultless, not only will I no longer sign but I will never have signed, is this not basically what I have always meant to say, and given that, for something to happen and for me finally to sign something for myself, it would have to be against G., as though he wanted to love in my stead, and to stop him I was finally admitting some perjury that his programming machine couldn't providentially account for, a thing all the more improbable in that his matrix, i.e. mine, that which faultlessly he formalizes and which in the past seized hold of me, but when will this giving birth have begun, like a "logic" stronger than I, at work and verifiably so right down to so-called aleatory phenomena, the least systemic, the most undecidable of the sentences

I've made or unmade, this matrix nevertheless opens, leaving room for the unantic-
ipatable singularity of the event, it remains by essence, by force, nonsaturable, non-
suturable, invulnerable, therefore only extensible and transformable, always unfinished,
for even if I wanted to break his machine, and in doing so hurt him, I couldn't do so,
and anyway I have no desire to do so, I love him too much.

9   Among the sentences that G. is right not to quote, all of them in short, there is one,
the only one, I recall it myself, but precisely as though I had not written it then, more
than ten years ago, as though I had not yet read the address thus kept in reserve for the
counterexample or the denial I want constantly to oppose to G., in other words to the
eternal survivress, to the theologic program or maternal figure of absolute knowledge
for which the surprise of no avowal is possible, and this sentence says that "one always
asks for pardon when one writes,"[3] so as to leave suspended the question of knowing if
one is finally asking pardon in writing for some earlier crime, blasphemy, or perjury or
if one is asking for pardon for the crime, blasphemy, or perjury in which consists
presently the act of writing, the simulacrum of avowal needed by the perverse over-
bidding of the crime to exhaust evil, the evil I have committed in truth, the worst,
without being sure of having even sponged it from my life, and it's the worst, but my
compatriot had a premonition of it, if a writing worthy of the name avows so as to ask
pardon for the worst, literally, *et nunc, domine, confiteor tibi in litteris*,[4] and turns away
from God through the very piece of writing addressed to his brothers on the death of
their mother, even were it supposedly to call them back to charity in the presence of
God, *legat qui uolet et interpretetur, ut uolet, et si peccatum inuenerit, fleuisse me matrem exigua
parte horae, matrem oculis meis interim mortuam, quae me multos annos fleuerat, ut oculis tuis
uniuerem, non inrideat, sed potius, si est grandi caritate, pro peccatis meis fleat ipse ad te, patrem
omnium fratrum Christi tui*,[5] no matter, writing is only interesting in proportion and in
the experience of evil, even if the point is indeed to "make" truth in a style, a book
and before witnesses, *uolo eam [ueritatem] facere in corde meo coram te in confessione, in stilo
autem meo coram multis testibus*,[6] and *make* the truth in this case that I'm not sure comes
under any religion, for reason of literature, nor under any literature, for reason of
religion, making *truth* has no doubt nothing to do with what you call truth, for in order
to confess, it is not enough to *bring to knowledge*, to make *known what is*, for example to
inform you that I have done to death, betrayed, blasphemed, perjured, it is not enough
that *I present myself* to God or you, the presentation of what is or what I am, either by
revelation or by adequate judgment, "truth" then, having never given rise to avowal,
to true avowal, the *essential* truth of avowal having therefore nothing to do with truth,
but consisting, if, that is, one is concerned that it consist and that there be any, in
asked-for pardon, in a request rather, asked of religion as of literature, *before* the one
and the other which have a right only to this time, for pardoning, pardon, for nothing.

11   No point going round in circles, for as long as the other does not know, and
know in advance, as long as he will not have won back this advance at the moment of
the pardon, that unique moment, the great pardon that has not yet happened in my
life, indeed I am waiting for it as absolute unicity, basically the only event from now
on, no point going round in circles, so long as the other has not won back that advance
I shall not be able to avow anything and if avowal cannot consist in declaring, making

known, informing, telling the truth, which one can always do, indeed, without confessing anything, without *making* truth, the other must not learn anything that he was not already in a position to know for avowal as such to begin, and this is why I am addressing myself here to God, the only one I take as a witness, without yet knowing what these sublime words mean, and this grammar, and *to*, and *witness*, and *God*, and *take*, take God, and not only do I pray, as I have never stopped doing all my life, and pray to him, but I take him here and take him as my witness, I give myself what he gives me, i.e. the *i.e.* to take the time to take God as a witness to ask him not only, for example, like SA, why I take pleasure in weeping at the death of the friend, *cur fletus dulcis sit miseris?*,[7] and why I talk to him in Christian Latin French when they expelled from the Lycée de Ben Aknoun in 1942 a little black and very Arab Jew who understood nothing about it, to whom no one ever gave the slightest reason, neither his parents nor his friends, but why do I address her like him, my God, to avow, while he is the very thing who, I know nothing else about him when I prepare for avowal, must already know, and indeed he knows that very thing, as you well know, *cur confitemur Deo scienti*, you the knower, in your science required by desire and the first impulse of avowal, the witness I am seeking, for, yes, for, without yet knowing what this sublime vocable, *for*, means in so many languages, for already having found him, and you, no, according to you, for having sought *to* find him around a trope or an ellipsis that we pretend to organize, and for years I have been going round in circles, trying to take as a witness not to see myself being seen but to re-member myself around a single event, I have been accumulating in the attic, my "sublime," documents, inconography, notes, learned ones and naive ones, dream narratives or philosophical dissertations, applied transcription of encyclopedic, sociological, historical, psychoanalytical treatises that I'll never do anything with, about circumcisions in the world, the Jewish and the Arab and the others, and excision, with a view to my circumcision alone, the circumcision of me, the unique one, that I know perfectly well took place, one time, they told me and I see it but I always suspect myself of having cultivated, because I am circumcised, *ergo* cultivated, a fantastical affabulation.

14 For example, and I'm dating this, this is the first page of the notebooks, "*Circumcision, that's all I've ever talked about, consider the discourse on the limit, margins, marks, marches, etc., the closure, the ring (alliance and gift), the sacrifice, the writing of the body, the pharmakos excluded or cut off, the cutting/sewing of Glas, the blow and the sewing back up, whence the hypothesis according to which it's that, circumcision, that, without knowing it, never talking about it or talking about it in passing, as though it were an example, that I was always speaking or having spoken, unless, another hypothesis, circumcision itself were merely an example of the thing I was talking about, yes but I have been, I am and always will be, me and not another, circumcised, and there's a region that is no longer that of an example, that's the one that interests me and tells me not how I am a case but where I am no longer a case, when the word first of all, at least, CIRCUMCISED, across so many relays, multiplied by my 'culture,' Latin, philosophy, etc., as it imprinted itself on my language circumcised in its turn, could not have not worked on me, pulling me backward, in all directions, to love, yes, a word, milah, loves another, the whole lexicon that obsesses my writings, CIR-CON-SI, imprints itself in the hypothesis of wax [cire], no, that's false and bad, why, what doesn't work, but saws [mais scie], yes and all the dots on the i's, I've greatly insisted on it elsewhere, Mallarmé, Ponge, but that's really what I*

was talking about, the point detached and retained at the same time, false, not false but simulated castration which does not lose what it plays to lose and which transforms it into a pronounceable letter, i and not I, then always take the most careful account, in anamnesis, of this fact that in my family and among the Algerian Jews, one scarcely ever said 'circumcision' but 'baptism,' not Bar Mitzvah but 'communion,' with the consequences of softening, dulling, through fearful acculturation, that I've always suffered from more or less consciously, of unavowable events, felt as such, not 'Catholic,' violent, barbarous, hard, 'Arab,' circumcised circumcision, interiorized, secretly assumed accusation of ritual murder" (12–20–76), the quoted time of this notebook pulls the white threat of a period cutting across the three others, at least, 1. the theologic program of SA, 2. the absolute knowledge or geologic program of G., and 3. the presently present survival or life by provision of Georgette Sultana Esther, or Mummy if you prefer, which cuts across everything, a synchrony running the risk of hiding what's essential, that is that the restrained confession will not have been my fault but hers, as though the daughter of Zipporah had not only committed the crime of my circumcision but one more still, later, the first playing the kickoff, the original sin against me, but to reproduce itself and hound me, call me into question, me, a whole life long, to make her avow, her, in me.

19   *"So I have borne, without bearing, without its ever being written"* (12–23–76) the name of the prophet Élie, Elijah in English, who carries the newborn on his knees, before the still unnamable sacrifice, and I must have carried myself and the impossible port without bank and without head of this porterage is written everywhere for anyone who knows how to read and is interested in the behavior of a ference, in what precedes and circumvents in preference, reference, transference, *différance*, so I took myself toward the hidden name without its ever being written on the official records, the same name as that of the paternal uncle Eugène Eliahou Derrida who must have carried me in his arms at the moment of the event without memory of me for they are the memories of an amnesia about which you wonder why *"I'm getting ready to write them, in this book of 'circumcision' dreamed of after the death of my father (1970) and certain events that followed, deliberately projected after* Glas *but never undertaken, no doubt carried since ever in this netherworld of scars, escarres, scarifications and cannibalism, of alliance through the blood that flows and that the* mohel, *sometimes charged with sacrificial slaughter, sometimes sucks, like the mother here or there eats the foreskin and elsewhere the boy that of excision"* (12–23–76), and now today (6–29–89) I telephone myself today to G. as to God, an hour before sliding my body stretched out on its back into the tomblike capsule of a scanner in Neuilly to tell him what I'm writing right up against him and tell him that for several days now my face has been disfigured by a facial paralysis holding my left eye fixed open like a glass-eyed cyclops, imperturbable vigilance of the dead man, eyelid stretched by the vertical bar of an inner scar, *an invisible scar*, I tell him, and my twisted mouth from which water falls a little onto my chin when I drink, recalling me to my mother each time that, one hand holding up her head, I pour water into her mouth rather than her drinking it, *ecce ubi sum! flete mecum, et pro me flete,*[8] for like SA I love only tears, I only love and speak through them, even if one must deny it, he commands, on the death of a mother, it's about them that I would telephone rather *restat uoluptas oculorum istorum carnis meae, de qua loquor confessiones, quas audiant aures templi tui,* what SA never says about *concupiscentia oculorum,*[9] not counting the supple-

ment of pleasure, the addition of the optical machine that comes to "scan" the beyond of a sensory immediacy, as I should like to brush away all the perjuries of my memory ("Dear Madam, I ask you for a scan of the trajectory of the left facial nerve"), tears, think credulous humanists, remaining impossible for machines, try to make a scanner weep, *How wisely Nature did decree, With the same eyes to weep and see!* [. . .] *For others too can see, or sleep, But only human eyes can weep,*[10] what stupidity (rictus on the right).

23   Well, I'm remembering God this morning, the name, a quotation, something my mother said, not that I'm looking for you, my God, in a determinable place and to reply to the question, *Sed ubi manes in memoria mea, domine, ubi illic manes? quale cubile fabricasti tibi?* [. . .] *tu dedisti hanc dignationem memoriae meae, ut maneas in ea, sed in qua eius parte maneas, hoc considero,*[11] etc., and neither my will nor my power is today to "go beyond," as SA wanted, *istam uim meam, quae memoria uocatur,*[12] but to quote the name of God as I heard it perhaps the first time, no doubt in my mother's mouth when she was praying, each time she saw me ill, no doubt dying like her son before me, like her son after me, and it was almost always otitis, the tympanum, I hear her say, "thanks to God, thank you God" when the temperature goes down, weeping in pronouncing your name, on a road in the "little wood," one summer, when a doctor had threatened me with a violent and dangerous operation, that serious operation that in those days left you with a hole behind your ear, and I'm mingling the name of God here with the origin of tears, the always puerile, weepy and pusillanimous son that I was, the adolescent who basically only liked reading writers quick to tears, Rousseau, Nietzsche, Ponge, SA, and a few others, that child whom the grown-ups amused themselves by making cry for nothing, who was always to weep over himself with the tears of his mother: "I'm sorry for myself," "I make myself unhappy," "I'm crying for myself," "I'm crying over myself" – but like another, another wept over by another weeper, I weep from my mother over the child whose substitute I am, whence the other, nongrammatical syntax that remains to be invented to speak of the name of God which is here neither that of the father nor that of the mother, nor of the son nor of the brother nor of the sister, and of that syntax coming slowly to me like the hope of a threat, I'm more and more scared, like the scared child who up until puberty cried out "Mummy I'm scared" every night until they let him sleep on a divan near his parents, fear today of what has just happened to me halfway through, just before I'm 59, with this facial paralysis or Lyme's disease which, gone now without leaving any visible trace, will have changed my face from the inside, for henceforth I have changed faces and my mother is not for nothing in this, not the eternal visage of my young mother but hers today, especially near the lips, that's the event, unpredictable both for G. and for me, in the writing of a circumfession for the death agony of my mother, not readable here but the first event to write itself right on my body, the exemplary counterscar that we have to learn to read without seeing, "*Kar: to do in Sanskrit, the thing done as sacred thing, what happens in circumcision, what is done, outside language, without sentence, the time of a proper name, the rest is literature . . .*" (8–1–81).

24   "Quid ergo amo, cum Deum meum amo? *Can I do anything other than translate this question by SA into my language, into the same sentence, totally empty and huge at the same time, the change of meaning, or rather reference, defining the only difference of the 'meum': what*

do I love, whom do I love, that I love above all? [. . .] *I am the end of Judaism*" (1981), of a
certain Judaism, they will understand it as they like, the fire I'm here playing with is
playing with me again, I am no longer the same since the FP, whose signs seem to have
been effaced though I know I'm not the same face, the same *persona*, I seem to have
seen myself near to losing my face, incapable of looking in the mirror at the fright of
truth, the dissymmetry of a life in caricature, left eye no longer blinking and stares at
you, insensitive, without the respite of *Augenblick*, the mouth speaks the truth sideways,
defying the diagnostics or prognostics, the disfiguration reminds you that you do not
inhabit your face because you have too many places, you take place in more places
than you should, and transgression itself always violates a place, an uncrossable line, it
seizes itself, punishes, paralyzes immediately, topology here both being and not being a
figure, and if it is a disfiguration, that's the trope I've just been hit right in the face with
for having violated the places, all of them, the sacred places, the places of worship, the
places of the dead, the places of rhetoric, the places of habitation, everything I
venerate, not the unpredictable event I have supposedly written, myself, namely
sentences fit to crack open the geologic program, no, that took place outside the
writing that you're reading, in my body if you prefer, this conversion ought to be the
surprise of an event happening to "myself," who am therefore no longer myself, from
the wood I warm myself with, that's the "conversion" I was calling with my wishes or
avowals, they were heard even if you remain deaf, even if I could not foresee what the
vows of avowal destined me to, but the fact that it is not decipherable here on the page
does not signify in any way the illegibility of the said "conversion," I have to learn to
read it while my mother is still alive, today is July 23, her 88th birthday, I must teach
you to teach me to read myself from the compulsions, there will have been 59 of them,
that make us act together, we the chosen of unhappiness, *non enim tantum auditoribus
eorum, quorum e numero erat etiam is, in cuius domo aegrotaueram et conualueram, sed eis
etiam, quos electos uocant,*[13] even if a circumfession is always simulated, the symptom said
figuratively to be "real," the conversion *which happens* ought no longer to cause any
fear, as though she had said to me: "I know you are innocent right up to the most
extreme of your perjuries, perhaps because I am a woman, I do not know if what I am
saying to you does good or harm, you cannot save on your torment, your angel
protects you, Elie."

25   *Sed excusare me amabam et accusare nescio quid aliud, quod mecum esset et ego non
essem,*[14] the question remains, after months of interruption, we are in November now,
it's almost a year since my mother went into her lethargy, her *escarres* are closing, what
health, she still does not recognize me but she smiled at me the other day, at least she
smiled at someone, replying, when I said, "You see, I'm here," "Ah, you're here," it
remains to be known who will be there, if she will still be alive if I arrive, before the
end of this year if I survive it, at the end of my 59 periods, 59 respirations, 59
commotions, 59 four-stroke compulsions, each an Augustinian *cogito* which says *I am*
on the basis of a *manduco bibo, already I am dead*, that's the origin of tears, I weep for
myself, I feel sorry for myself from my mother feeling sorry for me, I complain of my
mother, I make myself unhappy, she weeps over me, who weeps over me, syntax to be
invented, neither the father's nor the mother's nor mine but what trinity's, if not a
compulsion grenade for I promised to God never to write anything more except on

the most irrepressible of drives, the double condition, no?, of the worst and the best in literature, but that's what you have always done, answers God, I'll answer for it, yes, but all the same, more or less, my father would specify who must for his part have seen the thing when his brother Eugène Eliahou held me on his knees, his brother Elie, i.e. me, already, "*holding myself on his knees, in my arms, I am sitting on the high chair and am holding the velvet cushion, little Jackie is howling, his hands in the air, hallucination, I am uncle Eugène Eliahou and I see Jackie, he already bears this name, not the other, he was born one 15th of July in this house,*" not in the rue Saint-Augustin, in town, where I lived with my parents until I was 4 except in the summer, I remembered a few months ago, in the middle of my facial paralysis, I was driving in Paris near the Opéra and I discovered that other rue Saint-Augustin, homonym of the one in Algiers where my parents lived for 9 years after their marriage, my elder brother René was born there, Paul-Moïse, whom I replaced, was born and then died there before me, a few months old, I remembered this when all that precedes this had already been written on the trace of SA, the only "images," very vague ones, that I still have of my early childhood coming from the rue Saint-Augustin, a dark hallway, a grocer's down from the house, we had returned there after the summer of the "*poker game, hot holiday night, I am also the mochel, my sacrificer, I write with a sharpened blade, if it doesn't bleed the book will be a failure, not necessarily the book produced, evaluable by others in the marketplace, but the self-surgery, my father is looking, but where is my brother, and my mother? no doubt in the next room with the women, she lost a son less than two years previously, scarcely older than myself*" (12-24-76).

30   "... *the mixture on this incredible supper of the wine and blood, let people see it how I see it on my sex each time blood is mixed with sperm or the saliva of fellatio, describe my sex throughout thousands of years of Judaism, describe it (microscopy, photography, stereophototypy) until the paper breaks, make all the readers drool, wet lips, high and low, stretched out in their turn on the cushions, right on the knees of 'godfather' Elie – high mourning – leave nothing, if possible, in the dark of what related me to Judaism, alliance broken in every aspect (Karet), with perhaps a gluttonous interiorization, and in heterogeneous modes: last of the Jews, what am I [...] the circumcised is the proper*" (12-30-76), that's what my readers won't have known about me, the comma of my breathing henceforward, without continuity but without a break, the changed time of my writing, graphic writing, through having lost its interrupted verticality, almost with every letter, to be bound better and better but be read less and less well over almost twenty years, like my religion about which nobody understands anything, any more than does my mother who asked other people a while ago, not daring to talk to me about it, if I still believed in God, *nutrierat filios totiens eos parturiens, quotiens abs te deuiare cernebat,*[15] but she must have known that the constancy of God in my life is called by other names, so that I quite rightly pass for an atheist, the omnipresence to me of what I call God in my absolved, absolutely private language being neither that of an eyewitness nor that of a voice doing anything other than talking to me without saying anything, nor a transcendent law or an immanent *schechina,* that feminine figure of a Yahweh who remains so strange and so familiar to me, but the secret I am excluded from, when the secret consists in the fact that you are held to secrecy by those who know your secret, how many are there, and do not dare admit to you that this is no longer a secret for them, that they share with you the open

secret, letting you reckon that they know without saying, and, from that point on, what you have neither the right nor the strength to confess, it is just as useless to make it known, to hand it over to this public notoriety you are the first and only one to be excluded from, properly theological hypothesis of a blank sacrifice sending the bidding up to infinity, God coming to circulate among the unavowables, unavowable as he remains himself, like a son not bearing my name, like a son not bearing his name, like a son not bearing a name, and if, to give rise to this beyond of the name, in view and by reason of this unacceptable appellation of self for my mother has become silenced without dying, I write that there is *too much* love in my life, emphasizing *too much*, the better and the worse, that would be true, love will have got the better of me, my faithfulness stands any test, I am faithful even to the test that does harm, to my euthanasias.

33   The satyr galatea that I am, a half-mourning satyr without confession which begins by getting lost in seduction, at the very moment it admits in me the dissidence of the true, "*the splitting of the ego, in me at least, is no transcendental claptrap, nor the double focus with-without monocular vision, I am, like, he who, returning, from a long voyage, out of everything, the earth, the world, men and their languages, tries to keep after the event a logbook, with the forgotten fragmentary rudimentary instruments of a prehistoric language and writing, tries to understand what happened, to explain it with pebbles bits of wood deaf and dumb gestures from before the institution of the deaf and dumb, a blind groping before Braille and they are going to try to reconstitute all that, but if they knew they would be scared and wouldn't even try...*" (12– 31–76), there will be neither monogram nor monograph of me, not only because I will always be too young for the contemporaries, then what G., the one or the other, will perhaps never have heard, I confided it to myself the other day in Toledo, is that if I am a sort of *marrane* of French Catholic culture, and I also have my Christian body, inherited from SA in a more or less twisted line, *condiebar eius sale*,[16] I am one of those *marranes* who no longer say they are Jews even in the secret of their own hearts, not so as to be authenticated *marranes* on both sides of the public frontier, but because they doubt everything, never go to confession or give up enlightenment, whatever the cost, ready to have themselves burned, almost, at the only moment they write under the monstrous law of an impossible face-to-face, *tu ... qui mecum es et priusquam tecum sim* [...] *sed neque me ipsum diiudico, Sic itaque audiar* [...] *ego uero quamuis prae tuo conspectu me despiciam et aestimem me* terram et cinerem, *tamen aliquid de te scio, quod de me nescio. Et certe* uidemus nunc per speculum in aenigmate, *nondum facie ad faciem* [...] *confitear ergo quid de me sciam, confitear et quid de me nesciam,*[17] at the moment of writing, neither before nor after but otherwise, I have the vision of SA, too, as a little homosexual Jew (from Algiers or New York), he has repressed everything, basically converts himself quite early on into a Christian Don Juan for fear of Aids, which he could see coming like me, from so far off, and, very well turned, very dignified, he does not recount his death, it is still too near, the only ally, the most secure, it's to death that already I owe everything I earn, I have succeeded in making of it, as I have with god, it's the same thing, my most difficult ally, impossible but unfailingly faithful once you've got him in your game, it costs a great deal, believe me, a great deal of love, you have to forgive yourself the hurt you do yourself, and the grace of the child is not certain, when I was a child they said I was "gracious" rather than "pretty," but my mother used to pass salt over my head of an evening in the kitchen to ward off the evil eye.

34   "*The 'alliance' was first of all for the 13-year-old child the name of the place one had to go to, a school really, a year after the exclusion, the numerus clausus and the other school, the Jewish one, rue Emile-Maupas, to learn and sit exams with a view to the bar mitzvah ('communion', as they called it), the word 'alliance' had no continuity with its simple homonym that [in French] designated the wedding ring, to describe the places...*" (12–31–76), and from that moment on I used to flee that Jewish school as well as the "alliance," I played truant without telling my parents for almost a year, I used to go to the rue de Chartres to the depths of the cousin's little watchmaker's to watch the soldiers, the "Allies," queuing up in front of the brothels, the Moon, the Sphinx, I knew how to "zap" even before television gave me that pleasure, as I have always zapped in writing, *Wechseln der Töne* which leaves the other rooted to the spot from one sentence to the next, in the middle of a sentence, dead or vigilant at last, ally for life or murderer, as though the reader had to wish for my death when for example I slip the *alliance* G. talks about on the other side to make it fall into the depths of my childhood, at the very surface of my tongue, reminding you that "alliance" for me will always be a Jewish building on the rue Bab Azoun, "What's new?" I asked her this 30th of December 1989, as if I were interrogating myself at every moment, that is without waiting for a reply, and indeed there was none, no more than to the question "Are you happy or sad?", not a sign of sadness when I leave without knowing whether I shall see her still living, she who wept as much as Monica at each of my departures, from the first, on the *City of Algiers* in the autumn of 1949, seasickness bad enough to make you give up the ghost, and so many times since, I lied to her all the time, as I do to all of you *sed quare hinc abirem et illuc irem, tu sciebas, deus, nec indicabas mihi nec matri, quae me profectum atrociter planxit et usque ad mare secuta est. sed fefelli eam violenter me tenetem* [. . .] *. . . et mentitus sum matri, et illi matri, et euasi, quia et hoc dimisisti mihi misericorditer seruans me ab aquis maris plenum exsecrandis sordibus usque ad aquam gratiae tuae, qua me abluto siccarentur flumina maternorum oculorum quibus pro me cotidie tibi rigabat terram sub uultu suo, et tamen recusanti sine me redire vix persuasi, ut in loco, qui proximus nostrae naui erat* [. . .] *maneret ea nocte. sed ea nocte clangulo ego profectus sum, illa autem non; mansit orando et flendo. et quid a te petebat, deus meus, tantis lacrimis, nisi ut nauigare me non sineres?,*[18] we euthanize ourselves in asking what a living woman would think *if* she saw death coming, whereas my mother had, when she was alive, before her lethargy, demanded from the doctor cousin, who told us this later, that he should never let her live in this way, never practice on her what the doctor is accusing us of, therapeutic harassment, as though —

36   And you ask if I write, G., because the Jews know nothing of confession, to which I reply that I am not confessing myself, rather I'm confessing the others for the imponderable and therefore so heavy secrets I inherit unbeknownst to myself, for example Esther or the two Elie's, for there is more than one now, and I have known for a few days that the first will not have held the second in his arms at the moment of circumcision as the second will have held the third, i.e. me, but me who deliberates passively, here or elsewhere, not about what there is to be said, the content, this or that, but if one must or must not, if I can desire to resist confession or not, for example if I ought to tell them that I pray, and describe how that could happen, according to what idiom and what rite, on one's knees or standing up, in front of whom or what books, for if you knew, G., my experience of prayers, you would know everything,

you who know everything, you would tell me whom to address them to, *et ubi essent tantae preces et tam crebrac* sinc intermissione? *nusquam nisi ad te*,[19] and you would tell me why I am interested in what at bottom, in the depths of me, precisely describes the "without-interest," what I am only, what "I" is only the misdirection, i.e. the presumed crime I am calling circumcision, and "*the role of the mother in circumcision for if she who desires, sometimes commits circumcision, compromises with the inhibited desire for child-murder, she is indeed in the position of obsequence (Glas, with its circumcisions, guillotines, incisions, still illegible tattoos), figure without figure, armed extra who is no longer present among us at the operation she now delegates after having previously performed it herself,*" (7–1–77), and I am trying to disinterest myself from myself to withdraw from death by making the "I," to whom death is supposed to happen, gradually go away, no, be destroyed before death come to meet it, so that at the end already there should be no one left to be scared of losing the world in losing himself in it, and the last of the Jews that I still am is doing nothing here other than destroying the world on the pretext of making truth, but just as well the intense relation to survival that writing is, is not driven by the desire that something remain after me, since I shall not be *there* to enjoy it in a word, *there* where the point is, rather, in producing these remains and therefore the witnesses of my radical absence, to live today, here and now, this death of me, for example, the very counterexample which finally reveals the truth of the world such as it is, itself, i.e. without me, and all the more intensely to enjoy this light I am producing through the present experimentation of my possible survival, i.e. of absolute death, I tell myself this every time that I am walking in the streets of a city I love, in which I love, on whose walls I weep myself and was weeping myself again yesterday in the night of the rue de l'Abbé de l'Epée not long after leaving you, G., at Gatwick.

42   "*Rediscover the (lost) taste for holding the pen, for writing well in a sense I have mistreated, reworked, lost a long time ago (double syntax of 'lose someone') and beyond the malediction which traverses my love for the person who has lost me, rediscover an easy, offered, readable, relaxed writing*" (10–14–77), oh how fine her hands are, my survivress, she had such beautiful handwriting, that can be said in the past, quite different from mine, and very legible, stylish, elegant, more cultivated than herself, I wonder if that's possible, and how to speak of her and SA without participating in their chirography, from the lowest part of my body and to the tips of my fingers, without even feeling the resistance the support must have opposed to both, but no more to you, G., nor to me, and I wonder again what can have happened when my writing changed, after thirty years, then again later, when machines took it over on the sea, for I got to the sea, first when the current passed through, then here when I swim against the tide, against the waves that write on my face from the screen to tell me how lucky my mother will be, if she is, to die before me, which I infer from my fear of not dying before my uncircumcised sons, objects of my infinite compassion, not that my compassion be extended to any uncircumcised but to my own, without religion apparently having anything to do with it, nor Moses the father of my mother, like for someone, me, who would be capable of inventing circumcision all alone, as I am doing here, and of founding another religion, refounding all of them, rather, playfully, doubtless according to the vague presentment that my uncircumcised sons, the only people whose judgment I fear, will have failed to fail, what culture is made of (and man, *vir*, so they say), and that for that reason they will

never finish envying me or hating me, for their love hates me, and I love them with love, a dissymmetry that nobody will believe except me and G., who is always right, like God, of course, who knows how much the love of the son can come to be lacking, it's God weeping in me, turning around me, reappropriating my languages, dispersing their meaning in all directions, *ita cum alius dixerit: "hoc sensit, quod ego," et alius: "immo illud, quod ego," religiosius me arbitror dicere: cur non utrumque potius, si utrumque uerum est, et si quid tertium et si quid quartum et si quid omnino aliud uerum quispiam in his uerbis uidet, cur non illa omnia uidisse credatur, per quem deus unus sacras litteras uera et diuersa uisuris multorum sensibus temperauit?*,[20] and as I am someOne that the One God never stops de-circumcising, in other words *hounds* herself to make bleed in dispersion, *salus in sanguine*, all those who can no longer sleep for it pretend to be waiting for me somewhere I've already arrived, like the truest of false prophets, they want to deport their Elijah obsession, attraction repulsion, sucked up thrown out to the periphery of a sentence, to the periphrases of my signature.

43   I invent the word *dhavec* this day of Purim 5750, while Esther still lives on and for almost a year and a half, without ever being interested in this name Esther, in spite of my appeals, still less at this moment at which she is surviving the conscience of me, of her name as of mine, I lean over her budding *escarres*, "they look good" said the reassuring nurse, they are roaring in the carnage of a protest, life has always protested in my mother, and if "bad blood" will always be for me *her* expression, if from her alone I have received it, heard it or learned it, from her impatient sighs, this is because I began with this fear, with being scared of her bad blood, with not wanting it, whence the infinite separation, the initial and instantaneously repeated i.e. indefinitely postponed divorce from [*d'avec*] the closest cruelty which was not that of my mother but the distance she enjoined on me from [*d'avec*] my own skin thus torn off, in the very place, along the crural artery where my books find their inspiration, they are written first in skin, they read the death sentence held in reserve on the other side of the screen for in the end since the computer I have my memory like a sky in front of me, all the succor, all the threats of a sky, the pelliculated simulacrum of another absolute subjectivity, a transcendence which I would finally do with as she would like, she who wants my death, "*the sublime scission, the bottomless bet: to learn how to love — that cannot fail to repeat one and many closed-up rents, open again the wound of circumcision, analyze that form of secret, the 'my life' which is neither a content to be hidden nor an inside of the solitary self but hangs on the partition between two absolute subjectivities, two whole worlds in which everything can be said and put in play without reserve, with the exception not of this fact but of the bottomless stake of the other world, I write by reconstituting the partitioned and transcendant structure of religion, of several religions, in the internal circumcision of 'my life' . . . I came up to write something else, for I come up now (into this loft, this 'sublime' to write*" (10–14–77), I do not have the other under my skin, that would be too simple, the other holds, pulls, stretches, separates the skin from [*d'avec*] my sex in her mouth, opposite or above me, she makes me sperm in this strange condition, it's my condition, on this suspended condition that I write to death on a skin bigger than I, that of a provisional and sacrificed spokesman, who can't stand it any more, *caelum enim plicabitur ut liber et nunc sicut pellis extenditur super nos. sublimioris enim auctoritatis est tua diuina scriptura* [. . .] *sicut pellem extendisti firmamentum libri tui, concordes utique sermones tuos, quos per mortalium ministerium superposuisti nobis.*

[. . .] *Cum hic uiuerent, non ita sublimiter extentum erat. non dum* sicut pellem caelum *extenderas, nondum mortis eorum famam usquequaque dilataueras.*[21]

51   I am no longer far from touching land at last, she is watching, she is waiting for me to have finished, she is waiting for me to go out, we will leave together, she was holding my hand, we were going up by the route known as the little wood and I began to invent the simulacrum of an illness, as I have all my life long, to avoid going back to nursery school, a lie that one day I forgot to recall, whence the tears when later in the afternoon, from the playground, I caught sight of her through the fence, she must have been as beautiful as a photograph, and I reproached her with leaving me in the world, in the hands of others, basically with having forgotten that I was supposed to be ill so as to stay with her, just, according to our very alliance, one of our 59 conjurations without which I am nothing, accusing her in this way of letting me be caught up again by school, all those cruel mistresses, and since then I've always been caught up by school, while she was smiling at me in silence for her capacities for silence and amnesia are what I share best, no arguing with that, that's what they can't stand, that I say nothing, never anything tenable or valid, no thesis that could be refuted, neither true nor false, not even, not seen not caught, it is not a strategy but the violence of the void through which God goes to earth to death in me, the geologic program, me, I've never been able to contradict myself, that's saying, so I write, that's the word, convenient for forgetting, one can always come and go, go off ahead light of foot, I am still so young, all I'm saying is nursery school, *la maternelle*, the unforgettable power of my discourses hangs on the fact that they grind up everything including the mute ash whose name alone one then retains, scarcely mine, all that turning around nothing, a Nothing in which God reminds me of him, that's my only memory, the condition of all my fidelities, the name of God in the ash of Elijah, an evening of rest that never arrives, seven days after the 52-week year, Domine deus, pacem da nobis – omnia enim praestitisti nobis – *pacem quietis, pacem sabbati, pacem sine uespera* [. . .]. *Dies autem septimus sine uespera est nec habet occasum,*[22] and as I say nothing, well-known program, I write to alienate, drive mad all those that I will have alienated by not saying anything, I am just to confide in them the memory of me who am in for nobody, since a date immemorial, since I've been scared, me, in the evening, of the fear I inspire, fear of the deathly silence that resounds at my every word, *"even if – Elie were to be written as a novel in 4 columns, at 4 discursive levels (cf. above . . . although I gave up the 4 notebooks at least a month ago), no doubt I should not make the distinction apparent in typographical of topographical form, from one sentence to the next of the apparently continuous tissue but according to strict internal criteria, the 4 breaths relaying each other"* (9–4–81).

57   Whether they expelled me from school or threw me into prison, I always thought the other must have good reason to accuse me, I did not see, I did not even see my eyes, any more than in the past I saw the hand raising the knife above me, but basically they were telling me, that's their very discourse, in the beginning the *logos*, that it was enough to seek, to track down the event by writing backward, never seeing the next step, it was enough to write to prepare the moment when things turn round, the moment at which you will be able to convert and finally see your sacrificer face on, not to accuse him in turn at last, but to make the truth, *"It would be enough to begin with any*

old shock, in apparently the most aleatory fashion, and all the rest, yes, would come RUN-
NING, lovely word, without delay, like some mad thing, and it would not be aleatory, but why,
to begin with scenes of guilt in some sense faultless, without any deliberate fault, situations in
which the accusation surprises you, and afterward the having-been at fault, even before any
reflection, has to be, not taken on board, for that is just impossible, but you have to let yourself be
'charged,' as they say in English, and struggle with that charge, doubtless significant enough to
serve later as a paradigm a whole life long, for there is nothing fortuitous in the fact that these
scenes play in their Confessions an organizing and abyssal role" (9–6–81), know that I am
dying of shame, but of a shame in which I persevere all the more in that I have nothing
to do with it, I'm not admitting anything and yet I am ready to justify or even repeat
the very thing I'm being accused of, even tirelessly to provide you with arguments of
my own vintage to establish this fault which nonetheless is all Hebrew to me, for I am
perhaps not what remains of Judaism, and I would have no trouble agreeing with that,
if at least people really wanted to prove it, and we'll have to get up early, at dawn on
this day with no evening, for after all but after all what else am I in truth, who am I if I
am not what I inhabit and where I take place, *Ich bleibe also Jude*, i.e. today in what
remains of Judaism to this world, Europe and the other, and in this remainder I am
only someone to whom there remains so little that at bottom, already dead as son with
the widow, I expect the resurrection of Elijah, and to sort out the interminably
preliminary question of knowing how they, the Jews and the others, can interpret
circumfession, i.e. that I here am inhabiting what remains of Judaism, there are so few
of us and we are so divided, you see, I'm still waiting before taking another step and
adding a word, the name from which I expect resurrection – and of my mother, *cum*
iam secura fieret ex ea parte miseriae meae, in qua me tamquam mortuum sed resuscitandum tibi
flebat et feretro cogitationis offerebat, ut diceres filio uiduae: iuuenis, tibi dico, surge, et
reuiuesceret et inciperet loqui et traderes illum matri suae.[23]

59   To speak of the child's hell you prefer "minimalist" decency, question of taste, *et*
solidasti auctoritatem libri tui,[24] at the moment when here you are trembling, Tuesday, May
1, 1990, 7 o'clock in the morning in Laguna Beach, she's still alive for you, over there in
Nice, 20, rue Parmentier, 4th floor, it is 4 in the afternoon there, your brother and sister
have not yet arrived, you will see her, perhaps you will still hear her when you get back,
it's enough to recount the "present" to throw G.'s theologic program off course, by the
very present you are making him, *Everybody's Autobiography*, yours which tells you so well
that *there is no thinking that one was never born until you hear accidentally that there were to be five*
children and if two little ones had not died there would be no G.S., you archive the system,
MacWrite Macintosh SE Apple of PaRDeS, you are unrecognizable, as you were to that
young imbecile who asks you, after your talk on the Final Solution, what you had done to
save Jews during the war, but though he may well not have known, until your reply, that
you will have been Jewish, it recalls the fact that people might not know it still, you
remain guilty of that, whence this announcement of circumcision, perhaps you didn't do
enough to save Jews, he might be right, you always think the other is right, at the
beginning or the end of the book, perhaps you didn't do enough, not enough to save
yourself first of all, from the others or again from the Jews, you have not yet "seen" like
those circumcised ones among the Wonghi, who receive the order to open one eye then
the other after the operation, immediate simulacrum of a resurrection, but you see

yourself beginning to overrun this discourse on castration and its supposed substitute, that old concept of narcissism, that worn edge topology, resurrection will be for you "*more than ever the address, the stabilized relation of a destination, a game of a-destination finally sorted out, for beyond what happens in the P.C., it is now the work to dispatch it that must win out, toward the secret that demanded, like a breath, the 'perversity' of the P.C., not to be finished with a destinerrancy which was never my doing, nor to my taste, but with a still complacent and therefore defensive account of the Moira*" (7–6–81), too late, you are less, you, less than yourself, you have spent your life inviting calling promising, hoping sighing dreaming, convoking invoking provoking, constituting engendering producing, naming assigning demanding, prescribing commanding sacrificing, what, the witness, you my counterpart, only so that he will attest this secret truth i.e. severed from truth, i.e. that you will never have had any witness, *ergo es*, in this very place, you alone whose life will have been so short, the voyage short, scarcely organized, by you with no lighthouse and no book, you the floating toy at high tide and under the moon, you the crossing between these two phantoms of witnesses who will never come down to the same.

Notes

1   "Why we confess to God, when he knows (everything about us)." This title is given to chapter 1 of book 9 of Saint Augustine's *Confessions* in the 1649 French translation by Robert Arnauld d'Andilly. It was in this very free translation that I first read the *Confessions*. In spite of my attachment for this bilingual edition (Garnier, 1925) in which, so long ago, I discovered the prayers and tears of Augustine, I henceforth use the translation in the edition of the Bibliothèque Augustinienne, by E. Tréhorel and G. Bouissou (Desclée de Brouwer, 1962). [Translator's note: English translations are taken, with some minor alterations, from the version by Vernon J. Bourke (Washington: Catholic University of America Press, 1953).]

2   "We hastily gathered about her, but she returned to consciousness quickly and looked at me and my brother as we stood by. Rather like a person in search of something, she said to us: 'Where am I?' Then, seeing that we were overcome with grief, she said: 'Bury your mother here.' I remained silent and restrained my tears" (IX, xi, 27).

3   *The Post Card – from Socrates to Freud and Beyond*, I think.

4   "And now, O Lord, I am confessing to Thee in writing" (IX, xii, 33).

5   "Let him who wishes read and interpret it as he wishes. If he finds it a sin that I wept for my mother during a little part of an hour, the mother who was dead for the time being to my eyes, who had wept over me for many years that I might live before Thy eyes – let him not be scornful; rather, if he is a person of great charity, let him weep himself for my sins, before Thee, the Father of all the brethren of Thy Christ" (IX, xii, 33).

6   "I desire to do this [the truth] in my heart, before Thee in confession; and in my writing, before many witnesses" (X, i, 1).

7   "Why tears are sweet to those in misfortune?" (IV, v, 10).

8   "See my position! Weep with me and weep for me" (X, xxxiii, 50).

9   "There remains the pleasure of these eyes of my flesh. I speak of it in the form of confessions which the ears of Thy temple may hear, [brotherly and pious ears] ... " (X, xxxiv, 51).

10   Marvell, "Eyes and Tears."

11 "But where dost Thou dwell in my memory, O Lord; where dost thou dwell there? What resting place hast Thou fashioned for Thyself? [What sanctuary hast Thou built for thyself?] Thou has granted this favor to my memory, to dwell in it, but in which part of it Thou dost dwell, this I now consider" (X, xxxv, 36).

12 "[I shall even pass over] this power of mine which is called memory, [desiring to attain Thee where Thou canst be attained]" (X, xvii, 26).

13 "[I was associating even then, in Rome, with those false and fallacious 'saints']: not just with their auditors, to which rank belonged the man in whose home I recuperated and regained my health, but even with those whom they call the 'elect'" (V, x, 18).

14 "[For, up to that time, it seemed to me that it is not we who sin, but some other unknown nature within us which sins . . .] but I loved rather to excuse myself and accuse some other unknown being which existed with me and yet was not I . . . [Thou hadst not yet set a watch upon my heart and a door of safekeeping about my lips (*custodiam ori meo et ostium continentiae circum labia mea*) [. . .] So, until then, I associated with their elect]" (V, x, 18).

15 "She had brought up her children, being in labor with them each time she saw them wandering away from Thee" (IX, ix, 22).

16 "[Fresh from the womb of my mother, who put much hope in Thee, I was marked with the sign of His cross and] seasoned with His salt" (I, xi, 17).

17 "Thou Thyself [. . .] art with me even before I am with Thee. However, 'I do not even judge myself.' Thus, then, may I be heard [. . .] In fact, though I despise myself before Thy sight and consider myself but earth and ashes, yet I do know something about Thee which I do not know about myself. Truly, 'we see now through a mirror in an obscure manner,' not yet 'face to face' [. . .] Therefore, I will confess what I know of myself and what I do not know of myself" (X, iv, v, 6, 7).

18 "Thou, O God, didst know why I left here and went there, but Thou gavest no sign either to me or to my mother. She complained bitterly at the prospect of my leaving, and followed me to the seaside. But I deceived her, while she was urgently holding on to me [. . .] I lied to my mother, and such a mother, and I slipped away. Thou hast mercifully forgiven me even this, preserving me from the waters of the sea, though I was full of abominable filth, unto the water of Thy grace, to be washed by it, when the rivers of my mother's tears might then be dried up, those with which in my behalf she daily in prayer to Thee did moisten the ground beneath her countenance. Yet, when she refused to return without me, I persuaded her with some difficulty to spend the night in a place which was near our ship [. . .] But on that night, I set out secretly, while she remained behind in prayer and tears. What did she ask of Thee, O my God, with so many tears, but that Thou wouldst not permit me to sail away?" (V, viii, 15–16).

19 "And where would then have been such great, such frequent, and uninterrupted prayers? Nowhere but with Thee" (V, ix, 17).

20 "So, when one man has said: '[Moses] meant the same as I,' and another: 'Not that but what I mean,' I think I can say in a more religious way: 'Why not both, instead, if both are true?' And, if there is a third, and a fourth, and any other truths that anyone sees in these words, why may it not be believed that he saw all these, and that, through him, the one God has tempered the sacred writings to the perceptions of many people, in which they will see things which are true and also different?" (XII, xxxi, 42).

21 "For 'the heavens shall be folded together as a book,' and now it is stretched over us like a skin. Indeed, Thy divine Scripture is of more sublime authority [. . .] Just so, Thou hast stretched out the firmament of Thy Book like a skin, Thy wonderfully harmonious words which Thou hast imposed upon us [. . .] while they were living here below, it was not so sublimely extended. Thou hadst not yet spread out the heaven like a skin; Thou hadst not yet broadcast the renown of their death in all directions" (XIII, xv, 16).

22   "O Lord God, grant us peace – for Thou hast provided all things for us – the peace of rest, the peace of the Sabbath, the peace without an 'evening' [. . .] Now the seventh day is without an 'evening' and has no setting" (XIII, xxxv, xxxvi, 50, 51).

23   " . . . since she already felt safe in regard to this aspect of my wretchedness, in which she wept for me as for one dead but destined to be restored to life by Thee. She was offering me on the bier of her thoughts, so that thou wouldst say to the son of the widows: 'Young man, I say to thee, arise!' and he would come back to life and begin to speak again and Thou wouldst return him to his mother" (VI, i, 1).

24   "Thou didst establish the firmament of the authority of Thy Book" (XIII, xxxiv, 49).

8

BELIEF ITSELF

Luce Irigaray

What I am about to tell you, or confide in you, today, will remain rather primary, loose. This is both deliberate and due to lack of time. But what time do I mean? The time that has not, or has not yet, been loosed by all that is too bound, too secondarily bound, thereby leaving so-called free energy chained up, in the crypt. But perhaps that energy is merely deprived of the space-time it needs to cathect, unfold, inscribe, play. . . .

So I shall be talking more or less freely, offering to your associations and interpretations certain of the still dark, oneiric experiences, trials, associations that I have had as woman and as analyst. At times it will be like a children's story.

To dream greatly, to hold onto sleep while letting everything float freely, is, among other things, the duty or the vocation of the analyst. Especially if she is a woman, perhaps. Bound and chained in and under the secondary processes? A "poste restante" or P.O. box[1] where messages for unknown persons with no fixed address are held, undeliverable by the usual, already coded, telecommanded, circuits.

So, at this poste restante, a woman's message came my way recently that could not be decoded by the usual interpretative methods. The woman told me she had given the message to one psychoanalyst with no success – no useful interpretation was afforded, they both agreed. The resistance set up by the analyst, by analysis, by the woman herself perhaps, was too strong, the associations were confused and confusing, a deaf ear was turned to such events.

Yet, this message is in my opinion the essential preliminary for any consideration of sexual difference. It tells us where the obstacle lies. What it is that lies across the threshold, blocking access, barring the very location.

Here is the message: "At the point in the mass when they, the (spiritual) father and son, are reciting together the ritual words of the consecration, saying, 'This is my body, this is my blood,' I bleed."[2]

The father and the son must celebrate the Eucharist together in her absence, and then hand out the consecrated bread and wine to the congregation to complete the communion service. This generally occurs on a Sunday. She makes the connection between her hemorrhaging and the mass only subsequently.

She adds that she loves the son. At least consciously, secondarily, she does not accept the men's current forms of belief. This is not to say that she is alien to that aspect of the divine which finds an impoverished form and fulfillment in their celebrations – a divine that comes as blood flowing *over and above*. The truth of father and son assails her, wounds her in that place where she remains excluded from the manifestation of their faith, though she is not necessarily far outside their tradition. Her fidelity to that tradition is shown in a sensual experience for which the words, the rites, the historic interpretation of the texts, are inadequate. It finds expression in a bodily immediacy that no mediation the woman knows can affect.

In her turn, she fears not being believed, even by herself, and goes so far as to look for proofs and demonstrations! Nothing changes. No word comes, or at least none that matches her problem, her sense of abandonment.

First association for me: what deceives some people and destroys others about belief is the way it makes us forget the real. Faith first stands in for confidence and loyalty, and then it aims to double its own reflection, to square or even cube all its numbers or letters and thereby make the other – with a capital O – the other of the same. But, for this to succeed, surely a sacrifice of a different body and flesh is made? Yet no one must ever see that, by means of the male twosome, it is she who is being offered in partial oblation, she who manages the communion between them and among the other men and women present.[3]

Belief is safe only if that in which or in whom the assembly communes or communicates is subject to concealment. Once this is exposed, there is no need to believe, at least as adherence is usually understood. But truth, any truth throughout the centuries, assumes a belief that undermines it and that seduces and numbs anyone who believes. Does not the fact that this belief asserts and unveils itself in the form of religious myths, dogmas, figures, or rites show us that metaphysics keeps watch over the crypt of faith? Theology and the ritual practices it demands would seem to correspond to one formulation of all that is hidden in the constitution of the monocratic patriarchal truth, the faith in its order, its word, its logic.

Therefore I shall term the preliminary to the question of sexual difference: belief itself.

Let me go back to my example. This woman I spoke of, whose age casts her as mother and daughter, between mother and daughter, tells me: I bleed. This is truly a strange *I*. It takes place both outside and inside the game, but in a radical hemmorhage of herself. She is faraway when she bleeds. She needs to be faraway when that (*ça*) takes place, too far to come back to him, to her, within herself, kept at a distance from the celebration and the communion that occurs between the men, among the men and the women.

These are the facts. With no family names. Are they useless? The first names would be more important, but it is not up to me to reveal them to you. As for the family names, these apparently have the characteristic of not doubling any of their letters.[4] Their first names, on the other hand, have some relevance.

So having this (*ça*) in poste restante, I read Jacques Derrida's *The Post Card*. Among other things in the book, I find – and this is the text that I will be concentrating on – the discussion of the *fort-da* of little Ernst. And, without any attempt to interpret as yet,

I associated or joined the two scenes together. Are there not some obvious similarities between the two – notably Sophie, the Sunday daughter, whose death is so hard for her father to accept?

So, here is the *fort-da* scene as translated by Jacques Derrida:* "The child was not at all precocious in his intellectual development. At the age of one and a half he could say only a few comprehensible words; he could also make use of a number of sounds which expressed a meaning (*bedeutungsvolle Laute*, phonemes charged with meaning) to those around him. He was, however, on good terms with his parents and their one servant-girl, and tributes were paid to his being 'a good boy' (*anstandig*, easy, reasonable). He did not disturb his parents at night, he conscientiously obeyed orders not to touch certain things or go into certain rooms, and above all (*vor allem anderen*, before all else) he never cried when his mother left him for a few hours. At the same time, he was greatly attached to his mother, who had not only fed him herself but had looked after him without any outside help. This good little boy, however, had an occasional disturbing habit of taking any small objects he could get hold of and throwing them away from him into a corner, under the bed, and so on, so that hunting for (*Zusammensuchen*, looking for and collecting up) his toys (*Spielzeuges*) and picking them up was often quite a business" (*Postcard*, p. 307). As Jacques Derrida stresses, the famous reel or spool has not yet made its appearance. Here it comes now, preceded by an interpretative anticipation. "As he did this (as he threw away his *Spielzeug*) he gave vent to a loud, long-drawn-out 'o-o-o-o', accompanied by an expression of interest and satisfaction. His mother and the writer of the present account were agreed in thinking (the daughter and the father, the mother and the grandfather are here conjoined in the same speculation) that this was not a mere interjection but represented the German word *fort* (gone, faraway). I eventually realized that it was a game and that the only use he made of any of his toys (*Spielsachen*) was to play 'gone' (*fortsein*) with them. One day I made the observation which confirmed my view. The child had a wooden reel (*Holzspule*) with a piece of string (*Bindfaden*) tied round it. It never occurred to him to pull it along the floor behind him, for instance, and play at its being a carriage. What he did was to hold the reel by the string and very skilfully (with great *Geschick*) throw it over the edge of his curtained cot (or veiled bed, *verhangten Bettschens*), so that it disappeared into it, at the same time expressing his expressive (*Bedeutungsvolles*) o-o-o-o. He then pulled the reel out of the cot again by the string and hailed its reappearance with a joyful *Da* (there). This, then, was the complete game (*komplette Spiel*) – disappearance and return (*Verschwinden und Wiederkommen*). As a rule one only witnessed its first act, which was repeated untiringly as a game in itself, though there is no doubt that the greater pleasure was attached to the second act" (*Postcard*, p. 309).

"'This, then,' says Freud, 'was the complete game.' Which immediately implies: this, then, is the complete observation, and the complete interpretation of this game" (*Postcard*, p. 309).

---

* The following passage consists of quotations from *Beyond the Pleasure Principle*, by Sigmund Freud (translated and edited by James Strachey, New York: Norton, 1961, pp. 8–9), with bracketed interpolations by Derrida. See *The Post Card: From Socrates to Freud and Beyond*, translated with an introduction and additional notes by Alan Bass (Chicago: University of Chicago Press, 1987). In his text, Bass has amended the Standard Edition translation to better match the French text used by Derrida. Most specifically, he has preferred the American word *spool* to the *reel* used by Strachey to translate *Spule*. I have kept the Strachey text intact. – Tr.

"Instead of playing on the floor (*am Boden*), he insisted on putting the bed into the game, into play, on playing with the thing over the bed, and also in the bed. Not in the bed as the place where the child himself would be, for contrary to what the text and the translation have often led many to believe (and one would have to ask why), it appears he is not in the bed at the moment when he throws the spool. He throws it from outside the bed over its edge (*Rand*) from the other side, which quite simply might be into the sheets. And in any event, it is from 'out of the bed' (*zog . . . an dem Bett beraus*) that he pulls back the vehicle in order to make it come back: *da*. The bed, then is *fort*, which perhaps contravenes all desire, but perhaps not *fort* enough for the (grand)father who might have wished that Ernst had played more seriously on the floor (*am Boden*) without bothering himself with the bed. But for both of them, the distancing of the bed is worked upon by this *da* which divides and shares it: too much or not enough. For the one or for the other" (*Postcard*, p. 310).[5]

The mother's presence in the re-presentation presumes, therefore, a rather white and transparent screen: air, canvas, veil. The curtain or veil that covered the bed or the crib was white or very light in color and probably was not wholly opaque. It's hard to imagine it all black, absorbing the light, or a bright, glaring red or indeed any color that would separate or confuse the two sides, the edges. The child throws something over there, beyond, but not behind a wall or behind a curtain that concealed, hid her, hid him definitively. Or at least, that's what he believes. Neither he nor she really goes away or disappears for good.

What Ernst wants is to master presence-absence with the help of a more or less white, more or less transparent veil. Freud does not seem to care about the nature or texture or indeed the color of this veil. Apart from the thread and the reel he has nothing to say about any of the things that ensure the return – how they are located in reference to the child, the presence or absence in the room or the house of the main actors in the play. He has nothing to say about what properties in the veil make the going-return possible. That (*ça*) has nothing to say to him – or not any more. Which is probably why he is able to tell the story of this drama in all good conscience without really knowing what he is telling or what he is talking about. He is just pleased that his grandson, in all innocence, gives him what he needs to go on writing his own text, his own life, both their lives.

So Freud says nothing, knows nothing, wants to know nothing about what stands between him and him, between him and her, disappearing and reappearing in the scene with the reel, before Ernst notices himself in the mirror. The veil is necessary as a setting, a mediation for the performance of presence in absence, for the process of re-presentation in this particular scene, where for the first time the son plays symbolically with the mother, but it is then neglected, censored, repressed, forgotten by Freud. The father of psychoanalysis notes what it is that enables Ernst to confuse the other in himself, the other in the same, with a skill that surprises and amazes his grandfather, in particular through its topology (it occurs in front, not behind, for example): he takes note of it in his description, but then goes right on. What is the child throwing away from himself? Is it himself, her and him, him and her, her in him, him in her? These are questions Freud never pauses to ask. He too just moves on.

But he, after all, is not playing: he is framing a theory. This tale, in which the child's naïveté is useful as an objective, scientific guarantee, can be interpreted as he likes, thus standardizing, prescribing the desire of his descendants, indeed retroactively his own, and that of his ancestors. She must be thrown over there, put at a distance, beyond the horizon, so that she can come back to him, back inside him, so that he can take her back, over and over again, reassimilate her, and feel no sorrow. Freud simply notices the reel and the thread. A physical substitute for her (he says), an object, and a link that allows him to send her faraway, and bring her back to him, back inside him.

But does, in fact, the reel have anything to do with her? Or with him? With him, foetus, playing at going in and coming out of her with a cord, a placental-veil, a womb-bed, for example. This assumes that the disappearance-reappearance, inside-outside, outside-inside can be mastered, whereas in fact they can no more be mastered than the life-death watch that is our obligation from birth, if not before. This darling little boy believes that coming into the world or going out of it can be made into a game in this way. He *believes* it because it is not the truth. This is an event that can never be controlled or planned, obeying a necessity that can never be so easily played with. Except by killing, and fasting to death.

This game, too simple when related to her absence or presence, will undermine his language of beliefs. At the moment when he believes he is best able to master her appearance-disappearance, he is most slave to belief. Belief in himself and his power of course, but also in her, since his link to her depends upon the belief that she is there, when she is not, that she is there more when she is not there (here), that she is where she isn't. Once this split between the two has been achieved, everything is possible. The thread by which the son holds her/holds her back, and makes a game of her life-her death, their life-their death, opens up the way to any presence or absence, in or out of the world. The truth of the world plunges downward, opening up like a set of Chinese boxes. Anything can climb up or down, climb back up or down. The framework of desire of the child-king or god closes and opens the session, the play, or the world to any kind of appearance or disappearance. It authorizes the confusion or substitution of reality and unreality, truth and untruth, between something and nothing, someone and no one, a living person and a ghost, self and someone other, someone other and someone other again, someone other and someone same.

The most important *fort-da* – as you know, even, or especially when you refuse to believe it – refers, past the mother's presence, in the mother, beyond-veil, to the presence of God, beyond the sky, beyond the visual horizon. It moves away from the presence of the mother beyond veil, petticoats, pants, etc. – though this does not mean that the son does not send himself there in the first veil, the amniotic fluid and the placenta that separate him from the womb – away from the mother's presence, then, toward that of god beyond and in heaven. All the threads and all the sons (*tous les fils et les fils**) come and go between these two places of the invisible, those two hidden presences, between which everything is played out, in which everything meets. And what is being sent of hers, quite apart from the whole rigmarole of toys and objects, is

---

* Play on the words *le fil*, thread, and *le fils*, son, both of which have the same plural, *les fils*. – Trans.

not some phallus she guards jealously – even if this is a condition he depends on – but rather the mystery of a first crypt, a first and longed-for dwelling place, the happy time when he had a space in her, and she in him, when he owed his whole life to her, before any call or claim. He lives off her, feeds on her, is wrapped up in her, drinks her, consumes her, consummates her…before any call or claim. This is a gift that permits no mastery during its term, an infinite debt, an infused, diffuse, profuse, exhaustive presence, and he can play with it only at the cost of relegating her, by a qualitative leap, into some place beyond life and death. This life in turn becomes merely a kind of exodus between two paradises: the one split between biology and mythology or left in silence, and the other for which a certain knowledge claims to account. For these two places, there are therefore two different measures and transcriptions, or so it seems at least. It remains to be seen how the one is folded and bent into the other, as an immemorial store of fiction, of belief, that secretly underpins its truth.

During that time in her womb, then, haven of skin, of membranes, of water – a complete world, in fact, in which and through which he receives all he wants, with no need for work or clothing – air, warmth, food, blood, life, potentially even the risk of death, come to him via a hollow thread. Everything comes that route, without being called upon. To believe that she will always be there takes only a step or two at most. The hollow cord and the thread of the reel don't quite amount to the same thing. Once the primal bond is severed, she will be there only if he summons. But was she ever there?

Step number two, which comes before or after the first, and he thinks he can keep a hold on her by alternating between the two: she was there and was not there, she gave place yet had no place, except her womb, and even then. Within her womb, an amnion and a placenta, a whole world with its layers, its circuits, its vessels, its nourishing pathways, etc., a whole world of invisible relations that adheres to her womb, that takes place in her womb, that gives him pain and gives her pain when the time comes for her to push him out and be delivered. But this world is not to be confused with her. It is destroyed forever at birth and it is impossible ever to return to it. All kinds of veils may claim to take its place, seek to repeat it, but there can be no return to that first dwelling place.

In fact she was never there, except in that ceaseless transfusion of life that passed from her to him, by a hollow cord. She offers the possibility of entry into presence but has no place in it. No encounter is possible with her during the pregnancy.

The son, obviously, always wants to go back there. And, if he can't, doesn't he tear away bit by bit the whole membrane that separated him from her but created an inconceivable nearness that he can never cease to mourn? She is so close, invisibly penetrating him, and she remains an unmasterable presence, if such a word can still be used in this way for a relationship in which she flows into him and for him, without face or form.

The placenta is clearly the first veil that the child knows as his own. Yet, he seems to forget that it is his own, even if it is produced for him within her, even if she thereby gives herself to him asking nothing in return, and even if this first home is not without some connection to her? The veil is his as much as hers, even if they share it. It stands between them, obviously: by its means she gives herself to him and within him.

But it seems that from now on he will impose the veil upon her much more than she on him. It is true that she has not begun to speak, that she has her place in the veil, that they have never really met each other face to face, as if their mouth-to-mouth, their mouth-to-ear were still mediated by an umbilicus. From his navel to his or their placenta and from the connection of that enveloping membrane to her womb, unconsciously there would continue to be a dialogue. This does not prevent him from wanting to master her, reduce her little by little to nothing, by constructing for himself all kinds of new enclosures, new homes, new houses, directions, dimensions, foods, in order to break the bond with her. Behind all these substitutes lies the belief that she stands, she stands there all-powerful.

Two steps, then. The string of the reel is *not* like the first cord and does *not* bring her to him: he merely believes this and weaves this absence into his language. And, what is more, she should *not* simply be equated with the first dwelling place. To have access to her – to woman – would come after the nostalgia for this return into her, for that move back into the lost paradise where she shelters him and feeds him with and through her/ their container. To have access to her demands another threshold than the one where she always stands behind the veil. The veil has served the life they once shared and can never be repeated. Later, it serves as a hideout or hiding place for all or nothing. In this game of hide and seek, the son plays with himself alone: with him in her, her in him, before any meeting face to face can occur. The game takes the place of that encounter, takes over from it, overtakes and overcomes it, weaving a whole world, from the depths of the earth to the highest heavens. Everything is set up in such a way that she is lost at the poste restante, never arrives at the destination, never comes face to face with him. This encounter between them can perhaps take place only in the form of a scar, a wound that he reopens in her, or fears truly to reopen, in order to close himself off. He opens the wound in her womb so that he can close up his navel, his heart, or his mouth over the wound left by her absence, her disappearance from him. This requires a whole game with his geometry, both Euclidian and more advanced, his vectorizations of space: horizontal and vertical, strings and veils, which exist only because she is faraway and because he believes that, when he sent her far off like this, she will come back the same, whereas she returns to the other in the same (*le même*). This difference undermines the truth of his language: a credulous-ness is introduced in the power of the subject that thereby constitutes itself, plays even as it is played with. He remains eternally in exodus from the place that transcends all that in which he might at last discover the truth of truth, in some ontological or theological heaven. The two are not unrelated, maintain their mutual situation, control what takes place, and what does not. Here too there is no lack of flights and soaring.

For all this to succeed, a more or less transparent veil was needed that ensures a certain number of passages between him and her within representation, a certain number of repetitions in which he believes he masters the mother, completely. In the scene as he sets it up, he stands in the middle, where the string-cord begins. She would come back to the middle. And, if he can only pivot around a little, always looking straight on, or, straight on but all around, he thus reconstructs – he believes – his first dwelling place.

And, as all this remains very much on the primary level, very loose even if all the strings are already in place, before he buckles it all up, closes or sutures the ways in and out, space itself is still capable of expanding almost infinitely, a cosmogony is possible in which the unconscious (*ça*) moves on, stretches, propagates, travels at lightning speed. So before the son has perfected his stage set, one can try and steal his veil away from him, take the curtain of his theater, the means or mediator of his *fort-da*, and loan it or give it back to the *angels*.

The veil that ludically separates him from her, from himself, from himself in her, from her in himself, this veil that will divide off and surround his drama, evokes or perhaps recalls something of the angel. Angels have been as misunderstood, forgotten, as the nature of that first veil, except in the work of poets, perhaps, and in religious iconography.

Yet the whiteness of angels, their semitransparence, their lightness, the question of their sex, their purity (in the Rilkean sense: as pure as animals), could all these attributes not be a reappearance or recollection of that by which and thanks to which messages from the beyond are transmitted? Beyond what? The ultimate veil. Whence they would emerge. Always coming from beyond the horizon. And yet the element traversed would not be opaque or very colored, but rather airy, allowing free passage – like the angel. Who is sent, or comes, from heaven, on a mission, to do a job. In fact the angel always returns to heaven, goes home, to the other side of the ultimate veil. Unless he stands there, if only for a fragment, a flight, a detached soar that is sent, addressed, to announce what comes after. Awesome call or recall that circulates so swiftly and lightly, an annunciation of more weight than any coded message, moving to and fro between the first and last dwellings that are withheld from present visibility or readability, to be deciphered only in the next world. From beyond the angel returns with inaudible or unheard of words in the here and now. Like an inscription written in invisible ink on a fragment of body, skin, membrane, veil, colorless and unreadable until it interacts with the right substance, the matching body.

We have to search back very far to find it, assuming it (*ça*) can be found, far beyond and deep within the language, in its first bed or nest or cradle of beliefs. There, always undecipherable and undeciphered, unless one passes–passes back through God and his angels, bent and folded up within every message and every code, forming the basis for every potential inscription, is this *veil*, through which there once took place and perhaps will again take place the sympathy between two bodies capable of mutually decoding one another. We shall need to go as far as the last veil and beyond if, one day, this (*ça*) is to pass back, through him, between him and her, her and him, not by means of some regressive return to a place that is lost forever nor in a completely other place from which that first place would be relegated for good.

While we wait for this to happen – assuming it can, or hasn't already, though not face-to-face – this sympathetic deciphering of bodies, skins, membranes, mucuses, while we are waiting then, sometimes a mediating angel or angels come to give us news about the place where the divine presence may be found, speaking of the word made flesh, returning, awaited.

The angels come down and go up, go up and come down in a vertical mediation, like that of the veil over the stage, which they claim is primary, and which, on this occasion, would go from highest to lowest, a structure permitting the movement to and fro, back and forth from heaven to earth, going from one to the other through the various containing layers, but upon which, apparently, *nothing is inscribed*.

If my children's story is applied to Ernst, the angel who helps him while his mother is gone is a good angel. There are, as you know, the bad angels, who want to become like God, who block the mediating channels, stand in the path of movement to and fro, back and forth. In this case, the stand-in angel seems good, at least as far as Ernst and his grandfather are concerned. Perhaps not for her since she ends up excluded from the party, sent away, for good in the end. The angel in this case is rather under the thumb of the child-king or god, even of his grandfather. The angel is interposed to allow and preserve or to allow the preservation of the relationship, the rapport. He seems to be in the service of the son as well as of the string and the reel that is thrown away and pulled back, far or near Ernst. There seems to be only one angel, who obeys the son, and perhaps the grandfather: the mother's father. She seems to have no angel. She is thrown away and pulled back by means of the angel, but she herself cannot use that mediation, that messenger. She fulfills the desire or the word of the child-god, and previously of her father, but sends no message of her own. She yields to his call, yields to being called back, thrown away − far from herself or from him − then brought back into him, beyond any veil. The angel even stands in the way between God and herself so that she can be sent away from the men and can come back outside herself, in him, in them, between them.

Does she stay the same once she has been thrown away, put at a distance, pulled back, brought near, in this way? No. On her return, he has wrapped her in his own veil, his own call, his, or their − the men's − own language. He has taken possession of the veil or canvas that traces the limits of his desire, his will, his pleasure, and, now, he plays with it. She will always be there, she will always be in, when he wants. He will only have to call her, call her back, and she will be re-present(ed) to him, in his world.

This protects him from disappearing into her. This return annihilates that other return that might swallow him up, take him back into that first dwelling place inside her. And anytime he comes near her he will be armed with this little toy: a reel with a more or less elastic string, a veil over her but also a mask (a phallic mask, for example) that shrouds his own reel. This invisible supplement to the body helps in time of danger, rather like a guardian angel − which may be something of a devil[6] − that he dispatches before sending any message. Mediation of the message before any message exists, it is the condition of representation and presentation. Always placed between presence and absence, if, in this case, this pairing has any meaning. But perhaps it has meaning only in this case.

So the angel dispatches himself, or receives himself, or listens to himself, earlier than any conception, birth, flight to heaven or back to heaven. *Even before the hymen* the angel makes the annunciation. Unless he takes the place of the hymen, unless he comes to its assistance from somewhere outside place, outside the game, as is generally believed. Everything, it seems, happens earlier, in a word in which something of the first veil is brought back in the name of God and the engendering of the son.

Mysteriously, she seems to receive through her ear all that has been taken away from her womb. Structure bearing the message but not its inscription, related to the sense of hearing without any need for skin or membrane to be broken or perforated. A great deal of sympathy is needed to decipher this, to unveil the secret of the game.

But does a complete unveiling occur? Or does this merely announce, prefigure, is it just the expectation of a resurrection, an ascension, a return? How are we to know if the angel is coming from beyond the ultimate veil or if he is simply announcing this coming? If the one who is expected is coming back again for some early encounter or is coming at last? If we are dealing here with a prologue or the fulfillment of presence? Or again: if what the angel does and says is the work of a ghost, sent back from the beyond to haunt us. Beyond what? And how are life and death to be kept apart in this case?

Could it be that this risk of assimilating life into death occurs because of the angel's one-way journey? The angel always goes in the same direction, even on his two-way trips: from heaven where the God-Father is supposed to be, to her, for example, with the mission of giving or entrusting her with his offspring. But isn't this all rather twisted around? When the angel goes toward her, might he not actually actually be coming from her? Hasn't the angel taken off from her, flown away from her? Skin and membrane that can hardly be perceived, almost transparent whiteness, almost undecipherable mediation, which is always at work in every operation of language and representation, ensuring that the lowest earth and highest heaven are linked, that first dwelling place in her, from which he makes and remakes his bed, and works out the transcendence of the Lord.

Doesn't the angel announce, in some way, that she is also an angel and that she will bring an angel into the world? A couple that will give rise to a new conception of the flesh, to those miracles owed to touch, with or without words, that we know as transfiguration, resurrection, ascension, or assumption? A couple of angels or in which all angels would concentrate their function as mediators – and beyond? But this couple does not appear as such, or at least not according to canonical revelation. She remains only mother and he son, the two obedient to the words of the Father. And when the angel announces the news to her, brings her the message, he already comes or comes back from God the Father. The veil and the reel, it seems, can be given back to her only through Him, after the mediation of his writing. Her duty is to remain the supporting structure that permits absence to be separated from presence in re-presentation. This substrate would be her property, or at least her lot, but the son seems to have taken it over, and the father with him, and it would come back to her only if moved by an Other, the All High, omnipotent Father, center and matrix of reference for all our beliefs.

The angel is terrible, terrifying, as Rilke says. He reminds us of something that is meant to be eternally forgotten. He conjures up something that has not been written legibly, with a word that moves through it without stopping, but without which she would not be that which can give place to the presence she has in his re-presentation.

But there also are the *devils*. These are not angels, who go and come from high to low, mediators for heaven and earth in their airy journeys across all frontiers, creatures of flight and soar, breath, veils, wings, airs, unfettered by allegiance to port or shore. Who make themselves known in cryptic messages, oracles, dreams. Who come to meet us openly, face-to-face, even if in confrontation or opposition.

The devils, on the other hand, don't work as discreet mediators. Their job is to disrupt and to confuse. They block mediation, blur its message, burn it sometimes, before it can be heard and heeded. Perhaps they were merely angels before the fall. But, by wishing to be like or more than the angels, and, ultimately, like and more than God, they ceaselessly cut and disrupt the path leading into presence. Their wish to be *like* means to wish always to be more than, to take over the place or the post and give them more power. By wishing always and still to outdo, overcome, they double the angels, and, ultimately, God, by claiming to intercept or turn the veil, fraying the barely perceptible thread of communication. They never stop crossing mediation with their doublings, mimes, interventions by means of an other yet like force that is quantitatively greater. They block the way by repeating, even within themselves, the circuit of transfer (of life and of death, of assimilation and disassimilation). They confuse ancestors and descendents, push genealogy off track, jumble communication, break communion. In their darkness they capture and make a screen against any transmission of light and send none back. They are seen or make more of an impact more often even though they are, or because they are, negatives. But the negatives of a positive that exists before any printed image, any fixed representation, immobilizing or blurring the call to or expectation of any possibility of presence. Perhaps they are the negatives of angels, easy to draw but difficult to photograph, given their relation to light. Angels can only be approached with extreme sympathy, great intimacy. The diabolic, on the other hand, would be an effect of overexposure or underexposure because it wills to double the other. It operates by blocking the attraction of presence – which can be perceived but yet not defined – and those gestures and words that announce it explicitly or succeed in making it flesh. The devil gets in the way. He blocks understanding, sets the stage by paralyzing it through a mimicry that turns it upside down, reproduces it in many copies, backwards: back/front, up/down, etc. In this way he rubs out one faint trail and blazes another. Ultimately, in the representation of history, we will remember him alone, even as we believe we are perpetuating the memory of the angel – and beyond of all that the angel brings and sends back. But the angel mediates by keeping space open and marking the trail from the oldest of days to the farthest future of the world. Serving as active memory, even if it remains unconscious, this mediation is turned by the diabolical will to reproduce the relation to light into an inscription that makes the rules, or at times into a writing that hides the source.

There's only one chance: the angel goes before the devil. He takes place earlier. If one can manage to clear a way past the devil's obstructive workings, sometimes one comes upon this awesome destiny, this daunting encounter. Otherwise, the whole stage is taken over by the devil, the devils, who turn everything upside down to make the leap and make us leap into dark, hidden, sulfurous beyond. Unless the whole thing goes suddenly up in flames? Otherwise, the future endlessly recycles the past, after assimilation and disassimilation that blinds the eyes.

The devil's work blinkers us, allowing us to see only itself, blocks any movement to and fro from past to future, traps us, stymies us, leads us round and about into a dead end. (Unless we yield to him wholly, pass completely over to the devil?) He blurs the future and any hint we may receive of it. He closes the frame to keep out light and air: he is only to be seen, even though he never appears. But he is there, already and forever dark. In our encounters, from now on, each of us, man and woman, meets only his or her image. Only doubles are present and represented, only reproductions, kinds of negatives, reduced prints – only the angel can give light and expansion. In encounters like these, no hint of the future remains. Everything seems to be programmed, predictable. All that remains is to pursue this strange continuum, series. Unless, perhaps, an essential difference befalls us.

It is true that there is some use in standing back, taking things only in retrospect, for someone who wanders in the heavens or drowns in the depths, who is overwhelmed by the immensity of time and space with no partitions, no possible demarcations, no people or objects to play with, no distance that can be mastered with a reel and a string.

So the answer is to use the other as a screen. Position the other in front of the heavens and the deep chasms, and look only at what the other has already been able to assimilate-disassimilate. While the other is framing and being framed in this way, the man who stands behind this device, this telesetup, can relax a bit. Nothing need be predicted for the moment of his own history, his own goals, his own moves. He analyzes a posteriori, sheltered by the *fort-da* from all that precedes him, from his body, or his flesh.

But why the devil – we may aptly exclaim – does Plato-the-son stand behind Socrates?[7] Why does the son, or sons, stand behind the (spiritual) fathers and not the mothers, given that the sons are really trying to possess the mothers? If we are to reframe the paternal scenario, see how it made its mark, play it backward, we cannot merely master the female whom the father was always seeking to take or take back in his threads, the female who, already, exceeded the father and whom he endlessly sought to bring back into his game. The son merely listens attentively to the father's game (or sometimes vice versa), tests out how he came to situate her, and to situate himself, within her and in relation to her. In order to learn in what history of hers he has been taken and has taken her, the son takes the measure of the father's game, intends to take him by surprise, take him by surprise in the figures of the game, their placings and enlacings. He is not encountering *her* but the father who encounters her, the father's links to her, his place in relation to her, his place as it issues from and with her. By this retroaction the son gives himself or gives himself back, with or without her, a *face* that can be present, rediscovered, behind the father's back. Equally, he gives himself or gives himself back a volume by moving around the father. But why not around her? Because she can only be encountered piece by piece, step by step. But if he arrived at the limits of known spatiality he would lose his favorite game, the game of mastering her.

There is another way of refusing or rejecting the angel, or angels, another way of not hearing the message, or distorting its direction and dimension: this is to deprive the mediator of his word, his presence, and blindly and cynically to implant it or anchor it in another site, another earth or heaven than the one it came from originally. Thus, seeking to capture the angel in the home, any home – be it house, hostel, temple, altar

– and covering what lives there in the guise of the messenger is another kind of diabolic paralysis that freezes movements and words. To seek to cage up within the domestic setting something that has always flowed uncontained is like turning free soaring, rapture, flight into parchments, skeletons, death masks.

If we do not rethink and rebuild the whole scene of representation, the angels will never find a home, never stay anywhere. Guardians of free passage, they cannot be captured, domesticated, even if our purpose is to see ourselves in them. They can light up our sight and all our senses but only if we note the moment when they pass by, hear their word and fulfill it, without seeking to show, demonstrate, prove, argue about their coming, their speaking, or appearance. Without trying somehow to keep them at our disposal, in a transfer of destination that obscures and befuddles everything: with no face or name corresponding anymore to the angel's place or his light, his faith or his truth.

This game that we play with the angel's whiteness and transparence, this claim that all things are equal in appearance, this crazy, demented gaze that reduces a multiplicity of objects, or at least two, to one perfect resemblance, surrounding them with that which makes matter out of form for each man or woman, and their spatiality, this game is certainly the most diabolic temptation that exists. This is how the veil and the angel are appropriated and destroyed, leaving the air empty of loving leadership.

The angel always engages with us face-to-face, even if it is to affront or to assail. Unlike devils and animals or at least the mammals who are our nearest relatives and who engage from behind, the angel returns in front, stands in front. But when he comes to us, returns to us in this way, he is often alone. If he is calling us and recalling us to some lost encounter, face-to-face, he is alone as he gives his message.

Except in the Holy of Holies? Behind the temple veil. Then there are two of them. There the angels face one another over the ark of the covenant, standing at the two ends of the mercy seat of which they make one piece. The mercy seat *covers* the ark, can be detached from it, and serves in atonement, in washing away sin. It is in this place that Yahweh appears to Moses and speaks to him from between the cherubim.

In Exodus 26, verses 17 to 22, Yahweh speaks to Moses and says: "And thou shalt make a mercy seat of pure gold: two cubits and a half shall be the length thereof, and a cubit and a half the breadth thereof. And then thou shalt make two cherubim of gold, of beaten work shalt thou make them, at the two ends of the mercy seat. And make one cherub at the one end, and one cherub at the other end: of one piece with the mercy seat shall ye make the cherubim on the two ends thereof. And the cherubim shall spread out their wings, with their faces one to another; toward the mercy seat shall the faces of the cherubim be. And thou shalt put the mercy seat above upon the ark; and in the ark thou shalt put the testimony that I shall give thee. And there I will meet with thee, and I will commune with thee from above the mercy seat, from between the two cherubim which are upon the ark of the testimony, of all things which I will give in commandment unto the children of Israel."*

---

*Later English translations use the expression "ark of the tokens" rather than "ark of the covenant" or "ark of the testimony," and refer simply to a "cover" over the ark, rather than a propitiatory or mercy seat. – Trans.

So here, two angels face one another to guard the presence of God, who may perhaps be turning away in his anger or absence. The angels face one another over the ark of the covenant. Beneath them, the tablets of the law, and between them, between their wings, the divine presence that cannot be sensed or seen. The doubling of the angel (and of the veil? You know that the veil of the temple covering the entrance to the Holy of Holies will be rent when the Son of Man dies, meaning also the coming of his resurrection) would keep Yahweh from being closed up in the text of the law. It seems to be setting up the future presence of God in the more airy element: he can come and go freely, the word that has already been offered and inscribed in stone is loosed, and a new covenant is prepared.

Two angels who face one another – this event could only take place here. They turn toward one another, guarding and calling the divine presence between them. They do not go in one single direction. There are two of them, halted in their paths. Face-to-face, they stand in almost timid contemplation, intent on something that hasyet to come, yet to be situated, not yet inscribed, written, spoken. They shelter what may take place because they are two and are turned toward one another. Coming from opposite directions, to meet one another, they halt the return from sameness to sameness, before any determination or opposition of presence or absence can be made. Here is there no course taken, no reel, no string, no mastery of re-presentation? They are turned toward, or – one might imagine – turned away from, according to what they are guarding or are no longer guarding. Face-to-face or back to back.

Are the two alike? We might believe so. But those who are alike tend to engage with each other from the back, moving step by step, in single file, the one taking the other's place, supplanting him or possessing him in his place, so as to move forward. Those who are different are more likely to face one another, except as animals, at least according to the most pregnant imaginary. So, is it true to say that like beings place themselves to the rear, unless some idealization is already at work – in the mirror? squared? – whereas different beings stand face-to-face, except in the transgression of the matrix of idealization?

Those angels, perhaps, heed none of these imperatives. Neither like nor other, they guard and await the mystery of a divine presence that has yet to be made flesh. Alike and different, they face each other, near enough and far enough for the future to still be on hold. Neither God, nor men nor women, nor beasts, nor language seem yet to have found their final destiny. Neither God, nor difference of the sexes, nor difference between man and animal seem decided upon once and for all, already really made flesh.

Something lives there out of site, or perhaps between sites, some airy, mobile and yet material structure serving to bear presence, for the one, for the other, and for the unique in this relationship, of this relationship.

Something, forever deferred until the divine comes or comes back, perhaps has never taken place in this advent setup between the two angels: the advent of flesh itself, which in its most airy, subtle rapture might go beyond or before a certain sexual difference, once that difference has first been respected and fulfilled.

Beyond and before this parting of ways, enveloping it as its future advent and ultimate home, here stand the angels in deep meditation. At least two of them, facing, close, just far enough apart to prevent the uncountable touch of the flesh from blending into contact with the two ends. Between them the flesh holds back and flows forth before any mastery can be exercised over it, or after a *fort-da* far more sophisticated than the reel, a *fort-da* of the possibility of presence and of sharing in something divine that cannot be seen but can be felt, underlying all incarnation, which two angels, facing but not looking at each other, set up between them.

My conclusion would be that if tradition says nothing about their sex, it is because they are of a different sex and because tradition knows nothing of sexual difference. So it must be if the flesh of God is to become flesh. Tradition does say that (*ça*), but without wanting to make any statements about the sex of the angels – who have yet to experience any sexual engagement.

Besides, the angels of the ark of the covenant are neither human nor animals. Sphinxes each of them, each for the other? they wait, and wait for each other. Lacking not the lure but the threshold of the entry into presence.

This threshold appears to be blocked, notably in the myth of Aristophanes in the *Symposium*, if I need to give an example. The yoking of two into one same one paralyzes the whole scene. There is no space between him and her, between the men and the women. Unless it be a diagonic space? A kind of match that has been squared *into sameness*, played out obliquely to closed stations. The stage is loaded with blurred shapes, blocked movements, duels for dominance. Whatever the struggle, no future is possible. Memory does not go back far enough. Or rather it returns home to master the other, without making any motion to go beyond.

But, in such a permutuation between, what remains to be achieved of the one and of the other? Unless the permutations are merely apparent, possible only because each remains what he or she was, for fear of flying off into envelopes that are lacking in all resources? Only death lies on this path, no interpenetration of different germ cells is now possible. The statue is fixed forever into a figure that equates one sex to the other, without any relationships between them henceforth, no possible creation or rejuven-ation.

Thus the body that gives life never enters into language. Ernst, the son, believes perhaps that, in his first language game, he holds his mother. She has no place there. She subsists before language as the woman who gives her flesh and her blood, and beyond language as she who is stripped of a matrix/womb, a veil, an enclosure or a clearing in which she might live according to the horizon of her games, symbolizations, representations. She remains the elemental substrate of life, existing before all forms, all limit, all skin, and of heaven, visible beyond–horizon. Between these extremes stand the angels and the annunciation of the fulfillment of the flesh.

In the meantime, the stake in the game is split between him and her. Both of them bleeding, the one openly, the other secretly, but he and she remain bound to their functions as son and mother. Yet he puts her at a distance, seeking the society of the father. Together he and the father organize the world, bless the fruits of the earth, identify them with their body and blood, and in this way effect the communion between the units of the people that have been neutered, at least apparently. In effect, the women in attendance must be mothers, mothers of sons, whereas *the other*, the woman lover, is kept away from the scene. No one must see that it is they, the wives and mothers, who are being offered up in communion here, who effect the communion, that, like the earth and its fruits, it is the body and the blood especially of virgin women that are being sacrified to that intermale society. The duty to bear children, to be silent, to be in attendance but off on the side – all this wounds the flesh and the spirit of women, and there is no representation of that sacrifice. In fact, it is doubled in the duty women have to believe and to be practicing believers. Dogmas and rites appear as substitutions and veils that hide the fact that women's carnal and spiritual virginity is being sacrificed and traded. The sons are separated from their mothers and from the women who love them out of duty to their Fathers.

But who is the Father if his will is that flesh be abolished? Is this the meaning of religion, as some would have us believe? Or are we dealing with the crypt of an order set up by one sex that claims to write the rules of truth at the price of life? Henceforth, are the sons not obliged to play weird games of *fort-da* between mothers who are by some extraordinary turn virgins and fathers who are mysteriously absent? How are the spirit and mind to be woven of the threads of remoteness, belief, paralysis, denial, and negation of life?

This is how men gather together in the mystery of the here and now present of a body and a blood that have not figured on the stage and thus allow that stage to be set. Many, many years ago, in our tradition, the pick was driven into the earth-mother's womb in order to build the sacred enclosure of the tribe, the temple, finally the house.

But there are still flowers, since after all we still feel a need to spend a little time on earth, in the sunshine, to open up to the joy of light and air, to pulse to the rhythm of the seasons. There are roses, if I may evoke the flower that, despite its thorns, has so often been celebrated by poets, philosophers, and divines. Mysteriously, the rose's bloom recalls something of blood and of the angel. It is reborn ceaselessly, causelessly, because it must bloom, having no care for itself, no need to be seen, following in its own cycle and the cycle of the world. The flower is like a pure apparition of natural generation, the angel is like a pure vector of spiritual spatiality, rapt purity before any conception occurs, any meeting of fixed dimensions or directions.

There is the rose, before and after the bloom, forever opening for the first and last time. And yet the arrangement of its petals knows all the roses that have been and are to come, but with no doubles, no replicas. Even as the rose opens up, it already knows about shedding petals, dying down, lying dormant, not as an end but as a recovery. Except for the petals surrounding or cradling the heart – those at the very center – the rose's petals are grouped front against back (or the opposite, depending on the presentation), in against out, with inside protecting outside. By thus pursing the lips that have already been opened, offered, the flower seems to guard against dispersion, in a movement contrasting with that of the son who keeps throwing away his many toys or, on each occasion, his woman-mother, either whole or in torn fragments. Sorrow and loss will accompany his memory as it seeks to shelter the inside from an overwhelming outside by clothing and closing itself in with roof, house, appearances. This may deceive him, lead him into error or temptation as to what goes to the heart, the inmost center, or the source. The rose within itself – if we can speak in this way –

seems imperceptibly veiled by its repose in or about an invisible composure. Its inmost secret calyx is never shown, it lies beneath all the gathered petals. When the petals have opened completely in immodest splendor, the place in which the rose once touched herself, lip to lip, has disappeared. You will never see it. You will never see what she is or has in her heart of hearts. Perhaps it – or he? or she – can be sensed by someone living close to the rose, breathing the space around her, which she creates with that caress in which she subsists freely offering herself, in a gift that wafts through the air unseen, untouched. But so easy to lose.

The heart of the rose opens without the need of a blueprint. In the heart of a flower there is nothing – but the heart. It opens for no reason. No teleology directs the petals to unfurl. They serve no function. Unless it is to be gazed upon? But what gaze? The rose looks at us from somewhere where it is not represented. A calendar for the world, the rose recalls sight to a presence virgin of mastery, to a gaze still innocent of all manufactured and reproducible presence. In a certain sense it is invisible, while being so much more visible than anything that is represented. It is neither object nor thing. It cannot speak itself in words, even though a certain set of syllables designate the rose in our language. It has no double. It always gives itself for the first unique time. It draws our eyes in its contemplation, arrests them – for no reason. Our gaze opens – for no reason, bathed in its blossoming.

Movements without forces. Features determined without the rigid requirement to apply some kind of energy. Petals without firm shapes. In-finite finitude, unlimited. Splendor of imperfection.

What is offered in this way is the very movement of blossoming, a growth that is not entrusted merely to the veiling-unveiling activity of the gaze but allows itself to be seen as it blooms. The *phuein* seems to escape the eye, which counts upon itself alone. *Upokeimenon* that is perceived only when complete, leaving in the shadow all that contributes to the availability of what is offered to the gaze.

In the movement of the *proteron te phusei* may be found the heart of thought, that which remains veiled in what thought says and which speaking obeys as some secret command. But already, when it speaks, thought no longer speaks what moves it. It no longer retains that emotion even as a fault in speech, as a dark night out of which it would expect to burst forth. Thought excludes the heart that moves it. That which makes thought live is spoiled, set outside of it. But it does not know this. Like a firm foundation that itself has no foundation upon which it would rely calmly, careless of the distress rising from the abyss.

As long as it does not touch upon that abyss, thought can still breathe. But it runs out of breath and food and takes no notice. And the sublime, which thought consumes, is transformed into utilities. Instead of singing the lost trace of vanished gods – the sacred ether that it leaves in the night – thought dismembers this being (*étant*) that is no being at all but shelters the mystery of every being. It shreds the air to coin it into values, trumpery values that no longer even shine with that mysterious light of being (*être*). Those garments, which can always be changed, no longer clothe any person in their own radiance, but are loaned out, substituted, calculated to function as a kind of pleasing that masks nothingness but not abandonment. Exercises in futility torn from the poet's flesh that has been left in distress, at the heart of all that oblivion allows, still, to appear. The poet alone remembers the bond that ties men and gods, recalls the nonappearance of the air in which some trace of the sacred remains. He questions, over and over, that presence which does not show itself and yet persists, as a shelter, in time of want, for all that resists calculation. Love, pain, life and death, are kept there, secret, enigmatic, barely breathing out their melody beyond or through all speakable words.

But can a mortal still sing? And how to speak of his song? Has the quarrel between the poet and the thinker already gone far enough to make a basis for their agreement? This will not occur without risk.

A risk that risks life itself, going beyond it barely by a breath.[8] A breath that, if it is held, saves through song, prophet of pure forces that call out and refuse shelter. Does not everything already in existence paralyze the breath? Imperceptibly occupying the air, preventing its free use, strangling with multiple coils anything still anxious to cross this captive atmosphere.

And anyone who does not go down into the abyss can only repeat and retrace the ways already opened that cover over the trace of the vanished gods. Alone, always alone, the poet runs the risk of moving outside the world and turning over what it opens up until touching the bottom of the bottomless, saying yes to something calling him from beyond the horizon. As he stands abandoned, he retains at most a breath, that first and final energy forgotten until it fails. Everywhere present, yet invisible, it grants life to everything and everyone, on pain of death. Risk taken at each moment by the poet, that seeker after the still sacred ether, which today is so covered over or buried that he can trust no heaven or earth, learn his path from no mouth, find no sure direction. For him no place is habitable, since his mission is to reopen a ferial site. Thus he has to leave the world, while yet remaining mortal, go off to some shore that bears no signpost, to love a life assured by none. To achieve this he has no firm ground. He must tear himself away from his native land to plunge his roots into a ground that is virgin, unknown, unpredictable. Free for risk.

He even lets go of that captivating magic that makes men kin to each other, becomes an exile from any will belonging to an existing community, descending into the hell of history to seek traces of life there, seeds still held in unturned subsoil. Seeds to set free, to lay in the air even though they may produce something that has never yet appeared, may give rise to a new blossoming, stripped of protection, of shelter, of home. No veil? To advance into danger is to lay the self bare before any answering confidence has been granted. Here, there is no betrothal, no site. Terror becomes consent to everything, permission for everything that touches, without refusal or withdrawal.

Risk protects anyone who, insensibly, invisibly, moves onward while remaining in his own heart. Who is still alien to existence as one who yields, offers himself freely to the other outside himself and receives himself back in return. Access to a space and a time whose dimensions surpass the stars as well as the imaginary of each conscience. Objective and subjective lose their limits thereby. Each person and all things rest in one another, flow one into the other unconfined. Recollection of a state so ancient that few are capable of it. Crossing the frontiers of their own lives, following far and near, risking their breath, they yield the very rhythm of their breath to the other, agreeing to lose the beat of their pulse in order to discover a new amplitude. In this way they expire one into the other, and rise up again inspired. Imperiling that citadel of being, language, so that this woman, that man, can find a voice, a song.

Leaving a temple already consecrated, they seek the traces of the ferial bond with the wholly other being. No longer having words, risking speech itself, they have no anxiety because nothing is calculated, they are strangers to exchange, business, marketplace. They tremble at the coming of that which has been announced, that other breath born to them after all known resonance has been broken, beyond everything that has already been achieved. Beyond the unheard sonority of the watchers who do not venture out into the infinite journey of the invisible. The only guide here is the call to the other, whose breath subtly impregnates the air like a vibration perceptible to these men lost for love. They go on, attentively, boldly moving forward over paths where others see only shadows and hell. They move forward, and at times a song comes to their lips. From their mouths issue sounds that have no meaning – only the inspiration that will strike the other with the feelings and thoughts that overwhelm them. Responses, mostly inaudible, to what they sense in the wind. They breathe confidently, carefree because they lack the anxiety of their security. They have willed to strip away all structure and rely only upon the attraction they perceive that pulls them beyond all frontiers. They agree to walk where they are borne, as far as the source that gives them themselves, unreservedly attaining all that draws them on and letting it flow out again in the fullness of the gift. In this movement to and fro no dwelling has been built, no shelter set up. This consent and its reward take place without additional protection for those who risk their lives in this way. They do not end up in some enclosure that guarantees they will come to no harm, they are not separated. In rapturous consent, they receive and give themselves in the open.

The way to this strange adventure is found in the renunciation of any path that has already been proposed. Anything that once offered a possible future must be abandoned, turned back, like a limited horizon: a veil that imperceptibly conceals the world facing us. Before the departure, all goals must at the very least be turned upside down, every plan must be upset. Those who dare all make their way without maps as blind men do. Free of the spell that made them afraid to be without a shelter, they yield unrestrainedly to the open, a place where men free from fear can embrace and blossom. Offering every aspect of themselves to straight scrutiny, joining their forces, acting upon one another in the integrity of a perception that has no refusal in the center of its pure gravity, they say yes, unreservedly, to the whole of the experience to come.

Even to death, as one other face of life? Yes. And to the other as other? Yes? Or is it still a matter of remaining in one's own realm? While accepting the reverse, of course, making the negative a positive, naturally, but always acting in the same way. Once the sphere of application has been extended, there enters into it something that shapes a horizon that turns back into a vast imperceptible film whose outside is endlessly given within, unveiling and reveiling what has been closed up in one site.

Beyond go one to the other those who give up their own will. Beneath every speech made, every word spoken, every point articulated, every rhythm beaten out, they are drawn into the mystery of a word that seeks incarnation. While trusting beyond measure in that which gives flesh to speech: air, breath, song, they reciprocally receive and give something that is still crazy, and are thereby reborn by giving each other the gift of a speech of forgotten inspiration, buried beneath logic and indeed beneath all existing language. This suspension of all meaning unveils the commerce that underlies meaning, and risks going back to a time when separation had not yet occurred, when there was as yet no attempt to rate this as more valuable than that. In this opacity, this night of the world, they discover the trace of vanished gods, at the very point when they have given up their safety. Light shines on them once they have agreed that nothing shall ensure their protection, not even that age-old citadel of man – being (être) – not even that guarantor of the meaning or nonmeaning of the world – God.

These prophets know that if anything divine is still to come our way it will be won by abandoning all control, all language, and all sense already produced, it is through risk, only risk, leading no one knows where, announcing who knows what future, secretly commemorating who knows what past. No project here. Only this refusal to refuse what has been perceived, whatever distress or wretchedness may come of it.

These predecessors have no future, They come from the future. In them it is already present. But who hears it? Silently their song irrigates the world of today, of tomorrow, of yesterday. The need for this destiny is never heard clearly, never appears in broad daylight without suffering disfigurement.

But the breath of one who sings while mingling his inspiration with the divine breath remains unattainable, unlocatable, faceless. Anyone who perceives him starts on the road, obeys the call, goes to encounter nothing, or else something greater than anything we now have.

Notes

1   This allusion to the postal service will become clear later.
2   It seems difficult, I think, to establish that these two events happen at exactly the same time. On the other hand, there is no question that the onset of bleeding coincides with the hour of the eucharistic celebration and the approximate moment when the host is consecrated.
3   The situation might be susceptible to sex permutations, but asymmetrically. That which is offered to be partaken is always a maternal body, unless we were to say equally: this is my sperm. It is worth considering why that formula is never used. Could it be that the eucharistic rite is bound up with an imaginary of the prenatal stage and earliest infancy? Unless the rite is stripped of its meaning – as Eucharist – when the fruits of the earth are appropriated by the male body. If meaning has indeed been twisted in this way, the whole horizon of Christianity would be perverse. The only interpretation of the earth man can make that would not take possession or evoke magic would be: we, men and women, are fruits of the earth and of our labor; in them, in us, among us, we commune, in the memory of Christ. The formula: "This is my body, this is my blood" that is pronounced over the bread and wine is in fact particularly unacceptable today when many celebrants and communicants care so little about the fate of the earth and its fruits and thus put the whole meaning of the eucharistic communion in doubt. Equally questionable is the appeal made in the mass to taste, as for example in the words of the consecration ("Take, eat ye all

of this, this is my body . . . "), which are strongly reminiscent of the great spiritual traditions of India.

4 Or at least that was what the woman thought at first. This was probably her way of expressing her wish for a union innocent of all doubling. Details of this kind do not amount to an indiscretion, otherwise they would probably have set up a system of defenses operating through a kind of complicitous game. As for this text, its intent is to raise a veil from the scene of belief and the scene of truth – whence the allusion to proper names, for example. The woman's revelation may seem violent and sacrilegious to some people, both male and female. But without that revelation which reaches beyond the canonic enclosure of revelation, fidelity in history and confidence in certain of its figures become beliefs, dogmas, rites that are in part sacrificial and repressive. All this is not necessarily religious but seems essential to the establishment of priestly power over the people, a power that is handed down from father to son, to the exclusion of women, in our patriarchal tradition.

5 As I was rereading this text before including it in the collection *Sexes and Genealogies*, I realized that I had always assumed that Ernst was playing with his own bed or crib, not with the bed of his mother or his parents. Which explains why I took no notice of Derrida's "into the sheets." My interpretation is an attempt to account for the constitution of the male cultural subject in its philosophic and religious dimensions. The other scene would conjure up, on the contrary, its at least partial other side or back side, through allusion to mother-son incest. What is more, in my reading, it is not amazing that the bed should be *fort*. The game occurs by day and children hate to stay in bed. On the other hand, they love to climb out of bed when they like, especially if the bed is rather high and difficult to climb down from. It seems to me that little Ernst's pleasure comes in part from this.

6 This is one way of understanding that all phallic norms make sexuality devilish in the sense that this order is interposed to blur the sympathy between the sexes.

7 See in this regard Jacques Derrida's *The Post Card: From Socrates to Freud and Beyond*, trans. Alan Bass (Chicago: University of Chicago Press, 1987)

8 Following the Cerisy conference in August 1980, these last pages were used in somewhat modified form in my book, *The Forgetting of Air in Martin Heidegger*, trans. Mary Beth Mader (Austin, TX: University of Texas Press, 1999). Sometimes this section echoes the essay "Why Poets?" in Heidegger's *Poetry, Language, Thought* (translated by A. Hofstadter, New York: Harper and Row, 1971).

PART II

CONTEMPORARY ESSAYS

9

THE FINAL APPEAL OF THE SUBJECT

Jean-Luc Marion

I

Has phenomenology ever had a more urgent challenge to confront than the determination of what or possibly who succeeds the subject?

Phenomenology has never definitively decided between two ways of thinking this succession: between either definitively abolishing the subject in order to replace it with the very absence of an heir (as Nietzsche claimed he had done) or pausing to repeat, each time, in a mode which is always new, the function of subjecti(vi)ty. On the subject of the subject, phenomenology has never ceased to oscillate from one to the other postulation, between heritage and "new beginning." Such a hesitation doubtless permits us to inscribe phenomenology both within the field of metaphysics and on its margins or even outside of its limits. It remains the case that, from itself, the phenomenological option does not allow us to designate, without further consideration, what or who succeeds the subject. The question of the posterity of the subject will therefore not even find the outline of a response as long as the way in which phenomenology claims to go beyond the subject, and hence the metaphysical subject, has not itself been sketched out. To ask this in another way: Does phenomenology offer a sure route for proceeding ahead, beyond the subject, taken in its transcendence but also in its pure and simple abolition? We shall examine this question through the clearly privileged example of *Dasein*, whose ambivalence Heidegger discerned in *Being and Time*.

As a consequence, we shall ask, To what extent does the existential analytic exceed the problematic (and thus also the abolition) of the metaphysical subject? *Dasein* attains its proper and authentic truth in the figure of care (*Sorge*), which identifies it as anticipatory resoluteness: "*Dasein* becomes essential in authentic existence which itself is constituted as anticipatory resoluteness (*vorlaufende Entschlossenheit*)."(§65) It is fitting therefore to examine whether this ultimate determination of the meaning of its Being permits *Dasein* to surpass and thus to succeed the subject – or whether we must still await an other.

II

There would be no sense in contesting that *Dasein* definitively subverts the subject, even and especially the subject understood in the sense that Husserl gave it in his transcendental phenomenology. *Being and Time* not only places in question the Kantian transcendental *I* (such as it might indeed still reappear after the *Ideas* of 1913); it places in question the phenomenological *I* in general, in its very foundation understood according to the *Logical Investigations* (against the pious legend of a direct continuity between 1899 and 1927 that one finds in the later Heidegger). In what does this questioning consist? It consists in a radical revolution: subjectivity no longer has as its objective the objectivization of the object, because the ultimate instrument of this objectivization – intentionality – no longer aims, as it did for Husserl, at accomplishing the Kantian project, that is, the constitution of objects, but rather it aims at the opening of a world. The intentionality constitutive of an object remains, certainly, but it is reduced to the status of a particular and derived case of the fundamental determination of the being-in-the-world of the one who from then on renounces the title of "subject," since the objective of the objectivization of the object is abandoned in favor of the title of *Dasein*. One must not be mistaken: the analysis of readiness to hand (*Zuhandenheit*) plays a decisive role in the entire analytic of *Dasein*, because it establishes not only that readiness to hand does not maintain a primarily theoretical relationship to the world, but most of all because that which is worldly is not at first there in the form of an object constituted according to the objectivization exercised by a subject, but according to the mode of a manipulability which, in return, determines *Dasein* itself – handled, as it were, by that which it handles. *Dasein* is no longer in the world as a spectator, even a constituting spectator, *Dasein* is in the world as someone taking part, as a party possibly challenged by that which it meets and encounters. Intentionality accomplishes itself at the same time as it disappears in Being-in-the-world, where the world is substituted for the object and *Dasein*'s existence is substituted for the constituting I. The world no longer amounts to a sum of constituted objects, since it does not consist of anything: it no longer consists at all, but is opened in making a (whole) world. However, this world can thus only open itself insofar as it is *Dasein* that makes the opening in general through its own extasis. The extasis of *Dasein* consists in the fact that, far from founding itself on its own essence or founding its essence on itself (according to the two Kantian and Aristotelian postulations of subjectivity), it is the being for which what is at stake, each time, is nothing less than its Being – even better: it is the being for which, when what is at stake is *its* Being, what is at stake is just as well *the* Being of all other beings. Such an appropriation of Being to the *I* – "the Being of this being is *in each case mine [je meines]*" (§9) – should not, moreover, be interpreted as a subjection of Being to the figure of the ego, even to a transcendental egoism (against Lévinas's doubtless unjust critique); if Being is each time witnessed as mine, this rather results from the impossibility of other beings attaining their Being and from the impossibility on the part of *Dasein* acceding to Being otherwise than placing itself in play in the first person – in risking itself as it is exposed to death. Being opens itself to *Dasein* in the way in which death affects *Dasein* as a possibility: in person, in the first person, according to the mode of unsubstitutability. The "mineness" of Being no longer indicates that the I subsists in an essentially unshakeable subjectivity, but that Being remains inaccessible to *Dasein* (and thus absolutely concealed) insofar as *Dasein* does not risk itself through exposing itself without reserve and without certainty, as the possibility of impossibility. Being-towards-death, which defines this ultimate possibility, should therefore be interpreted, without any morbid nihilism, as the "mineness" of Being. From intentionality to "mineness," the *I* who is master of its objects and possessor of its Being vanishes in order to let *Dasein* appear, which sets against the subject a double paradox: *Dasein* fails to constitute any object, and thus cannot be assured of any substantiality, but attains its proper being only when it risks itself in the first person.

III

To accomplish its own Being in risking itself in person defines *Dasein* as the one who takes over from the subject. The "mineness," where what is at stake is Being itself, doubtless disqualifies any pretension to the auto-foundation of an unconditional I. This advance does not dispense with the need for a new interrogation: On what condition does *Dasein* accomplish the "mineness" that is characteristic of its proper way of Being? The literal response to this question is contained in a formula: "Resoluteness (*Entschlossenheit*) is a privileged mode of openness (*Erschlossenheit*)."(§60) The openness of *Dasein* is displayed according to a privileged mode, that of resoluteness. Indeed, resoluteness, understood as anticipatory, defines the being of *Dasein* as care (*Sorge*) and allows the attainment of the meaning of being from the perspective of the future. It is therefore a question of determining how the ecstatic structure of care is accomplished phenomenologically: briefly stated, what does resoluteness resolve? To what does resoluteness resolve itself for *Dasein*? Towards what does the decision bear? Resoluteness prepares itself and concretely locates itself in several phenomena which are ordered around it in a constellation: it is a question of anxiety, of the guilty or indebted conscience, and of Being-towards-death (as anticipation). All of these phenomena offer a common and essential character to resoluteness; it remains for us to elucidate it.

Anxiety leads to the phenomenological ordeal of the nothingness of all beings, that is to say, all manipulable or ready-to-hand beings and all subsistent or present-at-hand beings: "in that before which one has anxiety, the 'it is nothing and nowhere' becomes manifest."(§40) That this nothingness may and even must be understood as the world does not modify the fact that anxiety opens onto nothingness, without anything more than this nothingness itself. The conscience which experiences its debt there perceives an appeal or call, whatever that appeal might be; yet this appeal does not evoke or demand any response, any reparation or any ontically assignable price: "What does the conscience call to him to whom it appeals? Taken strictly nothing. The call asserts nothing, gives no information about world events, has nothing to tell."(§56) The indebted conscience therefore opens *Dasein* not onto whatever innerworldly beings there may be but rather to its own transcendence in the encounter with beings in general, a transcendence which alone opens a world. Strictly speaking, the conscience of fault opens nothing for *Dasein* except itself insofar as it transcends beings. And finally,

Being-towards- death: at first glance Being-towards-death marks an exception; never, to our knowledge, has Heidegger indicated that Being- towards-death would open onto nothingness, but yet the entire analysis seems to intend this – indeed it opens onto the possibility of impossibility. The anticipation of (or rather in) Being-towards-death finally opens *Dasein* to the absolute possibility – absolute since the impossible is here being attained – which alone qualifies *Dasein* as the ontological being par excellence; here therefore *Dasein* fully experiences its transcendence towards all beings and there-fore experiences itself as such. If therefore "in Being-towards-death, *Dasein* comports itself towards itself as a distinctive potentiality-for-Being,"(§51) one must conclude from this that *Dasein* does not comport itself towards anything other, to any being, and therefore comports itself towards nothing. Thus, strictly speaking, the three phenomena which determine the Being of *Dasein* as care only define anticipatory resoluteness as an open extasis towards nothing. *Dasein* discovers itself and experiences itself at the very moment of risking itself as that being for whom Being is an issue, an identity which is in itself empty.

For, if it leads to nothing, that does not mean that anticipatory resoluteness leads to nothing at all; through this nothing anticipatory resoluteness "isolates" (*vereinzelt*) *Dasein* by returning it to the ontico- ontological transcendence which sets *Dasein* apart form innerworldly beings. Such an isolation does not only or primarily signify that *Dasein* acedes to its final form (in the sense that Aristotle speaks of "*e gar entelecheia korizei*")(1039a7), or that *Dasein* should *in se redire* (following the Augustinian theme taken up once again by Husserl). Isolation does not purely and simply lead *Dasein* back to itself, but rather to its fundamental determination: being without any possible substitution, itself, in person without another person, at play within Being as within what is its own. That which was formulated at the beginning of the *Dasein* analytic as "mineness" (*Jemeinigkeit*) is stated at the end of the analysis as "ipseity" (*Selbstheit*): "the ipseity of *Dasein* has been formally determined as a way of existing."(§54) *Dasein* therefore exists qua itself. Resoluteness does not resolve anything, because it should not resolve anything, since what is at stake is the possibility of *Dasein* risking itself for that which is its own: namely, to be the being in whose Being what is at stake is Being itself. If resoluteness leads *Dasein*, beyond any ontical relation, to be itself, then ipseity must be understood resolutely as a constancy of self in person, or as a self-constancy (*Selbst- ständigkeit*) – and it is thus that Heidegger does not hesitate to name resoluteness in a development at once strange and capital:

Ipseity (*Selbstheit*) can be discerned existentially only in one's authentic Being-able-to-be-oneself (*Selbsteinkönnen*), that is to say in the authenticity of *Dasein* "understood" *as care*. The constancy of the self (*Ständigkeit des Selbst*), as the supposed permanence of the subject, gets clarified in terms of care. But at the same time the phenomenon of authentic–inability-to-be opens our eyes to the constancy of a self (*Ständigkeit des Selbst*), in the sense of its having achieved some sort of position. *The constancy of the self (Ständigkeit des Selbst), in the double sense of solidity and "constancy," is the authentic (eigentliche)* counter possibility to the absence of constancy (*Unselbst- ständigkeit*) or of irresolute falling. The *self- constancy (Selbst-ständigkeit)* does not signify anything else existentially than anticipatory resoluteness."(§64)

Thus, ipseity prolongs itself in a constancy of the self, which offers two characteristics: on the one hand, ipseity is prolonged as a self-constancy which confirms that care leads back the self to itself and leads *Dasein* back to a manner of self- identity; on the other hand, the constancy of the self permits us not only to comprehend an evidently metaphysical figure (the "supposed permanence of the subject") but again to understand it from the perspective of authenticity. The analytic of *Dasein* thus rediscovers, in a way that is familiar, but is yet derived from the care which is distant from familiarity, the metaphysical avatar of constitutive subjectivity. Thus arises the prodigious paradox of 1927: the extasis of care, which radicalizes the destruction of the transcendental subject in Descartes, Kant, and Husserl, nonetheless leads to a miming of the subject by reestablishing an autarky of *Dasein*, identical to itself through itself up to the point where this ipseity stabilizes itself in a self-positing. *Autarky*, however strange it might sound, is the suitable term, for resoluteness only opens the world in the ectasis of care through eventually disclosing that the self of *Dasein* leads back to itself. Even if the autarky and self-positing of *Dasein* do not regress back to the self-constitution and permanence of subsistence or the present-at-hand, they mime the latter. The shadow of the ego falls across *Dasein*.

IV

The ipseity of the self positing itself as such, absolutely unsubstitutable by virtue of care and through anticipatory resoluteness, defines *Dasein* through an autarky which is existentially proper to it and supposedly authentic. The entire analytic of *Dasein* is concentrated into this result. Assuming it is actually achieved, this result gives rise to two interrogations, both of them directly linked to the enterprise of surpassing the subject and to the choice of its successor.

The first interrogation points to an aporia that is exterior to the project of *Being and Time*: if the autarky of the Self still essentially defines *Dasein*, whatever the phenomenological or existential justification might be for this autarky of constancy of the self (*Ständigkeit des Selbst*) or self-constancy (*Selbst-ständigkeit*), to what extent does *Dasein* still "destroy" the metaphysical project of a transcendental *I* which is unconditioned because it is self-constituted? Doubtless, *Dasein* challenges the permanency of the *ousia* or the *res cogitans*. Yet the autarky of the Self goes as far as toying with the strange title of *ständig vorhandene Grund der Sorge*: "if the ontological constitution of the Self is not to be traced back either to an Ego-substance or to a 'subject,' but if, on the contrary, the everyday fugitive way in which we keep on saying 'I' must be understood in terms of our *authentic* potentiality-for-Being, then the proposition that the Self is the basis of care and constantly presence-at-hand is one that still does not follow."(§64) Beyond the fragility of this denegation, how does one explain this proposition if the metaphysics of a "constantly present-at- hand foundation" is only rejected as premature ("*noch nicht*"), and not absolutely? How, moreover, is one to distinguish so clearly between such a constant presence-at-hand (*ständig vorhanden*) of the foundation and the constancy of the self (*Ständigkeit des Selbst*) which is going to follow? In fact, the reflexive character of the verbs, to decide for oneself, to exhibit oneself, to precede oneself, to anguish oneself, and so forth, which are each time enacted for nothing other than the self (for the nothing and for the Self) appear to always mime the hitherto self-founding reflexivity of the transcendental subject and, indeed, of all subjecti(vi)ty. It might well be that *Dasein*'s confrontation with metaphysical egology (from Descartes to Hegel) will remain incomplete and even undecided, like a battle that is suspended before the winner is known. Most importantly, it might well be that *Dasein* does not completely surpass the thematic of the subject that the project of a "destruction of the history of ontology" nevertheless expressly implied in the proposed second section of *Being and Time*. We shall therefore risk the following hypothesis: the analytic of *Dasein*, rather than designating that which succeeds the subject, is the last heir of the subject itself, to the extent that *Dasein* offers not so much an overcoming of the subject as a path by which one may eventually come to the subject. To the extent that the overcoming of the subject can only be envisaged by passing through *Dasein*, and therefore in destroying *Dasein* as well.

Hence the second interrogation, which designates an aporia internal to *Being and Time*: If the autarky of the Self still defines the proper constancy of *Dasein*, how might this autarky be concerned with the question of Being in general? The imbalance, powerfully visible if not always repeated, between the question of Being in general and the analytic of *Dasein*, which traverses the entirety of *Being and Time* and which almost necessarily implies the incompleteness of the book, does not stem from a fault in *Dasein*'s demonstration. On the contrary, it is precisely the exemplary accomplishment of this demonstration that installs *Dasein* in the autarky and the constancy of the Self, without any other opening than itself – to the extent that if the existential analytic definitely leads, in the two sections of the published part of *Being and Time*, to the identification of *Dasein* with the self of anticipatory resoluteness and therefore to itself, the analytic does not, to our knowledge, even sketch the goal, which was explicitly fixed in the introduction, of connecting the Being of *Dasein* to Being in general and of finally reducing the existential analytic to fundamental ontology. Moreover, the final paragraph 83 of *Being and Time* might perhaps be read as the confession *in fine* of the final impossibility of passing from the existential analytic to fundamental ontology: "Can one provide *ontological* grounds for ontology, or does it also require an *ontical* foundation? And which being must take over the function of providing this foundation?" – it is thus that the "fundamental yet still 'veiled' problem" (§83) is finally acknowledged. The aporia of fundamental ontology appears all the more radical to the extent that it arises from the very success of the existential analytic: the Self, through positing itself autarkically in its proper constancy through anticipatory resoluteness, no longer admits any extrinsic relation – neither the world (which it opens and precedes) nor entities (which it transcends) nor time (to which alone its authenticity accedes) can lead *Dasein* to evoke Being. Far from exercising its neutrality, Being here finds itself obfuscated. The neutrality of the Self disqualifies any transition from *Dasein* outside of itself towards Being.

Therefore, *Dasein* would not accede to the question of Being in general by virtue of its most authentic determination as an autarkic self. Indeed, *Dasein* cannot appeal or call to Being, since in anticipatory resoluteness *Dasein* calls only to itself: "*Dasein* is the one who calls or appeals and, at the same time, the one who is called or appealed to." (§57) Heidegger only found the solution to this paradoxical aporia at the price of the *Kehre*, which, in a sense, sacrifices everything that *Being and Time* had succeeded in making manifest (the analytic of *Dasein*) in order to manifest what was lacking from *Being and Time* (Being in general). And moreover, this heroic reversal is immediately marked, among other innovations, by the disqualification of the autarky and constancy of the Self. Since anticipatory resoluteness, as a self-calling or auto-appeal, fails through neutralizing the question of Being, it must be opened, from the outside, to an appeal or call that it no longer controls, decides, or performs; in the postface to *What is Metaphysics?* and then in the *Letter on Humanism*, this appeal is named as the *Anspruch des Seins*, which is the appeal by which Being claims the human being (rather than *Dasein*) as the phenomenological instantiation of its manifestation. Contrary to *Being and Time*, where the appeal always comes down to an appeal to itself, here the appeal claims the human being in the name of Being, from the outside and in advance. One must choose between anticipatory resoluteness and the claim [*la revendication*] of the human being by Being: Heidegger finally chose to "destroy" the constant autarky of the Self by a recourse to the claim that Being exercises over the human being. By "human being" it is therefore necessary to understand, contrary to any humanism, that which comes after the subject but also after the Self, since the human being lets itself be instituted through the *Anspruch des Seins*. Claimed before allowing itself to be resolved, the human being should thus be named *der Angesprochene* – the one who is claimed [*le revendiqué*].

This thesis marks the second advance of Heidegger beyond subjecti(vi)ty, a more decisive although less often realized advance. And yet, this thesis gives rise to a question that is still more redoubtable than the preceding difficulties it has managed to vanquish. For, while *Dasein* indeed received an analytic, the one who is claimed [*le revendiqué*] does not, explicitly at least, receive any. And this is indeed why no other Heideggerian term comes to replace that of *Dasein*. Now if it is as the one who is claimed, and not as a constant and resolute Self, that the "human being" gives itself up to the question of Being in general, then the "new beginning" remains suspended over an analytic of the claiming call (*l'appel revendicateur*) in general – which is precisely what is missing. Furthermore, the interpellation that Being exercises over the human being discovers itself to be subordinated to the very possibility of determining the human being as the one who is interpellated or claimed through and through. To break with the subject? To hear the call of Being? This is of little importance in the final analysis: in both cases it is first of all necessary to determine how, why, and up to what point I can hear a call or appeal in general.

V

The claim, then, interpellates me. Before I have even said "I," the claim has summoned me, named me, and isolated me as myself. Moreover, when the claim resounds, the claim that hails me in my name, it is only appropriate to respond – and perhaps respond as silently as the call was silently intimated to me – and to respond by saying, "Here I am!" or, "See me here!" (*Me voici!*), without saying or claiming to advance the least "I." The claim gives rise to a "Here I am!" and thus delineates a *me* without leaving any place to an *I*. The nominative gives way decidedly to that which – provisionally at least – appears to be an accusative case. Contrary to all appearances, it is no longer a question here (as in previous analyses) of a classical critique of the transcendental *I* by and through an empirical and constituted I/me (*je/moi*) in the manner of Kant, Husserl, and Sartre. For this critique finally and much more radically reestablishes a transcendental *I*, which is not constituted but constituting, and which is always originary precisely because it remains unknowable and unconstitutable as an object; indeed, within this metaphysical regime, the relativity of the empirical *I* all the more clearly underlines the absolute primacy of the transcendental and constitutive *I*. Here, on the contrary, in this regime where the claim interpellates *me*, the *I/me* that the claim imparts to *me* and where it assigns *me*, does not designate a return to any transcendental, constitutive, or absolute *I*. The claim, in claiming *me*, refers, across this effect, to its originary interpellation. The experience of the *me*, namely that I hear *myself* speaking, does not offer any proof of some transcendental *I*, an I which comes from some world behind the scenes, but rather, as this pure and simple experience, affects me by its claim and its status as interpellation. The pole to which I must refer *myself*, or more exactly to which the *I* must henceforth refer itself as a *me*, does not lead back to any *I* behind the scenes – an *I* which remains in an invisible reserve as a more originary pole which would open and command the phenomenological horizon – but rather designates an inconceivable, unnameable, and unpredictable instance or agency exercised by the claim itself. Doubtless, to hear *myself* thus interpellated, I experience myself as claimed and, therefore, called in or summoned like some suspect whose identity needs to be verified. But, precisely, this identity no longer returns to me as my own: I cannot produce it as if I were my own master, and were this identity ever to become accessible to me, I would owe this to a speech uttered from elsewhere. I experience *myself* (or more exactly, the *I* experiences itself) as a *myself/me* (un *moi/me*), that is to say, as the pure and simple identification through the passive experience of a *myself* which is submissive and receptive: In the experience that the claim imposes on it, the *I* does not duplicate itself in a *myself*, which would rather underline it; it transmutes itself into *himself (lui)* and loses itself. The interpellated *me* ratifies the disappearance of any *I* under the irremediable empire of the claim. The disaster of the *I* marks the accomplishment or completion of the claim.

Here then, this *myself/me* that is assigned to *me* in the claim arises from the disaster of the *I*. Henceforth we will designate the *me* as the interlocuted (*l'interloqué*). We shall determine the interlocuted by four characteristics: convocation, surprise, interlocution itself, and, finally, facticity. Firstly convocation: when the claim has taken place, the interlocuted experiences an appeal which is powerful and conscriptive enough for it to be obliged to render itself, in the double sense of displacing itself and submitting itself. Thus, the interlocuted should renounce the autarky of every self-affirmation and self-effectuation: It is only insofar as it is altered by an originary relation that the inter-locuted recognizes itself as eventually identified. The pure and simple shock (*Anstoss*) of the claim identifies the *I* only by transmuting it immediately into a *me*. This mutation of the nominative case into the accusative case also marks the inversion of the hierarchy between metaphysical categories: the individualized essence (the *ousia protè*) (as the *tode ti*), no longer precedes the relation (*pros ti*) and no longer excludes it from its ontic perfection; here, on the contrary, the relation precedes and produces individuality. And moreover individuality loses it autarkic essence by being derived from a relation which not only is more originary than it but is half unknown; for, the claim delivers up to evidence only one of its two poles – *myself* or rather *me* – without necessarily or for the most part delivering up the other pole, namely, the origin of the call or appeal. Indeed, the call or appeal is perfectly well able to exercise itself as such without displaying itself or placing itself in evidence. Individual essence undergoes a double relativization: it results or derives from a relation and, moreover, from a relation whose origin is unknown. Thus, a fundamental paradox: through convocation, the interlocuted identifies itself, but this identification escapes it straight away by affecting it and rendering it ecstatic in relation to any self-producing autarky of the *I*. Convocation annuls subjecti(vi)ty to the benefit or an originally altered identity.

Surprise: the interlocuted, which results from a convocation, recognizes itself to be taken and covered over (taken over) by an extasis; but this extasis determines the interlocuted because it remains indeterminate with regard to its pole of origin. Such an extasis, imposed on the *myself/me* without its knowledge, contradicts every epistemological extasis, where the self-constituted I displays or shows the constituted object which stands before it in an evidence which is in principle transparent. Surprise is obscure extasis which is somehow undergone: it contradicts intentionality, which is itself a known and knowing extasis displayed by the *I* and derived from itself; far from covering over the clear terrain of knowable objectivity, when the *I* is transmuted into a *myself/me* it recognizes itself as covered over by an unknowable claim. The inversion of this covering over (*surprise*) is at once with the disqualification of the grasp (*prise*) of epistemology (sur-*prise*). The one and the other are confounded in the same loss of knowledge, in the double sense of the loss of any original self-consciousness and of the incapability of knowing the original pole of the claim as if it were an object. Descartes can here serve as a guide in his definition of admiration or wonder: "when our *first* encounter with some object *surprises* us and we find it novel, or very different from what we formally knew or from what we supposed it ought to be, *this causes us* to admire it and to be astonished and because all this may happen *before we know* whether or not this object is beneficial to us, it seems that admiration or wonder is the first of all the passions." According to Descartes, the surprise of admiration is nothing less than the first passion of the *ego* and therefore of the subject. In distinction from this, we are here describing here a more originary affection, which precedes metaphysical subjectivity; and even if this subjectivity might eventually proceed from this affection, surprise would render the subject destitute rather than instituting it. Surprise arises before the metaphysical admiration of the subject, it is more original than the *thaumazei*, from which philosophy is born.

Interlocution: of course, it is not at all a question of a situation which would already be dialogical, where two interlocutors would converse in an equal relation, but rather of that which is designated under this name in the ancient French judiciary language: "to ordain that a thing will be proven or verified, before one pronounces on the essence of a state of affairs," "to interrupt the legal procedure by an interlocutionary sentence."(Littré) Juridically speaking, to launch an interlocutionary appeal amounts to the suspension of an action, insofar as the facts have not been established, and therefore to suspend the question of right in favor of fact; in phenomenological terms, one would say that interlocution operates a reduction: no longer a reduction of the given by a constituting consciousness (Husserl) or *Dasein* (Heidegger) but a reduction of the purely given understood as such. To determine the given as pure given demands the suspension within the *I* of everything which does not directly result from the claim itself, and therefore to reduce the *I* to the pure giving or donation of a *myself/me*. It is no longer a question of comprehending this giving according to the nominative case (Husserl) or according to the genitive case (of Being: Heidegger) nor even according to the accusative case (Lévinas), but rather according to the dative case – I receive *myself* from the call or appeal which gives me to myself. It would almost be necessary to suppose that this strange dative case was not here distinguished from the ablative case (as in Greek), since the *myself/me* accomplishes, insofar as it is the first gift which derives from the appeal or call, the opening of all other donations or gifts and particular givens, which are possibly ethical. As a given dative, an ablative giving, one might say that the *myself/me* is played out in the manner of the oblative. Receiving itself from the call or appeal which summons it, the *myself/me* undergoes an interlocution – defining the fact of its pure donation – by reducing every other possible phenomenon to pure donation according to interlocution. Interlocution thus marks the ultimate phenomenological reduction.

Facticity: the interlocuted endures the appeal or call and the claim as if it were a fact always already given, and therefore received de facto; the given fact of the appeal or call lets one infer the irremediable facticity of the interlocuted. None amongst mortals has ever lived for an instant without having received a call and being disclosed as interlocuted by facticity. Or, which strictly comes back to the same thing, no mortal has ever lived for an instant without discovering itself to be preceded by a call or appeal that was already there. The paradigm of this irremediable facticity is derived from the fact, always already attained, of speech itself: the first speech for any mortal was always heard or understood before being able to be uttered. Speaking is primarily and always equivalent to hearing or understanding speech; to understand speech is always and primarily equivalent to passively hearing or understanding a speech that comes from an other, a speech that is primarily and always incomprehensible, which announces no sense and no signification, except the very alterity of the initiative which the pure fact gives us to think about for the first time. It is not only that the first speech is not said by the *I* who can only undergo it by receiving it, nor is it only that the first speech does not give any knowledge of an object or of reason. It is rather that the first speech opens onto the fact that a gift originally comes to *me* or befalls *me*, because this gift precedes me to the extent that I must recognize that I proceed from this gift. The human being merits the title of the mortal (or, to say the same thing, the animal) gifted with speech, on the condition that the phrase "gifted with speech" be understood in its strict sense: "endowed with speech," that is, having received the gift of speech. Therefore, to express this with phenomenological rigor, endowed by the gift of speech as it is heard or understood, heard or understood as a given. A decisive consequence follows from this: since the call radically precedes the interlocuted which proceeds from it, the one who calls can never coincide with the one who is called, precisely because, however it occurs and whatever its eventual meaning, the call or appeal accomplishes the separation of the two. The facticity of the call precludes the possibility that the one who is called may perfectly understand the call, in whatever sense one gives to this. To suppose, moreover, that the one who is called attains complete understanding of the one who calls forgets the fact that the one who is called can recognize this call only by admitting that it comes from elsewhere, by recognizing the antecedency of its donation or giving – to the extent that any identity (which is impossible de facto) of the call, would de jure reinforce the immemorial originality of the one who calls over the one who is called. Far from the call or appeal guaranteeing that the one who is called can take possession of its property in the figure of the one who calls, and therefore becoming the matrix of authenticity, it rather indicates that the one who is called can come to itself only by receiving (itself) (as) a *myself/me* and, therefore, by also receiving through the same gesture an infrangible separation from that which assures or guarantees the self. The call or appeal gives *me* to and as *myself*, because, through its facticity, it separates me from all propriety, property, or possession of the proper and of what is my own. It is not only necessary to say that the call or appeal, through its facticity, imposes inauthenticity as the original posture (or rather as the originally nonoriginal posture) of the *myself/me*. It is much rather necessary to admit that the facticity of the call or appeal produces a strict equivalence between the access of the one who is called to itself as a *myself/me*, and thus its ipseity, and its original difference from and with itself as an *I*, and thus its inauthenticity. The original and irreducible posture of the *myself/me* – its ipseity – is thus accomplished in inauthenticity. From which follows a paradox: authenticity, far from being de jure primary, rather masks or covers over the fact of the call – the fact that it is the call alone which always already gives (me) (as) myself. The call, and not the *I*, decides upon the *myself/me* before myself – as that for which I precisely am myself; or, better: the *I* is as such only insofar as the call or appeal has always already claimed it and therefore given it to itself as a *myself/me*. Authenticity, far from opening upon an untainted origin or leading back to such an origin, dissimulates after the fact the originally inauthentic movement of the gift. For, the fact of the call or appeal – calling to *me* before *I* even hear anything – makes me originally differ from this origin and from whatever *I* might be.

Summoned outside of my autarky, according to an originary relation, surprised in itself before any knowledge of the one who calls, but reduced to the pure given, the interlocuted, which is claimed by an anterior fact, differs essentially from itself, because it arises from this very call.

VI

However, the thesis that the interlocuted alone succeeds the subject exposes itself to a major and indeed massive objection: the claim can install the interlocuted as such only if some agency performs it. It is necessary, then, that the claim ultimately be referred to a pole whose initiative rends or tears subjecti(vi)ty, by its silence or by its sound. Therefore, it is unavoidably necessary to ask, who or what claims the interlocuted? As to that which could exercise the claim, rival candidates are not lacking: God (by revelation), the Other (by obligation), Being (by the event), Life (by auto–affection), and so forth. But these various candidates permit us only to define a difficulty but not at all to confront it. For, more than the problem of the identity of the one who calls, the difficulty consists in the consequently devalued status of the interlocuted: in all the above cases, when the interlocuted is placed as a derived, regional, and thus contingent agent, does it not necessarily regress to the humble status of an anthropological given (or even a prosaically psychological or subjective given), without any de jure necessity, purely factual and empirical describable, but conceptually indeterminate? The difficulty of designating exactly what or who calls leads, then, before receiving the least solution, to the following difficulty: that the interlocuted is interpreted as phenomenologically fallen. The anonymous indeterminacy of the one who is called. However, this objection, as strong as it may seen, does not hold. It is not only that the anonymity of the one who calls and the facticity of the one who is called do not in any way oppose the interlocuted; they rather positively confirm its disposition.

The anonymity of the one who calls (what or whom?) does not invalidate the concept of the claim but rather confirms it: since *I* recognize *myself* as interlocuted before any consciousness of my subjecti(vi)ty, which precisely results from this convocation, any eventual knowledge of the one who calls would be added to the claim after the fact, rather than preceeding it as if it were a presupposition. At the origin, the claim is accomplished, and not the consciousness of this claim by the interlocuted, still less the knowledge that would permit the identification of the one who calls in the call or appeal. Moreover, the surprise character of the call forbids the interlocuted from comprehending or knowing its convocation as if it were a determinate, permanent, and named object. To discover *myself* summoned would have no rigor if the surprise did not definitively deprive *me* of knowing, for a time at least, in the instance of the convocation, by what and by whom the claim is exerted. Without the anonymity of the what and the whom, the convocation would not surprise us. Reciprocally, if I knew in advance that Being, or indeed the Other, or indeed God, or indeed life, summoned me, then I would immediately escape from the full status of an interlocuted, since I would be free of any surprise; and thus, knowing in advance (or at least immediately) to what and to whom I was related in the speech that I heard, I would know (what) or I would respond (who) by way of a covering over of a constitution or the equality of a dialogue, that is to say, without the interlocuted passivity of a surprise. In brief, I would become once again an *I* who would be delivered from the status of a *me*. Thus, anonymity belongs strictly to the conditions of possibility of the claim, because it defines the unconditional poverty of the latter: in conformity with the principle of insufficient reason, the claim does not have to become cognized in order to become recognized, nor does it have to be identified in order to be exerted. Only this poverty is sufficient to wound subjecti(vi)ty and exile it outside of any authenticity.

But there is more: the anonymity of the one who calls can be deduced absolutely from the characteristics of the claim. Indeed, the call or appeal resounds first of all prior to any understanding and any hearing, since it surprises – or takes by surprise – a consciousness which was not previously awakened. The call or appeal thus produces the original difference: at the origin, in the fact of the origin, no coincidence, no identity, and no authenticity are found, but rather the separation between the call or appeal and the *myself/me* that it surprises. The delay of *my* surprise with respect to the appeal or call which is always already launched, marks the unique origin of difference, or rather the origin as difference. That which differs is derived from the claim: prior to the partition between Being and beings, also more ancient than the delay between the intuition and the intention (or between the sign and presence), the claim differs. This difference produces the separation between the summoning call or appeal and the understanding of that appeal. Indeed, the interlocuted can do justice only to the convocation from within this surprise and following this essential delay. Surprise says that the appeal or call has already begun to summon, or indeed has already ceased to resound, and that the interlocuted has not finished or indeed has not yet begun to understand it. The facticity of the call or appeal, which rightly implies its anonymity, bears the traces of this difference: effect without cause, fact without reason, the call or appeal comes to an understanding only belatedly awoken, after having already begun to finish, already in the twilight of its dawn. The call or appeal surprises the interlocuted not so much because of its facticity but rather because it remains in origin unknown. The anonymity of the call or appeal, which is implied by its facticity, essentially surprises the interlocuted by its archetypal difference. Deferred through the differing call or appeal, the interlocuted – latecomer, belatedly awoken, originally orphaned by the movement which opens it – thus defines itself by this very delay.

The interlocuted is delayed. It is delayed from its birth, precisely because it is born; it delays its birth, precisely because it must first of all be born. Any living thing must first of all have been born, that is to say, have arisen after or in a delay from its parents, in the attentive circle of an anticipation of the words which would summon it, before the living thing can itself understand or guess; in brief, already surprised by the summons. This latter statement is not at all trivial, since it inscribes the interlocuted, before and more essentially than its mortality, in a difference with respect to the call or appeal. It follows that the interlocuted bears the stigmata of the differing call or appeal, and the full intimacy of its originary inauthenticity, in the very proper name that it bears. Each person has one, two, or sometimes three names, which are, in principle, sufficient to designate a person without any confusion in their ultimate individuality (*haecceitas*). And yet, these names that each one of us bears insofar as we are interlocuted – if it can be supposed that they fully identify us – would not ever be equivalent to a proper name. Or rather, no "proper" name merits this title de jure or de facto. The "proper" name is the result par excellence of an appeal or call: it was given to *me* before I could choose it, know it, or even understand it; it was given to *me* because in fact *I* was given (interlocuted) as and to *myself* (literally: the *I* has been given as and to *me/myself*) by the fact of this name. My right to be me results from the fact that others, without and before me, have given and are giving rise to *me*. I can never say that "I call myself by this (proper) name" (*je m'appelle de ce nom (propre)*); I should always say that *I* have been preceeded by a *me*, namely, as that which others have always already called *me*. In other words, *I* am only called by that name that others (and *myself*) recognize as such, through launching the syllables like a call or appeal (for better but also for worse). It is they who recognized me first of all (surprising me) in and by this name. And they can only do this and should only do this because it is they and not me (I am delayed in advance) who have given *me* this name. Thus, I am called "myself" only insofar as others have always already appropriated me to a name which, without their convocation, would never have been able to name me properly. My proper name has been given to *me* by those who have appropriated *me*: what is proper to me or my own results from an improper appropriation and thus only identifies *me* through an originary inauthenticity – namely, the difference of the claim. Before the supposedly proper name – which is de facto and de jure improper – might be appropriated to me by others (in convocation), it was necessary that the call or appeal preceded it. From whence arises a first consequence: the anterior and thus differentiating call or appeal constitutes the forename (*le pré-nom*) of the name; the fore-name anterior to the name; and which is proper, while the "proper" name in fact marks an inappropriation; a fore-name which does not itself constitute any name, since it gives, announces, and instigates the name. The forename – and it alone – silently satisfies the conditions of possibility for the appropriation of the name that is called "proper" through the convocation. The fore-name precedes the name in the same way as someone calling my name precedes me. The name, by which I alone accede to myself, or more exactly by which *I* accede to the self as a *me*, precedes (and surprises) me only on the basis of the call or appeal (fore-name) which gives it to me (interlocution) and which thus purely and simply gives me to myself as deferred from myself. From whence arises a second consequence: The *myself/me* is born from the appeal or call whose origin is essentially unknown; what is proper to it resides not in its name but rather in the mute fore-name which inauthentically calls it and appropriates it to itself. *I* is called "me" (*Je s'appelle moi*) – henceforth *I* appears only as a differed neutralization of originary difference (that of the convocation), a surface abstraction, a tactical denegation of the diffentiating claim. As a consequence, what is truly proper to a name – the fore-name without name – resides in the very movement of recognizing oneself as called, of admitting the inauthenticity of the surprising convocation, that is to say, in vocation. The only proper name of the interlocuted lies not in such and such a series of names which are by definition improper but in the confession of the call or appeal – that is, in vocation. *Vocatus*, in itself invoked and provoked as a *myself/me*, the interlocuted admits itself to be preceeded by a call or appeal from which it proceeds. Convocation delivers vocation into the appropriating fore-name of all the appropriated names (said to be "proper"). From this arises a third conclusion: the uniquely proper, that which may still respect the differentiating gap of the fore-name, consists in the response [*répons*]. By "response" we understand the resumption of the appeal or call (convocation) by the interlocuted, to the extent that what comes to the interlocuted in the mode of difference (surprise) finds itself acknowledged, admitted, and repeated by the inter-locuted as something all the more authentic because it has come to it through an essential inauthenticity. Indeed, the response literally says nothing other and nothing more than that which the call or appeal said in the first place; it thus repeats the originary inauthenticity; but in this way it makes it its own and therefore acknowledges it as paradoxically authentic. At this second level, authenticity does not consist in claiming to produce the equal appropriation of "*I* to *I*," or of leading back the *myself* to the *I*; authenticity consists in taking for itself, that is, for myself, the original and differentiating inauthenticity of the claim; taking it for itself as if it were a charge or a burden, a weight, or perhaps a danger, in the sense that, during a battle, I might cry out, "the next bullet has my name on it!" There is no authenticity in this appropriation but rather the recognition, often forced but at least admitted, and therefore free, that inauthenticity, alienation, and alteration concern me despite myself, to the point where they are more *myself* than I ever am. Thus the response transmutes the claim into its "*interior intimo meo.*"(*Confessions* III, 7)

What succeeds the subject is the very movement of irremediable difference which precedes it, insofar as the subject is given to itself as a *myself*, to which any *I* claiming authenticity only offers a mask, doubly belated and radically secondary, or even originally deceptive. More essential to the *I* than itself, the gesture that interlocutes appears, freely but not without price, in the figure of the claim – as that which gives the *I* as a *myself* rendered to *itself*. Grace gives the *myself* to *itself* before the *I* even notices itself. My grace precedes me.

10

"VEERINGS" FROM *THE THEOLOGICAL TURN OF FRENCH PHENOMENOLOGY*

Dominique Janicaud

In carrying out our inquiries on quite recent works, we still do not abandon the most ancient questions and their constraints. These gather round the fold already immanent in Aristotle's thought, divided between a science of being [*être*], such as it is given in general, and a science of the Highest Being, the noetic illumination of the divine. The theme of onto-theology has so intimately penetrated reflection on the history of metaphysics that it seems quite legitimate to turn this magic wand back on contemporary writings whose "postmetaphysical" character is often more proclaimed than proved. With Lévinas's thought, we faced a complex puzzle and a paradoxical and strategic blurring of the boundaries between the phenomenological and the theological. I say a strategic blurring, for, by installing the transcendence of the Other [*Autre*] at the heart of a phenomenology that can no longer quite be considered one, Lévinas expressly divests the philosophical regard of the neutrality of which he ought, in principle, to make it his duty to protect. I say a paradoxical blurring, for the trouble stirred up in the phenomenological field does not at all sit well with mystical drunkenness and does not prevent Lévinas, moreover, from vigorously re-posing the question of the philosophical status of the idea of God. "Questions relative to God are not resolved by answers in which the interrogation ceases to resonate or is wholly pacified.... One asks if it is possible to speak legitimately of God without striking a blow against the absoluteness that his word seems to signify."[1] How can we contest the philosophical legitimacy of this question?

Whereas a gunslinging rationalism (today less and less prevalent) would enclose itself in a double refusal – of the opening [*ouverture*] of philosophy onto the "unapparent," and of the elevation of thought to the question of God – our critical inquiry means, on the contrary, to make room for all phenomenological and philosophical possibilities. Thanks to a methodological discrimination, we mean to permit each project to retrieve its specificity and to respect the type of rigor special to it. For example, Wassily Kandinsky magnificently enriched abstract art, and it would be aberrant to challenge his pictorial oeuvre in the name of "social realism" or any other theory. Nevertheless, the manifesto entitled *Concerning the Spiritual in Art*, however stimulating it may be, exposes itself to contradiction when it claims to actualize the great spiritual rebirth it announces by means of the paths of theosophy.[2] Every allowance being made, we find ourselves in a comparable situation in philosophy: in this special marketplace, we are not forced to take or leave any oeuvre as a whole. We have the right, and even the duty, not only to hem and haw and wrangle, but to finger the stuff of thoughts, to test their solidity, and to expose to the light of interrogation inspirations, concepts, and prospects. And so it will be in the discussions that follow, and principally in regard to Jean-Luc Marion's *Reduction and Givenness*, where our objections will be directed not at the theological as such, but at certain of its translations or intrusions into the phenomenological field.

Phenomenology and Metaphysics

Whereas, until Wolff, and still today in neo-Thomism, rational metaphysics played the role of a propaedeutic to theology, its scope was inverted by Heidegger. For him, access to the "God most divine" depends on a disengagement from the metaphysical mode of thinking. In *L'idole et la distance* and *God without Being*,[3] Marion, for his own part, took this Heideggerian reversal in the direction of a nonontological, nonrepresentative theology of Christly love. *Reduction and Givenness* is infinitely more discreet in this regard, and for this discretion we can only praise its author: this work is presented as an ensemble of phenomenological investigations. This presentation does not, though, rid it of all difficulties. What is questionable, from the methodological point of view, is the status of phenomenology – and of the phenomenological – between a metaphysics that has been "overcome" (or challenged) and a theology that has been made possible (at once prepared and held in reserve).

Not only has Marion lucidly perceived this problem, but he has resolved it in his own manner, putting in place in 1984 (in the "Foreword" to the collection *Phénoménologie et métaphysique*) a framework by means of which phenomenology becomes the privileged inheritor of philosophy at the era of metaphysics' completion.[4] He writes: "Clearly, since metaphysics found its end, whether in fulfillment with Hegel, or in twilight with Nietzsche, philosophy has been able to pursue itself authentically only under the figure of phenomenology."[5] This thesis is reaffirmed and even emphasized when Marion suggests that we have thus swung "toward a thought [that is] perhaps already postmetaphysical."[6]

These affirmations call for, at first, a kind of head-on examination. What is their validity; are they acceptable in themselves? If they are not self-evident, but instead dubious, we must ask why the thesis of the "metaphysical extraterritoriality of phenomenology" has been pushed so far and what it permits or authorizes.[7]

Chiefly contestable is the "evidence" concerning the end of metaphysics and the historicist form given to this Heideggerian thesis (that we have entered into the "postmetaphysical" era). Admittedly Marion nuances this thesis with a "perhaps" and concedes its "unilateral violence," its dogmatic massiveness. It remains the case, nonetheless, that this schema is adopted as quasi-evident. Here we encounter a twofold series of difficulties. On the one hand, must the Heideggerian thesis of the accomplishment of metaphysics be so completely accepted? And on the other hand, and more importantly, is it a question here of a historial thesis – not only a historical one? The response to the second point will permit us to clarify our first objection. If Heidegger never employs the expression "postmetaphysical," this is because its use would lead us to believe that the exit out of metaphysics has already been reached. In truth, he thinks the contrary: planetary technique brings metaphysics to its "unconditional rule."[8]

"Experienced in the dawn of its beginning, metaphysics is, however, at the same time past [*vergangen*], in the sense that it has entered into its ending [*in ihre Ver-endung eingegangen ist*]. The ending lasts longer than the heretofore history of metaphysics."[9] We do indeed, then, have to do with a historial thesis in whose name we cannot at all justify presenting a philosophical current as escaping the *Ver-endung* of metaphysics.

Given as much, the attitude to adopt before the first question must not be unilateral, insofar as Heidegger's thinking on the "overcoming" of metaphysics is, paradoxically, both complex and simplifying. Complex, because it requires us to make a double connection between the *Vollendung* and the *Verwindung* – to comprehend, and even to make our own, the contemporaneity of the accomplishment of metaphysics and the withdrawal this means for it. Simplifying, however, to the extent that this thesis unifies under the same term "metaphysics" *metaphysica generalis* (as condition of the articulation of the senses of being [*sens de l'étant*]) and *metaphysica specialis* (as principled foundation of being [*l'étant*]) to respond to one and the same injunction, both epochal and destinal. The onto-theological structure accedes to a credit so large and so enveloping that it suffocates or minimizes all exceptions or marginalities. So attests the case of Nietzsche, concerning whom contemporary research doubts more and more (and with justification) that he "led to its end and accomplished all the possibilities – even inverted – of metaphysics" (to cite, once more, a formulation of Jean-Luc Marion).[10]

It is evident that this discussion, bearing on the purported end of metaphysics and directed at the Heideggerian thesis as well as the formulation Marion gives it, puts into play important stakes implicating phenomenology. For putting metaphysics into perspective by means of a historical schema (or, more grandly, a historial one) implies a complementary ordering of phenomenology. According to Marion, phenomenology would be, since Hegel, the place of an essentially antimetaphysical breakthrough: "Phenomenology does not introduce metaphysics, it exits from it [*elle en sort*]."[11]

The argumentation in regard to Hegel merits examination. It authorizes itself to deduce, from the renewed debate among interpreters on the relationship of the *Phenomenology of Spirit* to the ensemble of Hegel's System, a "conflict with the knowledge of metaphysics."[12] But this argumentation rests on an altogether illegitimate elision (in any case, one not justified in Marion's text) between System and metaphysics. No one will contest that there is a divide, if not a distortion, between the masterpiece of 1807 and section III, I B, of the *Encyclopedia*. But it does not follow that there is a question here of a "conflict" between phenomenology and metaphysics. Even if the *Phenomenology* is detached from the System – whether from the anthropological point of view, as by Alexandre Kojève; in a Marxist sense, as by Herbert Marcuse; or in an existential sense, as by Jean Hyppolite – the Heideggerian question of the metaphysical status of Hegelianism nevertheless arises. There is nothing more metaphysical than the final chapter of the *Phenomenology* on *Geist*, and it is the same for the initial chapter on "Sense Certainty" as for the conceptual armature of the whole work. Heidegger himself, in the remarkable commentary he devoted to the introduction, interpreted the "science of the experience of consciousness" as an inspired tissue of ambiguity, within metaphysics (that is to say, the parousia of the absolute), between the present and presence. He affirms this quite clearly: "At the time of the first publication of the *Phenomenology of Spirit*, science is for Hegel the onto-theological knowledge of what truly is insofar as it is [*wahrhaft Seienden als Seinden*]."[13] The tension between the *Phenomenology* and the *Logic* is in no way interpreted by Heidegger in terms of a decisive break with metaphysics (in the first work), but in terms of a change in emphasis (from ontology to speculative theology) within onto-theology, that is to say, metaphysics. It is then illegitimate, even from the Heideggerian point of view, to hold that "the first entry of phenomenology in metaphysics came to its end, with Hegel, in [phenomenology's] being put aside."[14]

Must we go so far as to claim that phenomenology separates Hegel from metaphysics? With Husserl, the undertaking becomes more delicate yet. For how can we find support for the thesis of a conflict between phenomenology and metaphysics in an itinerary that, despite the breakthrough of the *Logical Investigations*, restores – by the admission of Marion himself – all the exigencies and structures of transcendental idealism? It is evident that, if Husserl brackets *metaphysica specialis* and initially dismisses ontology, he does not do the same in regard to *metaphysica generalis*. As eidetic, the reduction is an eminently Platonic act; as transcendental, it encounters the problem of foundation across that of autoconstitution (which Marion very justly notes).[15] These clear facts ought to lead to a revision of Marion's thus imperiled thesis. The example of Husserl shows quite clearly that a metaphysical phenomenology is possible; ought we to add, more categorically perhaps, that phenomenology, radically implemented and methodically conducted, can only be metaphysical (in the sense of *metaphysica generalis*)? Marion prefers to take a step back, to a position that does not altogether mask his discomfiture: "The strangeness, as troubling as fascinating, of the Husserlian institution inheres in its radical impuissance to take a position regarding the essence of metaphysics."[16]

But is Husserl only interesting on account of his "impuissance"? This negative appraisal – paradoxical, if not disingenuous – of the Husserlian institution is only explicable, in fact, by the double presupposition that it is Heidegger who radicalizes and deepens the Husserlian reduction and that he does so by opening phenomenology to the ontological question and confronting it with the essence of metaphysics. But this retrospective unification, if it is not qualified by precautions, sets down a grid of interpretation that only prepares the way for further schematizations. Concerning the relation to metaphysics, if it is evident that Husserl does not explore its essence, it follows neither that we must neglect his refusal of *metaphysica specialis*, nor overlook or scorn the positive sense he intended to give to *metaphysica generalis* in reinstituting transcendental idealism. If the relation between phenomenology and metaphysics is more open and complex than Marion's presentation of the problem would have us believe, by the same stroke the linearity he projects onto the Heideggerian "radicalization" of the reduction must be called into question.

The Schematism of the Three Reductions

We have called into doubt the "postmetaphysical" character of phenomenology as Marion tries to unify it. But we must go further in dismantling a framework within which the "schematism of the three reductions" permits us to imagine a relation of inverse proportionality between reduction and givenness. The purpose of this frame-work is to establish an appearance of formal continuity between the best known nucleus of the phenomenological method and "the pure form of the call"[17] a most elliptical operation that does not fear to disconcert us by announcing other "new and rigorous paradoxes,"[18] but whose brio cannot spare the author of having to warrant our belief. Let us review in order, then, the demands he makes of us. Let us examine the methodological solidity of the triad of reductions, their supposed relations with givenness, and, finally, the astonishing promotion of a pure givenness.

The schema of the three reductions is summarized at the end of *Reduction* and *Givenness*, but obviously we must refer to developments within the body of the text to appreciate its ramifications.[19] According to Marion, the first reduction is transcendental, the second existential, and the third pure, almost unqualifiable. These correspond quite simply to three signatures: Husserl, Heidegger, Marion. But is the situation so clear? Let us take a closer look.

Let us also immediately correct what was just suggested: for Marion, the transcendental reduction is not uniquely Husserlian, but "Cartesian" or even "Kantian" as well. "It matters little here," the author bizarrely specifies. On the contrary, it matters a lot, even ultimately, for the question is whether it is possible to amalgamate, for the needs of the cause, such different undertakings. The scare quotes, however, mean to make us set aside any historical suspicions, and so be it. But what is the relation between the "Cartesian" reduction and that of Descartes, and so on? The recapitulative movement of "phenomenological" truth, we are to believe, enables us to circumscribe the enterprise of reduction in four (hastily enumerated) strokes: constitution of objects (1) for a constituting I (2), the transcendental reduction opens onto only regional ontologies (3) and excludes all that exceeds the horizon of objectivity (4).[20]

But this unified presentation of the transcendental reduction fails to recognize the difference, introduced by Husserl in the *Ideas*,[21] between regional reductions and the *epoché* as such. The epoché is no longer simply directed at objects related to psychological events, but at pure lived experiences [*vécus*] in their intentional correl-ations. While claiming Cartesian inspiration, Husserl shows in §10 of his *Cartesian Meditations* in what sense Descartes missed the transcendental orientation: he made the ego a separate "*substantia cogitans.*"[23] This point is not a secondary one, for, if it is not appreciated, the very sense of the epoché and the radical novelty of intentionality will be misunderstood. In "the free and unlimited field of consciousness," it is the "world-phenomenon" itself that is disengaged, and not simply "objects" for a "constitutive I." The reference to Kant (to the "paralogisms of pure reason")[24] in Marion's text equally obliges us to correct this idea. According to the "paralogisms of pure reason," the I think as liaison of representations is not substantially constitutive of objects, but is only the foyer − problematic and formal − of the transcendental correlation. Kant writes:

Through this I, or he, or it (the thing) which thinks, nothing further is represented than a
transcendental subject of the thoughts = x, which is known only by the thoughts that are
its predicates, and of which, apart from these, we could never have the least concept.[25]

No more in Kant than in Husserl, the transcendental horizon cannot be diminished
to an egology constituting objects. We must instead maintain the profundity of this
field and the precautions (including those concerning the transcendental scope, or not,
of the Cartesian cogito) that *Reduction and Givenness* seems to lack, and not only in its
final pages. Throughout the book, the phenomenon in the Husserlian sense is system-
atically presented as "flat,"[26] which implies that the quest for integral and objective
presence annuls the opening [*ouverture*] of the *epoché* onto the correlation with the
world as such. More royalist than the king, Marion systematizes the Heideggerian
critique of the Husserlian reduction (which Heidegger formulated, in particular, in the
Basic Problems of Phenomenology[27] to such a point that it becomes impossible to discern
either the interest or the originality of Husserl. Let us turn, then, to the second
reduction in order to discover the "true" meaning of phenomenology.

Basing himself, essentially, on the *History of the Concept of Time* and the *Basic Problems*
(courses Heidegger gave in 1925 and 1927, respectively), Marion presents the Heideggerian ontology as a radicalization and revival of Husserlian phenomenology. And
during the years of his elaboration of *Being and Time*, this was indeed how Heidegger
opposed himself to Husserl. "For us," Heidegger writes in the *Basic Problems*, "the
phenomenological reduction means leading the phenomenological regard back from
the apprehension of the entity [*Erfassung des Seienden*] – whatever the character of this
apprehension – to the understanding of the being [*Verstehen des Seins*] of this entity
[*dieses Seienden*]."[28] To this extent, it is justifiable to interpret the Heideggerian
"reduction" as a "redoubled reduction." As Marion writes:

> The privilege of Dasein comes to it only from its disposition to undergo a redoubled
> phenomenological reduction. This [reduction] makes the transition from the entity
> [*l'étant*] to the "sense of being" ["*sens d'être*"] only by working through that entity [*cet
> étant*] that being [*l'être de l'étant*] determines par excellence.[29]

Being [*être*] is no longer understood as immanent to intentional consciousness, but
inversely as the horizon of phenomenality, that is, in terms of the uncovering of the
entity [*l'étant*]. Phenomenality will thus be interrogated, in a privileged manner, on the
basis of the ontico-ontological articulations offered by Dasein, whose sense of being
[*sens d'être*] no eidetic ever exhausts.

Only, to whatever extent it is true that Heidegger questions "the very appearing
[*l'apparaître*] of the phenomenon,"[30] must we agree that his ontological soundings
operate exclusively by the reduction and toward "reviving" phenomenology? This is
what Marion would have us believe in his study "The Entity and the Phenomenon
[*L'étant et le phénomène*],"[31] and by design: we discover the rationale of the schema of
the three reductions, within which Heidegger's "way" is stylized in a manner so
elliptical that it becomes unrecognizable. In effect, why pass over in silence, first, the
fact that "fundamental ontology," as it is deployed in *Being and Time*, is already
presented no longer as reduction, but as an analytic of Dasein; and, second, that

Heidegger will later completely abandon all terminology of Husserlian origin? And why neglect this even more significant detail: Heidegger's relativization, starting with the *Basic Problems*, of the reduction itself? "The phenomenological reduction, as the leading-back of the regard from the entity to being [*vom Seienden zum Sein*]," Heidegger writes in that book, "is not, however, the unique *nor even central* fundamental part [*Grundstück*] of the phenomenological method."[32] He adds that the question of being [*être*] stands in need not only of the reduction, but of the destruction and reconstruction of the fundamental concepts of philosophy. Even reinterpreted in the ontological sense, the reduction is, for Heidegger, only a "part" or a phase of an ampler procedure that will require both a more and more thoroughgoing destruction of the history of metaphysics and its rereading in function of the ontological difference.

Following the internal logic of Heidegger's path from the *History of the Concept of Time* to *What Is Metaphysics?*, we find no evidence for the extension of the problematic of the reduction toward an existential or ontological reduction that would stand as an autonomous, philosophical finality. Still less do we discern, in the latter lecture, a "phenomenological framework" that would allow us to recognize in it "a sort of phenomenological reduction."[33] On the contrary, Heidegger immediately delimits the field of phenomenological reductions, transcendental and eidetic, within the horizon of intentionality.[34] Further, circumscribing this horizon in a critical manner on account of its idealist and Cartesian character, he more and more distances himself from what it implies. He retains from the reduction only its ontological differentiation, whose proper accentuation will oblige him to pose the question of metaphysics still more radically. But at the epoch of fundamental ontology, Heidegger has recourse to the reduction only under implicit or explicit scare quotes – a recourse occasioned by his difficulty in settling upon a method proper to the mode of thought still trying to find itself across the existential analytic. The problem becomes more complicated yet if we consider that, as Jean-François Courtine has seen, the "ontological reduction" still remains burdened with transcendentalism.[35]

Over and against the claim that "Heidegger remains, therefore, a phenomenologist, since he resumes [*reprend*] the reduction,"[36] it is rather the inverse that is true: he directs himself toward the true sense of phenomenality, the "ek-static" horizon of time, only to the extent that the elaboration of the question of being [*être*] is substituted for the reductions. (Heidegger does not, then, focus on the phenomenon of being [*être*] "in itself" ["*en personne*"], as Marion writes, but on its mode of uncovering.[37]

The reader will perhaps excuse this detailed reappraisal when reminded that it allows us to understand the purpose (but also the fragility) of the framework by which Marion makes his way to the third reduction. In the end, this game is not hidden. We read, regarding this tertium quid, "[O]ur whole enterprise has tended toward nothing other than to render the recognition of it inevitable."[38] But it is obvious that this recognition cannot take place, nor certainly appear inevitable, if the path that was supposed to lead to it proves to have been too artificially flattened.

If it is difficult to linger for long with this pseudoreduction, of which we learn only what it is not (we shall return to this thinness), the strategy of the seizure of phenomenology must nevertheless see its assurance confronted by what it masks and risks. "[T]he transgression of the claim of being [*être*] by the pure form of the call," Marion writes, "belongs to the phenomenological field for exactly the same reason that would allow the analytic of Dasein to replace the constitution of the transcendental I."[39] We have here an admission of the mimetic methodology by which Marion wants to pass off the *salto mortale* toward the "pure call" as proceeding from the same rigor as Heidegger's deepening of the Husserlian reduction. But this trick has already been pulled off by Lévinas (whom it is not surprising to see cited on page 197 of *Reduction and Givenness* [page 295 of *Réduction et donation*]), as it will be again by more than one comrade: repeating, in displacing to advantage, the Heideggerian "overcoming" of idealist intentionality (or metaphysics, or ontology). Only here Marion raises the bar still higher in claiming that his transgression is rigorous and scrupulous, arising "eminently from phenomenology."[40] But what remains phenomenological in a reduction that, "properly speaking, *is* not,"[41] and refers back to "a point of reference [that is] all the more original and unconditioned as it is more restricted"?[42] Many pains have been taken, in purportedly methodological arguments, to lead us to this absolute and above all to make us believe in its phenomenological character. We must turn now to this pure givenness so as to specify how it is incompatible – for as much as it is utterable – with the astute detours by which Marion wants, at any price, to render phenomenological what cannot be.

What Givenness, What Call, and What Promise?

We have already seen that the more doubtful the phenomenological character of the procedure, the more emphatically this character has been affirmed. The passage from the second to the third reduction was as if hooked onto the model of the passage from the first to the second. But the trajectory of this first passage, given as a model for the second, seemed to us much too complex to be formalized as Marion did, thus imperiling the whole operation. What do we end up with? With a call, given as the "originary schema," whose pure form "plays before all specification, even of being [*être*]."[43]

From here onward, whether it is a question of the reduction, givenness, or the call, we find ourselves confronted by a *coincidentia oppositorum* in the truly classical sense, on the theological, mystical way. The more phenomenality becomes attenuated, to the point of annihilating itself, the more the absolute inflates and amplifies itself, to the point of apotheosis. We have to do, here, with a rather dry mystical night; the superabundance of grace has been put through the Heideggerian ringer. But the qualifying terms, in any case, are neither human nor finite: pure, absolute, unconditioned – such is this call. It addresses itself, it is true, to a reader, an interlocutor [*interloqué*], however ideal. But *voilà!* the interlocutor is in his or her turn reduced to his or her pure form, to the interlocuted "as such."[44] Is not this experience, slimmed down to its a priori sheathe, too pure to dare to pass itself off as phenomenological? And will not the reader who is thus interlocuted be tempted to cede to the facilities of irony before sentences like these: "Literally, surprise prohibits the interlocuted from comprehending the convocation that it nevertheless receives"?[45] Or again, "The imprecision, the indecision, indeed the confusion of the claiming instance attests much rather that, at the origin, is found the pure form of the call as such"?[46]

We want to believe that it is by design, and not without a certain complaisance, that farewell is thus bid not only to common sense, but to the stuff of phenomena. In fact, the only tie that binds these citations to whatever kind of experience is religious. When we read, "Listen, Israel, Jahweh our God, Jahweh alone,"[47] we no longer doubt the nature of the call, nor that of the promised givenness; as for the response, it depends on each of us. But who introduces "imprecision, indecision, nay confusion," if not the philosopher who means to transform references of another order, as Pascal would have put it, into an a priori instance and general schemes?

Now Marion invokes none other than the leitmotif of Pascal to respond to the excellent question posed by the editors of the *Revue de métaphysique et de morale* concerning the very "problematic" character of the third reduction and the "equivocality of the very term givenness [*donation*]."[48] As much as his response is justified in relating the problematic of his *On Descartes' Metaphysical Prism* to the Pascalian destitution of the "vanity" of philosophy,[49] it becomes just as much acrobatic in claiming that *Reduction and Givenness's* terminal point "beyond being [*hors d'être*]" – conceded "empty" – does not base itself on "external givens [*données*] admitted by hypothesis." The reasoning is strange: Marion admits that, since it is a question here of phenomenology (a point to which he clings), we need an immediate intuition. But he concedes that this intuition is absent: "Therefore *Reduction and Givenness* limits itself to a kind of negative phenomenology, following after the negative theology deployed by God without Being. Only derivative phenomena appear – the interlocuted, ennui, and others – and indices or effects of phenomena still indescribable as such – the call, nonindifferent assignation, and others."[50] We had to cite this sentence to its end; it makes a capital concession (the phenomenological element in *Reduction and Givenness* is "derivative," in any case when we come to the threshold of the third reduction), but immediately takes it back in a somewhat captious form. This consists, on the one hand, in playing on the notion of "negative phenomenology" – which calls for examination, as it is not evident that it coincides with the most founded phenomenology – and, on the other hand, in introducing the idea that there would be "phenomena not yet manifest"[51] – a strangely surreptitious displacement toward a kind of progressivism in phenomenality. If the "pure form of the call" appears empty in 1991, it seems that the happy, humming days to come of a phenomenology more and more negative will draw out the contours of, alas, a "more difficult" work.

In Marion's work, there is no respect for the phenomenological order; it is manipulated as an ever-elastic apparatus, even when it is claimed to be "strict." In the same way, his response concerning "givenness" [*donation*] makes use of the term's very ambiguity to avoid truly responding to the question posed, which did not contest the recourse to the notion of givenness, but the precise use (or misuse) the ultimate stage of *Reduction and Givenness* makes of it. Marion makes the argument, among others, that Merleau-Ponty gave a conceptual treatment of givenness, in spite of (or because of) its ambiguity: if we look at page 360 of the *Phenomenology of Perception* [page 413 of *Phénoménologie de la perception*] (which Marion cites), we will note that the givenness in question is that of a reflection "open on the unreflected [*irréfléchi*]." This is, par excellence, situated givenness, since it is that which unveils the tie between my subjectivity and the world. "My freedom, the fundamental power that I have to be the subject of all my experiences, is not distinct from my insertion in the world,"

Merleau-Ponty writes. Here the question is one of a totally phenomenal givenness, which is precisely not the case with the third, "Marionesque" givenness. The question then stands, and it does not suffice to displace it toward a hypothetical future, whether to exploit the ambiguity of the notion of givenness, or to use the "phenomenology of the unapparent" as a kind of talisman or alibi.

In fact, Marion's end point is clear, and its phenomenological emptiness can be explained only by a double reference, which the acute reader of his texts recognizes: to the problematic of the overcoming of ontology (or metaphysics), and to the properly theological or spiritual dimension. It is the running together of these two schemas under the cover of phenomenology that is contested here. Not only does this strategy afford itself no few rhetorical facilities, but it leads us back to an autosufficiency (pure givenness "gives *itself*"!) that restores *metaphysica specialis* – and its favorite trick, autofoundation – rather than giving it the boot.

If the paradoxes of *Reduction and Givenness* were restricted to questioning the notion of givenness and interrogating its phenomenological sense (such is the posture Marion adopts at the end of his first response to the *Revue de métaphysique et de morale*), we would have no objection.[52] But we must not let the "radicality" of Marion's interrogation prejudice us as to the radicality (real or pretended) of his furnished response. By now it is evident that *Reduction and Givenness* does not at all limit itself to interrogation: this book, by Marion's own admission, is destined "to lay the foundation platform available for a higher edifice."[53] The metaphor is revelatory, and we will see a comparable veering, both metaphoric and methodological, in the work of Jean-Louis Chrétien, *La voix nue. Phénoménologie de la promesse* [*The Naked Voice: Phenomenology of the Promise*].

This book is remarkable for many of its traits: the quality of its writing, the richness of its references, the fineness of its analyses. The criticisms that follow must not, then, be misunderstood: they are uniquely methodological and will concentrate, too briefly, on the sense of the book's subtitle, "phenomenology of the promise." Our challenge bears less on the intentions Chrétien acknowledges in his introduction than on their realization. His project wishes to be phenomenological: on the nakedness of the voice and of the body as well as on the lie, equivocality, admission, and testimony. His question is altogether legitimate: "Is it phenomenologically possible to think a body without secret and without reserve, whose glory would be full manifestation and perfect visibility?"[54] Likewise legitimate is his question about whether the study of the "oblique character of manifestation" is not preeminently phenomenological. The answer here is that without any doubt, it is – on condition one respects minimal rules that cleave to the spirit of phenomenology. Proclaimed on the first page of the introduction, the "critique of philosophies of presence" will be, we are led to believe, a leitmotif in this regard. We anticipate, then, that the intertwining of analyses and phenomenological descriptions will show up the metaphysical closure on the illusion of thoroughgoing transparence (as the title of the first part, "Critique of Transparence," indicates).

Now, on the first page consecrated to "the glory of the body," and after several beautiful lines consecrated to the body offered to vision, the extended sleeper or twirling dancer, we read: "In rendering itself visible, the body does not render itself alone visible, but lets come into the light of the world the invisible soul that, in vivifying [the body], is its perpetual origin, without which it would show nothing."[55] In the following, recourse to this concept of soul is constantly made, as if it were self-evident; how it escapes from metaphysics – given that it is "perpetual origin" indispensable to corporal manifestation – is also not explained. Admittedly, the text criticizes the idea of a complete manifestation of the soul across the body, a criticism phenomenology upholds. But this critique of the glorious body operates to the advantage of a more secretive metaphysics where the soul wraps itself up in the "body's nights." From here flow the suggestive evocations of a body "haunting the distances," once more making sign toward glory, but a glory that is the "very assumption" of the secret and not a complete manifestation. From here also flows the conclusion on eternal life as "act of praise," and the firm hope that the secret of the body will be "finally given in glory, without our being able to retake it."

Let us be clear: it is not at all a question here of contesting the interest, for a Christian thinker, of rethinking corporeality, including in the perspective of the resurrection promised by the Scriptures. But we must observe, as a matter of fact, that in the text in question the recourse to phenomenology is constantly biased by both a "call" that is purportedly original and a reference, imposed on the reader, to religious experience. It is a question here, we might put it, of a Christian phenomenology [phénoménologie chrétienne], but whose properly phenomenological sense must fall away, for a nonbeliever, midway through the journey (assuming, even, that he or she accepts the reference, properly metaphysical, to the notion of soul).

This same kind of utilization of phenomenology recurs throughout the rest of this work, so rich in philosophical, theological, and patristic references. Chrétien apprehends and thinks the Christian sense of the Incarnation against (and on the basis of) successive and insistent figures of the metaphysics of transparence: the nakedness of essence, the angelic horizon, the obliquity of the divine, freedom as transparent causality, the experience of paradise, the generosity of the One, God's purely speculative intelligence, the translucence of excessively intellectual love. He thus succeeds in writing up, often with touching grace, a spiritual experience whose corporal envelope gestures toward both the word's invisible ties and the exaltation of a promise in excess to itself. "The naked soul is the naked hand, the naked voice, the naked shadow of the promise that always already surrounds us."[56] A challenge to the metaphysics of transparence, this thought of the pure promise gives itself off as "phenomenology" only to reintroduce, subtly but with an altogether strategic constancy, a metaphysics of the secret divine and the transcendent call.

Our questions on the sense of givenness, the call, and the promise were, then, quite naïve: the "phenomenologies" of Marion and Chrétien, however different in their twists, turns, and qualities, are woven with the same immaculate thread. The theological veering is too obvious. And it does not suffice in order to minimize it, to claim as a pretext that it "is obviously not a question here of invoking revealed authority in order to broaden phenomenology's field."[57] That has been, in a sense, clearer yet. In fact, and despite all the denials, phenomenological neutrality has been abandoned, just as the reasons that explicitly led Husserl to put the transcendence of God "out of circuit" have been put aside (or neglected). "Upon this 'absolute' and 'transcendent,'" Husserl writes, "we naturally extend the phenomenological reduction. It [the transcendence of God] must remain excluded from the new field of study we have to create, insofar as this field must be a field of pure consciousness."[58] This Husserlian methodological precaution applied itself not only to the explicit reference to God in the method's practice, but to reasons drawn from "religious consciousness,"[59] among whose number it is not, without doubt, illegitimate to count "the call" or "the promise" as figures of Transcendence.

A second characteristic of the theological veering is that it leads to analyses that verge on edification – if they do not succumb to it with delectation. Whether it is a question of a call always ready to claim a listening interlocuted, or of a promise that precedes itself and holds in reserve the unhoped-for, phenomenality knows the negative or the absurd only under the passable form of ennui or the lyrical evocation of a fear ready to be reassured. Would not a phenomenology whose dice have not been loaded have more attention for the atrocious, despairing, unqualifiable, or even only undecidable – where our condition is also woven? Does not E. M. Cioran reveal himself, then, to be at least as phenomenological as our authors, in many of his ruthless descriptions of our human condition? We borrow from him this conclusion: "For the unbeliever, infatuated with waste and dispersion, there is no spectacle more disturbing than these ruminants on the absolute. . . . Where do they find such pertinacity in the unverifiable, so much attention in the vague, and so much ardor to seize it?"[60]

Notes

1   Lévinas, *De Dieu qui vient à l'idée* (Paris: Vrin, 1986), p. 8; English trans., *Of God Who Comes to Mind* (Stanford, CA.: Stanford University Press, 1998), trans. Bettina Bergo, pp. xi–xii.

2   Wassily Kandinsky, *Du spirituel dans l'art* (Paris: Denoël-Méditations, 1969), trans. P. Volboudt, pp. 59–60; English trans., *Concerning the Spiritual in Art* (New York: Dover Publications, 1977), trans. M. T. H. Sadler, pp. 53–5. Cf. Michel Henry, *Voir l'invisible. Sur Kandinsky* (Paris: François Bourin, 1988). For Henry, the abstraction of "inner necessity" that Kandinsky liberates has nothing to do with geometrical abstraction. We will return to this thesis and to the phenomenological interest of Henry's book in chapter 5.

3   Marion, *L'idole et la distance* (Paris: Grasset, 1977), *Idol and Distance* (New York: Fordham University Press, 2001), trans. Thomas Carlson; and *Dieu sans l'être* (1982; Paris: Presses Universitaires de France, 1991); English trans., *God without Being* (Chicago: University of Chicago Press, 1991), trans. Thomas A. Carlson.

4   *Phénoménologie et métaphysique* (Paris: Presses Universitaires de France, 1984), ed. Jean-Luc Marion and Guy Planty-Bonjour.

5   Ibid., p. 7.

6   Marion, *Réduction et donation: Recherches sur Husserl, Heidegger et la phénoménologie* (Paris: PUF, 1989), p. 7; Eng. trans. *Reduction and Givenness: Investigations of Husserl, Heidegger, and Phenomenology*, trans. Thomas Carlson (Evanston: Northwestern University Press, 1998), p. 1.

7   *Phénoménologie et métaphysique*, p. 7.

8   Martin Heidegger, *Vorträge und Aufsätze* (Pfullingen: Neske, 1954), p. 63; English trans., *The End of Philosophy* (New York: Harper & Row, 1973), trans. Joan Stambaugh, p. 85.

9   Ibid. (trans. modified).

10 Marion, *Réduction et donation*, p. 7; trans., p. 1 (trans. modified).

11 *Phénoménologie et métaphysique*, pp. 10–11.

12 Ibid., p. 10.

13 Heidegger, *Holzwege* (Frankfurt am Main: Vittorio Klostermann, 1967), pp. 183–4; English trans., *Hegel's Concept of Experience* (New York: Harper & Row, 1970), trans. anonymous, p. 142. Heidegger adds: "This truth is the essence of metaphysics [*Diese Wahreheit ist das Wesen der Metaphysik*]," trans., p. 143; trans. modified.

14 *Phénoménologie et métaphysique*, p. 11.

15 Ibid., p. 12.

16 Ibid.

17 Marion, *Réduction et donation*, p. 305; trans., p. 205. [See chapter 9 of this Volume. (Ed.)]

18 Ibid.

19 Ibid., pp. 304 and 97–103, 289–96; trans., pp. 204 and 62–6, 192–8.

20 Ibid., p. 304; trans., p. 204.

21 Husserl, *Ideen zu einer reinen Phänomenologie und phänomenologischen Philosophie: Erstes Buch*, Husserliana Band 3 (The Hague: Martinus Nijhoff, 1950), ed. Walter Biemel, §33, pp. 73–4; English trans., *Ideas Pertaining to a Pure Phenomenology and to a Phenomenological Philosophy: First Book* (The Hague: Martinus Nijhoff, 1983), trans. F. Kersten, pp. 65–6.

22 Ibid., §36, p. 80; trans., p. 73.

23 Husserl, *Cartesianische Meditationen und Pariser Vorträge*, Husserliana Band 7 (The Hague: Martinus Nijhoff, 1950), ed. S. Strasser, §10, p. 63; English trans., *Cartesian Meditations* (The Hague: Martinus Nijohoff, 1960), trans. Dorion Cairns, p. 24.

24 Immanuel Kant, *Kritik der reinen Vernunft*, A-341/B-399ff.; English trans., *Critique of Pure Reason* (New York: St. Martin's, 1929), trans. Norman Kemp Smith, pp. 328ff.

25 Ibid., A-346/B-405; trans. p. 331 (trans. modified).

26 Marion, *Réduction et donation*, p. 90; trans., p. 56.

27 Heidegger, *Die Grundprobleme der Phänomenologie*, Gesamtausgabe Band 24 (Frankfurt am Main: Vittorio Klostermann, 1975), ed. Friedrich-Wilhelm von Hermann, p. 29; English trans., *The Basic Problems of Phenomenology* (Bloomington, IN: Indiana University Press, 1982), trans. Alfred Hofstadter, p. 21.

28 Ibid. (trans. modified).

29 Marion, *Réduction et donation*, p. 110; trans., p. 70 (trans. modified).

30 Ibid., p. 99; trans., p. 63.

31 Ibid., pp. 65–118; trans., 40–76.

32 Heidegger, *Die Grundprobleme der Phänomenologie*, p. 29; trans., p. 21 (italics added by Janicaud; trans. modified).

33 Marion, *Réduction et donation*, p. 111; trans., p. 71.

34 Heidegger, *Prolegomena zur Geschichte des Zeitbegriffs*, Gesamtausgabe Band 20 (Frankfurt am Main, Vittorio Klostermann, 1979), ed. Petra Jaeger, p. 137; English trans., *History of the Concept of Time: Prolegomena* (Bloomington, IN: Indiana University Press, 1982), trans. Theodore Kisiel, p. 100.

35 Jean-François Courtine, "L'idée de la phénoménologie et la problématique de la réduction," in *Phénoménologie et métaphysique*, p. 226.

36 Marion, *Réduction et donation*, p. 102; trans., p. 65. Translator's note: Carlson translates "reprend" as "resumes," and I have followed him, though it might be argued that this translation misses the nuance and that "retakes" might be better – if it were not so awkward. As Marion sees it, Heidegger not only takes up the reduction, but both takes it back from Husserl and "retakes" it in the sense that a film director retakes a cut.

37 Ibid., p. 117; trans., p. 75.

38 Ibid., p. 305; trans., p. 204.

39 Ibid., p. 296; trans., p. 197 (trans. modified).

40 Ibid., p. 297; trans., p. 198 (trans. modified).

41 Ibid., p. 305; trans., p. 204.

42 Ibid., p. 303; trans., p. 203 (trans. modified).
43 Ibid., p. 297; trans., p. 198.
44 Ibid., p. 302; trans., p. 202.
45 Ibid., p. 301; trans., p. 201.
46 Ibid., p. 302; trans., p. 202 (trans. modified).
47 Ibid., p. 295 (citation of Deuteronomy 6.4); trans., p. 197.
48 *Revue de métaphysique et de morale* No. 1 (1991): 65.
49 Trans. See Marion, *Sur le prisme métaphysique de Descartes* (Paris: Presses Universitaires de France, 1986), pp. 293–369; English trans., *On Descartes' Metaphysical Prism* (Chicago: University of Chicago Press, 1999), trans. Jeffrey L. Koskey, pp. 277–345.
50 *Revue de métaphysique et de morale*, p. 68.
51 Ibid.
52 Ibid., p. 69.
53 Ibid., p. 67.
54 Chrétien, *La voix nue*, p. 8.
55 Ibid., p. 13.
56 Ibid., p. 60.
57 Marion, *Réduction et donation*, p. 295; trans., p. 197 (trans. modified).
58 Husserl, *Ideen zu einer reinen Phänomenologie*, §58, p. 140; trans., p. 134 (trans. modified).
59 Ibid., p. 139; trans., p. 134.
60 E. M. Cioran, *Précis de décomposition* (Paris: Gallimard, 1949), p. 196; English trans., *A Short History of Decay* (New York: Viking Press, 1975), trans. Richard Howard, p. 139 (trans. modified).

11

THE EXPERIENCE OF GOD

Kevin Hart

"Who comes after the God of metaphysics?"

"What comes after onto-theologic?"

I recognize these questions. The first recalls "*Qui vient après le sujet?*" which Jean-Luc Nancy put to French philosophers in 1986. And both obliquely recall passages of the *Critique of Pure Reason* and the *Critique of Practical Reason*. When Nancy framed his query it created a space where new thoughts could gather. Yet the questions John D. Caputo has asked seem to have been answered long ago by Kant. "Ontotheology" is the attempt to pass from the idea of a transcendent being to its reality, and it always fails. Were we to have practical reasons for presupposing that God exists, Kant says, we should determine this idea "on its transcendental side" in order to scrape away all anthropomorphisms.[1] And in the second *Critique* he shows that we have every right to grant the antecedent. It is the God who reveals himself through reason alone who comes after metaphysics.

Both questions also rehearse much of Heidegger's *Gesamtausgabe*. Poetry and thinking come after onto-theologic, some of those dark volumes whisper to one another and to us. Nevertheless, they entertain many reservations about the future and the past, for the ending of metaphysics may last as long as its entire epoch, and not everything thought or written has been simply metaphysical. Who comes after the God of metaphysics? Heidegger was less sure he could answer this. From time to time he spoke of "the last god" and "the divinities," and commended the mystical writings of Meister Eckhart and Angelus Silesius, while also encouraging Christian theologians to answer the questions themselves. As I hear them, both questions have more of a Heideggerian than a Kantian inflection, partly because in "onto-theologic" I discern more than the ontological argument, and partly because both questions are left ajar, the second more widely than the first. Because these are open questions, they have elicited diverse responses from those who have encountered Heidegger while following a philosophical or theological path.

Of these many people, from Rudolf Bultmann to Jean-Luc Marion, I take Jacques Derrida as a partner in conversation not because of any theology he has taught me but because he reads Heidegger beyond his meaning. Since onto-theologic does not form a unity on Derrida's understanding, the proposition that something might come "after" it, as Heidegger imagined at times, cannot be well-formed. One must proceed otherwise. However, when he responds to the second question it is in a style that affiliates him with Kant. A religion at the limits of reason alone, such as Derrida proposes, would have sources in faith and holiness. If holiness is the singularity of the other, as he says it is, faith is "the very experience of the non-relation or of the absolute *interruption*."[2] This seems reasonable for a "religion without religion," although I am looking for something a little richer and would therefore like to try another track leading from Heidegger.

Attempts to free theology from metaphysics are not new. In the modern period Albrecht Ritschl and Adolf von Harnack tried to theologize without metaphysics, but as Heidegger implicitly showed they could not succeed until the scope, strength and status of metaphysics were properly delineated. To do that, one must see how metaphysics "fails to think the unity of beings as such in the universal and that which is highest."[3] On Heidegger's analysis, metaphysics seeks the λόγος of beings as beings, the ὄν ἧ ὄν, in a double manner: it pursues both their universal traits, ὄν καθόλον, and their highest ground, θεῖον, which is a timeless presence. Metaphysics is therefore onto-theo-logical in character, and only when this is grasped can we understand metaphysics and what if anything comes after it. For Heidegger, metaphysics conceives being as "being present," although this notion reveals itself differently in the epochs of western history. He is plain that ontotheology emerges in philosophy, without reference to theology. Strictly speaking, one should write "onto-theio-logy," not "onto-theo-logy." Even so, he suggests, because ὄν unconcealed itself in this way it attracted Christian thinkers.

Heidegger does not offer an historically nuanced account of how theology fuses or confuses the θεῖον and θεός, and this, amongst other things, exposes him to the criticisms of theologians who wish to preserve metaphysics.[4] However, he allows two logical possibilities to follow from his description of how ὄν unconceals itself. First, one may approach being in a way that is not onto-theological. Heidegger calls this "thinking", and shows how it is practised by sages and poets; it involves a reference to the gods, as I have said, but I leave Heidegger's neo-paganism aside. Second, one may approach God, θεός, outside the sphere of the θεῖον. Before this could assist a Christian theologian, θεός would need to be redefined in order not to name the totality of the θεοί but the unique, personal God whose son was born as one of us. Taking that as done, although without distinguishing Aristotle's θεός from the ὁ θεός of the New Testament, Heidegger calls this approach "faith," and separates it from the theological appropriations of the οὐσία of the ὄν that help to make up Christendom. Therefore it seems reasonable to answer "What comes after onto-theologic?" by replying: thinking and faith. And it would seem just as sensible to answer "Who comes after the God of metaphysics?" by replying "God": not the *ens realissimum*, and not even the *ipsum esse subsistens*, for "new discriminations and differentiations" are needed.[5]

In his first years as a teacher Heidegger may have been intrigued by the lure of such fresh distinctions although he never formulated any. And after 1922, with *Die Aris-*

totles-Einleitung and its insistence on the methodological atheism of philosophy, he lost interest in exploring them. Of course, this stress on method does not stop him in 1957 from reproaching philosophy for its shabby treatment of the divinity: "The god-less thinking which must abandon the god of philosophy, god as *causa sui*, is thus perhaps closer to the divine God. Here this means only: god-less thinking is more open to Him than onto–theo–logic would like to admit."[6] This openness must have concerned him earlier, though, since in 1951 we find him toying with the idea of investigating it: "If I were to write a theology, as I am sometimes tempted to do, the word 'being' ought not to figure in it."[7] Although this remark is often taken to suggest that a Heideggerian theology would not construe God in terms of being, Heidegger does not propose organizing theology around the God beyond being. A phenomenology of the holy does not sustain his interest, either, and he quietly rejects conceiving theology as the science of God. Instead, as early as *Being and Time* (1927) he says that theology should ground itself in human relations with God. Does this mean that we begin with *fides qua* and find *fides quae* in revelation? Yes, except that Heidegger abandoned a Catholic acceptance of *fides* for a Lutheran affirmation of *fiducia* which, for him, resonates more fully with πίστις. It might seem as though Heidegger loosens theology from philosophy and courts fideism. The separation is never envisaged as complete, however. We hear in 1936 that, "*All* theology of faith is possible only on the basis of philosophy, even when it rejects philosophy as the work of the devil."[8]

Karl Barth might have partly recognised himself in the latter half of that description. The first volume of the *Church Dogmatics* had appeared in 1932, a *Glaubenstheologie* if ever there were one. Its project was to know God through experience of the word of God, and if it remains close to Anselm of Canterbury it draws from the saint's linking of faith and understanding, *fides quaerens intellectum*, not from what others have called an ontological "argument" or ontotheology.[9] For Barth, Christianity was to be presented not as a religion, in which man searches for God, but as the drama of God's quest for man. Christianity for him was a religion without religion, and his work was a theology without philosophy, one that rejected even the barest suggestion that revelation can be conditioned by an epistemology or ontology.[10] When we open Barth's prolegomenon we read, "As a theological discipline, dogmatics is the scientific [*wissenshaftliche*] test to which the Christian Church puts herself regarding the language about God which is peculiar to her."[11] The distance between Heidegger and Barth can be appreciated by recalling Heidegger's Tübingen lecture of 1927, "Phenomenology and Theology," where he argues that, unlike philosophy, theology is a positive science. Barth could agree with the first sentence: "The positive science of faith does not need philosophy for the founding and primary disclosure of its *positum*, Christianness, which founds itself in its own manner." He could never agree with the second: "The positive science of faith needs philosophy only in regard to its scientific character [*Wissenshaftlich-keit*]."[12]

Heidegger conceives faith as rebirth, and in a bold Hegelian gesture insists that the believer's pre-Christian existence is "sublated [*aufgehoben*]" when turning to Christ. One's pre-Christian existence is "existentially, ontically, overcome in faith" while remaining "ontologically included within faith-full existence" (18). A theologian speaks of the cross, grace, revelation and sin, none of which has a philosophical origin. Nevertheless, each meaning is ontologically determined and therefore rests on philosophy: "*the possible ontological corrective which can formally point out the ontic and, in particular, the pre-Christian content of basic theological concepts*"(20).

Thirty years after the Tübingen lecture, when reflecting on Hegel's *Logic* in order to adduce the onto-theo-logical character of metaphysics, Heidegger explicitly contrasts the basis of the dialectic, the *Aufhebung*, with his "step back."[13] For all that, one cannot conclude he had changed his mind concerning the priority of philosophy with respect to theology. He had not.[14] In 1928, the year after the Tübingen lecture, we find him maintaining that philosophy is not a science because it is more than a science; and in a later and more elegant formulation, philosophizing is "an extra-ordinary inquiry into the extra-ordinary."[15] Nor had Heidegger replaced the Hegelian argument with one of his own. What he had done, in 1942–3, is to show that "Hegel does not conceive experience dialectically; he thinks of the dialectic in terms of the nature of experience."[16] *Aufhebung* derives from *Erfahrung* conceived as the being of beings. If Heidegger will not endorse this Hegelian notion of experience it nonetheless remains true that experience orients his thought, early and late, even though the words it translates are seldom prominent.[17]

So one would not expect to find *Erlebnis* or *Erfahrung* when Heidegger affirms that thinking relies on hearing. He does so repeatedly. 1927: "hearing constitutes the primary and authentic way in which Dasein is open for its ownmost potentiality-for-Being"; 1933–4: "Mortals hear as those who cannot hear; their hearing is a *deaf ear* and the will not to hear;" 1951: "We have heard [*gehört*] when we *belong to* [gehören] the matter addressed"; and 1955: "Thinking is a listening [*Erhören*] that brings something to view."[18] The biblical source for this imagery is well-known; it is Galatians 3:2 where Paul affirms that grace comes "by the hearing of faith." Heidegger had lectured on Galatians in 1920–1, and over time he resets the biblical note of hearing o Λόγος in a philosophical key.[19] It is a shift from the ontic to the ontological, a doubling of being and language: "the Being (presencing) of being appears as o Λόγος as the 'Laying that gathers'."[20] One becomes a Christian by "the hearing of faith," and one becomes a theologian by also hearing the call of being. In effect, Heidegger distinguishes the good theologian, who hears twice, from the bad theologian who, mishearing two calls, receives just the one ("God is being"), or who hears the call of faith but does not ground it scientifically and consequently succumbs to fideism.

Heidegger's safeguard against fideism is therefore an ontological analysis of faith in God, not the exercise of reason and certainly not the development of a natural theology. Historical revelation remains primary, as he insists when speaking in Zurich in 1951: "I believe that being can never be thought as essence and ground of God, but that nevertheless the experience [*Erfahrung*] of God and his revelation (provided it meets humans) occurs in the dimension of being, which doesn't mean that being could be a predicate of God."[21] We may experience God in being, but the divine aseity is affirmed over claims that God is being.

What comes after onto-theologic? Heidegger's final answer to Christians is "the experience of God." It recalls his early lectures when he sought the lived experience from which theoretical knowledge arises and which is also the "primal form in the religious."[22] This is the Heidegger who, even before he foresook Catholicism, was reading scholastic philosophy with modernist sympathies. Already, in 1915, in the *Habilitationsshrift* on Duns Scotus, he argues that the original forms of cognition are not known but lived [*erlebt*], and once the anti-modernist strictures of *Lamentabili* and *Pascendi* (1907) can be left behind, he will push the argument further, drawing strength from Schleiermacher and Dilthey. Even if we underline that the older Heidegger is oriented to *Erfahrung* rather than *Erlebnis*, and is more interested in a theology of experience than experiential religion, the phrase "experience of God" remains obscure. It can be clarified a little but will never be transparent. To begin with, we can say that Christian experience is often more a process than a distinct event, that it is invariably mediated by community, symbol and tradition, and that interpretation is integral to it at every level. We might wish to set aside mystical experiences, at least in their higher reaches, for testimony about them tends to suspend God as an object of experience, while the events themselves dissolve or shatter the subject who enjoys them. Yet there there is no clear or continuous line between ordinary belief and mystical experience: God never gives himself as a positive object of experience, and no one is ever fully formed as a subject before an encounter with him. Besides, for the ordinary believer as for the mystic, Christian experience is for the most part an experience of non-experience, that is to say, of faith. To be a Christian is not to live at the limit of experience but to realise that a limit passes through all experience.

All this must be kept in mind when following Heidegger's guiding insight: to discover who comes after the God of metaphysics we must leave transcendental for revealed theology while never leaving philosophy as ground. Before going very far along this path we will surely hear Derrida raise two objections. First, he will urge that "God is the name and the element of that which makes possible an absolutely pure and absolutely self-present self-knowledge."[23] I reply that this is the God of metaphysics, and that elsewhere he allows the possibility of a non-metaphysical theology.[24] Second, he will observe that "'Experience' has always designated the relationship with a presence, whether that relationship had the form of consciousness or not."[25] If this seems to be a knock-down argument against appeals to experience we have only to keep reading. For Derrida invokes the passage from regional to "transcendental experience," although "transcendental" must be deconstructed. We are told what will follow this operation, "experience as arche-writing," though nothing more is said about it here.

Were there to be a theologian who examined transcendental experience, suitably adjusted, perhaps he or she would be able to tell us what comes after onto-theologic. There is a candidate in Karl Rahner, the most distinguished of Heidegger's students to have become a theologian. Like Heidegger, Rahner does not believe in the autonomy of theological propositions; they must be traced back to ontological structures, not for correction by philosophy but because a man must "attune his ear" to his historical being in order to hear revelation.[26] Yet where Heidegger moves away from the metaphysics of the subject in regarding these structures as modes of original temporalizing, Rahner firmly ties theology to a metaphysics of knowledge. Like Joseph Maréchal, whom he read deeply, he seeks a transcendental philosophy that sets a new point of departure for metaphysics. It will involve the unity of being and knowing, "the (conscious) being-present-to-itself of being," and this anchors him to onto-theologic rather than leads him beyond it.[27] That said, Rahner's theology is not all of a piece. When he turns to the Bible, he finds both metaphysical and non-metaphysical dimensions: "It is not so much to the Absolute and Necessary – and thus easily impersonal and abstract – that the New Testament turns its gaze in metaphysical contemplation; its eyes are upon the *personal* God in the *concreteness* of his free activity."[28]

Even so, one could rightly say that Rahner's guiding question is "Who comes to the subject?" Experience of self and God, he argues, form a unity that overcomes divisions between thinking God as speaking outside or inside consciousness.[29] Each act of knowing or willing involves a self-reflection which can be traced back to the structures of subjectivity. Now in phenomenology the question "What?" yields to the question "How?": consciousness seeks horizons of intentionality that would otherwise remain implicit. Rahner goes further than Husserl would permit, though. He is not concerned to determine the meaningfulness of phenomena but to show that the subject is always led beyond any set of objects or categories. In his early work on St. Thomas, Rahner will say that the *conversio ad phantasma*, the intellect's turn to sensibility, has always and already occurred: there is never a moment when spirit is outside our sensory engagement with the world.[30] I prefer the boldness of his later declaration, "Transcendental experience is the experience of *transcendence*."[31] Experience then is co-ordinate with transcendence in Heidegger's sense of the word although not in his sense of the world. For when Heidegger speaks of transcendence he conceives *Dasein* as thrusting into non-being, which is ontologically disclosed as anxiety. Rahner rejects this view, asserting that it is self-contradictory to claim that human openness to the world can be grounded in non-being. And so it would be, except that for Heidegger an experience of nothingness does not reveal non-being as *Abgrund* but rather the irreducible fragility and strangeness of the world to which poets testify endlessly. Rahner does not see this and, quickly seeking a theological solution to a philosophical question, says we are open to "being in an absolute sense." There is no ontologism here, for "being" is conceived as a horizon. And this horizon does not delimit a field of activity, as in Heidegger, but rather forms the limit of every experience. In recognising this limit we begin our *itinerarium mentis in deum*. It is as though the question "How?" implies "Who?"

Never apprehended as such, Rahner's God is nonetheless pre-apprehended, not by the emotions or intellect but in a vaguely formulated conviction that quotidian events are fraught with eternal significance. Each event invites us to feel around its depths and heights for what we cannot name but what in the end we must call Being, God or the Holy Mystery.[32] It is an invitation that ultimately comes from the incarnation. Although Kant and Heidegger are usually cited as the vanishing points of Rahner's philosophical world, and with good reason, a central reference here is surely Descartes. I am thinking of the assertion that "in some way I have in me the notion of the infinite earlier than the finite – to wit, the notion of God before that of myself."[33] Unlike Descartes, though, Rahner does not uncover infinity as a rationalist implant but as a perpetually withdrawing ground against which beings cut their figures.

It is tempting to object here, in the voice of Emmanuel Lévinas, who also draws deeply from Descartes, that "the relation with infinity cannot, to be sure, be stated in terms of experience [*expérience*]," for "the inexhaustible surplus of infinity overflows the actuality of consciousness" and resists "metaphors referring to light and the sensible."[34] This objection is not as straightforward as it seems, for he quickly redefines "experience" so that "the relation with infinity accomplishes experience in the fullest sense of the word."[35] True enough, Lévinas will tell us that "the infinite is the absolutely other [*autre*]" and that "God is the other [*Autre*]"; but he will also point out that "Once come into a correlation, the divinity of God dissipates."[36] And what is experience if not a correlation?

To resolve this tension in the word "experience" Lévinas distinguishes "phenomenon" from "enigma." For a phenomenologist, experience turns on the transcendental reduction: transcendence is bracketed, and what remains is a phenomenon for me. Now if, as Lévinas believes, ethics is coordinate with the transcendence of the other person, phenomenology reaches a limit in ethics. Unable to be brought into an intentional correlation with me, the other person cannot be an object of my experience. Instead, I am faced with an enigma that disturbs the settled order of my life. It is not a permanent confrontation; for in the testimony of a saying, the other person irrupts in my world as sheer transcendence while retreating into the assurance of a said. Here, saying is neither an anterior experience nor the house of being; it is the trace of the infinite that approaches, never arrives, but summons me, in an unthematic manner, to responsibility. The trace signifies "beyond being," not in the Platonic sense, which calls for a negative theology, but beyond the metaphysics of knowledge implied by the transcendental reduction. "Beyond," here, indicates an immemorial past: the other is always and already within me, as a trace, imposing a meaning – responsibility for the other – that cannot be reduced to either knowing or being.

For Lévinas, "experience of God" as the expression tends to be used makes no sense because, as Kant showed, "God" cannot be synthesized by the categories of the understanding. Yet the expression signifies all the same. God stymies all correlation between me and the other person, while declining to enter into a correlation himself. I encounter God in a relation with infinity, a "relation without relation," though only as a disturbance in immanence which awakens in me responsibility for the other person. Since the deity does not reveal himself in the present, and my responsibility for the other person derives from a past that was never present, it seems that Lévinas has disclosed what comes after onto-theologic: a religion at the limits of ethics alone.

Attractive as this view of religion might seem, especially to anyone sympathetic to the Kantian tradition, I would like to sound a note of caution. In a lucid and powerful essay, "God and Philosophy," Lévinas says, "God is not simply the 'first other,' or the 'other par excellence,' or the 'absolutely other,' but other than the other, other otherwise, and other with an alterity prior to the alterity of the other, prior to the ethical obligation to the other and different from every neighbor, transcendent to the point of absence, to the point of his possible confusion with the agitation of the *there is* [il y a]."[37] Lévinas regards this "possible confusion" of God with indeterminate being as an ambiguity of nobility and glory. This may be acceptable for ethics; it is not for theology. The confusion arises for Lévinas because his ethics requires an absolute privilege for transcendence, and because both God and the *il y a* are transcendent. It leaves us with an ethics which is based on responsibility but which does not allow us to respond to nature, let alone take responsibility for using and abusing it. At this juncture one longs for a theology in which God's transcendence does not annul his immanence, in which the difference of grace and nature is understood by way of "the radical unity of God's free self-communication as love."[38] The mature Christian concept of God "makes a radical distinction between God and the world," Rahner concedes, yet "God himself is still the very core of the world's reality and the world is truly the fate of God himself."[39] It is what we need. And so without forgetting Lévinas we return to Rahner.

What if infinity interrupted me in another manner, by summoning me through my own deeds endlessly to transcend myself? This is the import of "transcendental experience." Certainly one may object to Rahner's model of the human subject. One can quote William James scolding rationalists for treating trans-empirical conjunctive relations "as being true in some supernal way, as if the unity of things and their variety belonged to different orders of truth and vitality altogether."[40] Or one can quote Walter Benjamin, correcting Kant by way of insisting on the need for a transcendental consciousness "stripped of everything subjective" in order to make "religious experience [Erfahrung] logically possible."[41] Or one can cite Johann Baptist Metz, himself seeking a way beyond onto-theologic by way of "political theology," and looking askance at the individualism and subjectivism of Rahner's anthropology. True enough, Rahner's theology presupposes a human subject; but it is not a pre-formed self. When he writes of the unity – rather than the identity – of experience of self and experience of God, he does so in order to indicate that the subject is not constituted before experience but is formed in its openness to experience. To begin to meet the objections of Benjamin and Metz, Rahner would have to go further and show that his subject is in fact linked to transcendental and material communities. At any rate, the infinite for Rahner both forms and exceeds the subject while testifying to an exteriority, although his infinite is not "beyond being."

Apart from that final point, there is one other sharp difference between Lévinas and Rahner. Lévinas regards the interruption of transcendence as exclusively ethical. It is not simply that his description of "the coming of God to mind" does not presume a theology but that he restricts God's activity in the world.[42] God is not allowed to disclose himself, even invisibly, as creator: all theology of nature is bypassed in the same step that leaves natural theology behind. Similarly, God is not allowed to manifest himself in positive revelation: humanism, even if it is the humanism of the other man, is elevated so high that one cannot see God. For Rahner, however, while God is transcendentally given in the love of one's neighbor, this gift is twinned with grace, and grace is dialectically involved with creation.[43] This transcendental experience fits exquisitely with positive revelation for Christians, while for others it fits less well but well enough to allow the possibility of salvation.

A Heideggerian might condemn Rahner as a bad theologian because he confuses the calls of being and faith and concludes that God is being. Were Rahner to argue only that the mind is structurally open to being, the claim that the absolute horizon of being is what we call God would be a version of St. Anselm's first statement of the ontological argument in which there is no appeal to experience.[44] Yet Rahner also maintains that the mind is never merely natural; its transcendentality is always elevated by grace. This gives him the right to call the absolute horizon of being "God" but makes his theology an account of Christian, not human, experience. Of course, there is one sure way in which Rahner can protect his theology of experience, and that is by calling all humans either Christians or "anonymous Christians." And to the consternation of some readers this is precisely what he does. Hans Urs von Balthasar for one is not sympathetic to this theology of religions, not least of all because the experience he values is a person's "act of entering into the Son of God" and not his passage "into his highest and best possibilities."[45] He maintains that Rahner's heavy accent on anonymous Christians devalues any theology of the cross that he might propose.[46] This slides too quickly over Rahner's theology of death for my liking, while overlooking his argument that our experience of the Spirit and our participation in Jesus's death are one and the same.[47]

Be that as it may, the doctrine of anonymous Christians exposes Rahner to the question, "Why then is the world not better than it is?" which he never answers convincingly at the deepest and most demanding level of the heart. To approach this level, we need to ponder the conception of transcendental experience as preapprehension of a horizon. That it is *Vorgriff*, a reaching out without assurance, not *Vorwissen*, a fore-knowing, is important, especially since Rahner's metaphysics of knowledge relies on a deep unity of being and knowing. However, *Vorgriff* is a consequence of reflection: we realise unthematically that our questions about the world presuppose an absolute horizon of being. That our questions can be answered is presumed by Rahner, as is that the question shapes what can count as an answer.

On Rahner's argument, the experience of God is a doubling of categorical and transcendental revelation. Our questions, prompted by transcendental experience, are answered, if not fully, then as fully as we may hope for, by the word of God. The experience of God is underwritten by unity. Now Rahner is careful to speak here of unity not identity in order to allow some interplay between the categorical and the transcendental. Even so, unity restricts the role that experience can play in his theology of experience. It presumes a fundamentally untroubled passage from the transcendental to the categorical, whereas this passage is precisely an *experience*: an exposure to the revelation of divine love that may be at odds with human love. Rahner tells us that we transcendentally experience God at the limit of human events, yet he fails to think "limit" with the kind of rigor that Hegel has made obligatory.[48] For a limit is both within and without an event, and its uncertain status requires us to think "experience of God" as a flaring of what is outside human understanding as well as within it. Divine love may confirm my erotic and friendly relations with others; also, though, it may grant me unmerited forgiveness or ask me to accept unmerited suffering. In construing not just transcendental experience but God himself as horizon, Rahner undervalues the verticality of the divine. This is not a matter of God's distance or closeness but of his surprise: "For my thoughts are not your thoughts, neither are your ways my ways, saith the Lord" (Isaiah 55:8). To conceive transcendental experience as *Vorgriff* without attending to the nature of a limit is to downplay the possibility that God can interrupt life absolutely; it is to confuse the horizon that renders revelation possible with the horizon of expectation. If the suffering, death and resurrection of Jesus constitute God's fullest answer to our most searching questions, we must admit that our questions about the world have been badly posed. For who could conceive *that* answer to any human question?

I turn to a quite different theological extension of Heidegger, one that derives from his later thought, avers not to be in fee to metaphysics, and that devotes itself to revelation as event. Eberhard Jüngel, the theologian I have in mind, is a sympathetic reader of Lévinas, even if he overstates things when proposing that for the Frenchman revelation is a predicate of interruption. Not so: the trace is the passing of God in withdrawal, not a self-giving of the divinity. Yet there is no doubt that for Jüngel interruption is a predicate of revelation.[49] Let us enter his meditation on this theme in midstream: "In view of the possibility of nonbeing, man has a qualitatively new experience with his being. I call it *an experience with experience* [*eine Erfahrung mit der Erfahrung*] because in it not only every experience already had, but experience itself is experienced anew." This "experience with experience" is profoundly ambiguous, for it "can take shape as *anxiety*," an insight prized "from Schelling to Heidegger," or it can "take shape as gratitude" that being is preserved from nonbeing.[50] To decide in favour of gratitude rather than anxiety, Jüngel tells us, "is possible only as the result of an event which is called in theology *the revelation of God*."[51] Jüngel is plainly casting the Heidegger of "What is Metaphysics?" as the enemy here, much as Rahner does, although it is worth noting at the outset that Jüngel's expression resembles a phrase that Heidegger valued as a young man. In 1919 the *Privatdozent* sought a pretheoretical science of experience. His quest was for a phenomenological reduction that, unlike Husserl's, would not objectify experience; it would be an "experience of experience" [*Erleben des Erlebens*] that occurs factically and works hermeneutically, while resisting any formulation as a theoretical principle of principles.[52]

It might seem that we could measure the distance between Jüngel and Heidegger by charting the differences between *Erlebnis* and *Erfahrung*. This is also a way of separating the younger from the older Heidegger. Where the former was drawn, under the influence of Dilthey, to conceive "to experience" [*Erleben*] as a reference of "life and lived experience back to the 'I'," the latter rejected the metaphysics of the subject implied there and preferred to think of "to experience" [*Erfahren*] as "to be under-way."[53] Another way of measuring the distance would be to span the shift from immanentism to extrinsicism. For Jüngel, like the older Heidegger, is a theologian of revelation. Perhaps the older Heidegger would have sympathized with Jüngel when he writes of faith as "an incomparably new experience, one which fundamentally ruptures the series of worldly experiences." What makes this experience with experience "new," now and forever, is that it is "an experience of God."[54] Experience is figured wholly in exterior terms: "only the speaking God himself can say what the word 'God' should provide us to think about."[55]

Like Barth, Jüngel wishes to distance himself from all correlational theology so that only God determines the meaning of the word "God." No doubt about it, this is a theology that takes verticality seriously, more seriously than it takes biblical criticism. The liberal Christian confesses that God has spoken but that he has spoken decisively in history, as man, and from the very beginning his words have been interpreted by men who were far from divine. Revelation may be singular, and may call us in our deepest recesses as nothing else can; but it is also iterable, and its repetitions produce differ-ences. Were this not so, "word of God" could not mean Jesus Christ, scripture and preaching as Barth and Jüngel assume it does. Indeed, without evangelization it would be impossible for someone who has felt the fragility of existence to correlate this experience with the God disclosed in Jesus. I wonder also about the scope of this correlation, since not all religions figure the void as German philosophers have done. And I wonder about the experience itself, whether the choice between anxiety and gratitude is so clear cut, or should be presented so simply within a thematics of choice. Meanwhile, for someone who has grown up in Christendom, there is also the question of hearing that needs to be considered. Jüngel tells us that "in the person Jesus is revealed what God as the one who speaks is all about." This must be the case for any Christian, one would think, yet a closer inspection would make us pause at the expression "the one who speaks."

In building a bridge from exegesis to dogmatics, Jüngel assumes there is a unified kerygma, but if modern biblical scholarship tells us one thing it is that the New Testament is a collection of kerygmata.[56] Jüngel assumes a unity because, like the older Heidegger, he insists that language is the event of being. The parables, for example, do not tell us about the Kingdom so much as "bring the Kingdom of God to speech."[57] I would like to suggest a different approach, one that confirms Lévinas's unease with language as the house of being, namely that a parable is a saying. It disrupts the order of impersonal being, and has an eerie ability to keep doing so because, unlike much biblical writing, a parable can unsay itself. The Kingdom does not come to speech in a parable. On the contrary, in addressing me – or, rather, in allowing myself to be addressed by the Jesus who speaks of a fig tree or a prodigal son – the parable provokes me to change my life. I am called to bring about the Kingdom in and through my daily actions in the world. The Kingdom is not a ground, it is a possibility: the possibility of the impossible.

For Jüngel, God is not subject to being because he disposes both being and nonbeing and therefore has no ground: aseity preceeds ontology. God must be distinguished from the *ens necessarium* of metaphysics, who is culturally dead, yet to the extent that theologians are constrained to speak of being we must use metaphysics without allowing it to determine our relation with God: first philosophy as the science of ὄν καθόλου, not the θεῖον. Is this what comes after onto-theologic? Yes, Jüngel tells us, with the condition that, ὁ θεός is rendered thinkable only by an ontological death: the crucified God. "For responsible Christian usage of the word 'God', the Crucified One is virtually the real definition of what is meant with the word 'God'."[58] Rather than incline me to agree with Jüngel, the words "virtually" and "real" give me pause. There can be a death of Jesus only because he was born and preached the Kingdom, and there can be a resurrection only because there was an execution. Whether one adopts a high or a low Christology, the three events of incarnation, crucifixion and resurrection form the one story, and Christianity is reduced whenever one event is valued above the others. More generally, and here I am in sympathy with Rahner, creation and salvation mesh in an open dialectic that involves both history and nature.

And yet the cross changes the very nature of what our experience of God can be. Jüngel's former colleague at Tübingen, Ingolf Dalferth, sees this clearly when distinguishing "the experience of the word of God *through* Jesus," as in the telling of the parables, from "the experience of Jesus *as* word of God," which became possible after the crucifixion. In Dalferth's terms, "The possibility of the primary reception of faith is thus crucially linked with the *absence* of Jesus."[59] This important insight is clouded, I think, when Dalferth introduces the appearances of the resurrected Christ as the beginning of the experience of the word of God. On the contrary, I would suggest, the experience of the word of God commences only when nothing is visible. If I may adopt one of Jean-Luc Marion's expressions without subscribing to all that he makes of it, the word of God is a "saturated phenomenon," for here intuition exceeds intentional correlation: no horizon can contain it, no subject can constitute its meaning.[60] Were there to be a horizon in which the word of God could appear, the divinity would become an object. At the same time, were there to be no horizon, not even one that is augmented, contested or divided, no revelation could manifest itself. Marion speaks of being dazzled by a saturated phenomenon, and regards Christ as the saturated phenomenon *par excellence*.[61] I would prefer "disturbed" to "dazzled." For the word of God is experienced as a disruption in our everyday lives; it refigures the subject of experience and what this subject will value in experience. Nothing is given to us in an experience of God except a calling forth of love and a desire for God. We reflect on what this means for our ordinary actions in fear and trembling.

In trying to understand the expression "experience of God" as what might come after onto-theologic one runs into difficulties when conceiving God by way of the horizontal or the vertical. That theologians weight the expression toward "God" is understandable, although even the most anthropologically grounded of them tends not to realize that "experience," *Erfahrung*, requires both. There is no experience without anticipation or model, and no experience without the possibility of interruption, surprise or danger. When the two arrange themselves in the negative form of an aporia, we have what Derrida imagined when he wrote of "experience as arche-writing"; not an experience of the trace but the trace passing through experience. Simply by attending to "experience," then, the experience of God would involve both the horizontal and the vertical. Yet we are talking of the God whose love can never form a horizon, however generously conceived, because that love fractures all horizons. It is tempting to speak of divine love as a horizon posited immemorially although freshly discovered each time one truly encounters God in nature, sacrament or scripture.[62] But this could never be a horizon as such, for any relation with the divine presumes the possibility of absolute interruption. The experience of God would therefore occur in a divided present: the already (for God has spoken in history) being taken in tandem with the not yet (for God is unseen and unforeseen: *deus absconditus* in nature, eschatalogical in history). Even in the life of faith which, as I have said, is an experience of non-experience, no one knows if he or she is truly imitating Christ. The *imitatio Christi* does not turn on Jesus as example but as exemplary, and consequently "to be Christian" is a verbal form that can be conjugated only in the future anterior. If this causes anxiety, as it must, even in a life of radical trust in God, the unease must be lived with humility, not sorrow.

    Those who dare to call ourselves Christians could dub this encounter with aporia an experience of the word of God, although I am tempted to recast the venerable expression and talk of the saying of God, simply to underline the fact that Christian experience involves exposure, promise, hope and testimony. Unsaying is a phase of this saying, Derrida will remind me, and I can only agree: were it not so Christianity would be a settled question and not, as it is, an induction into a mystery that exceeds metaphysics. Whatever else it is, the experience of God is always an experience of the saying of God: disturbance and irruption, to be sure, but also the possibility of a response to abandonment and vulnerability.

Notes

I wish to thank Tony Kelly and Mark C. Taylor for their comments on an earlier version of this essay.

1   Immanuel Kant, *Critique of Pure Reason*, trans. and ed. Paul Guyer and Allen W. Wood, The Cambridge Edition of the Works of Immanuel Kant (Cambridge: Cambridge University Press, 1998), 584 (A632/B660), 588 (A639/B667).

2   Jacques Derrida, "Foi et savoir: Les deux sources de la 'religion' aux limites de la simple raison," in *La Religion*, sous la direction de Jacques Derrida et Gianni Vattimo (Paris: Éditions du Seuil, 1996), pp. 84–5.

3   Martin Heidegger, "The Onto-Theo-Logical Constitution of Metaphysics," *Identity and Difference*, trans. and introd. Joan Stambaugh (New York: Harper and Row, 1969), p. 61.

4   See, for example, Jürgen Moltmann, *The Crucified God: The Cross of Christ as the Foundation and Criticism of Christian Theology*, trans. R. A. Wilson and John Bowden (London: SCM Press, 1973), pp. 216–19, and Wolfhart Pannenberg, *Metaphysics and the Idea of God*, trans. Philip Clayton (Grand Rapids, MI: William B. Eerdmans, 1990), pp. 8–14. While Moltmann is right to say that a theology without philosophy would be intellectually isolated, he misses the point that metaphysical theology, in Heidegger's sense of "metaphysics," involves a fundamental misorientation of theology. Pannenberg's critique of Heidegger remains unconvincing because he fails to recognize the distinction between θεῖον and θεός.

5   Heidegger, "Zürcher Seminar," *Gesamtausgabe*, 15 (Frankfurt am Main: Vittorio Klostermann, 1986), p. 437.

6   Heidegger, "The Onto-Theo-Logical Constitution of Metaphysics," 72.

7   Heidegger, "Zürcher Seminar," 437.

8   Heidegger, *Schelling's Treatise on the Essence of Human Freedom*, trans. Joan Stambaugh (Athens: Ohio University Press, 1985), p. 51. My emphasis.

9   See Karl Barth, *Anselm: Fides Quaerens Intellectum* (London: SCM Press, 1960). It should be added that although Barth sought to avoid all philosophical grounding, there are traces of Hegel in his writings, early and late.

10 See, for example, Barth, *Church Dogmatics* II: 1, ed. G. W. Bromiley and T. F. Torrance (Edinburgh: T. and T. Clark, 1957), p. 44. Barth criticises Heidegger in *Church Dogmatics* III: 3, trans. G. W. Bromiley and T. F. Torrance (Edinburgh: T. and T. Clark, 1960), pp. 334–49. Although Christianity, for Barth, is a "religion without religion" it is not what Marcel Gauchet calls "a religion for departing from religion." Barth would not agree with Gauchet that "What is currently alive in the Christian faith has no connection with the circumstances surrounding its birth, the conditions that allowed it to assert itself and develop, or the role through which its major themes and variations have been played out," Gauchet, *The Disenchantment of the World: A Political History of Religion*, trans. Oscar Burge, foreword Charles Taylor (Princeton: Princeton University Press, 1997), p. 4.

11 Barth, *Church Dogmatics* I:1, trans. G. T. Thomson (Edinburgh: T. and T. Clark, 1936), p. 1.

172   KEVIN HART

12 Heidegger, "Phenomenology and Theology," in *The Piety of Thinking*, trans., notes and commentary James G. Hart and John C. Maraldo (Bloomington: Indiana University Press, 1976), p. 17. It must be added that Barth never doubted that reason is presupposed by any and all theology. What he objected to, right to the end of his writing life, are attempts to relate God to man rather than man to God. The latter results in proper theology, he thought, while the former holds theology captive to an ontology or anthropology. See his comments in *Evangelical Theology: An Introduction*, trans. Grover Foley (London: Fontana, 1965), pp. 13–14.

13 Heidegger, "The Onto-Theo-Logical Constitution of Metaphysics," p. 49.

14 See, for example, *What is Called Thinking?*, trans. and introd. J. Glenn Gray (New York: Harper Colophon, 1968), p. 131.

15 See Heidegger, *Einleitung in die Philosophie*, § 5, *Gesamtausgabe*, 27 (Frankfurt am Main: Vittorio Klostermann, 1996), *An Introduction to Metaphysics*, trans. Ralph Manheim (New York: Anchor Books, 1961), p. 11.

16 Heidegger, *Hegel's Concept of Experience*, no trans. detailed (San Francisco: Harper and Row, 1985), p. 119. In his 1942–3 lecture course on Parmenides Heidegger speaks of experience, *Erfahrung*, as fundamental. He observes in an addendum, "experience is in essence the suffering in which the essential otherness of beings reveals itself in opposition to the tried and usual," *Parmenides*, trans. André Schuwer and Richard Rojcewicz (Bloomington: Indiana University Press, 1992), pp. 166–7.

17 An exception is the *Beiträge* which Heidegger did not publish in his lifetime. See *Contributions to Philosophy (From Enowning)*, trans. Parvis Emad and Kenneth Maly (Bloomington: Indiana University Press, 1999), esp. section II.

18 Heidegger, *Being and Time*, p. 206; *Hölderlins Hymnnen 'Germanien' und 'Der Rhein'*, *Gesamtausgabe*, 39 (Frankfurt am Main: Vittorio Klostermann, 1980), p. 200; "Logos" in *Early Greek Thinking*, trans. David Farrell Krell and Frank A. Capuzzi (San Francisco: Harper and Row, 1975), p. 66; *The Principle of Reason*, trans. Reginald Lilly (Bloomington: Indiana University Press, 1991), p. 47.

19 See Heidegger, *Einleitung in die Phänomenologie der Religion*, §§ 14–22, in *Phänomenologie des Religiösen hebens*, *Gesamtausgabe*, 60 (Frankfurt am Main: Vittorio Klostermann, 1995).

20 Heidegger, "Logos," p. 76.

21 Heidegger, "Zürcher Seminar," p. 437.

22 Heidegger, *Zur Bestimmung der Philosophie*, *Gesamtausgabe* 56/57 (Frankfurt am Main: Vittorio Klostermann, 1987), p. 212.

23 Derrida, *Of Grammatology*, trans. Gayatri Chakravorty Spivak (Baltimore: The Johns Hopkins University Press, 1976), p. 98.

24 See my *The Trespass of the Sign: Deconstruction, Theology and Philosophy*, rev. edn. (New York: Fordham University Press, 2000).

25 Derrida, *Of Grammatology*, p. 60.

26 Rahner, *Hearers of the Word*, trans. Michael Richards (New York: Herder and Herder, 1969), p. 111. Also see p. 160.

27 Rahner, *Hearers of the Word*, pp. 39–40.

28 Rahner, *Theological Investigations*, I, trans. and introd. Cornelius Ernst, OP (London: Darton, Longman and Todd, 1961), p. 114.

29 In theological jargon, the distinction is between "extrinsicism" and "immanentism." See Rahner, "Experience of Self and Experience of God," *Theological Investigations*, XIII, trans. David Bourke (London: Darton, Longman and Todd, 1975).

30 See Rahner, *Spirit in the World*, trans. William Dysch, SJ (Montreal: Palm, 1968), pp. 66, 238.

31 Rahner, *Foundations of Christian Faith: An Introduction to the Idea of Christianity*, trans. William V. Dych (New York: The Seabury Press, 1978), p. 20.

32 See Rahner, "The Concept of Mystery in Catholic Theology," *Theological Investigations*, IV, trans. Kevin Smyth (London: Darton, Longman and Todd, 1982), p. 50.

33 Elizabeth S. Haldane and G. R. T. Ross, eds., *The Philosophical Works of Descartes*, 2 vols (Cambridge: Cambridge University Press, 1972), I, p. 166.

34 Emmanuel Lévinas, *Totality and Infinity: An Essay on Exteriority*, trans. Alphonso Lingis (The Hague: Martinus Nijhoff, 1979), pp. 25, 207.

35 Lévinas, *Totality and Infinity*, p. 25.

36 Lévinas, *Totality and Infinity*, pp. 49, 211; *Collected Philosophical Papers*, trans. Alphonso Lingis (The Hague: Martinus Nijhoff, 1987), p. 62.

37 See Lévinas, *Of God Who Comes to Mind*, trans. Bettina Bergo (Stanford: Stanford University Press, 1998), p. 69.

38 Rahner, "Grace," *Sacramentum Mundi: An Encyclopedia of Theology*, ed. Karl Rahner *et al.*, trans. W. J. O'Hara, 6 vols (New York: Herder and Herder, 1968), II, p. 417.

39 Rahner, "The Specific Character of the Christian Concept of God," *Theological Investigations*, XXI, trans. Hugh M. Riley (London: Darton, Longman and Todd, 1988), p. 191.

40 William James, *Essays in Radical Empiricism* (London: Longmans, Green, and Co., 1912), p. 44.

41 Walter Benjamin, "The Coming Philosophy," in *Selected Writings*, Vol. I: 1913–1926, ed. Marcus Bullock and Michael W. Jennings (Cambridge, MA: Harvard University Press, 1996), pp. 104–5.

42 Lévinas, *Of God Who Comes to Mind*, p. ix.

43 See, for example, Rahner, *The Love of Jesus and the Love of Neighbour*, trans. Robert Barr (Middlegreen: St Paul, 1983), p. 71–2.

44 Anselm stated the ontological argument in two forms. As Iris Murdoch clearly shows, in its second form we have "a metaphysical argument which is also an appeal to experience ... We have instinctive faith in God, and also conceive of him by looking at the world; and when we consider what we conceive of we understand that it exists necessarily and not contingently," *Metaphysics as a Guide to Morals* (London: Chatto and Windus, 1992), pp. 295–6.

45 Hans Urs von Balthasar, *The Glory of the Lord: A Theological Aesthetics*, vol. I: *Seeing the Form*, trans. Erasmo Leiva-Merikakis, ed. Joseph Fession SJ and John Riches (San Francisco: Ignatius Press, 1982), p. 222. Also see "Experience God?," in *New Elucidations*, trans. Mary Theresilde Skerry (San Francisco: Ignatius Press, 1986).

46 Von Balthasar, *The Moment of Christian Witness*, trans. Richard Beckley (San Francisco: Ignatius Press, 1994), p. 109.

47 See Rahner, "Experience of the Holy Spirit," *Theological Investigations*, XVIII, trans. Edward Quinn (London: Darton, Longman and Todd, 1983), pp. 206–7.

48 See G. W. F. Hegel, *Science of Logic*, trans. A. V. Miller, foreword J. N. Findlay (London: George Allen and Unwin, 1969), pp. 127–9.

49 Eberhard Jüngel, *Theological Essays*, II, ed. and introd. J. B. Webster, trans. Arnold Neufeldt-Fast and J. B. Webster (Edinburgh: T. and T. Clark, 1995), p. 91.

50 Jüngel, *God as the Mystery of the World: On the Foundation of the Theology of the Crucified One in the Dispute between Theism and Atheism*, trans. Darrell L. Guder (Grand Rapids, MI: William B. Eerdmans, 1983), p. 32. The formulation survives Heidegger. See, for example, Jean-Luc Nancy's observation that "the 'foundation of foundation' is experience itself: experience does not experience anything, but it experiences the *nothing* as the real that it tests *and* as the stroke of luck it offers ... ," *The Experience of Freedom*, trans. Bridget McDonald and foreword by Peter Fenves (Stanford: Stanford University Press, 1993), p. 86.

51 Jüngel, *God as the Mystery of the World*, p. 33.
52 Heidegger, *Zur Bestimmung der Philosophie*, p. 117. I am indebted to Theodore Kisiel's analysis of the *Kriegnotsemester* of 1919 in *The Genesis of Heidegger's "Being and Time"* (Los Angeles: University of California Press, 1993).
53 Heidegger, *On the Way to Language*, trans. Peter D. Hertz (New York: Harper and Row, 1971), pp. 35, 74.
54 Jüngel, "'My Theology' – A Short Summary," *Theological Essays*, II, p. 5.
55 Jüngel, *God as the Mystery of the World*, p. 13.
56 See, for example, Ernst Käsemann, "The Canon of the New Testament and the Unity of the Church," in his *Essays on New Testament Themes*, trans. W. J. Montague (London: SCM Press, 1964).
57 Jüngel, *Paulus und Jesus. Eine Untersuchung zur Präziserung der Frage nach dem Ursprung der Christologie* (Tübingen: J. C. B. Mohr, 1962), p. 135.
58 Jüngel, *God as the Mystery of the World*, p. 13.
59 I. U. Dalferth, "Christian Discourse and the Paradigmatic Christian Experience: An Essay in Hermeneutics," *New Studies in Theology*, I, ed. Stephen Sykes and Derek Holmes (London: Duckworth, 1980), p. 65.
60 See Jean-Luc Marion, *Étant donné: Essai d'une phénoménologie de la donation* (Paris: PUF, 1997), § 20.
61 Marion, *Étant donné*, § 24.
62 See, for example, Bernard J. F. Lonergan, *Method in Theology* (London: Darton, Longman and Todd, 1972), p. 106.

12

ESCHATOLOGY OF THE POSSIBLE GOD

Richard Kearney

God is not but may be. This was the conclusion of my first book, *Poétique du Possible*, published in Paris in 1984. It was, at the time, a position that set me apart from atheists, for being too theistic, and from theists, for being too atheistic. In fact, my then head of department at University College Dublin (who subsequently became Archbishop of Dublin) called me into his office and said that he felt like saying to me what Yahweh said to Adam after the Fall – "where are you?" To be frank, some sixteen years later I still don't know quite where I am. But I do stand over my position that an eschatological notion of the possible can blaze trails to a new understanding of God in our time. By way of trying to consolidate this contention here I will outline what I believe to be four crucial if preparatory approaches in twentieth-century thought to what I call the "possible God": (1) teleological (Husserl); (2) dialectical (Bloch); (3) ontological (Heidegger); and (4) deconstructive (Derrida). I will conclude by suggesting that it is in fact a new eschatological rethinking of God which offers an account most consistent with the Messianic promise of theism.

In traditional metaphysics, the category of the possible was understood as a dimension of being pre-contained within reality. Possibility was conceived as a latency or lack to be realized into act. It was a material striving towards fulfillment. Aristotle called this *dunamis* (*Meta* 9.8.1059); Aquinas and the scholastics called it *potentia*. But what all agreed was that whatever you called it, God didn't have it. The Aristotelian and medieval deity was deemed to be a self-causing, self-thinking Act lacking nothing and so possessing no "potencies" which might later be realized in time. Aquinas states this canonical position succinctly: "God is pure act without any potentiality whatsover" (*Deus est actus purus non habens aliquid de potentialitate. Summa Theologica*, I pars. Q.3–4).

A second influential concept of possibility was that of intellectual representation. The rationalists and idealists referred to this as *possibilitas*. (A famous example of this position was Leibniz's theory of "possible worlds.") But whether this logical category of represented possibility was understood from a metaphysical or nominalist viewpoint, it was invariably contrasted with various notions of "reality." And since almost every theistic metaphysics considered God to be the Supreme Reality, it would have been little less than blasphemy to describe the divine in terms of the merely "possible." Possibility, as a category of modal logic, fell far short of a true grasp of God.

A third metaphysical approach which exerted a profound influence on our Western understanding of the possible is that of evolutionist thought. This is no doubt best outlined by Bergson in the "The Possible and the Real" (1930), a seminal text for the notion of God as "Process" (a notion also advanced by thinkers like Whitehead and Hartshorne).[1] What this vitalist model argued was that the possible is the *retrospective* result of reality as it invents and creates itself. The possible doesn't pre-exist the real in any ontological sense; it post-exists it as precisely that which can be recognized as a possibility *after the event*. The possible exists therefore only as a retroactive image which spirit projects backwards into the past once it has been historically realized! "According as reality creates itself, new and unpredictable, its image reflects itself behind it into an indefinite past," writes Bergson. "The possible is therefore the mirage of the present in the past."[2]

In all three approaches – realist, representationalist and evolutionist – the possible is thought of as a sub-category of the real (understood as substance, being, act, existence or history). In no way, according to such readings, could the possible be construed as the royal road to a new understanding of the divine. Now it is just this metaphysical opposition between the divinely real and the non-divinely possible that I want to challenge here: first, by rehearsing a number of pioneering modern attempts to revise this opposition – Husserl, Heidegger, Bloch and Derrida; and, second, by sketching out a new eschatological category of the possible which invites us to consider God in a very different fashion (e.g., as *posse* rather than *esse*).

1   Teleological notion of the Possible (Edmund Husserl)

In his last work, *The Crisis of Transcendental Phenomenology and European Science* (1934–8), Edmund Husserl speaks of the ultimate aim of western philosophy as a teleological Idea of reason. This telos plays the role of a Kantian limit-Idea which surpasses the categorial intuition of essences towards an horizon of *pure possibility*.[3] As such, it signals a radical openness to the on-going perfectioning – or as the phenomenologists would say "filling-out" – of meaning. It recognizes the possible as the *future of meaning*.

This Husserlian insistence on the futurity of the possible was to inaugurate a whole series of subsequent studies by phenomenologists into the temporal and historical character of consciousness. Heidegger would talk of the "pre-understanding" of Dasein, Lévinas of the "otherness" of time, Sartre of our being-towards-our-possibles, and Derrida of *différance*. These are various names for the temporalizing transcending of the present towards the possible.

Husserl had already touched on this protentive-projective character of our intentional possibilities in various early works – e.g., volume 6 of the *Logical Investigations* and section 129 of *Ideas* – but it was not until *The Crisis*, and especially Appendix 13, that Husserl tackled the issue of teleological possibility in both its theoretical and ethical aspects. Identifying philosophy as the conscience of a universal humanity, Husserl declared that "to be human is to have a teleological meaning, to have a duty-to-be."[4] Both our theoretical and ethical consciousness, Husserl insists, are structured according to the teleological possibility of an Idea which is unconditioned and therefore surpasses any determined intuitive fulness (or presence) we may presume to have. Any attempt by our consciousness to grasp the telos as a fixed or complete object fails, for the goal of meaning is forever escaping us, *immer wieder*. The telos is always *beyond* us.

In a sense, Husserl is rehearsing here Kant's claim, in his critique of transcendental illusion, that the highest goal of all human endeavour is the ultimate Good – *die Absichte aufs hochste Gut*.[5] This teleological Good is a "postulate of reason" which expresses itself as a hope in the order of things to come – a hope which is the philosophical equivalent of a "God resurrected from the dead."[6] For both Husserl and Kant such a rational project takes the form of a practical aim (*Absicht*) which transcends all modes of cognitive intuition, manifesting itself instead as a perpetual extension and expansion (*Erweiterung und Zuwachs*) of our experience in the direction of a higher goal.[7] The teleological Good is what Kant, in the third formulation of the categorial imperative in *Foundations of a Metaphysics of Morals*, calls the "possible kingdom of ends." But where Kant crosses over from a strictly philosophical notion of a teleological Good to a Christian notion of a resurrected God (albeit within the limits of reason), Husserl is more reserved – at least up until his final Manuscripts.

Husserl might also be said to differ from Kant in seeing the ultimate telos of Reason as motivating an *historical* striving, that is, a long and progressive trajectory leading from the origin of geometry and mathematics in the ancient Greeks to Newton and Gallileo, right up to the transcendental turn in the modern philosophy of Descartes and Kant culminating in phenomenology.[8] For Husserl the perfectioning of philosophical reason is a teleological vocation for all humans, from the genesis of human reason to its end. Indeed from the time he wrote *The Crisis*, a latent Hegelianism appears to modify Husserl's Kantian transcendentalism: "We may understand that everywhere limit-forms are announcing themselves," he now claims, "emerging from the praxis of conceivable perfectioning, and towards which are tending each series of perfectionings, as towards an invariant and inaccessible pole."[9]

This teleological Idea which governs the history of our intellectual-practical endeavors is not subject to intuitive realization (sensible or categorial). It remains a *possibility* which only manifests itself to us in the symbolic mode of the "as-if." Qua possibility, the Idea announces itself without ever actually appearing in the presence of a present. Derrida offers the following illuminating gloss on Husserl's retrieval of the Kantian notion of teleological Idea: "The Idea in the Kantian sense of the regulating pole of every infinite task, assumes diverse but always analogous and decisive functions at various points in Husserl's itinerary . . . However, while granting a growing attention to what it conditions, Husserl never made the Idea itself into the theme of a phenomenological account."[10] The ultimate possibility of Husserl's teleology of reason remains irreducible to a finite object or determinate essence; but this does not prevent it from serving as both origin (*Urstiftung*) and end (*Endstiftung*) of all our intellectual-practical labors.

No matter how much Husserl strives to elucidate this teleological possibility in the *Crisis* or elsewhere (e.g., *Ideas* para 143 or *Formal and Transcendental Logic* para 16), he never manages to offer a full phenomenological description. The teleological possible eludes every knowledge we can have of it. It operates as a pure, prospective intention without intuition.[11] It is an "essential possibility" (*Wesenmoglichkeit*) which transcends the reality of essences (*Ueberwirklichkeit*) while constituting the final meaning (*Zwecksinn*) of all historical reality.[12] For Husserl it is both "innate in humanity" *and* that goal towards which we are "called" – making all thinkers "functionaries of humanity" who must never "abandon faith in the Possibility of philosophy as a task, in the possibility of universal knowledge."[13]

In a striking passage in his late E Manuscripts (III, 4), Husserl identifies this teleological possibility of reason as "God." Again using language more akin to Hegel or Aristotle than to Kant, Husserl speaks of this "God" taking the form of an evolving telos-logos whose "hidden meaning" goes beyond the world of actual being in itself (*Ueberwirklich/Ueber-an-sichlich*) towards a goal yet to be realized.[14] It is, as Husserl puts it, "teleologico-historical." At a more personal level, he confided to his student Edith Stein in December 1935, that "the life of man is nothing other than a path towards God."[15] But while he leaves us such tantalizing hints and guesses, Husserl never chose to elaborate on his understanding of God in his published work.[15a]

Several of Husserl's phenomenological followers developed his notion of teleological possibility. None of them, however, with the ambivalent exception of Heidegger, explored the theological character of Husserl's wager. Thus while Sartre described the human desire to be God as our ultimate teleological possibility in *Being and Nothingness* (1943), he deemed this possibility to be both ontologically and logically absurd, and so utterly meaningless.[16] And though Merleau-Ponty was less dogmatic in his pronouncements on the issue, for him even the most "essential possibility" (*Wesenmoglichkeit*) of being remained always an immanent "world possibility" (*Weltmoglichkeit*) which had little or nothing to do with the transcendent God of Revelation.[17]

Finally, Nicolai Hartmann developed Husserl's category of teleological possibility in the direction of a logical ontology devoid of any theological dimension. Resolved to pursue Husserl's insights, Hartmann published a book entitled *Moglichkeit und Wirklichkeit in* 1939, just one year after Husserl's death. But Hartmann remained a captive of the metaphysical priority of the actual over the possible. Dividing the category of the possible into the "real" (an empirical condition of possible existence) and the "ideal" (a principle of logical non-contradiction), Hartmann fell back into the traditional dualism between realist *potentia* and idealist *possibilitas*. Thus reinforcing the old dichotomy between historically actualizable possibles (*Real-Möglichkeiten*) and purely essential ones (*Wesensmöglickkeiten*), Hartmann declared a clear preference for the former as candidates for a true ontology. Indeed, he concluded by subordinating ideal and fictional possibilities to a *Realontologie* which discloses the existence of authentic possibles *within* the actual-actualizable order of being: *Was real moglich ist, das ist auch real wirklich*. To say truely of something that it is possible, even as a telos, is tantamount to saying that it is realizable here and now: *Hier-und-jetzt-wirklich-werden-konnens*. If the conditions for the actualization of something do not or can not obtain, one is not really entitled to say that it exists as a possibility.[18] In the process, the possible is reduced to a merely secondary or subjacent category of reality, and any dimension of alterity or transcendence is denied. For Hartmann, the possible is not beyond the real but beneath it.

In developing the Husserlian notion of the teleological possible in the direction of an unambiguously immanentist ontology, Hartmann might be said to have deprived it of its inchoate potential for theistic transcendence, recasting it instead in the evolutionist categories of the possible enunciated by non-phenomenological thinkers like Whitehead and Bergson.[19] Either way, the intriguing eschatological implications of Husserl's innovation are as neglected by Hartmann as by Sartre and Merleau-Ponty. We will have to wait until Heidegger and Derrida for some of these implications to be retrieved and extrapolated.

2   Dialectical notion of the possible (Ernst Bloch)

A second approach which I believe is conducive to an eschatology of the possible is Ernst Bloch's dialectical utopianism. The notion of God as a dialectical end of historical struggle finds its most explicit religious expression in the theology of liberation (Boff, Guttierez, Secundo, Cardenal, Moltmann, Metz); but it draws much of its theoretical inspiration from neo-Marxist dialectical thinkers like Ernst Bloch and the critical theorists.

Advancing a singular brand of humanist utopianism, Bloch speaks of a coming kingdom which reveals itself as an "objectively real possible" (*Das objektiv-real Mögliche*).[20] Nicknamed the "theologian of the Revolution," Bloch was determined to show that the pivotal "principle of hope" evinced by all great religious traditions is nothing less than the utopian quest for a future society of revolutionary justice and peace. He thus restores the energies of spiritual striving from a heaven of transcendence and transcendentalism to their proper place in the immanent dialectic of history. Interpreting what he calls the "symbolism of hope" as it expresses itself in the signs and images of a wide variety of cultures, myths, dreams, literatures and liturgies, Bloch identifies a universal project for the New (*Novum*) precontained in each of them. The *Novum* is the promise of a "renewed nature" implicit in all progressive social expressions. It is the prefiguration of a materially equal and emancipated society which is "not yet" (*noch nicht*). And in this sense it takes Marx at his word when he says that as soon as we become conscious of what the world has dreamed of up to now, it will be obvious that there is no real "rupture between past and future but rather a realization of the projects of the past" (Marx in a Letter to Ruge, 1843).

Spiritual and religious aspiration thus finds its appropriate material correspondent in the revolutionary horizon of history. And in the process, the old Hegelian definition of being as that which has been (*das Wesen ist das Gewesene*) is replaced by the neo-Marxist notion of utopia as a latent possibility of history, as that which has not yet actually been (*noch nie so gewesen*). Yet far from constituting a simple "negation" or "nihilation" of historical reality, as in the manner of Sartre's imaginary possibilities, the possibility of utopia takes the form of a "maieutics" which brings the tacit imaginings of history to birth.[21] As such, the revolutionary category of the possible previews the "leap ahead" from present alienation to future peace.[22] Indeed, Bloch will not hestitate to critique fellow humanist Marxists, Lukács and Adorno, for reducing the "prophetic" potencies of cultural dreams to distorted forms of ideological false-consciousness.[23] He castigates Lukács in particular for wearing "sociological-schematic blinkers" which prevent him from recognizing that works of art can transcend existing ideologies and point towards "creative cultural surpluses" which serve as both a "pre-vision" (*Vor-Schein*) and "prefiguration" (*Vor-Bildung*) of utopia.[24]

It is, however, in a chapter of his monumental *The Principle of Hope* (1938–47), entitled "The Category of the Possible," that Bloch makes his most detailed contribution to this debate. Here Bloch outlines a notion of "real possibility" – as opposed to a purely ideal, formal or transcendental one – which shakes up any metaphysical given (*fixum*) in the name of a coming newness (*novum adventurum*). To interpret the world in the light of "real possibility" is to understand it as both "being-according to the possible" (*Kata to dunaton*) and "being-in-the-possible" (*to dunamei on*). Bloch thereby intends to reinject a dose of utopian historicity into the old Aristotelian metaphysics of "potency" (*dunamis*). Indeed he will go so far as to claim that the revolutionary discovery – by Hegel-Marx – of a "concrete theory-praxis" is inextricably linked to the "inquiry of the modality of objectively-real possibility."[25]

So doing Bloch historicizes Aristotle's concept of potency. But this move has nothing to do with a reductive materialism which would dismiss possibility as mere "sub-being." Rather Bloch rehabilitates the Aristotelian concept of "being-according to the possible" (*Kata to dunaton*) as a dynamizing magnet which draws matter towards its future. And he likewise restores the category of "being-in-the-possible" (*to dunamei on*) to an equally active role, serving as a "lap of fertility which gives rise to all the figures of the world...the hopeful visage of real possibility."[26] Bloch thus dispenses with the metaphysical understanding of potency as inchoate matter awaiting the meaning-giving imprint of form (*morphe*) or act (*entelecheia*) and elevates it to the primary role of a mobilizing catalyst: "the consideration of what is to be achieved in this moment or that depends on the being-according-to-the-possible" of matter.[27] Moreover, it is thanks to this enabling potential that a hermeneutics of utopia can help us critically discriminate between authentically "real" possibilities – capable of historical realization – and mere empty ego-fantasies.

In short, the most effective critique of ideological paralysis stems from a recognition of the correspondence between the goals of historical struggle and the inherent potencies of the material cosmos which surround us. As he puts it in *A Philosophy of the Future*: "The meaning of human history from the start is the building of the commonwealth of Freedom, yet without a positively-possible, possibly-positive meaning in the surrounding cosmology which all historical events ultimately merge with, the progress of this historical process might as well never have happened."[28] This, Bloch believed, was one of the great insights of the heretic Giordano Bruno who, brushing traditional ontology against the grain, discovered the root of divine fecundity in the "potentiality and potency" of history.[29]

The dialectical category of the possible thus serves double duty. In so far as it signals the world according-to-possibility, it plays a critical role regarding the limits of what is possible (almost a Kantian condition of possibility); while as token of the world-in-possibility it mobilizes an unlimited dynamism of meaning, forever extending into the "utopian *novum* of all of history."[30] It would be a mistake, therefore, to construe the *novum* as some kind of ontological *entelecheia*, understood in the sense of a "form of forms" or "self-thinking-thought" – timeless, immutable, devoid of potency. The *novum*, qua end of history, is not a transcendent *actus purus*; nor is it some Supreme

Being already accomplished beyond time and awaiting the culmination of history to reveal itself. No, the *novum* is that promise of possibility inscribed in the not-yet-now of time and the not-yet-there of space. And as such, far from being an indifference that leaves us, human agents, indifferent in turn, the *novum* galvanizes our utopian drive towards the kingdom whose realization "here on earth human labour so powerfully helps to accelerate"[31]. For Bloch, what connects this distant goal to our everyday earthly labors is precisely the intermediary realm of "dream", both aesthetic and religious. For without the "visible pre-appearing" of our images and icons, our struggling towards the *novum* would be blind and directionless. With it, by contrast, we are liberally instructed and guided in the "power-to-be" (*Kann-Sein*) of human history.

But if art and religion open up history to utopia, history grounds art and religion in the real. The dialectical category of *Kann-Sein* plays a crucial role here as a reminder not only of the still undetermined ends of revolutionary endeavor but also of the socio-material conditions which can bring such goals about. For utopia, as Bloch insists, "is only possible if it is partially conditioned."[32] Utopian possibility is thus redefined as what is not-yet-realized but realizable. Or to use Bloch's own terms, the "real possibility" of utopia is at once (a) the measure *of* things (as ultimate goal: *das sachlich-objectiv Mögliche*) and (b) the measure *within* things (as yardstick of feasibility: *das sachhaft-objectgemass Mögliche*).[33] In contrast to Kant, Bloch sees possibility not as an a priori condition of formal knowledge but as a precondition of historical transformation. Utopian possibility is less a power-to-know than a power-to-become-other than what is at present the case. This transmutational capacity reaches its highest expression in Bloch's secularized concept of salvation (*Heilsbegriff*): "Interdependence is here such that without the potentiality of the power-to-become-otherwise, the power-to-make-otherwise of potency would not have the space in which to disclose itself; just as without the power-to-make-otherwise of potency, the power-to-become otherwise of the world would have no mediating meaning with humans. Consequently, the possible reveals itself as being what it is . . . thanks to the activating intervention of humans in the field of the transformable: the concept of salvation."[34]

Far from guaranteeing redemption, therefore, the utopian possible presents itself as a free invitation from history to humanity – an offer which may be rejected or accepted.[35] And on our choice of response to the summons of the possible latent within history, rests the future of its realization or non-realization. This dynamic notion of possibility is directly opposed, in Bloch's view, to the inherited notions of "essence" as something already achieved, to be simply "remembered" (Platonic *anamnesis*) or "recollected" (Hegel's *Erinnerung*). Such metaphysical spiritualism is the kiss of death to true utopia, reducing the "possible" to a mere lack of being – a form of negative non-being with no status or value outside of actuality. In sum, Bloch was uncompromising in his resistance to any metaphysics for which "there is no possibility that is not already realized, no essence that has not already appeared."[36]

Equally vehement, however, was Bloch's critique of rival models of logical possibility. In a polemical section of *The Principle of Hope*, entitled "The Struggle of Static Logic against the Possible," he maintains that all purely logical-positive definitions of possibility, from Duns Scotus to nominalists like Ockham and later Vermeyer, evacuate the radically transformative power of *das Mögliche*, replacing it with a purely abstract category of modality. One could say, Bloch quips ironically, they wrote nothing "very real about the possible."[37] Against, therefore, *both* the metaphysical reduction of the possible to the primacy of form/act/essence *and* its logical reduction to a formal modality of ratiocination, Bloch militates for the retrieval of its radical utopian power. He resolves to reinstate it as the future-oriented determination of history itself (*zukunft-tragende Bestimmtheit*).[38]

3   Ontological Notion of the Possible (Heidegger)

In the Introduction to *Being and Time* (1927), Martin Heidegger makes the startling claim that for phenomenology "possibility stands higher than actuality." He probably had his mentor, Husserl, in mind; but he also, as would become clear, had thoughts of his own on the matter. Later in the same book (section 76), Heidegger goes on to speak of the "quiet power of the possible" (*die stille Krafte des Möglichen*). This, he suggests, is a privileged way in which Being reveals itself to us as temporal-historical beings. The question we are left with, however, is whether this power of loving possibility is something humans express towards Being (*Sein Uberhaupt*) or something Being expresses towards humans? In other words, which possibilizes which – Being or man? *Sein* or *Dasein*?

Given Heidegger's phenomenological analysis of Dasein's different categories of possibility in *Being and Time* – Seinkonnen, Möglichkeit, ermöglichen – one might be forgiven for supposing that the "power of the possible" refers to an essentially human property.[39] However, in the *Letter on Humanism* (1947), Heidegger claims that such a humanist supposition is in fact mistaken. In a pivotal if much neglected passage in his post-war letter to Jean Beaufret, Heidegger recites this exact reference to the "quiet power of the possible," redefining it this time as an unambiguous gift of Being itself. Theological connotations abound, albeit elusively. And we are tempted to ask: what, if anything, does this "quiet power" of Being have to do with God?

The passage in question opens as follows: "Being as the element is the 'quiet power' of the loving potency (*Vermogens*), i.e., of the possible (*des Möglichen*)." Already the interpolation of the new term *Vermögen*, to qualify the standard term for the possible in *Being and Time* – namely, *das Mögliche* – signals a shift from an existential-transcendental perspective (easily confused with humanism) to a more unequivocally Being-centered one. This new ontological assignation for Being's own power of possibilizing is clearly more topological than anthropological. It marks a clear departure from the logical and metaphysical residues of "possibility" still evident in the existential analytic of Dasein in *Being and Time*. Determined to avoid any further humanist misreadings, Heidegger is emphatic on this point. "Our words 'possible' and 'possibility' are," he explains, "under the domination of 'logic' and 'metaphysics', taken only in contrast to 'actuality', i.e., they are conceived with reference to a determined – viz. the metaphysical – interpretation of Being as *actus* and *potentia*, the distinction of which is identified with that of *existentia* and *essentia*." But Heidegger explains that when he speaks of the "quiet power of the possible," he means neither (1) the "possible of a merely represented *possibilitas*" (a Leibnitzian–Kantian category of modal logic), nor (2) "the *potentia* as *essentia* of an *actus* of the *existentia*" (an Aristotelian–Thomistic–scholastic category of metaphysics). He means, as he states here, "Being itself, which in its loving potency (*das Mögend*) possibilizes (*vermag*) thought and thus also the essence of man, which means in turn his relationship to Being." Heidegger concludes this decisive passage thus: "To possibilize (*vermögen*) something is to sustain it in its essence, to retain it in its element."[40]

The significance of this dense pronouncement on the "possible" cannot be under-estimated. It offers a unique insight into the famous "Turn" in Heidegger's thought from "phenomenology" (with its residual transcendental, existential, Dasein-centered idioms) to "thought" (with its shift of emphasis to Being-as-Being, *Sein als Sein*).[41] Heidegger I's humanist sounding liturgy of Being as temporality and historicality is now replaced with a more sacred-sounding language of love and grace, consistent with Heidegger II's rethinking of Being as Gift (*Es gibt*). Playing on the latent etymological affinities between the German verbs for loving (*mogen*) and making possible (*vermogen*), Heidegger invites us to rethink Being itself as the power that possibilizes the authentic being of things: "It is on the strength of this loving potency or possibilization of love (*das Vermögen des Mögens*) that something is possibilized (*vermag*) in its authentic (*eigentlich*) being. This possibilization (*Vermögen*) is the authentic 'possible' (*das eigentlich 'mögliche'*), that whose essence rests on loving"[42].

The proper response of human beings to such loving-possibilizing is, Heidegger suggests, to love-possibilize Being in return by thinking things and selves in their authentic essence. "Thought is . . . to concern oneself about the essence of a 'thing' or a 'person', that means to like or to love them."[43] The possibilizing of Being may thus be understood in terms of a double genitive referring both to Being's loving-possibilizing of thought and thought's loving-possibilizing of Being. Thus might we translate Heidegger's phrase – "*Aus diesem Mogen vermag das Sein das Denken*" – as "Being possibilizes thought which possibilizes Being." A translation whose sense is confirmed, it seems, in Heidegger's immediately subsequent sentence: "The one renders the other possible. Being as the loving-possibilizing is the '*posse*-ible' (*Jenes ermoglichte dieses. Das Sein als Vermogend-Mögende ist das 'Mög-liche'*)"[44].

By choosing to translate the operative term, '*mog-liche*', as '*posse-ible*', I am suggesting that the shared semantic sense of *mogen* (to love) and *vermogen* (to make possible) is perhaps best captured by the Latin term *posse* – a term which according to Nicholas of Cusa, lies at the very heart of divine being, qua God's power to love. Cusanus coined the term *Possest* to capture this double belonging of possibility and being which he identified with God.[45]

Heidegger does not go so far. And there are no mentions of Cusanus. Yet much of his language is deeply resonant with the religious language of Christian eschatology. Indeed in a related passage in the same letter to Beaufret, Heidegger actually equates the essence of Being with the "sacred" and the "divine."[45a] This, in conjunction with his posthumously published claim in *Der Spiegel* that "only a god can save us now," certainly invites the surmise that some rapport might exist between the "possibilizing" power of Being and the *Possest* of God. Moreover, Heidegger's liberal borrowings from Christian mystical theology – for example, Eckhart's *Gelassenheit*, Angelus Silesius' "rose-that-blooms-without-why" or Paul's eschatological *Kairos* – all suggest a deep and residual affinity with the author's early fascination with Catholic and Lutheran theology. And even if it is probably more the "god of the poets" (than of revelation) that the later Heidegger has in mind when he invokes a "saving god," one cannot gainsay some kind of relation (even if it is only one of proportional analogy) between ontological and theological readings of the "loving-possible."

Indeed when Heidegger speaks of poetic dwelling as an invitation to abide in "that which has a loving for man and therefore needs his presence" (*was selber den Menschen mag und darum sein Wesen braucht*), one has every reason to suspect that some kind of deity is hovering in the vicinity.[46] And this suspicion is substantiated when one observes how several of Heidegger's last writings recast the Husserlian notion of teleological possibility in terms of a quasi-eschatological drama. A typical example is *The End of Philosophy*, where Heidegger claims that the "end of philosophy is the place in which the whole of philosophy's history is gathered in its most ultimate possibility" – a final possibility which is also the "first possibility" from which all genuine thought originates.[47] Such a possibility is clearly beyond all human powers of determination, for "its contours remain obscure and its coming uncertain."[48] So we are back once again, it seems, with that possibilizing-appropriating of human thinking by Being itself: a form of happening (*Ereignis*) and giving (*Es gibt*) which remains beyond our ken and control. Being is thus reinterpreted as "that which is capable of being," the *esti gar einai* of Parmenides now being rethought by Heidegger as the "possibility of Being." From a human point of view this means, quite simply, letting things be what they *can be*.[49]

But whatever this "possibility of Being" may be said to be it is certainly *not* the mere *potentia* of some metaphysical substance, nor the *possibilitas* of some representational logic (alongside reality and necessity).[50] The loving-possible is for Heidegger something that surpasses the understanding of both metaphysics and logic. It is nothing less than the giving of Being itself.

4   Deconstructive notion of the Possible (Derrida)

In an essay entitled "As if it were Possible, 'Within such Limits...'" (1998), Derrida revisits the notion of possibility in terms of what he calls the "irreducible modality of 'Perhaps' (*peut-être*)."[51] Cautioning against all talk of "last words," in philosophy no less than in "history," Derrida declares this "perhaps" to be the necessary condition of possibility of every experience – to the extent that every experience is an event which registers that which comes from the unpredictable otherness of the future. Such an experience of the "perhaps" is at once that of the possible *and* the impossible. Or as Derrida puts it, the possible *as* impossible. If what happens is only that which is possible in the sense of what is anticipated and expected, then it is not an event in the true sense. For an event is only possible in so far as it comes from the impossible. An event (*évènment*) can only happen, in other words, when and where the "perhaps" lifts all presumptions and assurances about what might be and lets the future come as future (*laisse l'avenir à l'avenir*), that is, as the arrival of the impossible. The "perhaps" thus solicits a "yes" to what is still to come, beyond all plans, programs and predictions. It keeps the ontological question of "to be or not to be" constantly in question, on its toes, deferring any last word on the matter. But if deconstruction suspends the security of ontological answers, it also, Derrida insists, eschews the levity of a purely rhetorical "perhaps" (*peut-être/Vieleicht*). The "perhaps" sustains the survival of the question. But what might such a possible-impossible actually mean?

In *The Politics of Friendship* (1994), Derrida had already ventured some kind of response to this question. Picking up on Nietzsche's talk of a "dangerous perhaps" as the thought of the future, Derrida argues that such a thought is indispensable to friendship precisely as a category of futurity. Distinguishing between the bad possible (of predictability) and the good possible (of impossibility), Derrida affirms that it is only the latter that can safeguard true friendship as a commitment to what is to come. It is also only the good possible (that is, the impossible possible) which can respect the dual fidelity of friendship to undecidability and decision.[52] Without the openess of a radically indeterminate "possible" – which like the phenomenological reduction brackets our prejudices about the future – there could be no genuine decision. But, equally, no decision could be made without somehow also lifting the "perhaps," while retaining its "living" possibility in a kind of living memory. Consequently if no real decision – ethical, political, juridical – is possible without conjuring the "perhaps" that keeps the present open to the coming event, there could be no decision either – no commiting of oneself to one possible rather than others – if there was not some limiting of this opening "perhaps" which serves as condition of the possibility of decision![53]

This circle is what Derrida calls the "lucky aporia of the possible im-possible"[54]. In "As If...," he expands on this aporia, as first outlined in the *Politics of Friendship*. In the event of decision, he writes here, "only the im-possible takes place; and the unfolding of a potentiality of possibility already there would never constitute an event or invention."[55] Why? Because, explains Derrida, "a decision that I *can* take, the decision *in my power* and which merely manifests the acting out (*passage à l'acte*) or unfolding of what is *already possible* for me, the actualization of my possibility, decision which only derives from me, would it still be a decision?".[56] The answer is no, for genuine decision – like genuine responsibility – is not just about *my* possibles but is also about *others'* possibles intervening which may well represent the impossibility of my own possible. Whence Derrida's preference for a paradoxically *receptive* decision, recalling Lévinas' notion of a "*difficile liberté*" which allows for the irruption of the other in the self. He notes: "the responsible decision must be this im-possible possibility of a 'passive' decision, a decision of the other in me which removes none of my liberty or responsibility."[57] Moreover, Derrida insists that every responsibility must traverse this aporia of the impossible-possible which, far from paralyzing us, mobilizes a "new thinking of the possible."[58]

Later in "As If..." Derrida gives further examples of this aporetic logic. He cites, for instance, the fact that an *interpretation* is only possible if it remains to some extent inadequate (that is, if an adequate interpretation is impossible). For an interpretation without any default – closed therefore to the possibility of misinterpretation – would represent not only the end of interpretation, as an on-going process of exploring meaning but the end of a historical future in any sense whatsoever. Closing off the future, it would make everything impossible.

Derrida notes a similar interplay of possibility and impossibility in the instance of *invention*. Invention is always possible in so far as it is the invention of the possible; but invention is really only possible when it does not invent something new out of itself – in which case it would not be new – but rather allows something *other* to come, occur, happen. Now, given the fact that this otherness that comes to it is not part or parcel of invention's own resources of possibles, it means that the "only possible invention would be the invention of the impossible."[59] Of course, we may object that the invention of the impossible is impossible; but in fact, insists Derrida, it is the only kind possible. "An invention must pronounce itself as invention of what does not appear possible," short of which it would be little more than an explicitation of a "program of possibles in the economy of the same."[60]

A similar logic of impossible-possibility applies to Derrida's analysis of "pardon." Pardon, Derrida claims, is only possible, as such, when faced with the unpardonable, that is, where it is *impossible*. For pardon – like hospitality, gift, justice etc – is an unconditional that has to deal with conditions as soon as it becomes an act or decision. In such instances, the possible "is" impossible. Or to put it in more formal, quasi-transcendental terms, the condition of possibility of pardon (hospitality/gift/justice) is also and at the same time the condition of its impossibility.[61] The possibility of pardon, therefore, requires us to *do the impossible*, to make the impossible possible. But this must occur, says Derrida, without resorting to some sort of morality of rules and prescriptions, of oughts or obligations. Pardon must, by its very unconditional nature, remain unpredictable and gratuitious (*gratuit et imprévisible*).

In all of these examples, Derrida argues that im-possibility is not the mere contrary of possibility but rather its mark of renewal and arrival as event. No event worthy of its name is simply an actualization of some precontained potential program. For an event to be possible it must be both possible (of course) but also impossible (in the sense of an interruption by something singular and exceptional into the regime of preexisting possibles-powers-potencies). The event happens not just because it is possible, qua ontological acting-out of some inherent *dunamis* or *potentia*, but because something impossible – that is, hitherto unanticipated and unplanned – comes to pass. It is precisely the impossibility of formerly predictable possibilities which makes new ones announce themselves beyond this very impossibility.[62] The impossible reminds us, therefore, that beyond our powers the impossible is still possible. There are impossible possibles beyond us, never dreamt of in our philosophies. Or as Derrida puts it in *Politics of Friendship*: "Perhaps the impossible is the only possible chance of something new, of some new philosophy of the new. Perhaps; perhaps in truth the *perhaps* still names this chance."[63]

Derrida does not directly engage, it has to be said, with the eschatological implications of this issue. But he does leave us one or two tantalizing hints. In a note which refers to my own notion of the "may-be" in *Poétique du Possible* (1984), and to my discussion of Heidegger's "loving possible" (*des mögende Vermögens*), Derrida makes mention of the possible as that which is "more than impossible" (*plus qu'impossible* or *plus impossible*). And he refers us here, tellingly if only in passing, to the starling maxim of the Christian mystic, Angelus Silesius: "*das uberunmöglichschste ist möglich.*" The deeply theological connotations of this claim are not addressed by Derrida here alas. But he does allude to his discussion of the "name of God" in "Sauf le Nom." And he does add this sentence – recalling the opening claims about the "desire of God" in that essay: "All the aporias of the possible-impossible or of the more-than-impossible would thus be 'lodged' but also dislodging 'within' (*au-dedans*) what one might calmly call the desire, love or movement towards the Good etc"[64].

The "etc" resists any temptation to pronounce a "last word" and leaves open, in my view, the option of adding a "possible God" – a God whom we might now be inclined to refer to, along with Silesius, as a "more than impossible" God. Indeed, it might be noted that Derrida himself does allude here to a certain connection between the possible-impossible aporia and the undecidable aporia of who/what which he relates to the question of *khora* (which precedes the very distinction who/what). And this question of *khora*, as we have had occasion to remark elsewhere, is deeply linked in Derrida's work, as in Caputo's, to the question of God. But such an eschatological possibility is not, it must be said, explored or extrapolated by Derrida himself.

What Derrida is trying to do, it seems to me, is to rethink a post-metaphysical category of the possible by rethinking the category of the im-possible in a way that is not simply negative or disabling. The impossible needs to be affirmed because, as we have noted above, it is precisely im-possibility which opens up possibility and makes it possible. Strangely, however, this can only occur when my power of possibility undergoes its own death as "my" possibility – acknowledging in mourning, passion, suffering and anxiety that it is this very impossibility which allows a new possible, another possible, another's possible, an im-possible possible, to come, or to come back. This "other" possible returns, says Derrida, as a specter. It assumes the guise of a *revenant*, rising up from the grave of my own possible in the form of an in-coming other. And we experience this as surprise, gift, openness, grace, resurrection.[65]

In one especially charged passage, Derrida offers a more phenomenological take on this moment. Here he endeavors to describe the more affective dimension of the impossible-possible aporia: "It names a suffering or passion, an affect at once sad and joyous, the instability of disquietude (*inquiétude*) proper to every possibilization. This latter would allow itself be haunted by the specter of its impossibility, by its mourning for itself: the mourning of the self carried in itself, but which also gives it its life or survival, its very possibility. For this *im*-possibility opens its possibility, it leaves a trace, at once an opportunity and a threat, *in* what it renders possible. The torment would signal this scar, the trace of this trace . . . All this recurs with respect to Freud's concept of *Bemachtigung*, of the limit or the paradoxes of the possible as power."[65a] Derrida even goes so far as to identify this paradox of the impossible-possible with the experience of *faith* itself. For how is it, he asks, that that which makes possible makes impossible the very thing it makes possible? How is it that promise is so related to ruin, affirmation to death, renewal to deprivation? He responds: "The *im*-of the im-possible is no doubt radical, implacable, undeniable. But it is not simply negative or dialectical; it *introduces* to the possible . . . it makes it come, it makes it revolve according to an anachronistic temporality or incredible filiality – which is, moreover, also, the *origin of faith*" (my italics).[66] Why? "Because it exceeds knowledge and conditions the address to the other, inscribing every theorem in the time and space of a testimony ('I talk to you, believe me')."[67] But, we may further ask, why testimony? Because we can only possess and practice faith in a possibility never adequately or fully *present* but always already anachronistic (remembered) or still to come (promised). In this sense, Derrida's relating of "virtuality" to "the origin of faith" alludes, I suspect, to a general "spectral" structure of *all* human experience rather than to any *specially religious* experience of a loving God.[68] As such, it may have as much to teach us about the postmodern phenomenon of virtual reality as about the revealed reality of Yahweh, Jesus or Mohammed.

For Derrida, in short, the aporia of the impossible-possible is another name for deconstruction: "the beating pulse of the possible im-possible, of the impossible as condition of the possible. From within the very heart of the impossible, one could thus hear the pulse or pulsion of 'deconstruction'."[69] For me, the impossible-made-possible signals the promise of new thinking about the "possible God." Resurrection rather than deconstruction. (Though I would not deny that the former traverses the latter and has constant need of its purging powers.) There is not opposition here but difference. And the difference is one of emphasis as much as of substance. Derrida sees in the play of impossible-possible a structure of "experience in general." (Indeed at one point Derrida admits that his entire reflection on the impossible-possible may be little more than a gloss on his early exegesis of Husserl's phenomenology of the possible as a never-adequate intuition, see his *Introduction to the Origin of Geometry*.)[70] I, by contrast, would want to claim it marks a specifically *religious* experience of God. And I would want to suggest that this is a difference not only of language games but of "reference." *Differance* and God, as Derrida is the first to remind us, are not the same thing.

I would claim that Derrida's reflections on this subject do indeed open up new ways of thinking about faith and eschatology; but, as a self-confessed atheist, it does not interest Derrida to pursue these issues in a specifically theological or theistic manner. He clearly admires and applauds thinkers like Caputo and others who do this, but it is not his thing. Yes, he will go so far as to declare the impossible-possible paradox of pardon/gift/justice/hospitality as a general "messianic" structure of all experience; but he will refuse to pronounce on the theistic or atheistic, authentic or inauthentic, import of any given *messianism* (monotheistic or other). The closest Derrida's reflection comes to religion is in the guise of a "messianicity without messianism," a form of vigilant openness to the incoming events of *all our experiences* – secular, sacred or profane; good or evil; loving or violent. Derrida, in short, is more concerned with the everyday (every moment) incoming of events than in the truth or otherwise of some divine advent. The other that leaps towards you from this in-coming moment may be a "monster slouching towards Bethlehem to be born" or a lamb who lays down his life for love of mankind. There is no way of knowing.

It is for this reason that Derrida refrains from responding one way or another to any particular God-claim. He speaks of the "spectral" rather than specifically "revealed" structure of such incoming. But what his deconstructive reading of the impossible-possible certainly does help us to perform is a thoroughgoing purge of all "purist" or "dogmatic" notions of possibility as an immanently unfolding power blind to the invention of otherness which alone makes events happen. This deconstructive critique of inherited onto-theological notions of both potentiality and presence marks, I believe, an invaluable opening to a new eschatological understanding of God as *posse*. Derrida points to such possible paths but he does not choose to walk them. In the heel of the hunt, he prefers ghosts to gods. He prefers, as is his wont and right, to leave matters open. He reserves judgment.

This is where we part company. But I would add that, on this matter, anyone concerned with tolerance – religious or otherwise – would do well to take Derrida very seriously indeed. The indispensable lessons to be learned from Derrida here are vigiliance, patience and humility.

5   Conclusion: Towards an eschatological notion of the Possible

All of the above "post-metaphysical" readings offer some guidance towards a properly *eschatological* understanding of "the possible God." But each, I suggest, has its limits. Husserl discloses the teleological idea of possibility which motivates the development of reason towards a universal goal – but there always remains some ambiguity in Husserl's phenomenology as to whether this telos is transcendent of history or immanent in it.[71] There is always a lingering suspicion that his elusive notion of "God" may slip back into some kind of rationalist or idealist theodicy where the possible is predetermined from the outset. Bloch, for his part, grounds the possible firmly in the dialectical history of striving towards utopia; but his neutral position on the eschatological status of the *noch-nicht* leaves this "theologian of the revolution" uncommitted at a theological level. One cannot avoid the surmise that the Utopian Possible in question is really nothing other than the dream-projection of a universalist humanism. Heidegger's notion of the "loving-possible" clearly goes beyond both the transcendental idealism of Husserl and the dialectical humanism of Bloch; but it stops short of identifying this "possibilizing power" (*das Vermogen des Mogens*), with a theistic or theological God. Heidegger is more interested in Being than in God; and the curious "saving god" he invokes in his final days is probably more akin to the God of Apollo and the poets than to Yahweh or Jesus. Finally, Derrida exposes the intriguing enigma of the impossible-possible – and even links this to the "origin of faith"; but the faith in question is a deconstructive belief in the undecidable and unpredictable character of incoming everyday events (what he calls "experience in general") rather than in some special advent of the divine as such.

Despite their respective reservations on the theological front, however, these approaches proffer crucial critical pointers for a new eschatology of God – what I term "the God who May-Be." What all four thinkers teach us is that the conventional metaphysical concepts of the possible – as *dumanis, potentia* or *possibilitas* – fail to appreciate its force as something higher rather than lower than the actual. We may read them accordingly as suggesting, even if they did not pursue this suggestion, that since onto-theology defined God as the absolute priority of actuality over possibility, it may now be timely to reverse that priority. The consequences are far reaching and I have attempted to explore them elsewhere in some detail.[72] Suffice to note here, in summary, the following crucial implications of such a "possible God":

(1)   It is radically transcendent – guaranteed by the mark of its "impossible-possibility";

(2)   It is "possible" for us as faith in the promise of advent – the scandal of "impossible" incarnation and resurrection! – but equally reveals itself as what "possibilizes" such messianic events in the first place;

(3)   It calls and solicits us – where are you? who are you? who do you say that I am?
      why did you not give me to drink or eat? – in the form of an engaging personal
      summons (unlike Husserl's Telos, Bloch's Utopia, Heidegger's *Vermögen* or Der-
      rida's Perhaps);

(4)   And, finally, the eschatological May-Be unfolds not just as can-be (*Kann-sein*) but
      as should-be (*Sollen-sein*) – in short, less a power of immanent potency laboring
      towards fulfillment than as a power of the powerless which bids us remain open
      to the possible divinity whose gratuiteous coming – already, now and not yet – is
      always a surprise and never without grace.

Notes

1   On Henri Bergson, "The Possible and the Real" (1930) in *La pensée et le mouvant* (Paris: Presses
    Universitaires de France, 1934): see our commentary in *Poétique du Possible* (Paris: Beauchesne,
    1984), pp. 34–5. On A. F. Whitehead's notion of possibility and God, see for example *Dialogues
    of Alfred North Whitehead*, ed. Lucien Price (New York: The New American Library, 1964), pp.
    134–5: "I wish I could convey this sense I have of the infinity of the possibilities that confront
    humanity – the limitless variations of choice, the possibility of novel and untried combinations,
    the happy turns of experiment, the endless horizons opening out. As long as we experiment, as
    long as we keep this possibility of progressiveness, we and our societies are alive . . . It is the
    living principle in thought which keeps us alive." See Whitehead's related notion of "potential
    schemes" and "the extensive continuum which expresses the solidarity of all possible stand-
    points throughout the actual world" in *Process and Reality* (New York: Macmillan, 1929), pp.
    66–7. For useful commentaries on Whitehead's concept of God see John B. Cobb, "A
    Whiteheadian Doctrine of God" in *Process Philosophy and Christian Thought,* ed. D. Brown,
    R. James and G. Reeves (Indianapolis: Bobbs-Merrill, 1971), pp. 215–43; and Lewis Ford,
    "Creativity in a Future Key" in E. Neville (ed.), *New Essays in Metaphysics* (Albany: SUNY,
    1987), pp. 179–97. I am grateful to my UCD colleague, Timothy Mooney, for bringing these
    passages in Whitehead to my attention and for instructing me on the various parallels between
    process thought and phenomenology in his splendid article, "Deconstruction, Process and
    Openness: Philosophy in Derrida, Husserl and Whitehead" in *Framing a Vision of the World*, ed.
    A. Cloots and S. Sia (Louvain University Press 1999).
2   Cited *Poétique du Possible*, p. 35.
3   See our detailed exploration of Husserl's notion of the possible in Chapter One of *Poetics of
    Imagining* (2nd edition, Edinburgh University Press/Fordham University Press, 1998)
    entitled "The Phenomenological Imagination," pp. 13–14 and in *Poétique du Possible*, pp.
    199–208. See also Jacques Derrida's innovative reading of Husserl's category of possibility as
    a Kantian Idea in his *Edmund Husserl's "Origin of Geometry": An Introduction* (University of
    Nebraska Press, 1989). The notion of "essential possibility" plays a particularly important
    role in Husserl's method as a realm of "free variation" leading to "eidetic intuition." In the
    realm of pure possibles, consciousness may prescind from merely empirical givens and
    explore, describe and eventually intuit the "essence" of some thing or idea as the invariant
    totality that emergences from the freely varied horizon of real and ideal, empirical and
    fictional, possibilities.
4   Cited *Poétique du Possible*, p. 201.
5   See Paul Ricoeur, "La Liberté selon l'Espérance" in *Le Conflit des interprétations* (Paris: Seuil,
    1969), p. 407.

6   Ibid., pp. 408–9: "(Les postulats) désignent un ordre de choses à venir... Les postulats parlent à leur façon d'un Dieu 'ressuscité des morts'. Mais leur façon est celle de la religion dans les limites de la simple raison; ils expriment l'implication existentielle minimale d'une visée pratique, d'une *Absichte*, qui ne peut se convertir en intuition intellectuelle. 'L'Extension' – *Erweiterung* – l'accroissement' – *Zuwachs* – qu'ils expriment, n'est pas une extension du savoir et du connaître, mais une 'ouverture', une *Eroffnung* ... et cette ouverture est l'equivalent philosophique de l'espérance."

7   For a more detailed account of Kant's philosophical and religious analysis of human openness to a future Kingdom of possible ends, see our *Poétique du Possible*, pp. 202–5. See also P. Ricoeur, "La Liberté selon L'Espérance," pp. 410–14 where Ricoeur discusses Kant's postulates of freedom and immortality as philosophical analogies for the religious "expectation" (*Erwartung*) and hope in Resurrection.

8   Quoted *Poétique du Possible*, p. 205, note 12.

9   Ibid., p. 204, note 11.

10   From Derrida's *Husserl's Origin of Geometry: An Introduction*, cited in *Poétique du Possible*, p. 204. See also J. Derrida, "Comme si c'etait possible, 'within such limits...'," *Revue Internationale de Philosophie*, 3, 1998, no. 205, pp. 497–529; and especially p. 521, note 27. See Derrida's admission of debt to Husserl on this subject, note 70 below. J. Caputo offers this useful gloss: "an 'infinite' idea or intention (is) a regulative ideal, an 'idea in the Kantian sense,' to which no finite complex of intuitive content is ever fully adequate. For Husserl and Kant, 'God' is the very paradigm of such an idea, as an intention of an 'infinite being' which has no intuitive content at all and no hope at all of ever acquiring any." (Introduction to *God, The Gift and Postmodernism* [Bloomington: Indiana University Press Bloomington, 1999, p. 193])

11   *Poétique du Possible*, p. 205; see also Derrida, "Comme si...," p. 519.

12   Ibid., p. 207, note 16.

13   Ibid., p. 207, notes 14 and 15.

14   Husserl Manuscripts, E III, 4 and VIII, 1 and F 24. See our *Poétique du Possible*, p. 207, note 16.

15   On Husserl's remark to Edith Stein, see J. Benoist, "Husserl au-delà de l'onto-théologie?", *Les Etudes Philosophiques*, October 1991. The full statement, cited by Benoist, reads: "La vie de l'homme n'est rien d'autre qu'un chemin vers Dieu. J'ai essayé de parvenir au but sans l'aide de la théologie, ses preuves et sa méthode; en d'autres termes, j'ai voulu atteindre Dieu sans Dieu." Benoist goes on to argue that the God of Husserl's unpublished manuscripts is essentially a neo-Aristotelian God qua Telos. "Le Dieu des inédits, sous les traits aristotéliciens de l'entélechie et du principe, ne réinstitute-t-il pas tout simplement ce qu'on appelle une onto-théologie?" (p. 436). For a more general account of the theological aspects and influences of Husserl's phenomenological project, see Dominique Janicaud's illuminating texts, *Le tournant théologique de la phénoménologie française*, (Eclat, 1991) and *La phénoménologie éclatée* (L'éclat, 1998).

15a See Louis Dupré's informative essay on "Husserl's Thought on God" in *Philosophy and Phenomenological Research*, vol. 29, 1969, and related articles on Husserl's "teleological" God by X. Tilliette, "Husserl et la notion de la Nature," *Revue de métaphysique et de morale*, vol. 70, 1965, pp. 257–69; S. Strasser, "Das Gottesproblem in der Spatsphilosophie Edmund Husserl," *Philosophisches Jahrbuch* (1967), pp. 131 ff; and H. L. Van Breda, "Husserl et le probème de Dieu," *Proceedings of the Tenth International Congress of Philosophy* (Amsterdam, 1949), pp. 1210–12. Husserl's most charismatic designation of God is, Strasser concludes, as the supreme Eidos which "gives all the constituting activities unity, meaningful coherence and teleology." It is "no mundane being," as Husserl himself concedes, "but a final Absolute" (cf. Strasser). Louis Dupré, for his part, argues that

Husserl's deity is an immanent pantheistic Telos rather than a transcendent and personal God. He suggests, moreover, that Husserl's philosophical God, like that of Kant and Descartes, usually serves as an ultimate solution to problems, ambiguities and aporias that would otherwise remain unresolved. On Husserl's complex notion of the Absolute, see also R. Eleveton (ed.), *The Phenomenology of Husserl* (Chicago: Quadrangle, 1970), pp. 43, 182 et seq. The sheer diversity of interpretations of Husserl's God – as teleological, rationalist, deist, pantheist, Kantian, Aristotelian, Hegelian, Cartesian etc – testifies to a radical indeterminacy, ambiguity and one might even say obliquity in Husserl's approach to God. It also betrays the fact that most of his declarations on the subject were made in unpublished manuscripts rather than in terms of clearly formulated arguments. This elusive treatment did, however, prevent Husserl's phenomenological sketch of a divine teleology of the possible from exerting a deep influence on subsequent thinkers like Heidegger and Derrida (as outlined below).

16   For Sartre's analysis of possibility – and of "God" as the ultimate project of human possibility – qua ideal-but-impossible synthesis of being-for-itself-in-itself – see his conclusion to *Being and Nothingness* (New York: Philosophical Library, 1956). See also our commentaries on the metaphysical complexities and contradictions of Sartre's notion of the imaginary horizon of the possible in *Poétique du Possible*, pp. 29–31 (especially notes 29–30) and *Poetics of Imagining*, Edinburgh University Press/Fordham University Press, 1998, Ch. 3, pp. 80–94.

17   See M. Merleau-Ponty's comments on "essential possibility" and "world possibility" in *The Visible and the Invisible* (Northwestern University Press, 1968); and our *Poétique du Possible*, p. 30, note 30 and p. 59, note 7.

18   Nicolai Hartmann, *Moglichkeit und Wirklichkeit* (Berlin, 1939), ch. 31; see our analysis in *Poétique du Possible*, pp. 205–6.

19   For Bergson and Whitehead on possibility see note 1 above.

20   Ernst Bloch, *The Principle of Hope* (Oxford: Basil Blackwell, 1986) (French edition, Paris: Gallimard, 1976) p. 284.

21   On Sartre's treatment of imaginary possibility as a nihilating gesture of both subjective freedom and pathological solipsism in *The Psychology of Imagination* (1940), see our analysis in *The Wake of Imagination*, ch. 5 (London and New York: Routledge, 1996) and *The Poetics of Imagining*, ch. 3.

22   *Poétique du Possible*, p. 243, note 33.

23   Ibid., p. 243, note 34.

24   Ibid., p. 243, note 35.

25   Ibid., p. 245, note 37.

26   Ibid., p. 245, note 38.

27   Ibid., p. 245, note 39.

28   Ibid., p. 246, note 40.

29   Ibid., p. 249, note 51.

30   Ibid., p. 246, note 41.

31   Ibid., p. 246, note 42.

32   Ibid., p. 247, note 44.

33   Ibid., p. 247, note 45.

34   Ibid., p. 247, note 46. See *The Principle of Hope* (French edition), p. 281. Also, ibid., p. 299: "Le facteur subjectif répresente ici la puissance inépuisée de changer le cours des choses, le facteur objectif est la potentialité inépuisée de la variabilité du monde...La puissance subjective coincide non seulement avec ce qui fait changer l'histoire de direction, mais aussi avec ce qui se réalise dans l'histoire, et elle se confondra d'autant plus avec ce qui se réalise que les hommes deviendront les producteurs conscients de leur histoire.

La potentialité objective coincide non seulement avec ce qui est modifiable, mais aussi avec ce qui est réalisable dans l'histoire et cela d'autant plus que le monde extérieur indépendant de l'homme deviendra davantage un monde en médiation avec lui."

35 Ibid., p. 248, note 47.

36 E. Bloch, *The Philosophy of the Future* (New York: Herder, 1970), pp. 55–6. Bloch continues that for such traditional metaphysics, "being itself is understood as the identity of what has been. The origin only emerges archaically as arche; and the dialectical cosmology of disciplines is nothing less than the anamnetic anti-voyage back to the logical-ontology *ante-rem*" (ibid.).

37 *Poétique du Possible*, p. 248, note 49.

38 Ibid., p. 249, note 52. For further explorations of the dialectical model of possibility as a sign of utopia or of the Messianic Kingdom, see our commentaries in *Poétique du Possible*, pp. 243f, notes 33–6 on such figures as Cornelius Castoriadis, George Lukacs and Herbert Marcuse (on utopia); and pp. 238–41 re: Jürgen Moltmann and the theology of liberation (on Messianic hope).

39 In his Introduction to *Being and Time* (Oxford: Blackwell, trans. MacQuarrie and Robinson, 1962), Heidegger states that for phenomenology, "possibility stands higher than actuality" (p. 63). Later in this text he refers to Dasein's pre-awareness of its own death in *Angst* as a specific mood in which it "finds itself faced with the nothingness of the possible impossibility of its own existence" (*BT*, H 266). This existential–human experience of "possible impossibility" may be usefully compared and contrasted with Derrida's notion of "impossible possibility" in "Comme si c'etait possible . . ." (1998), discussed below. For a detailed critical discussion of Heidegger's various concepts of possibility in *Being and Time* and subsequent texts see our "Heidegger's Poetics of the Possible" in *Poetics of Modernity: Toward a Hermeneutic Imagination* (New Jersey: Humanities Press, 1995), pp. 35–48.

40 See our *Poetics of Modernity*, p. 219, note 34 on Edgar Lohner's contentious translation of *Vermogen* in his version of the "Letter on Humanism" in *Phenomenology and Existentialism*, ed. R. Zaner and D. Ihde (New York: Capricorn Books, 1973), pp. 147–81.

41 On the significance of this "Turn," see W. J. Richardson, *Heidegger: Through Phenomenology to Thought* (The Hague: Nijhof, 1963).

42 See our more elaborate commentary on this key passage in our "Heidegger's Poetics of the Possible," pp. 44–8 and p. 220, note 36; and in our "Heidegger, Le Possible et Dieu" in *Heidegger et la Question de Dieu*, ed. J. O'Leary and R. Kearney, (Paris: Grasset, 1980), pp. 125–67. On the various theological interpretations of Husserl's and Heidegger's phenomenology, especially by figures like Marion, Lévinas and Henry in France, see Dominique Janicaud, *Le tournant théologique de la phénoménologie française*, l'éclat, 1991. See also our "Heidegger's Gods" in our *Poetics of Modernity*, pp. 50–64; J-F. Courtine (ed.), *Phénoménologie et Théologie* (Paris: Criterion, 1992) and George Kovacs, *The Question of God in Heidegger's Phenomenology* (Evanston: Northwestern University Press, 1990).

43 Ibid., p. 220, note 37.

44 Ibid., p. 45 f.

45 See Cusanus, *Trialogus de Possest*, ed. R. Steiger (Hamburg: Felix Meiner Verlag, 1973); and P. J. Casarella, "Nicholas of Cusa and the Power of the Possible" in *American Catholic Philosophical Journal* 641 (1990), pp. 7–35. Casarella makes some interesting comparisons between Cusanus' divine *possest* and Heidegger's power of the "loving possible."

45a M. Heidegger, *Letter on Humanism*.

46 M. Heidegger, " . . . Poetically Man Dwells . . ." in *Poetry, Language, Thought* (New York: Harper and Row, 1971), p. 215.

47   This essay is published as a complimentary text in Heidegger's *On Time and Being*, trans. J.
     Staumbaugh (New York: Harper and Row, 1972), p. 54.
48   Ibid., pp. 59–60.
49   Ibid., p. 8. See also our *Poetics of Modernity*, pp. 220–1, note 41 on the crucial link between
     "possibility" and "Being understood as time which absences as it presences." See also the
     recent fascinating study by Hent de Vries, "Heidegger's Possibilism" in *Philosophy and the
     Turn to Religion* (Baltimore: The Johns Hopkins University Press, 1999), pp. 279–96.
     Unfortunately this analysis only came to my attention after completing the present essay.
50   See here Heidegger's deconstructive reading of Kant's critical project in *Kant and the
     Problem of Metaphysics* (Bloomington: Indiana University Press, 1962) as it pertains to his
     understanding of possibility, p. 252: "Kant must have had an intimation of this collapse of
     the primacy of logic in metaphysics when, speaking of the fundamental characteristics of
     Being, 'possibility' (what-being) and 'reality' (which Kant termed 'existence'), he said: 'So
     long as the definition of possibility, existence and necessity is sought solely in pure under-
     standing, they cannot be explained save through an obvious tautology'." But Heidegger
     does not ignore Kant's subsequent retreat to the logicist model: "And yet, in the second
     edition of the *Critique* did not Kant re-establish the supremacy of the understanding? And
     as a result did not metaphysics, with Hegel, come to be identified with 'logic' more
     radically than ever before?" (ibid.).
51   J. Derrida, "Comme si c'etait possible, 'Within such Limits'...," *Revue Internationale de
     Philosophie* 3 (1998), no. 205, pp. 497–529. (Henceforth referred to as "Comme si").
52   Ibid., p. 498. See also *Politique de l'amitié* (Paris: Galilée, 1994) (*Politics of Friendship*
     [London/New York: Verso, 1997]), p. 46: "Or la pensée du 'peut-être' engage peut-être
     la seule pensée *possible* de l'événement. De l'amitié à venir et de l'amitié pour l'avenir. Car
     pour aimer l'amitié, il ne suffit pas de savoir porter l'autre dans le deuil, il faut aimer
     l'avenir. Et il n'est pas de categorie plus juste pour l'avenir que celle du '*peut-être*'. Telle
     pensée conjoint l'amitié, l'avenir et le peut-être pour s'ouvrir à la venue de ce qui vient,
     c'est-à-dire nécessairement sous le régime d'un *possible* dont la *possibilisation* doit gagner sur
     l'impossible. Car un possible qui serait seulement *possible (non impossible)*, un *possible* surement
     et certainement *possible*, d'avance accessible, ce serait un mauvais *possible*, un *possible* sans
     avenir, un *possible* déjà mis de côté, si on peut dire, assure sur la vie. Ce serait un
     programme ou une causalité, un développement, un déroulement sans événement. La
     possibilisation de ce possible impossible doit rester à la fois aussi indécidable et donc aussi
     décisive que l'avenir même."
53   J. Derrida, *Politiques de L'Amitié*, p. 86.
54   "Comme si," p. 498.
55   Ibid., p. 515.
56   Ibid., p. 498.
57   Ibid., p. 498.
58   Ibid., p. 519.
60   Ibid., p. 516. Citing "Invention de l'autre' in *Psyché, Inventions de l'autre*," (Paris: Galilée),
     p. 59. It is useful to compare and contrast Derrida's position here with that of Whitehead,
     see W. Dean, "Deconstruction and Process Theology" in *The Journal of Religion* 64 (1984),
     pp. 1–19 and D. Griffin, "Postmodern Theology" in *Varieties of Postmodern Theology*, ed. J.
     Holland, W. Beardslee and D. Griffin, (Albany: SUNY Press, 1989), pp. 29–61.
61   Ibid., pp. 504–5.
62   Ibid., p. 520.
63   *Politics of Friendship*, p. 36.
64   "Comme si," p. 505. Also see J. Caputo and M. J. Scanlon, "Apology for the Impossible:
     Religion and Postmodernism" and J. Caputo, "Apostles of the Impossible: On God and

the Gift in Marion and Derrida" in *God, The Gift and Postmodernism* (Bloomington: Indiana University Press, 1999), pp. 1–19 and pp. 185–222. "For Derrida, the experience of the impossible represents the least bad definition of deconstruction... everything *interesting* for Derrida is impossible, not simply, logically or absolutely, impossible, but what he calls *the* impossible.... That is why Derrida can say he has spent his whole life "inviting calling promising, hoping sighing dreaming". Of the gift, of justice, of hospitality, of the incoming of the wholly other, of *the* impossible" (pp. 3–4). This leads Caputo to contrast "the impossible" to the "possible" in the form of a polar opposition or exclusion, e.g., "experience is really experience when it is an experience of *the* impossible, not when it experiences the possible" (p. 191). But while there are indeed passages in Derrida which can suggest such a move, the more nuanced position outlined in "Comme si" shies away from such a polar alternativism and speaks instead in terms of a chiasm of "impossible possibility." Of course, if one intends the "possible" in the traditional metaphysical and logical senses of *potentia* and *possibilitas*, then Caputo is correct to oppose it to "*the* impossible"; but as will be clear from the above, we are speaking in this essay – as is Derrida when he speaks of the "perhaps" in "Comme si" – of a radically post-metaphysical notion of possibility as *posse*: at once the possibility *and* impossibility of God/ alterity/transcendence/infinity/incoming event. That is why, eschatologically understood, the divine *posse* or "may-be" is *both* already here *and* always still to come (again), *both* incarnation *and* in-coming. In short, the God of eschatological possibility is simultaneously given *and* not given, possible *and* impossible – or to put it in denominational terms, Christian *and* Jewish. For Caputo's characteristically feisty, intriguing and challenging discussion of Derrida's notion of the impossible, in comparison with Marion's concept of "saturation," see "Apostles of the Impossible," pp. 199–206.

65   "Comme si," 516–17.
65a   Ibid., pp. 516–17.
66   My Italics. Ibid., p. 519.
67   Ibid. p. 519. This crucial passage reads in full as follows: "Mais comment est-il possible, demandera-t-on, que ce qui rend possible rende impossible cela même qu'il rend possible, donc, et introduise, mais comme sa chance, une chance non négative, un principe de ruine dans cela même qu'il promet ou promeut? Le *in*-de l'im-possible est sans doute radical, implacable, indéniable. Mais il n'est pas simplement négatif ou dialectique, il *introduit* au possible, il en est *aujourd'hui l'huissier*, il le fait venir, il le fait tourner selon une temporalité anachronique ou selon une filiation incroyable – qui est d'ailleurs, aussi bien, l'origine de la foi. Car il excède le savoir et conditionne l'adresse à l'autre, incrit tout théorème dans l'espace et le temps d'un témoignage ('je te parle, crois moi'). Autrement dit, et c'est l'introduction à une aporie sans exemple, une aporie de la logique plutôt qu'une aporie sans exemple, une aporie de la logique plutôt qu'une aporie logique, voilà une impasse de l'indécidable par laquelle une décision ne peut pas ne pas passer. Toute responsabilité doit passer par cette aporie qui, loin de la paralyser, met en mouvement une nouvelle pensée du possible" (p. 519). At a practical level we might draw a parallel here with Leonardo da Vinci's "impossible machines" – from flying and diving apparatuses to a system of shafts and cogwheels for generating enormous heat to rival the sun – which were sketched in his unpublished notebooks but whose "possibility" remained a perpetual promise and spur to further creativity and inventiveness (see Owen Gingerich, "Leonardo da Vinci: Codex Leicester" in *Museum of Science* magazine, Boston, winter 1997).
68   Ibid., p. 518–19
69   Ibid., p. 519
70   Ibid., p. 517: "possibilité de l'impossible, impossibilité du possible, l'expérience en générale etc." See Derrida's admission of his debt to Husserl's notions of possibility/

impossibility on p. 521, note 27: "J'avais d'ailleurs, il y a bien longtemps, dans l'espace de la phénoménologie husserlienne, analysé de façon analogue une possibilité de forme apparemment négative, une im–possibilité, l'impossibilité de l'intuition pleine et immédi-ate, la 'possibilité essentielle de la non–intuition", la 'possibilité de la crise' comme 'crise du logos.' Or cette possibilté de l'impossibilité, disais-je alors, n'est pas simplement négative: le piège devient aussi une chance: "...cette possibilité (de la crise) reste liée pour Husserl au mouvement même de la vérité et à la production de l'objectivité idéale: celle-ci a en effet un besoin essential de l'écriture" (*De la grammatologie* [Paris: Minuit, 1967, p. 60]; et d'abord *Introduction à l'Origine de la géométrie de Husserl* [Paris: PUF, p. 162 passim]).

71   On this ambiguity see Louis Dupré, "Husserl's Thought on God," cited in note 15 above.

72   On this notion of God as "May-Be" and as "transfiguring posse," see our *Poétique du Possible*, part 3; and our more recent, "Transfiguring God" in the *Companion to Postmodern Theology*, ed. Graham Ward, Oxford: Blackwell (forthcoming 2001). Both reproduced in Richard Kearney, The God Who May Be: A Hermeneutics of Religion, forthcoming Indiana University Press.

13

GOD IS UNDERFOOT: PNEUMATOLOGY AFTER DERRIDA

Mark I. Wallace

In the beginning God created the heavens and the earth. The earth was a vast waste, darkness covered the deep, and the Spirit of God hovered over the surface of the water. (Gen. 1:1–2)

Religion requires a metaphysical backing; for its authority is endangered by the intensity of the emotions which it generates.[1]

God and Being are not identical, and I would never attempt to think the essence of God by means of being . . . If I still sought to write a theology, an idea to which I am sometimes inclined, then the word "being" ought not to figure in it. Faith does not need the thinking of being. If it needs it, it is already no longer faith.[2]

Theology and Metaphysics

The question of this volume is, "Who or what comes after the criticism of the God of metaphysics?" My response is that the critical analysis of the God of philosophical theism paves the way for a countermetaphysical, biblically-rooted, and earth-centered reenvisioning of the Spirit as the "green face" of God in a world under siege. At a time when the horror of ecocide is present to all living things, I contend that hope for a renewed earth is best undergirded not by the metaphysical quest for certainty but by recovering the biblical witness to God as Earth Spirit, the benevolent and sustaining force within the biosphere who is enfleshed within, and seeks to maintain the integrity of all forms of life on our planet.

Historically, thought about the Spirit in the West has been speculative and philosophical. In such discussions the Spirit has been defined in terms of the "ground of Being" or the "principle of consciousness," transforming the earthly reality of the Spirit, as witnessed to in the Bible, into a metaphysical abstraction that has little purchase on solving the crisis that now besets us. The philosophical determination of the Spirit as the ground of Being has consistently removed the topic of the Spirit from the concerns of culturally engaged theological reflection. Metaphysical pneumatology undermines a biblical understanding of the Spirit as the renewing power of God in a world suffering from chronic environmental abuse. In response, I propose postmodern green pneumatology as a way to revivify our thinking about the intimate relationship between God and the earth. Thus, I will draw in this essay on the rich and fecund nature tropes for the Spirit within the Bible – the Spirit as water, light, dove, mother, fire, breath, and wind – as an alternative to the regnant metaphysical models of the Spirit in historic Western thought.

My pneumatological response to the question "What follows after the God of philosophy?" steers a different course from the philosophical tack followed by much of traditional religious thought. In order to extricate itself from its tribal beginnings, the long-held desire of historic theology has always been to develop a metaphysically rooted system of beliefs with enough certitude to be considered a science. Unless and until theology becomes grounded on universal truths, so the argument goes, it runs the risk of remaining mired in the parochial origins of the early faith communities that gave rise to primitive theological reflection in the first place. My proposal may appear, then, to raise the specter of returning theology to the twilight of its prephilosophical beginnings. My suggestion that theology rediscover its biblical roots and abandon the ideal of universal, metaphysical reason looks like a frontal challenge to theology's time honored goal of rendering itself an intellectually credible discipline on a par with all other forms of inquiry within the academy. To now question this ideal, it seems, runs the risk of allowing theology to degenerate into a private language game, a confessionalist ghetto, inadequate to the public criteria for meaning and truth to which all forms of rational inquiry must subscribe.

As the natural sciences have been able to secure foundational knowledge about the order and predictability of physical objects, so theology, historically understood, sought to specify the transcendental conditions for the possibility of every form of being and existence, including the being and existence of God. The dream of historic theology, therefore, has always been the ideal of metaphysics, that is, "inquiry beyond or over beings which claims to recover them as such and as a whole for our grasp."[3] It is the ideal of a systematic transcendental investigation, as Kant put it, into the conditions of thought and experience built into the nature of reality itself. In Western culture, the various practitioners of metaphysical theology have hoped to articulate a body of intuitive beliefs about God, self, and world that are incorrigibly self-evident. The denial of these certain beliefs would so fundamentally alter the received understandings of reality with which we all operate that these beliefs cannot be seriously questioned. Insofar as the task of metaphysics is to explicate the conditions constitutive of being as such, theology, properly understood, is the highest form of metaphysics because it interrogates the nature of the one strictly necessary being, God, who is the source and end of all possible beings.

This metaphysical tradition continues into the present. For many contemporary Christian theologians and philosophers of religion, belief in God should have the same intellectual status as other incorrigible, self-evident truths. Many of the primary exponents of normative theology maintain that the problem of theology today is that it has not adequately patterned its efforts after the models of its counterparts in philosophy and science. They argue that the iteration of the right conceptual system for establishing the cognitive claims of Christianity has gone begging and that without an adequate intellectual undercarriage the faith of the church will retreat into the twilight world of fideism untouched by the light of reason and argument.

Alfred North Whitehead, for example, laments that while Christianity "has always been a religion seeking a metaphysic" it has suffered from "the fact that it has no clear-cut separation from the crude fancies of the older tribal religions."[4] Whitehead argues that if Christianity is to achieve the status of an authoritative, universal system of coherent beliefs, it must divorce itself from the intense experiences characteristic of its erstwhile tribal origins – that is, its pagan, Jewish, and early Christian origins – by adopting a body of formal truths concerning the conditions for understanding the nature of reality. "Religion requires a metaphysical backing; for its authority is endangered by the intensity of the emotions which it generates. Such emotions are evidence of some vivid experience; but they are a very poor guarantee of its correct interpretation."[5]

Wolfhart Pannenberg operates with the same anxiety as does Whitehead about the descent of Christian thought into its parochial, experiential origins without the aid of metaphysics. His response is to demonstrate the universality of Christian claims about God as Infinite on the basis of an analysis of the most general features of finite human existence. Much like Whitehead and other process thinkers, and in a manner similar to the tradition of neo-Thomist thought, Pannenberg avers that insofar as we are able to ask the question of being *as such*, and not simply inquire into the character of individual beings, we uncover our fundamental and implicit orientation toward the One who is the ground of all being(s).[6] Beyond the finitude and multiplicity that characterizes human existence, our common inquiries into the unity of experience and consciousness is an index to the reality of the One within all experience. "In the nature of things there is always a connection with the questions raised by the idea of God when an understanding of reality as a whole is articulated, since the question always arises of what the ultimate basis is for the unity of reality in any particular conception."[7] The reality of God is already implied in the question concerning the unity and ground of finite experience. As the thematization of an unthematized awareness of unity-within-difference, theology and philosophy, rightly understood, consist of converging metaphysical orientations.

The compatibility between metaphysical theology and philosophy stems from an agreement that genuine thought about God follows the classical trajectory of intellectual *ascent* beyond the plurality of everyday objects and experiences toward the One who grounds all things in itself. Philosophy and theology share the same metaphysical content, since both disciplines articulate the return path back to the Source who is above the created order: our destiny is our origin as we recover the reality of God as the ground and end of all existence. The call to thought to "rise above" and "ascend" to the Absolute beyond the finite is the proper telos of all religious reflection, theological or philosophical. Pannenberg writes: "Whenever philosophy uses the label 'God' for the absolute One – the goal of the metaphysical ascent above everyday experience – it already makes use of the language of religion ... [thus] there is a thematic unity between the absolute One of philosophy and the one God of the monotheistic religions."[8] While the existence of God cannot be proven *per se* according to Pannenberg, reason pressed to its limits entails the reality of God as its "term" or "whence," rendering the complementary modes of identifying God in both disciplines flip sides of the same metaphysical coin.

For Whitehead, Pannenberg, and others the assumed goal of metaphysical inquiry is the critical correlation between general philosophical truth and special revealed truth in order to provide an account of the truth of being as such. "If," as Whitehead argues, "our trust is in the ultimate power of reason as a discipline for the discernment of truth," then appeals to truth in religion must be brought to the bar of universal reason where the question is adjudicated concerning which truth-claims are demonstrably constitutive of all reality.[9] Balkanized as an exercise in religious subjectivism, theology has no place in the academy unless it can establish the validity of its claims on the basis of universal, metaphysical reflection.

The called-for reliance of theology on metaphysical presuppositions raises a number of questions, however, for a theology that seeks primary fidelity to the biblical witness. Should theology seek to ground its proposals on a metaphysical foundation, or should it abandon its quest for such foundations? Even if theology chooses the latter, can it do so? Can theology and metaphysics be disentangled so easily? As Heidegger asks, can theology "overcome" or "step back" beyond metaphysics by asserting its independence from any and all extratheological influences?[10] Or, as Derrida insists, "if one does not have to philosophize, one still has to philosophize" – in other words, even when one seeks to think outside the question of being, all thought, nevertheless, must circulate within a metaphysical economy?[11] Even if theology could insure its autonomy from the question of being, should it do so? Will theology not slide into tribalism and privatism unless it is conceived as homologous to metaphysics? Or does the practice of theology under the horizon of being threaten to undermine the novelty and hetero-geneity that is distinctive of all modes of authentic religious life and discourse?

To use God-language, does God need the openings that a metaphysical vocabulary can provide? Or are the openings proffered by such vocabularies in fact foreclosings of the presence of the Other who transgresses all categories and concepts? Given the historic elision of God and Being, how is the divine life to be understood in a contemporary setting? Is God a metaphysically certain *existent* within common human experience, or is God the unknowable (but not unspeakable) *Other* who is absolutely free of all metaphysical delimitations? Is God the necessary Being, the *ens realissimum*, who is knowable as the supreme origin of our beings, or is God, as the one who is *not-being* but still *is*, the violation of all categories and determinations? Is God best understood as the necessary ground of universal and contingent selfhood, the one who as Being-itself renders all derivative existence possible, or is God a reality anterior to and beyond all determinations (metaphysical or otherwise), a reality who meets us in ironic faith and discordant hope as we seek to encounter this reality in lives of openness to others?

Is Heidegger right that the question of Being in theology has saddled Christianity with a philosopher's God, the metaphysically certain God of supreme causality who mechani-cally functions as the cosmological ground and unity of all beings in the world? Relegating God to the part of a place-holder in a chain of cosmic causality, is theology captive to metaphysical assumptions that limit God to the role of highest existent, *ens a se*, pure actuality, being-itself, and *prima causa* – a distant, frozen, and abstract deity who, as "the god of philosophy," is such that one "can neither pray nor sacrifice to this god. Before the *causa sui*, man can neither fall to his knees in awe nor can he play music and dance before this god"?[12] Using Heidegger's formulation, must one engage in "god-less thinking which must abandon the god of philosophy" in order to approach the God of biblical faith?[13] If this is the case, is God, in short, not the *Being* known within the horizon of metaphysics, but the *occasion* for fostering new modes of scripturally nuanced existence that are no longer founded on the metaphysical securities of Western thought?

Derridean Iconoclasm

Jacques Derrida's thought is a fruitful resource in my attempt to reenvision the possibility of God outside the confines of metaphysics. Born in 1930 as a Jew in Muslim Algeria on a street named after St. Augustine, the rue Saint-Augustin, Derrida was raised in the lap of the three Western religions of the Book. Born a Jew, but whose "alliance" with Judaism was "broken in every respect," Derrida grew up praying to God in "Christian Latin French," but writes, nonetheless, that "I quite rightly pass for an atheist."[14] He is not an observant or confessing member of any religious denomination. And yet in his quasi-autobiographical musings entitled *Circumfession*, a running commentary on Augustine's *Confessions*, Derrida evinces a prayerful, spiritual yearning that he says everyone (including his own mother) has missed and misunderstood over the years. In these memoirs he laments a general misunderstanding of

> my religion about which nobody understands anything, any more than does my mother who asked other people a while ago, not daring to talk to me about it, if I still believed in God ... But she must have known that the constancy of God in my life is called by other names ...[15]

Derrida writes that in the vocabulary of the heart, God's presence and constancy is felt and understood, but that this God can only be identified through indirection, never directly. God is the object of Derrida's prayers and longings but, at the same time, this God is objectless and has no one definitive name (or to put it another way, God is the infinite bearer of many names). "All my life," he writes, "I have never stopped praying to God."[16] But *who* is this God he prays to? What is the *name* of this God? God cannot be *named*, according to Derrida, but many names can be *assigned to* God, nevertheless. No one name *per se* is adequate to describing God, but God can be named, prayed to, worshipped and adored. Like Augustine, whose voluminous writings assign a panoply of different names to God, Derrida says his own work operates under various designations for God as the undeconstructible – including names such as justice, spirit, hospitality, and the coming of the gift.[17] In order to shatter the idols that purport to name God with univocal certainty, Derrida implies here in his memoirs, and says explicitly elsewhere, that true religion must abandon all names for God in order to preserve God's freedom from captivity to the metaphysics of self-presence.[18] Could we say, then, that God is not at our disposal, but, rather, that God disposes us?

In his article "Sauf le nom," Derrida argues that in order to *save* the name of God it is necessary to *suspend* all names for God: to put into abeyance all names for God in order to identify the object of divine naming as without determinable object or reference.[19] As John Caputo says, one must save (*sauf*) "the name of God by keeping it safe (*sauf*); sacrificing the name of God precisely in order to save it. Sacrifice everything, save or except (*sauf*) the name of God. Save everything about God (keep God safe) save (except) the name of God, lest it become an idol that blocks our way."[20] In this regard, Derrida's religious thought has deep affinities with the tradition of so-called negative theology, which says God is neither this nor that in order to emancipate the possibility of God beyond the reach of the classical economy of ideas and names for God.[21] Although Derrida is quick to question the "hyperes-sentialism" of many forms of negative theology that understand God as Being, he writes approvingly, nevertheless, of certain negative theologies, such as Angelus Sile-sius's, that appear to avoid the sirens of crypto-essentialism by articulating an a/theology that "loses" God in order to "find" God (but not as Being). Commenting on Silesius's *The Cherubinic Wanderer*, Derrida writes that:

> It is necessary to leave all, to leave every "something" through love of God, and no doubt to leave God himself, to abandon him, that is, at once to leave him and (but) let him (be beyond being-something):
> *One must leave the something*
> Man, if you love something, then you love nothing truly:
> God is not this and that, leave then forever the something.
> *The most secret abandon*
> Abandon seizes God; but to leave God himself,
> Is an abandonment that few men can grasp [quoting *The Cherubinic Wanderer*, 1:44, 2:92][22]

Ironically, then, the best religion, in a certain sense, is no religion at all; the best name for God is no name at all. The "constancy of God in my life," Derrida writes, "is called by other names,"[23] but not by the name(s) of God as such, which allows Derrida to write about God, much in the way Silesius does, in the spirit of pseudonymous indirection, permitting God language a certain freedom and spontaneity that is denied it when it is under the control of strict philosophical or theological orthodoxy. Writing and talking about God indirectly allows God to relate to human persons in disruptive, heterogeneous freedom unconstrained by the controls of any sign-system – philosoph-ical, religious, or otherwise. The refusal to name God allows God, as an alien other, to arrive as the unassimable, indeterminate "something more," as William James puts it, who can productively transform human expectations. This refusal to name God preserves as much as possible the freedom of God to be God and unpredictably impact human experience as the question who subverts our answers – as the nameless, abyssal, ungraspable one who is coming but is nonetheless here as the heteronomic Other of our deepest longings.

Postmodern Theology

If God is wholly other as Derrida argues, can anything positive and determinate be said about this God other than the negative theological claim that God is unknowable? If God is unknowable and unnameable, what role, if any, can positive theology play in dialogue with Derrida's thought? I believe Derrida's iconoclasm encourages contem-porary theology, in spontaneity and freedom, to retrieve language and imagery of the divine life that has been repressed or forgotten. By avoiding the temptation to ground its enterprise on a philosophical foundation, theology is liberated to perform this retrieval by critically returning to its living wellspring – the founding stories and images of biblical faith. In eschewing the task of naming God as a knowable certainty, theology vis-à-vis

Derrida is set free to uncover neglected dimensions of the biblical witness that are desperately needed in our time. Glossing Derrida, my wager is that theology today is best served by returning *ad fontes* to its roots in the biblical narratives and cutting its moorings to the philosophical tradition of understanding God as supreme cause and ground of being. For theological purposes, the metaphysical tradition is sterile and fruitless because it has imparted to Christianity a distant and unfeeling deity, an apathetic unmoved mover, who can be neither feared nor loved, pleaded with nor danced to, blasphemed nor glorified. Such a God cannot be wrestled with and struggled against, as was the God of Jacob at the river Jabbok in Genesis; feared in terror, as was the God of Moses at the burning bush in Exodus; railed against in anger and bitterness, as was the God of many of the protagonists of biblical wisdom literature, such as David and Solomon and Job; petitioned in blood, as was the God of Jesus in Gethsemane in the Gospels; nor loved and worshipped, as was the God of Stephen who, upon being stoned to death by an angry mob in Acts, raised his eyes to heaven and said, "Lord, receive my spirit and do not hold this sin against them."

While recognizing that the metaphysical tradition has no resonance with the rich and variegated portraits of God within the biblical heritage, we may remain anxious that without the public security of a philosophical substructure, theology will lose its academic status and sink back into the netherworlds of privatism and tribalism. But this worry about the public versus private status of theology presupposes a sterile binary distinction that obscures a hidden middle path beyond the impasse generated by this false opposition. As an alternative to understanding theology in either strictly public or private terms, my proposal is for a *postmodern theology with an emancipatory intent* that critically retrieves language and imagery from previous (especially biblical) sources in order to enable personal and social transformation in a world at risk.

Postmodern theology is akin to other similar movements in contemporary thought. On one level, it bears affinities with postmodern architecture, which eclectically uses historical quotation in order to bring together materials, motifs, and styles from the past into a new urban design.[24] Like postmodern architecture, postmodern theology is an exercise in pastiche. It is self-consciously a *constructive* enterprise that selects from previous works thought forms and vocabulary that can be usefully recombined and refashioned in an idiom expressive of the hopes and desires of our age. On another level, however, postmodern theology goes beyond historical quotation and stylistic pastiche with its explicit commitment to enabling transformative praxis. Postmodern theology utilizes a wide variety of historical styles and motifs in order to craft a new theological framework that can productively engage the critical challenges of our time. Such an approach sacrifices neither intellectual rigor nor fidelity to the textual origins of Christian faith. On the one hand, postmodern theology abides by common norms of argument and rationality in order to articulate a body of beliefs that can withstand critical scrutiny and possible refutation; in so doing, however, it refuses to be held hostage to any philosophical assumptions (metaphysical or otherwise) that will blunt its move toward understanding the complexity of its subject matter, the mystery we call God. On the other hand, postmodern theology seeks rhetorical resonance to its documentary sources in order to construct a full-bodied vision of the divine life that can engender vitality and well being; in so doing, however, a biblically sonorous theology is vigilant in resisting the sectarian temptation to limit theology to the role of defending biblical or church orthodoxy. Eschewing both philosophical limits and ecclesial conformity, postmodern theology seeks creative and, at times, subversive fidelity to the biblical and historical traditions that can fund visions of liberation and change for a world in crisis.

Postmodern theology is methodologically parallel to Jeffrey Stout's notion of *bricolage* in contemporary moral philosophy. Quoting Claude Lévi-Strauss, Stout writes that *bricolage* is the process whereby a *bricoleur* constructs original artifacts (be they physical or conceptual constructs) based on the contingent resources and arbitrary materials at hand. The *bricoleur* takes the assorted odds and ends at her disposal and fashions them into a useful product; the random tools and elements at hand are the raw materials for the construction of the new project envisioned by the *bricoleur*.[25] Postmodern theology is a *bricolage* activity wherein the theorist cobbles together a framework for conversation between ancient source materials and contemporary realities and problems.

Green Pneumatology

Understanding postmodern theology as a constructive exercise in *bricolage*, my aim in the balance of this essay is to sketch the outlines for a coherent and liberating spirituality founded on the biblical texts that eschews the temptation to ground itself on the pseudo-security of a philosophical foundation. In particular, I propose to retrieve some key biblical tropes of *God as Spirit* as the most promising theological response to the growing crisis that defines our era – the immanent threat of global ecological collapse, the death of planetary life at the threshold of the third millennium. Few observers of the contemporary situation doubt that we face today an ecological crisis of unimaginable proportions. Whether though slow and steady environmental degradation or the sudden exchange of nuclear weapons, the specter of ecocide haunts all human and nonhuman life that share the resources of our planet home.[26] My case is that the most compelling religious response to the threat of ecocide lies in a rediscovery of God's presence within and love for all things earthly and bodily. A rediscovery of the ancient doctrine of the Holy Spirit as God's power of life-giving breath (*rûah*) within the cosmos is the doctrine that is ripe for recovery in our troubled times. I contend that an earth-centered reenvisioning of the Spirit as the "green face" of God in the world is the best grounds for hope and renewal at a point in human history when our rapacious appetites seemed destined to destroy the earth.[27] From this perspective, hope for a renewed earth is best founded on belief in God as Earth Spirit, the benevolent, all-encompassing divine force within the biosphere who continually indwells and works to maintain the integrity of all forms of life.[28]

In an ecological vein, the Spirit is best understood not as a metaphysical entity but as a healing life-force who engenders human flourishing as well as the welfare of the planet. Green pneumatology, as it were, positions the Spirit outside of the philosophical question of being and squarely within a nature-based desire for the integrity and health of all life-forms – human and nonhuman. This model understands the Spirit not as divine intellect or the principle of consciousness but as a healing and subversive *life-form* – as water, light, dove, mother, fire, breath, and wind – on the basis of different biblical figurations of the Spirit in nature. Philosophers of consciousness (for example, Hegel) have bequeathed to contemporary theology a metaphysically-burdened idea of the Spirit that has little purchase on the role of the Spirit in creation as the power of benevolent unity between all natural kinds. My wager is that an earth-centered understanding of the Spirit (beyond the categories of being) can both rehabilitate the central biblical affirmation of the Spirit's carnal nature and provide resources for confronting the environmental violence that marks our time.

My plea for a postmetaphysical green pneumatology stems from a desire to preserve the complete freedom of God as Spirit apart from the limitations imposed on the concept of God by metaphysics. I have argued that in the history of metaphysics (which includes such otherwise disparate thinkers as Aristotle, Hegel, Whitehead, and Pannenberg) God is understood as the supreme Being who is the source of unity among all other beings. In this model the otherness of God (including the otherness of God as Spirit) is colonized by a reductive philosophical analysis of God as a reality within, or coterminous with, Being itself. But in order to preserve divine freedom and novelty, I suggest that God as Spirit is not by any metaphysical necessity the Being of beings; rather, God as Spirit, in free and indeterminate decision, desires to be the life-giving breath who animates and maintains the whole natural order. In the biocentric model, God as Spirit is best understood, paradoxically, as *beyond* Being and still radically *immanent* to all beings within the natural order. Dialectically understood, therefore, God as Spirit should be figured as both *wholly other* to creation and *wholly enfleshed* within creation as the green love who nurtures and sustains all living things. The move away from defining God according to Being toward imagining God as life-source is not an exchange of one metaphysical absolute ("Being") for another ("Life" or "Nature"). Rather this move attempts to open up conceptual space for reenvisioning the freedom of God as Spirit to "blow where she wills" and not be determined by the question of Being within the domain of speculative philosophy.[29]

The sad legacy of historic Western theology, however, blunts our ability to envision the Spirit as an earthen life-form. In the history of the West, the Spirit is not understood as a friend of the earth but as a ghostly, bodiless entity far removed from the concerns of the created order. Conventional understandings of the Spirit evoke images of a vapid and invisible phantom ("the Holy Ghost") divorced from the tangible reality of life on this planet as we know it. These popular notions are rooted in the canonical definition of the Spirit as an incorporeal, bodiless, nonmaterial being that stands over and against the physical world, which is not of the same nature as the Spirit. As one theological dictionary puts it, the Spirit is "immaterial or nonmaterial substance . . . The term *spiritus* can therefore be applied to God generally [or] to the Third Person of the Trinity specifically . . ."[30] Much of Western thought – including religious thought – operates according to a series of binary oppositions that separate spirit from body, mind from matter, and God from nature. These dichotomies not only divide the spiritual world from the physical order. They also order the two terms in the polarity in a valuational hierarchy by positing the first term (spirit, mind, God) as superior to the second term (body, matter, nature). In general, therefore, Western thought has not only pitted the spiritual world and the physical order against one another but also subordinated the one to the other. In this schema, the Spirit is regarded as an eternally invisible and incorporeal force superior to the earthly realm which is mired in contingency and change.

This bipartite division between spirit and matter has a long and tenacious history in Western philosophical and religious traditions.[31] Plato's philosophical anthropology, for example, is controlled by metaphors of the body as the "prison house" and the "tomb" of the soul. The fulfillment of human existence, according to Plato, is to release oneself – one's soul – from bondage to dumb, bodily appetites in order to cultivate a life in harmony with one's spiritual, intellectual nature.[32] Origen, the third century CE Christian Platonist, took literally Jesus' blessing on those who "made themselves eunuchs for the kingdom of heaven" (Matt. 15:1) and at age twenty had himself castrated. As a virgin for Christ no longer dominated by his sexual and physical drives, Origen became a perfect vessel for the display of the Spirit.[33] But in the Christian West, Augustine is arguably most responsible for the hierarchical division between spirit and nature. Augustine maintains that human beings are ruled by carnal desire – *concupiscence* – as a result of Adam's fall from grace in the Garden of Eden. Adam's sin is transferred to his offspring – the human race – through erotic desire leading to sex and the birth of children. In their fleshly bodies, according to Augustine, infants are tainted with "original sin" communicated to them through their biological parents' sexual intercourse. Physical weakness and sexual desire are signs that the bodily, material world is under God's judgment. Thus, without the infusion of supernatural grace, all of creation – as depraved and corrupted – is no longer amenable to the influence of the Spirit.[34] This long tradition of hierarchical and antagonistic division between Spirit and matter continues into our own time – an era, often in the name of religion, marked by deep anxiety about and hostility toward human sexuality, the body, and the natural world.

At first glance, some of the biblical writings appear partial to this binary opposition between body and spirit. Consider Paul's rhetoric of spirit versus flesh in the Books of Romans and Galatians as cases in point. In Rom. 8:5–13, Paul emphasizes that "life in the flesh leads to death while life in the Spirit leads to life." This juxtaposition lends credence to the received notion that the material and spiritual orders are fundamental opposites in the New Testament. But while this reading of Paul is understandable given the force of his rhetoric here and elsewhere, this reading is a mistake. In reality, Paul's thought utilizes a threefold anthropology that trades on the terms *sarx* ("flesh"), *soma* ("body"), and *pneuma* ("spirit"). In this tripartite schema, the Christian subject is an embodied self (*soma*) who experiences the inner warfare between impulses that resist life in Christ (*sarx*) and a power within the self that brings the self into relationship with Christ (*pneuma*). Each of these terms carries a certain value in Paul's "systems" theory of the self: *soma*, as the human person in her essential bodily state, is positively understood as the environment within which the battle between the negative tendencies of *sarx* and the beneficial influence of *pneuma* is carried out. Far from denigrating the body (*soma*), Paul views bodily existence as essential to human being: it is not that we *have* bodies but that we *are* bodies as corporeal, enfleshed selves. As well, Paul's generally positive attitude toward the body is further expressed in I Cor. 6:19, 20 where he writes, "Do you not know that your body (*soma*) is a temple of the Holy Spirit (*hagiou pneumatos*) within you, which you have from God? . . . So glorify God in your body." The embodied, somatic Christian subject is a sacred dwelling place – a temple – inhabited by the Spirit of God. The Spirit and the body, therefore, are coterminous ideas in Paul's thought.[35]

Along with Paul, the vast majority of the biblical texts undermine the split between God and nature by structurally interlocking the terms in the polarity with one another. In particular, on the question of the Spirit, the system of polar oppositions is consistently undermined. In terms of the Spirit, rather than prioritizing the spiritual over the earthly, the scriptural texts figure the Spirit as a carnal, creaturely life-form always already interpenetrated by the material world. Granted, the term "Spirit" does conjure the image of a ghostly, shadowy nonentity in both the "popular" and "high" thinking of the Christian West. But the biblical texts stand as a stunning counter-testimony to this conventional mindset – including the conventional theological mindset. The Bible, rather, is awash with rich imagery of the Spirit borrowed directly from the natural world. In fact, the four traditional elements of natural, embodied life – *earth, air, water,* and *fire* – are constitutive of the Spirit's biblical reality as an enfleshed being who ministers to the whole creation God has made for the refreshment and joy of all beings. In the Bible, the Spirit is not a wraithlike being separated from matter but an embodied subject (like Jesus who was also an enfleshed life-form) made up of the four cardinal substances that compose the physical universe.

Numerous biblical passages attest to the foundational role of the four basic elements regarding the biocenric identity of the Spirit. (1) As *earth*, the Spirit is figured as a terrestrial being, a corporeal life-form that brings healing and renewal in her wings. The Spirit is both the *divine dove*, with an olive branch in its mouth, that brings peace and renewal to a broken and divided world (Gen. 8:11, Matt. 3:16, John 1:32), and a *fruit bearer*, such as a tree or vine, that yields the virtues of love, joy, and peace in the life of the disciple (Gal. 5:22–26). (2) As *air*, the Spirit is both the *vivifying breath* that animates all living things (Gen. 1:2, Ps. 104:29–30) and the *prophetic wind* that brings salvation and new life to those it indwells (Judges 6:34, John 3:6–8, Acts 2:1–4). (3) As *water*, the Spirit is the *living water* that quickens and refreshes all who drink from its eternal springs (John 4:14, 7:37–38). (4) And as *fire*, the Spirit is the *purgative fire* that alternately judges evildoers and ignites the prophetic mission of the early church (Matt. 3:11–12, Acts 2:1–4). In these texts, the Spirit is figured as the potency in nature who engenders life and healing throughout the biotic order.

Far from being ghostly and bodiless, the Spirit reveals herself in the biblical literatures as an earthly *life-form* who labors to create, sustain, and renew humankind and otherkind in solidarity with one another. As the divine wind in Genesis, the dove in the Gospels, or the tongues of flame in Acts, the Spirit does not exist apart from nature as a separate reality externally related to the created order. Rather, nature itself in all its fecundity and variety is the primary and indispensable mode of being for the Spirit's work in the world. The Spirit, then, is always underfoot, quite literally, as God's power in the earth who makes all things live and grow toward their natural ends. The earth's waters and winds and birds and fires that move within and upon the earth are not only *symbols* of the Spirit – as important as this nature symbolism is – but share in the Spirit's very *nature* as the Spirit is continually enfleshed and embodied through natural organisms and processes.

Conclusion

In this essay, I have proposed ecological pneumatology as an answer to the question, "Who or what follows in the wake of the critical analysis of the God of philosophical theism?" I have argued, in conversation with Derrida's iconoclasm, that the task of contemporary Spirit theology, in spontaneity and freedom, is to retrieve language and imagery of the divine life that has been repressed or forgotten. By eschewing the task of *naming* God as a knowable certainty, postmodern theology *rediscovers* God to be a carnal life-form through the agency of the Spirit. While not making a full turn to positive theology himself, Derrida, nevertheless, helps contemporary theology initiate the rediscovery of Earth God by encouraging it to abandon the pseudo-certainty of metaphysics in favor of uncovering neglected dimensions of the biblical witness that are desperately needed in our time of ecocidal despair. Unlike, say, Descartes's divine ground for self-knowledge or Kant's transcendent source for the moral law within, Derrida, much as Karl Barth did a generation before him, argues for the preservation of the freedom of God beyond metaphysics – to liberate theology, as Derrida puts it, from its "philosophical ego" in order to set free "a faith lived in a venturous, dangerous, free way."[36] From this angle, Derridean deconstruction is best understood not as a weapon in the war against faith, as its many critics argue, but as an exercise in philosophical hygiene that helps theology purge itself of its desire for metaphysical security. Rather than putting an end to theology as its judge and execu-tioner, deconstruction now becomes theology's helpmate and enables it to realize its true aim: a release from its dependency on philosophy in order to set free the evangelical testimony to a God who daily enfleshes Godself within the rich flora and fauna of the biotic order.

Can a recovery of the ancient, biblical idea of the Spirit as the green face of God provide the necessary focus for the practice of earth-healing in our time? I have proposed here that one of the most compelling *theological* responses to the threat of ecocide lies in a recovery of the Holy Spirit as God's power of life-giving breath (*rûah*) who indwells and sustains all life-forms. The answer to the increasing environmental degradation in our time is not better technology – a matter of more know-how – but a Spirit-motivated conversion of our whole way of life to sustainable living – a matter of the heart. Such a change of heart can occur through an encounter with Christian earth wisdom. This wisdom for our troubled times can be found in the rich biblical imagery of God as Spirit who sustains and renews all forms of life on the planet; the cor-responding belief, since the Spirit vivifies all things, in the interdependence that binds together all members of the biosphere in a global web of life; and the concomitant ethical ideal of working toward the healing of various biotic communities whenever they suffer ecological degradation.

Notes

1   Alfred North Whitehead, *Religion in the Making* (New York: Macmillan, 1926), p. 81.
2   Martin Heidegger, a conversation with Zürich students in 1951, quoted in Joseph S. O'Leary, *Questioning Back: The Overcoming of Metaphysics in Christian Tradition* (Minneapolis: Winston Press, 1985), p. 18.
3   Martin Heidegger, "What is Metaphysics?" in *Basic Writings*, trans. David Ferrell Krell (New York: Harper & Row, 1977), p. 109.
4   Whitehead, *Religion in the Making*, p. 50.

5   Whitehead, *Religion in the Making*, p. 81.

6   For a thoughtful comparison of the similarities among this group of philosophical theologians, see O'Leary, *Questioning Back*, pp. 1–112.

7   Wolfhart Pannenberg, *Theology and the Philosophy of Science*, trans. Francis McDonagh (Philadelphia: Westminster Press, 1976), p. 313.

8   Wolfhart Pannenberg, *Metaphysics and the Idea of God*, trans. Philip Clayton (Grand Rapids, MI: Wm. B. Eerdmans Publishing Co., 1990), p. 20.

9   Whitehead, *Religion in the Making*, p. 74.

10 Martin Heidegger, "The Onto-theo-logical Constitution of Metaphysics," in *Identity and Difference*, trans. Joan Stambaugh (New York: Harper & Row, 1969), pp. 42–76.

11 Jacques Derrida, "Violence and Metaphysics," in *Writing and Difference*, trans. Alan Bass (Chicago: University of Chicago Press, 1978), p. 152.

12 Heidegger, "The Onto-theo-logical Constitution of Metaphysics," p. 72.

13 Ibid.

14 Jacques Derrida, *Circumfession: Fifty-nine Periods and Periphrases*, in Geoffrey Bennington and Jacques Derrida, *Jacques Derrida* (Chicago: University of Chicago Press, 1993), pp. 154–5. I classify Derrida's musings in *Circumfession* as "autobiography" or "memoirs" insofar as these writings are exercises in writing the self, without making any claim as to the historicity of the "self" figured in these texts by Derrida.

15 Derrida, *Circumfession*, pp. 154–5. On the character of Derrida's philosophy of religion, see John Caputo, *The Prayers and Tears of Jacques Derrida: Religion without Religion* (Bloomington: Indiana University Press, 1997), Kevin Hart, "Jacques Derrida: The God Effect," in *Post-Secular Philosophy: Between Philosophy and Theology*, ed. Phillip Blond (London: Routledge, 1998), 259–80, and Mark I. Wallace, "God Beyond God: Derrida's Theological Self-Portraiture," in *Method as Path: Religious Experience and Hermeneutical Discourse*, ed. Elliot R. Wolfson (New York: Seven Bridges Press, 2001).

16 Derrida, *Circumfession*, p. 56.

17 John Caputo has identified in Derrida these and other unnameable names for God in *The Prayers and Tears of Jacques Derrida*.

18 Jacques Derrida, "Post-Scriptum: Aporias, Ways and Voices," trans. John P. Leavey, Jr., in *Derrida and Negative Theology*, eds. Harold Coward and Toby Foshay (Albany, NY: State University of New York Press, 1992), p. 317. I am referring to this article here as "Sauf le nom." See a slightly different version in Jacques Derrida, "Sauf le nom (Post-Scriptum)," trans. John P. Leavey, Jr., in *On the Name*, ed. Thomas Dutoit (Stanford: Stanford University Press, 1995), pp. 35–85.

19 See Derrida, "Post-Scriptum: Aporias, Ways and Voices" [aka "Sauf le nom"].

20 Caputo, *The Prayers and Tears of Jacques Derrida*, p. 43.

21 Jacques Derrida, "How to Avoid Speaking: Denials," in *Derrida and Negative Theology*, eds. Harold Coward and Toby Foshay (Albany, NY: State University of New York Press, 1992).

22 Derrida, "Post-Scriptum: Aporias, Ways and Voices" [aka "Sauf le nom"], p. 317.

23 Derrida, *Circumfession*, p. 155.

24 For an analysis of postmodern architecture, see David Harvey, *The Condition of Postmodernity* (Cambridge, MA: Blackwell, 1990), pp. 66–98.

25 For this discussion, see Jeffrey Stout, *Ethics After Babel: The Languages of Morals and Their Discontents* (Boston: Beacon, 1988), pp. 71–81.

26 See Bill McKibben, *The End of Nature* (New York: Random House, 1989), and Jeremy Rifkin, *Biosphere Politics: A Cultural Odyssey from the Middle Ages to the New Age* (San Francisco: HarperSanFrancisco, 1991), pp. 71–91.

27   In her earlier work Sallie McFague argued that the model of God as Spirit is not retrievable
     in an ecological age, criticizing traditional descriptions of the Spirit as ethereal and vacant.
     But in her recent writing McFague performs the very retrieval of pneumatology she had
     earlier claimed was impossible: a revisioning of God as Spirit in order to thematize the
     immanent and dynamic presence of the divine life within all creation. See *The Body of God:
     An Ecological Theology* (Minneapolis: Fortress Press, 1993), pp. 141–50. For an appreciation
     and critique of McFague's ecotheology see my *Fragments of the Spirit: Nature, Violence, and
     the Renewal of Creation* (New York: Continuum, 1996), pp. 139–44. Some of the material
     in this paper is borrowed from *Fragments of the Spirit* and subsequent articles I have written.

28   In recent years, there has been a surge of interest in Spirit-discourse from a variety of
     disciplinary perspectives. Many of these works have been essential to my own thinking
     about the Spirit in nature in this essay. In theology, see José Comblin, *The Holy Spirit and
     Liberation*, trans. Paul Burns (Maryknoll, NY: Orbis Books, 1989), Peter C. Hodgson,
     Winds of the Spirit: A Constructive Christian Theology (Louisville: Westminster John Knox
     Press, 1994), Adolf Holl, *The Left Hand of God: A Biography of the Holy Spirit*, trans. John
     Cullen (New York: Doubleday, 1998), Chung Hyun-Kyung, "Welcome the Spirit; Hear
     Her Cries: The Holy Spirit, Creation, and the Culture of Life," *Christianity and Crisis* 51
     (July 15, 1991): 220–3, Elizabeth A. Johnson, *She Who Is: The Mystery of God in Feminist
     Theological Discourse* (New York: Crossroad, 1992), Jürgen Moltmann, *God in Creation: A
     New Theology of Creation and the Spirit of God*, trans. Margaret Kohl (San Francisco: Harper
     & Row, 1985), Moltmann, *The Source of Life: The Holy Spirit and the Theology of Life*, trans.
     Margaret Kohl (Minneapolis: Fortress Press, 1997), Mark McClain Taylor, "Tracking
     Spirit: Theology as Cultural Critique in America," in *Changing Conversations: Religious
     Reflection and Cultural Analysis*, ed. Dwight N. Hopkins and Sheila Greeve Davaney (New
     York: Routledge, 1996), pp. 123–44, Nancy Victorin-Vangerud, *The Raging Hearth: Spirit
     in the Household of God* (St. Louis, MO: Chalice Press, 2000), and Michael Welker, *God the
     Spirit*, trans. John F. Hoffmeyer (Minneapolis: Fortress Press, 1994); in philosophy, see
     Jacques Derrida, *Of Spirit: Heidegger and the Question*, trans. Geoffrey Bennington and
     Rachel Bowlby (Chicago: University of Chicago Press, 1989), Derrida, *Specters of Marx:
     The State of the Debt, the Work of Mourning, and the New International*, trans. Peggy Kampf
     (New York: Routledge, 1994), and Steven G. Smith, *The Concept of the Spiritual: An Essay
     in First Philosophy* (Philadelphia: Temple University Press, 1988); and in cultural studies, see
     Joel Kovel, *History and Spirit: An Inquiry into the Philosophy of Liberation* (Boston: Beacon
     Press, 1991).

29   On the history of the problematic relation between metaphysics and pneumatology, see
     Alan M. Olson, *Hegel and the Spirit: Philosophy as Pneumatology* (Princeton: Princeton
     University Press, 1992), pp. 3–35, 107–62. For a defense of a countermetaphysical
     model of God, see Jean-Luc Marion, *God Without Being: Hors-Texte*, trans. Thomas A.
     Carlson (Chicago: University of Chicago Press, 1991). Finally, a note here about my use of
     different pronouns for the Spirit – including the female pronoun. As God's indwelling
     presence throughout the created order, the Spirit is variously identified with feminine,
     maternal characteristics in the biblical witness. The mother Spirit bird in Gen. 1 "broods"
     or "hovers" over the earth bringing all things into life and fruition; this same hovering
     Spirit bird appears in the gospels at Jesus' baptism to inaugurate his public ministry. In
     Proverbs 1, 8, 9 and the Book of Wisdom, God as Wisdom or *Sophia* is understood
     analogously to the maternal Spirit of Gen. 1 and the gospels: the nursing mother of
     creation who protects and sustains the well-being of all things in the cosmic web of life.
     Some early Christians believed that the Hebrew feminine grammatical name of the Spirit –
     rûah – was a linguistic clue to certain woman-identified characteristics of God as Spirit. On
     the history of feminine language for the Spirit, see Susan Ashbrook Harvey, "Feminine

Imagery for the Divine: The Holy Spirit, the Odes of Solomon, and Early Syriac Trad-
ition," *St Vladimir's Theological Quarterly* 37 (1993): 111–40, Gary Steven Kinkel, *Our Dear
Mother the Spirit: An Investigation of Count Zinzendorf's Theology and Praxis* (Lanham, MD:
University Press of America, 1990), and Johnson, *She Who Is*, pp. 128–31.

30 This definition is from the entry on "spiritus" by Richard A. Muller, *Dictionary of Latin and
Greek Theological Terms* (Grand Rapids, MI: Baker Book House, 1985), p. 286.

31 The literature on this question is extensive. See *inter alia* Caroline Walker Bynum,
Fragmentation and Redemption: Essays on Gender and the Human Body in Medieval Religion
(New York: Zone Books, 1991), Susan Griffin, *Woman and Nature: The Roaring Inside Her*
(New York: Harper & Row, 1978), Mark Johnson, *The Body in the Mind: The Bodily Basis
of Meaning, Imagination, and Reason* (Chicago: University of Chicago Press, 1987), and
William R. LaFleur, "Body," in *Critical Terms for Religious Studies*, ed. Mark C. Taylor
(Chicago: University of Chicago Press, 1998), pp. 36–54.

32 Plato *Timaeus* 42–9, 89–92.

33 Peter Brown, *The Body and Society: Men, Women, and Sexual Renunciation in Early Christianity* (New York: Columbia University Press, 1988), pp. 160–89.

34 Augustine *The Confessions* 7–8. Also see Peter Brown, *Augustine of Hippo* (Berkeley:
University of California Press, 1969), pp. 158–81, 340–97, and Elaine Pagels, *Adam, Eve,
and the Serpent* (New York: Random House, 1988), pp. 98–154.

35 On Paul's anthropology, see J. Christiaan Beker, *Paul the Apostle: the Triumph of God in Life
and Thought* (Philadelphia: Fortress Press, 1980), pp. 213–302.

36 The quotation by Derrida is from Anselm Haverkamp, ed., *Deconstruction in America: A
New Sense of the Political* (New York: New York University Press, 1995), p. 12. At first
glance, this Derrida-Barth association may appear forced. Nevertheless, each thinker's
countermetaphysical concern with ineradicable alterity in language – what Barth calls the
Word in the words and Derrida now refers to as the *undeconstructible* – provides a fertile field
of comparative analysis in spite of their important differences. On the potential of
deconstruction in theological reflection (with special reference to Barth), see Graham
Ward, *Barth, Derrida and the Language of Theology* (Cambridge: Cambridge University
Press, 1995), and my "Karl Barth and Deconstruction," *Religious Studies Review* 25 (October 1999): 349–54. On the potential of deconstruction in theological reflection in general,
see *Religion*, eds. Jacques Derrida and Gianni Vattimo (Stanford: Stanford University Press,
1998) and Kevin Hart, *The Trespass of the Sign: Deconstruction, Theology and Philosophy*
(Cambridge: Cambridge University Press, 1989). For a less sanguine reading of the
relationship between deconstruction and theology among radical orthodox thinkers in
which Derridean thought is labeled nihilistic, necrophilic, and fascistic, see John Milbank,
Catherine Pickstock, and Graham Ward, "Introduction: Suspending the Material: The
Turn of Radical Orthodoxy," in *Radical Orthodoxy: A New Theology*, ed. Milbank, et al.
(London: Routledge, 1999), pp. 1–20, Catherine Pickstock, *After Writing: On the Liturgical
Consummation of Philosophy* (Oxford: Blackwell, 1998), and Phillip Blond, "Introduction:
Theology Before Philosophy," in *Post-Secular Philosophy: Between Philosophy and Theology*,
ed. Blond (London: Routledge, 1998), pp. 1–66.

14

BEYOND BELIEF?: SEXUAL DIFFERENCE AND RELIGION AFTER ONTOTHEOLOGY

Ellen T. Armour
For Dr. Gail McClay (1937–1999)
in memoriam

A survey of the body of work on religion and continental philosophy finds an interesting gender gap around the significance of the issue of sexual difference to continental philosophy of religion and theology inflected by it. Sexual difference occupies center stage in the work of feminist scholars in this area, and opens new areas of inquiry to them.[1] While male philosophers and theologians in this field frequently note sexual difference as a feature in this landscape, it rarely affects the shapes their projects take.[2] A consensus has yet to emerge, then, about the nature and scope of the relationship between sexual difference and religion within continental philosophy, and thus about the significance of sexual difference to continental philosophy of religion and theology. In this paper, I attempt to move the conversation forward by arguing that the presence of symptoms of sexual (in)difference at the place where religion and continental thought intersect is (1) not coincidental and (2) important not only to feminist religious reflection, but to any claim to move religion beyond ontotheology.

Like other feminist scholars in this field, I think continental philosophy – particularly the work of Jacques Derrida and Luce Irigaray – calls for a radical rethinking of traditional ways of framing issues in philosophy of religion and theology. I will focus on one such frame here, the primacy given to belief. Traditionally, theology and philosophy of religion have served as guardians of belief. By subjecting particular beliefs to rational scrutiny, they provide support for those beliefs that survive the light of reason and reject those that do not. The relationship between faith and philosophy cuts differently in recent engagements between religion and continental philosophy.[3] Rather than offering the means for adjudicating and refining religion's truth, philosophy is frequently deemed the primary source of religion's infection by ontotheology. Under the guise of aiding belief, philosophy has led religion astray by providing only the false idols of ontotheological gods. Indeed, Jean-Luc Marion (1991) suggests that the so-called death of God is a boon to Christianity rather than a bane. Philosophy's god has died, says Marion, making room for the (re)emergence of the true god of faith. Rather than a god whose being is in question, this god is as pure gift, as self-giving love made manifest in the Eucharist (properly administered by priests in proper relationship to the ecclesiastical hierarchy).[4]

The reading I will offer here of two essays that appear within this volume – Irigaray's "Belief Itself" (Irigaray, 1993) and Derrida's "Circumfession" (in Bennington and Derrida, 1993) – will call into question this tendency to limit ontotheology's reach to philosophy and to reason. I will argue that, like philosophy, belief exhibits symptoms of sexual (and racial) indifference, which are central to the text of metaphysics, as I have argued elsewhere.[5] The Eucharist will play a central role in this inquiry into belief. Rather than a site exempt from ontotheology, as Marion proposes, the account I will give suggests that the Eucharist is an overdetermined locus of its inscription.

As Derrida and Irigaray both show, the text of metaphysics is ontotheological, logocentric, and phallogocentric. That is, at the foundation of this text lies a concept of God as absolute presence, absolute transcendence, unadulterated unity and pure being. This God, the founder of all that is (the theos that grounds ontos), serves as the guarantor of truth because his Word (logos) is reality. My reference to this God as "he" is neither coincidental nor incidental to the shape the text of metaphysics takes. The economies of truth, value, and desire that the text of metaphysics structures and sustains are phallocentric. That is, the phallus serves as the standard of value, the marker of the capacity for truth, and the object of desire that keeps these economies in circulation. Exchanges between masculine figures structure these economies, while female figures serve as their currency and raw material.

The intrinsic connection between ontotheology, logocentrism and phallocentrism would suggest that sexual and racial difference would be central to any vision of what might succeed ontotheology. This essay will also develop that suggestion with regard to sexual difference.[6] Irigaray's astute diagnosis of religion's place in sustaining sexual indifference challenges Marion's proposal of the Eucharist as a site beyond ontotheology. Derrida's quasi-autobiographical essay, which is replete with religious motifs, opens up a different route through the context Irigaray exposes. Its references to circumcision, to God, to prayers and tears, have received considerable attention to date, most notably in John D. Caputo's account of Derrida's "religion without religion" in *The Prayers and Tears of Jacques Derrida* (1997). However, reading "Circumfession" in light of "Belief Itself" brings other equally significant motifs (the maternal body, mourning, the interplay between life and death) to the fore whose religiosity lies just below the surface. Through reading these two texts together, I hope to show that sexual difference reshapes and reframes our vision of what might come after ontotheology.

Luce Irigaray on Religion and Sexual Difference

Understanding the role that religion plays in Irigaray's work requires some sense of the aim of her work as a whole. As several of her Anglophone commentators have noted, Irigaray describes her overarching project in Heideggerian terms. Each epoch has its question to think through; for Heidegger's day, it was the meaning of the question of being. Irigaray argues that our era faces the question of sexual difference. Beginning with her first book on philosophy, *Speculum of the Other Woman* (1985), Irigaray has relentlessly exposed sexual indifference as the heart of our cultural economy or grammar. Symptoms of sexual indifference appear in our culture's primary discourse of sexual subjectivity (psychoanalysis), in the discourse that attempts to articulate what is fundamental to reality (philosophy), and in the discourse of economic liberation (Marxism). Through often dazzling readings of texts central to these traditions, Irigaray exposes the cultural economy's repeated attempts to "fix" woman in her place; a place that denies her speech, subjectivity, and rights as a woman even as it uses her as a resource to sustain culture. Within the current economy, women as such serve as resources for exchanges between men. Their potential use defines their value (as virgins and as mothers). At the same time, Irigaray also shows that woman (and female figures like matter and nature) perpetually eludes these attempts to fix her. Woman/ matter/nature continually (but silently) exceed the grasp of this economy.

Irigaray is not content simply to expose the inner workings of sexual indifference. Answering the question posed to our era requires enabling genuine sexual alterity to come into being. This will make possible genuine relations between women and women (mothers/daughters, friends, lovers) and women and men (mothers/sons, friends, lovers). Women must come into their own as women, not as men's others who reflect them back to themselves as they would like to believe they are.

Religion plays a central role in both sides of Irigaray's project. Religious sites exhibit the symptoms of the disease of sexual indifference that Irigaray diagnoses. At the same time, Irigaray often turns to religious motifs when she invokes possible passages to a future economy of sexual difference. Both aspects of religion have been present in Irigaray's work from the beginning. At the heart of Speculum's architectural structure lies an essay entitled "*La mystérique*," which discusses medieval women mystics and visionaries as possible examples of a female subjectivity.[7] The essays in *Sexes and Genealogies* (1993), the anthology from which "Belief Itself" is taken, offer perhaps Irigaray's most sustained attention to religion currently available in English translation. Central to this essay (and to this volume) is Irigaray's critique of western Christianity as a site where the primordial maternal sacrifice both occurs and is hidden. Irigaray also recovers resources within the Christian tradition that contain traces of sexual differ- ence. These resources appear at points of rupture within the order of sexual indiffer- ence that point beyond it. For example, she points toward the figures of Mary and Anne (Mary's mother) as portraying a female genealogy. The figure of the angel, central to "Belief Itself" as well as other essays, signals the crossing of the borders that constitute religion and the text of metaphysics (matter/spirit, earth/heaven, mind/ body, male/female, divine/human).

Both sides of Irigaray's work with religion appear in "Belief Itself." Written for a colloquium at Crisy-la-Salle on Derrida's essay, "The Ends of Man," "Belief Itself" explores a link Irigaray sees between the presenting problem of one of her analysands and Derrida's analysis of Freud's *Beyond the Pleasure Principle* (1961) in *The Post Card* (1987). Irigaray's analysand presents her with a religious problem. Irigaray's analysand reports that, at the moment during the Eucharist when the priest intones the words of institution, she bleeds. Two additional facts heighten the strangeness of this situation. Irigaray's analysand is not present at the Mass when the bleeding occurs. Moreover, she claims not to believe in the dogmas of the Catholic church (though she "loves the son," Irigaray writes elliptically). In a move reminiscent of Freud's *Totem and Taboo* (1962) Irigaray reads this incident as symptomatic of cultural dynamics. *Totem and Taboo* located the origin of religion in a primordial patricide, which is both forgotten and commemorated (via a substitute) in religious rituals. Similarly, Irigaray suggests that her analysand's experience witnesses to a sacrifice of woman/matter/nature hidden beneath the sacrifice of the son explicitly commemorated in the Eucharist. Irigaray locates this sacrifice in the cultural imaginary, not in some distant (real or imagined) past event. Irigaray's maternal sacrifice is arguably less speculative than Freud's patricide (located in an imagined prehistory). As Irigaray's oeuvre shows over and over again, the maternal sacrifice is enacted and reenacted throughout the fabric of our culture (in families, in the value assigned to women in our economy, in philosophical texts, and so on). Yet complex mechanisms (psychoanalytic and otherwise) obscure its face.

Belief turns out to be one of those mechanisms. As Irigaray notes, belief by definition (and as opposed to confidence or fidelity) presupposes a denial of the real. Belief asserts an account of what is in spite of what appears to be real. In order to work, the real must remain hidden from view. In this case, the sacrifice of the maternal body (that the eucharistic sacrifice simultaneously commemorates and covers over) must be obscured in order for the sacrificial economy that it sustains to function.[8] Neither the sacrificial economy nor belief, however, resides solely within the religious realm; rather, the sacrificial economy IS our cultural economy, which is structured and sustained by belief. For this reason, Irigaray argues, an inquiry into belief itself is crucial to any inquiry into sexual difference. Hence the link between her analysand's experience and *The Post Card*.

Among the many scenes of (mis)communication that *The Post Card* discusses is Freud's famous analysis of the *fort/da* game played by his grandson, Ernst. The game consists of physical and verbal actions. The little boy tosses a spool on a string onto a curtained bed and then pulls it out again. When the spool disappears, Ernst says "o-o-o-o" (an approximation of "Fort," "away/lost/gone"). When it reappears, Ernst says, "Da" ("there"). Freud concludes that the repetitive game is the little boy's attempt to handle his frustration at his mother's comings and goings. The game commemorates the child's "great cultural achievement − the instinctual renunciation (that is, the renunciation of instinctual satisfaction) which he had made in allowing his mother to go away without protesting" (Freud 1961, p. 14).

As Derrida reads this episode in *The Post Card*, the narrative and the game open onto an abyssal set of mirrors that reveal multiple *fort/da* games played by multiple subjects, including Freud himself − as founder of psychoanalysis and as a family man (father, grandfather, husband, and son). These specular reflections are set in motion by the figure of the mother/daughter which occupies the (mute) center of *Beyond the Pleasure Principle*. *Beyond the Pleasure Principle* was published in 1920, the same year in which Freud's daughter, Sophie (who is Ernst's mother) died of influenza. Sophie's death leaves a series of traces − implicit and explicit − in this text, as Derrida reads it. In a footnote added to his account of the *fort/da* game after Sophie's death, Freud connects the game to the way Sophie's son (now almost six) handled his mother's death. "Now that she was really 'gone' ('o-o-o') the little boy showed no signs of grief" (Freud, 1961, p. 16, n. 7). Some of Freud's contemporaries used the connection between Sophie's death, this autobiographical episode, and the timing of *Beyond the Pleasure*

Principle's publication to challenge psychoanalysis's claim to scientific status. In *The Post Card*, Derrida returns to the question of autobiography and psychoanalysis in *Beyond the Pleasure Principle*, but in a very different vein. He, too, argues for a connection between Sophie's death and the text through a pairing of grandson and grandfather that repeats the pairing of Socrates and Plato from which *The Post Card* takes its title. The observing eye of Freud-the-scientist is also the specular mirror in which numerous reflections and refractions of Freud-the-family-man appears. Reflected in Freud-the-scientist's account of the son's displacement of the work of mourning his mother Derrida finds the father's displacement of the work of mourning his daughter. Reflected in Freud-the-scientist's account of Ernst's jealousy toward his brother (Freud links Ernst's lack of grief to this additional cause) is Freud-the-family-man's jealousy of his daughter's husband. These ever expanding circles ripple into the future, as well – toward the anticipated death of Freud's mother, toward his anticipation of his own death, toward the death of Ernst's brother (Freud's favorite grandson) and through him, backward in time toward the death of Freud's brother, Julius.

Derrida's interest, however, does not lie in Freud's psychobiography. Rather than calling into question the text's legitimacy as a scientific contribution, the connection between Freud and little Ernst calls forth a rethinking of the relationship between autobiography and psychoanalysis; indeed, a rethinking of the auto–bio–graphical (the links between autos, bios/thanatos, and graphos) itself.[9] Irigaray's reading highlights particular figures that shed important light on connections between the dynamics just described and questions of ontotheology, religion, and sexual difference.

Irigaray sees significant links between this game, its place in psychoanalytic theory, and her analysand's experience. She notes a commonality between Sophie's role in the *fort/da* game (and Freud's account of it) and her analysand's relationship to the Eucharist. Like Sophie, the age of Irigaray's analysand positions her as both mother and daughter. Just as Sophie's absence is crucial to the ritual of the *fort/da* game and Freud's account of it, so the bleeding woman's absence from the scene of the actual performance of the mass is central to its success. In both cases, though, the (unremarked) presence of female figures makes the ritual possible. The elements that circulate in the Eucharistic ritual are body and blood, bread and wine – elements marked as female by our cultural grammar. Their connection to the maternal body is, then, peculiarly present and absent.

The veil or curtain around Ernst's bed through which he tosses his spool occupies a similar (non)place of presence/absence in Freud's description of the *fort/da* game. As Irigaray notes, the veil is simply background in Freud's account. He fails to take account of its texture, its color, or the degree of its opacity. Yet without the veil/curtain, there would be no disappearance/reappearance, and no *fort/da* game.

In bringing the role of the veil/curtain to her reader's attention, Irigaray follows through on a particularly interesting passage (textual and geographical) in Derrida's analysis of the *fort/da* game. Derrida calls attention to the role of the curtained bed (with all of its sexual connotations) in the game. He remarks on the ease with which connections between the curtained bed and figures like the hymen, veil, umbrella, etc. – figures about which he has written so much – could be drawn. A few pages later, he even refers to the curtain as "the hymen of the fort:da" (Derrida, 1987, p. 316). But Derrida passes by that path of inquiry, remarking as he does so that he has "neither the time nor the taste for this task, which can be accomplished by itself or done without" (1987, p. 309).

For Irigaray, however, this path will not be so easily bypassed. In fact, within the figure of the veil lies the key to an even more deeply hidden subtext of the *fort/da* game. The veil rises on a yet more primordial loss common to both grandson and grandfather, the loss of their original dwelling place, the maternal body. At a deeper level, Irigaray argues, it is this gift without return (uncompensated and gone forever) that the game seeks to master rather than to mourn. It is this same gift that funds the Eucharist, and to which Irigaray's analysand witnesses without knowing it.

So far, my account of Irigaray's reading of this scene has uncovered thematic similarities to her analysis of her analysand's experience: that is, both the *fort/da* game and the Eucharist cover over and commemorate the loss of female figures. However, Irigaray argues that belief itself – not just this particular content – plays a structural role in both rituals. Belief's role in the Eucharistic feast is perhaps too obvious to need comment. But Irigaray finds belief at work in little Ernst's game and in Freud's narrative of it. Ernst believes that the ritual of the *fort/da* game grants him mastery over his mother's presence and absence. And he believes it because it is not true. "At the moment when he believes he is best able to master her appearance-disappearance, he is most slave to belief. Belief in himself and his power of course, but also in her, since his link to her depends upon the belief that she is there, when she is not, that she is there more when she is not there (here), that she is where she isn't" (Irigaray, 1993, p. 31). Belief plays a central role in what stands in for mourning. Ernst believes that he has mastered his mother's presence and absence, his own presence and absence, indeed, the dynamics of life and death themselves (indicated by his lack of grief at his mother's death).

Ironically, given Freud's desire that psychoanalysis be regarded as a science, Irigaray argues that the entire account rests on belief for its validity. The boy's naïve belief serves as the guarantee of Freud's scientific account and of its appeal to Freud's readers who must believe Freud's account of the boy's naïveté, in order to find Freud's analysis persuasive.

Theorizing belief as a source of compensation and/or escape from the pains and sufferings of life and death is nothing new. Indeed, such views are arguably hallmarks of modernity's view of religion. Each major hermeneut of suspicion (Marx, Freud, Nietzsche) offers different versions of it. But Irigaray's account is distinctive on several fronts, especially in relationship to questions about what comes after ontotheology. Whereas Freud and Marx advocate the triumph of the secular over the religious, Irigaray challenges that very division itself. She is, of course, hardly proposing a return to a traditional sacramentalism of any sort. Rather, she exposes the presence of one of western religion's structuring concepts, belief, in a setting that thinks it has outgrown religion. Moreover, her account suggests that psychoanalysis and Christianity share the same (effaced) object of belief, the maternal body. Irigaray's claim goes even farther. Psychoanalysis and Christianity may offer particularly clear views of the obscured female sacrifice and the unmourned maternal body, but such altars and crypts are not limited to these sites. Psychoanalysis and religion are symptomatic of a larger context, the cultural imaginary. Rather than being confined to discrete cultural arenas, Irigaray's analysis suggests that belief structures our cultural imaginary.

"Belief Itself" suggests that faith per se – and Christian faith, in particular – is also circumscribed by ontotheology, which challenges Marion's claims for the Eucharistic god. As I noted earlier, phallocentrism, logocentrism and ontotheology go together; thus, failure to escape from one calls into question claims that one has escaped from the other. If, underneath explicit invocations of a paternal sacrifice of a son lies an unacknowledged and unmourned maternal sacrifice, phallocentrism extends to the very heart of Christian faith. The death of philosophy's god may reopen access (if it was ever really lost) to the god of Christian faith, as Marion claims, but that god as invoked by Marion is still inscribed within the circuit of phallocentrism, logocentrism, and ontotheology. As I have argued elsewhere (n.d.), Marion's god remains inscribed within a phallocentric economy. Access to this (masculine) god's self-giving love comes through the chain of fathers and sons that stand in for him and through whose hands circulate the (feminine) elements of the Eucharistic feast.

This is not to suggest that we are now bereft of any route beyond ontotheology. Nor does it mean that religion – Christian or otherwise – cannot survive without ontotheology. Irigaray's exposure of the truth of belief in "Belief Itself" shifts attention away from theological or philosophical abstractions to the material realm of rituals and bodies, material practices and their symbolic meanings. If belief works only as long as the underlying dynamics that fund it remain hidden, what will happen when those dynamics are exposed and explored? What if, rather than covering up the maternal sacrifice, the pains of life and death, and one's mourning for the maternal body, one were to render these themes explicit? Could these resources traditionally mined without acknowledgement for ontotheological support actually go elsewhere? And would that "elsewhere" be religious in any sense? When read with the texts and issues discussed so far in mind, Derrida's "Circumfession," offers a provocative and suggestive perspective on these questions.

Circumfession

> Never will the man flayed alive that I am have written like this, knowing in advance the nonknowledge into which the imminent but unpredictable coming of an event, the death of my mother, Sultana Esther Georgette Safar Derrida, would come to sculpt the writing from the outside, give it its form and its rhythm from an incalculable interruption, never will any of my texts have depended in its most essential inside on such a cutting, accidental and contingent outside, as though each syllable, and the very milieu of each periphrasis were preparing itself to receive a telephone call, the news of the death of one dying. ("Circumfession," Bennington and Derrida, 1993, p. 207)

"Circumfession" consists of "59 periods and periphrases" (Bennington, 1993, p. vii) that form a countertext to Geoffrey Bennington's "Derridabase." The two, text and countertext, run together across the bottom and top (respectively) of the book entitled *Jacques Derrida* (Bennington 1993). In a sense, the two texts stage a battle over the proper ownership of "Jacques Derrida." In "Derridabase," Bennington sets out to "describe . . . at least the general system of [Jacques Derrida's] thought" ("Derridabase," Bennington, 1993, p. 1). "Circumfession" is Derrida's attempt to thwart Bennington by writing a text that resists systematization, surprising Bennington at every turn. I describe this battle as staged for a number of reasons. First of all, as both Bennington and Derrida acknowledge, *Jacques Derrida* is as much a labor of love between friends as it is a contest. Second, the relationship between this project and its supposed subject/object, the "real" Jacques Derrida, is problematic at best. As I will note below, "Circumfession" seems designed to obscure as much as it reveals about its author. As Bennington notes in "Acts of Genre," the biographical text appended to *Jacques Derrida*, the versions of Derrida's life produced between these covers are particular to the context of this project. Other contexts would have produced other lives with their own tangled relationship to their purported subject. Similar dynamics attend Bennington's relationship to *Jacques Derrida*. As a protagonist/antagonist of this project, the author of "Derridabase" is also a product of this collaboration. For this reason, I will follow their practice of referring to each other's textual personae by their initials (J.D. and G., respectively).

One approaches the task of interpreting "Circumfession" with trepidation. It is, as John D. Caputo has said, "a book of formidable difficulty (even by Derridean standards)" (1997, p. 285). It simultaneously seduces and repels its readers, placing them in a kind of *fort/da* game of approach and withdrawal, attraction and repulsion. The promise of self-revelation held out by its position as the text on Jacques Derrida by Jacques Derrida draws readers in only to become quickly overwhelmed. Its perpetual references to bodily sufferings, oozing wounds, and personal dramas and traumas seem to reveal too much. At the same time, its stream of consciousness style seems designed to obscure as much as it reveals.

For the theologian or philosopher of religion, the double movement of attraction and repulsion can take place at yet another level. Religious motifs – references to God, even – pepper this text and, as Caputo notes, tempt "religious thinkers" to enclose it within traditional and comforting schemas. And yet, as Caputo also makes clear, "Circumfession" resists all attempts at such comforting enclosures. Indeed, religion serves as the battleground on which this contest between disciple and master takes place.[10] J.D. invokes religious terms to describe both what "Circumfession" resists and what it seeks to enact. J.D. describes G.'s project over and over again as ontotheological. In aiming to display a hidden (to the uninitiated, at least) logic within the raw material of J.D.'s thought, J.D. accuses G. of playing God. He knows J.D.'s past, his present, and – since the logic of "Derridabase" implies a predictive power – perhaps even his future as well or better than J.D. himself.

J.D.'s resistance to G.'s project is figured in religious terms as well. J.D. appropriates a religious classic, Augustine's *Confessions*, as the template for his countertext. At first glance, the two texts – and their authors – seem polar opposites. Augustine was a devout Christian, J.D. an ostensibly secular Jew. Augustine embraced and took refuge in an ontotheological metaphysic, the very monolithic structure whose boundaries J.D. seeks to disrupt and escape. The *Confessions* mixes prayer, autobiographical narrative, and philosophical analysis, all designed to lead the reader toward the one true God. "Circumfession" seeks to mix prayers, tears, and blood, J.D. writes. Rather than guiding its readers toward a singular conclusion, its stream of consciousness style and periphrastic organization leaves them rudderless in a relentless sea of run-on sentences and fragmentary musings.

Yet at least two important similarities bind these two texts together. Both Augustine and J.D. employ the artifice of autobiography for larger, although antithetical, purposes. Augustine tells the story of his life to illustrate divine providence while J.D. turns to self-revelation to contest a teleological agenda. Both authors' mothers are central to their texts and to their larger purposes. Augustine's mother serves as key witness to the working out of the divine teleology. J.D.'s mother provides the means through which J.D. resists G.'s teleological agenda. J.D. surprises G. with what surprises him, what eludes his control; namely, the slow deterioration and impending death of his mother.

At about the time that J.D. begins "Circumfession," Georgette Derrida suffers a stroke. Her debilitation and lengthy dying process plays a centrifugal role in "Circumfession" by prompting J.D. into a chain of reflections set in motion by grief, loss, and guilt. The stroke has robbed Georgette of her subjectivity and reduced her to little more than body. Most of the time, she no longer knows him, J.D. reports. But J.D.'s grief for his mother is nothing new, it turns out. He grieves as much for what never existed between them as for what used to be. Georgette may rarely recognize him now, but she seems to have hardly known him before. He searches for the letters and notes that he sent her faithfully over the years, and finds almost none of them. It is as though, like the *Envois* in *The Post Card*, they never arrived.

The link between J.D.'s grief for his mother and his writing runs even deeper, however. According to Lacanian psychoanalysis, the separation from the mother initiated at birth and completed in the resolution of the Oedipal complex produces a scar that splits the subject. The loss of the maternal body leaves behind a residual longing for the (m)other within the subject that renders self-enclosure impossible. J.D. is acutely aware of this otherness within himself. Indeed, he describes it as the source of his desire and compulsion to write. All of his work is an address to his (m)other. If so, these *envois*, like his personal notes to her, have also never arrived. According to J.D., Georgette never read a word of her son's work.

Where *Beyond the Pleasure Principle* obscures the relationship to the mother, J.D.'s account of anticipatory mourning exposes the effects of the current sacrificial economy that Irigaray analyses in "Belief Itself" on the mother/son relationship. Within that economy, no genuine relationship between mother and son – no face to face relationship, as Irigaray says – is possible.[11] The mother serves as the silent sacrificial ground of the son's subjectivity and the resource for his work in the world. He serves as her imaginary but altogether unreal ideal.

I have argued elsewhere that Derrida's interventions in economies of sexual indifference from the masculine side make him a useful ally for feminism.[12] My reading of this text so far suggests that, in exposing these effects of the current sacrificial economy, "Circumfession" performs this service once again. In this essay, however, I aim to show that sexual difference bears on the shape religion might take on the other side of ontotheology. To make that case, I need to turn my attention to another aspect of this text.

Central to the portrait of grief and guilt in "Circumfession" lie two wounded bodies. Readers familiar with John D. Caputo's *Prayers and Tears* will already know that the figure of circumcision, which plays a central role in Caputo's account of Derrida's religion without religion, constitutes a major (dis)organizing figure within

"Circumfession." J.D.'s text plays on circumcision's links with familiar Derridean thematics (truth as castration, the proper name), with religion (Judaism and anti-semitic Christianity), and with autobiography (J.D. and Judaism) – all themes discussed by Caputo. *Prayers and Tears* proves that approaching "Circumfession" through this body-wound provides provocative access to the question of religion's place in Derrida's work. Caputo leaves uninvestigated, however, another bleeding and perforated body that also plays a central role within "Circumfession," that of J.D.'s dying mother whose bedsores (*escarres*) provide a constant leitmotif to her son's musings. The effects of this wounded body on the text take on particular interest when read in light of "Belief Itself."

I noted earlier that the stroke has reduced J.D.'s mother to little more than a body. Georgette's bedsores have turned her body into "an archipelago of red and blackish volcanoes, enflamed wounds, crusts and craters, signifiers like wells several centimeters deep, opening here, closing there, on her heels, her hips and sacrum." They turn Georgette inside out, in more ways than one. They uncover what usually remains hidden, "the very flesh exhibited in its inside, no more secret, no more skin" ("Circumfession," Bennington and Derrida, 1993, p. 82). In place of an absent internality, they also signify. Because of the mental confusion caused by the stroke, Georgette cannot serve as reliable witness to her own bodily state. Her healthcare workers read the waxing and waning of her disintegration and decay through the state of her bedsores (and other bodily signs). In this sense, then, the bedsores substitute for her (always) lacking (by Irigaray's account of femininity) subjectivity.

When read in light of "Belief Itself," Georgette's body turns "Circumfession" into an expos, of the sacrificial economy. The reader will recall that Irigaray uncovers a maternal body at the core of the sacrificial economy. Both the Eucharist and the *fort/da* game obscure and commemorate the loss or sacrifice of female figures (mothers, daughters, maternal bodies). Both substitute belief in the achievement of mastery over absence and death for acknowledgement of loss. "Circumfession," on the other hand, puts loss and mourning on display. J.D.'s mother's wounded body is central to that display. In following the trail blazed by his mother's body, J.D. uncovers its place within an economy of sacrifice. Like Irigaray's analysand, Georgette bleeds without knowing why and without suffering. It is up to another (J.D.? Us?) to read that body's messages. Insofar as Georgette's wounds fund J.D.'s writing, "Circumfession" continues to use the maternal body as a resource. J.D.'s authorial voice feeds on Georgette's soon-to-be-perpetual silence. Yet this is the sacrificial economy with a difference. Though Georgette's access to subjectivity remains forever blocked (leaving the problem of woman's subjectivity unaddressed), the wound at the heart of normative (masculine) subjectivity is laid bare. J.D. has not mastered this resource on which he draws or the loss that provides it. It is lack of mastery, not its achievement, that J.D. puts on display. Grief and loss are not overcome, but rather give rise to a series of abyssal compensations and losses that replicate rather than staunch the original wound.

In the course of writing "Circumfession," J.D. develops a neurological disorder that causes severe facial tics. These tics transform his face into a grotesque mask of his usual visage, and turn ordinary activities (like drinking water) into extraordinary feats. Though eventually diagnosed as Lyme disease, J.D. and one of his doctors think that his mother's current state may also be a factor. The loss of her body registers now as a literal wound to his body; a wound, like hers, that inverts the ordinary relationship between body and subjectivity, a wound, like circumcision, that is more–than–bodily. The facial tic, like his mother's bedsores, renders visible J.D.'s inner pain. It writes on his body the repeated loss of his mother's body (through separation at his birth, through the Oedipal drama, and now through her death). It writes his lack of mastery over her loss through his lack of mastery over his own body – a lack also evoked by circumcision, which he links to this experience. Indeed, these scenes of woundings render impracticable distinctions between inside and outside.

This displacement of interiority and exteriority inverts J.D.'s earlier description of his work as an address to his (m)other. In yet another remarkable passage from "Circumfession," J.D. describes his own work as a series of *escarres*. "I love words so much because I have no language of my own, only false *escarres*." J.D. writes ("Circumfession," Bennington and Derrida, 1993, p. 92). Later, he describes his work as "One book open in the other, one scar deep within the other, as though I were digging the pit of an *escarre* in the flesh" ("Circumfession," Bennington and Derrida, 1993, p. 308). Even after the symptoms have disappeared, J.D. describes himself as forever changed by "this counter-scar which we must learn to read."

Reading "Circumfession" through "Belief Itself" renders visible its interventions in a sacrificial economy in which the maternal body serves as a resource. What are the implications in this reading for religion on the other side of ontotheology?

Writing the Impossible

I gave in to the counterexemplary thing – "only write here what is impossible, that ought to be the impossible-rule" (10–11/77), of everything G. can be expecting of me ... a supposedly idiomatic, unbroachable, unreadable, uncircumcised piece of writing, held not to the assistance of his father, as Socrates would say, but to my assistance at the death of a mother about whom I ask to ti en einai before witnesses. ("Circumfession," Bennington and Derrida, 1993, p. 194)

Anyone who does not go down into the abyss can only repeat and retrace the ways already opened that cover over the trace of the vanished gods ... Beyond go ... those who give up their own will ... Light shines on them once they have agreed that nothing shall ensure their protection, not even that age-old citadel of man – being (être) – not even that guarantor of the meaning or nonmeaning of the world – God. These prophets know that if anything divine is still to come our way it will be won by abandoning all control, all language, and all sense already produced, it is through risk, only risk, leading no one knows where, announcing who knows what future, secretly commemorating who knows what past. No project here. Only this refusal to refuse what has been perceived, whatever distress or wretchedness may come of it. ("Belief Itself," Irigaray, 1993, pp. 51–3)

Another central theme that guides Caputo's *Prayers and Tears* is "a certain passion for the impossible" (Caputo, 1997, p. 285) crucial, according to Caputo, to Derrida's religion without religion. The name of God interests Derrida in part because of its links with impossibility. And yet, Caputo asks whether God is not perhaps the most dangerous name for the impossible?[13] Is it moreover, the only name for the impossible?

These questions provide an opening through which my concluding remarks will pass. Following the figure of the dying mother through this impossible confession addressed to her takes the figure of impossibility beyond the gods of logocentrism, ontotheology, and belief. As I noted at the outset, accounts of deconstruction's import for religion on the other side of ontotheology have tended to view ontotheology as a philosophical problem. If Christianity, for example, can jettison philosophy, it can retrieve its kernel of truth from its ontotheological husk. The reading of "Circumfession" and "Belief Itself" that I offer herein challenges that narrow definition of ontotheology and its relationship to belief. It also marks out a different path for religion after ontotheology. The reference to Socrates and a paternal figure in the epigraph above recalls Derrida's discussion of writing in "Plato's Pharmacy" (in Derrida, 1981, pp. 61–171). Writing's distance from a paternal origin – from a father who guarantees truth because his word is being – renders writing suspect in the Platonic scheme. Logocentrism, then, is caught up with a desire for mastery, an assertion of its accomplishment – if not by men, then by God. "Belief Itself," however, has shown that logocentrism is not only a philosophical construct. The *fort/da* game and the Eucharist depend upon (faith in) the union of word and being for their efficacy.

To logocentrism, J.D. opposes a writing held to the figure of a dying mother whose connection between word and being (such as it was, in this economy) has been severed. J.D. aims to escape G.'s desire for mastery not by engaging directly in a contest for (self)control, but by writing what lies outside his – indeed, anyone's – control, namely, the ateological but inevitable decay, decline, and death of his mother. Submitting to the gravitational pull of this loss offers J.D. particular purchase on the ontotheological system he wishes to elude because the maternal body serves as this system's resource.

What does this suggest, then, not just about where ontotheology's traps lie, but about the (im)possibility of religion after ontotheology? Religion in the modern west has been predominately a matter of a vertical relationship between a normative (masculine) subject and his perfected mirror image (God). Grounded in belief in transcendence over death, the God/man relationship has been funded by the sacrifice of sexual alterity, which in turn sustains the economy of sameness that western religion reflects.[14] "Belief Itself" and "Circumfession" call attention to the price paid by women and men – believers and non-believers alike – for participation in this economy. These essays also evoke the impossible possibility of breaking through this economy and the religion that sustains and reflects it toward an other sacrality. Access to sacrality on the other side of ontotheology will not come without significant risk. "Circumfession" suggests that working from the recognition of a primordial maternal sacrifice (rather than belief in a transcendent Father God) requires confrontation with pain and loss, not compensation for them. "Belief Itself" depicts a vertiginous path into the unknown with only fragile figures (angels and roses) for company and without the consolation of belief. As Amy Hollywood (1998) argues, Irigaray is not asking readers to believe in angels, but to take the risk that these figures of immanent transcendence embody and enable. Irigaray invites us to risk self and substance in order to encounter alterity in each other and beyond. Such an undertaking is not for the faint of heart. Yet the intertwined future of religion and sexual difference lies with the lure of the (im)possible.

Notes

My thanks to Amy Hollywood, Cynthia Marshall, and Dee McGraw for their assistance.

1   A number of feminist thinkers find the work of Luce Irigaray, which will figure prominently
    in what follows, particularly provocative and helpful for reframing philosophy of religion
    through the lens of sexual difference. See, e.g., Anderson 1998, Deutscher (1994, 1997),
    Hollywood (1994, 1998, n.d.), Jantzen (1999).
2   The attention given to sexual difference varies considerably. Early treatments of religion and
    deconstruction, for example, posited a basic incompatibility with feminist concerns. See,
    e.g., Hart 1989. More recent texts give some time to Julia Kristeva's work (Taylor 1987 and
    Winquist 1995). Caputo (1997) attends to issues of sexual difference in Derrida's work.
    Issues of sexual difference play an integral role in Ward 1999, which engages feminist
    theorists of various stripes.
3   See, e.g., Lowe 1993, Winquist 1995, Caputo 1997, Marion 1991.
4   The Eucharist also figures centrally in the work of Catherine Pickstock (1998), a proponent
    of so-called radical orthodoxy. As the antidote to modernism's nihilism (carried to its logical
    conclusion, she argues, in Derrida and Lévinas), she offers transubstantiation as the true
    source of all meaning. I will return to Pickstock's proposal later in this essay. I did not
    include her in my list of scholars working on religion and continental philosophy above
    because continental philosophers serve only as straw enemies for her. Pickstock's readings of
    Derrida and Levinas, in particular, are in my view unconscionable and irresponsible.
5   In particular, see Armour 1999.
6   By focusing on sexual difference here to the exclusion of other forms of difference, I risk
    perpetuating the very problem I criticize in *Deconstruction, Feminist Theology, and the Problem
    of Difference*. That I find myself in this position illustrates the pervasiveness of the
    divide between race and gender that I analyze there. I want to note, however, that race
    shadows my text, much as it does the contexts I analyse in the book – here, as ethnic
    and religious difference. The central figures in "Circumfession" bear marks of ethnic and
    religious alterity. Derrida and his mother are Algerian Jews, a double dose of alterity in a
    French context. The links between Judaism, in particular, and Derrida's mother are frequent
    in "Circumfession." Fully exploring those connections would require an interpretive appar-
    atus that takes account of European racisms; one I do not have at my disposal at this point.
    Two other aspects of the context feed into race's elision here. Since Irigaray focuses on a
    Christian scene, reading "Circumfession" with "Belief Itself" further elides the play of
    religious and ethnic alterity. Psychoanalysis's prominence in both "Circumfession" and
    "Belief Itself" highlights sexual difference at the expense of ethnic difference – at least, on
    the surface (see Derrida's *Archive Fever*, however, on the question of Freud and Judaism).
    Thus, the reading of "Circumfession" that I offer here is somewhat truncated. A fuller
    reading awaits a more fully developed contextualization.
7   On Irigaray's reading of mysticism, see Hollywood 1994.
8   The implications of Irigaray's reading also troubles Pickstock's confidence in transubstantia-
    tion as the ground of all meaning. Loading transubstantiation (which exemplifies a belief in
    Irigaray's sense, a denial of *prima facie* reality) with an all-or-nothing responsibility for all
    meaning truly courts nihilism. Meaning would seem to be possible only so long as (and only
    for those in whom) that belief can be sustained. A particularly problematic position when
    Irigaray's account suggests that the truth of the Eucharist is not what it appears to be, at first
    glance.

9   There are a number of interesting links between "Freud's Legacy" and "Circumfession" on the question of autobiography, life, and death. The present essay cannot give those links the attention they deserve, though I do want to note that a similar pattern of displacements (deliberate, in this case) marks Derrida's text. His mother's imminent demise calls to mind past losses and evokes imagined future ones, including those of J.D.'s sons and, most significantly, his own.

10 The interplay between G. and J.D. recalls Derrida's analysis of the interplay between Plato and Socrates in The Post Card, commemorated therein by a postcard featuring Socrates (presumably dictating) standing behind Plato (presumably writing). However, the flattened perspective in the painting/etching renders undecidable any definitive positioning of one or the other as master. Bennington and Derrida include a photo of themselves that plays on that image (see Bennington and Derrida, 1993, p. 11).

11 Irigaray's point provides an interesting counterpoint to Freud's claim that the relationship between mother and son was the least ambivalent of all human relationships.

12 See Armour 1997 and 1999.

13 Amy Hollywood argues that this danger motivates Derrida's desire to distance himself from negative theology (n.d.).

14 See Hollywood 1998 for a particularly cogent account of this claim.

Works Cited

Anderson, Pamela Sue. 1998. *A Feminist Philosophy of Religion*. Oxford: Blackwell. Armour, Ellen T. 1997. "Questions of Proximity: 'Woman's Place' in Derrida and Irigaray." *Hypatia* 12 (1), 63–78.

——.1999. *Deconstruction, Feminist Theology, and the Problem of Difference: Subverting the Race/ Gender Divide*. Chicago: University of Chicago Press.

——. N.D. "The (Im)possible Possibility of Theology Beyond God." Presented to the Theology and Religious Reflection Section at the American Academy of Religion, November 20, 1995, Philadelphia, PA.

Bennington, Geoffrey and Jacques Derrida. 1993. *Jacques Derrida*. Chicago: University of Chicago Press.

Caputo, John D. 1997. *Prayers and Tears of Jacques Derrida: Religion Without Religion*. Bloomington: Indiana University Press.

Derrida, Jacques. 1981. *Dissemination*. Translated by Barbara Johnson. Chicago: University of Chicago Press.

——. 1987. *The Post Card: From Socrates to Freud and Beyond*. Translated by Alan Bass. Chicago: University of Chicago Press.

Deutscher, Penelope. 1994. "'The Only Diabolical Thing About Women...'": Luce Irigaray on Divinity." *Hypatia* 9 (4), 88–111.

——. 1997. *Yielding Gender: Feminism, Deconstruction, and the History of Philosophy*. London: Routledge.

Freud, Sigmund. 1961. *Beyond the Pleasure Principle*. Edited and translated by James Strachey. New York: W.W. Norton and Co.

——. 1962. *Totem and Taboo: Some Points of Agreement Between the Mental Lives of Savages and Neurotics*. Translated James Strachey. New York: W.W. Norton.

Hart, Kevin. 1989. *The Trespass of the Sign: Deconstruction, Theology, and Philosophy*. Cambridge, England: Cambridge University Press.

Hollywood, Amy. 1994. "Beauvoir, Irigaray, and the Mystical." *Hypatia* 9 (4), 158–85.

——. 1998. "Deconstructing Belief: Irigaray and the Philosophy of Religion." *Journal of Religion* 78(2), 230–45.

——. N.D. "Apophasis and Ethics in the Early Derrida." Ms. provided by author. Irigaray, Luce. 1985. *Speculum of the Other Woman*. Translated by Gillian C. Gill. Ithaca, NY: Cornell University Press.

——. 1993. *Sexes and Genealogies*. Translated by Gillian C. Gill. New York: Columbia University Press.

Jantzen, Grace. 1999. *Becoming Divine: Towards Philosophy of Philosophy of Religion*. Bloomington: Indiana University Press.

Lowe, Walter. 1993. *Theology and Difference: The Wound of Reason*. Bloomington: Indiana University Press.

Marion, Jean-Luc. 1991. *God Without Being*. Translated by Thomas Carlson. Chicago: University of Chicago.

Pickstock, Catherine. 1998. *After Writing: On the Liturgical Consummation of Philosophy*. Oxford: Blackwell.

Taylor, Mark. 1987. *Altarity*. Chicago: University of Chicago Press.

Ward, Graham. 1999. "Bodies: The Displaced Body of Jesus Christ." *Radical Orthodoxy: A New Theology*. Edited by John Milbank, Catherine Pickstock, and Graham Ward. London: Routledge. Winquist, Charles E. 1995. *Desiring Theology*. Chicago: University of Chicago Press.

15

"BARELY BY A BREATH . . .": IRIGARAY ON RETHINKING RELIGION

Grace M. Jantzen

Modernity has constructed itself on the absence of God. The fundamental premise of western science, economics, politics and philosophy since the seventeenth century is that we live in the *saeculum*, literally the time between creation and the final judgment, the time during which the world must be investigated, understood and mastered without reference to divine presence or intervention. Whether or not one continues to believe in God is one's own private business, irrelevant to the conduct of the world, since such belief is not allowed to interfere with how one conducts an experiment, an argument, or dealings in the stock exchange. Thus even the growth of fundamentalist or evangelical Christianity in some parts of the western world, a Christianity focused on beliefs in a god outside the world and a heaven after death for those who hold those beliefs, does not impinge on this fundamental secularism, since even the believers conduct their public and professional dealings by the same standards as anybody else.

There are many voices, now, decrying the evils of modernity: its false, destructive, death-dealing trajectory; its greedy consumption of the earth; its construction of otherness and domination of gender, race and status. Increasingly, also, there are voices calling for rethinking religion, for greater awareness that secularism as the fundamental premise of modernity has banished the divine from the world so that "the divine radiance has become extinguished in the world's history."[1] This extinguishing of the divine, Martin Heidegger sees as a "destitute time," "the time of the world's night" which is continually deepening. "It has already grown so destitute, it can no longer discern the default of God as a default."[2]

But which god is absent? Is it the "good old God"[3] who could change the weather, intervene on the side of his favorites in battle, and watch while those who called themselves his (Christian) children slaughtered Jews, Muslims, and one another? Is it the "god called God,"[4] the god-father in whose name continents were appropriated, people enslaved, women oppressed, lesbians and gay men harassed, while incense and candles and boy-choirs chanting psalms deflected attention from the atrocities? If so, then we should hope that this god will stay away for a long time; and we should do all we can to prevent his return. That includes rethinking religion, which has a way of turning up in unexpected disguises. As Luce Irigaray has warned:

It seems we are unable to eliminate or suppress the phenomenon of religion.
It reemerges in different forms, some of them perverse: sectarianism, theoretical or
religious dogmatism, religiosity... Therefore it is crucial that we rethink religion, and
especially religious structures, categories, initiations, rules and utopias, all of which have
been masculine for centuries. Keeping in mind that today these religious structures often
appear under the name of science and technology.[5]

Anyone who deplores the dogmatism and violence of a religion which is centred on
sacrifice and death should be vigilant against the re-emergence of this god, whose
extinguishing is no cause to consider ourselves destitute.

After Nietzsche, christendom must be recognized as morally and intellectually
bankrupt. Far better an outraged atheism than a complacent christendom – or indeed
than any christendom that colludes with and thus reinscribes the deadening of the soul
and of the earth, the oppression of its peoples. There can be no going back to a
medieval or premodern religion of certainties and securities (if there ever was such a
thing); nor indeed should its substitute in "radical orthodoxy" be desired where
doctrines or revelations are given or premised without equally radical engagement
with the ways in which such orthodoxy has been death-dealing.

Therefore when Irigaray, pondering Heidegger, sees this time of the absence of god as
a destitute time, her comments should not be read as nostalgia for old time religion.
Rather, her summons is to re-think religion, reconceive divinity. Religion does not go
away. Nor should we wish it to: according to Irigaray religion in postmodernity is crucial
to countering the destructiveness and oppression of secular modernity. As I shall explain
below, it is in becoming divine, not in the elimination of divinity, that Irigaray sees hope
and beauty. The task concerning religion at the end of modernity is a religious task.

It is significant that Heidegger in "What are Poets For?" and Irigaray, in her essay
"Belief Itself"[6] which engages with Heidegger's work, both begin with the eucharist.
Heidegger, taking up Hölderlin's elegy "Bread and Wine" proceeds to a discovery of
the absence of the divine. Irigaray, however, discovers a different absence, the absence
of woman. And the reason she is absent pulls us up short. A woman, a client in
psychoanalysis, tells Irigaray, "At the point in the mass when they, the (spiritual) father
and son, are reciting together the ritual words of the consecration, saying 'This is my
body, this is my blood,' I bleed." As Irigaray recounts it:

> The father and the son must celebrate the Eucharist together in her absence, and then
> hand out the consecrated bread and wine to the congregation to complete the commu-
> nion service. This generally occurs on a Sunday. She makes the connection between her
> hemorrhaging and the mass only subsequently.[7]

Heidegger has been so caught up in tracing the elusive absence of the divine that he
has failed to notice this other absence that is glaring him in the face: the absence of
women in the constitution of religious belief and ritual. Yet as the woman with the
issue of blood stopped Jesus in his tracks when he was on his way to what those around
him deemed far more important (and far less embarrassing), so Irigaray inserts the
message of the menstruating woman. On whose body, on whose blood, will the
religion of postmodernity be constructed?

Heidegger has written at length about the forgetting of Being in modernity, particularly in the philosophical tradition. Irigaray is deeply influenced by him. As she engaged with his work in her characteristically detailed and elusive style, she suggests that Heidegger in his quest for the meaning of Being has, together with the philosophical tradition which he castigates, forgotten something else as well. This "something else" has been specified as sexual difference;[8] and this of course is crucial. But what I want to pursue is the further question: what does Irigaray suggest might happen if we did *not* forget? What happens to religion if we do stop and notice bleeding women? I suggest that in Irigaray's texts remembering bleeding women is importantly connected with rethinking religion and developing a new religious imaginary for postmodernity.[9]

When Heidegger, forgetting women, considers the absence of god in a destitute time, his response is to valorize the quest of the poet-philosopher. "Poets are the mortals who, singing earnestly of the wine-god, sense the trace of the fugitive gods, stay on the gods' tracks, and so trace for their kindred mortals the way toward the turning."[10] This he writes about as a venture, daring, risk: it is the venture of Nature, but it is also the unshielded dangerous openness in "the dark of the world's night,"[11] the task of the poet but also the philosopher like himself who "dwells poetically."[12] But feminists, while not unmoved by Heidegger's sensitivity to the beauty of Being and its destruction in the age of technology, also recognize here an old familiar dream of masculinity. Heidegger writes in a manner reminiscent of solitary hero stories, of the great adventurer going off on his lonely and dangerous quest. The roots of this story are deep in the history of the west: Odysseus and Sir Lancelot shape the symbolic of masculinity which in modernity is reinscribed under the sign of Faust and enacted by Livingstone, Stanley, Captain Cook, and whole companies of adventurers and exploiters.[13] This central western mythology of masculinity is now valorized in the form of the great heroic poet-cum-philosopher, who will be intrepid in his ventures into the meaning of Being in a destitute time.

But why is it that women usually have to stay at home? How is it that in this great adventure, where the heroic poet seeks the traces of the god who has abandoned him, he in turn abandons the woman, and even forgets that he has done so? Could these two abandonments be related? "What are the stakes of such a forgetting?" asks Irigaray.[14] If the poet-philosopher re-enacts the forgetting and abandonment which lie at the heart of western metaphysics, might it not be predicted that the god whose traces he seeks will turn out to have uncanny and unwelcome affinities to the old patriarchal "god called God" who cannot stay too far away and against whose return we must be ever vigilant?

Thus when Heidegger, forgetting woman, turns to poetry, Irigaray is reminded by the bleeding woman to return to Freud, to reconsider abandonment and its roots in childhood experience. In *Beyond the Pleasure Principle* Freud used the famous example of his grandson throwing a reel with a piece of string attached over the edge of a bed – *Fort!* (away) – and pulling it back – *Da!* (there) – with great satisfaction. This Freud interprets as the way in which a child learns to cope with his mother's absence and his feelings of abandonment. By keeping the reel (his mother) attached to a string, he can master her, throw her away and pull her back as he chooses, thereby overcoming her absence, which ultimately is the consequence of the two of them no longer being one, the irreparable abandonment of birth.[15] "She must be thrown over there, put at a distance, beyond the horizon, so that she can come back to him, so that he can take her back, over and over again, reassimilate her, and feel no sorrow."[16] Her body, her blood are mastered, taken back into himself; and so long as he has the symbols, the string by which he controls her, the absence of the actual mother/woman can be forgotten.

Irigaray points out, however (as Freud does not) that the flat truth of the matter is that the mother is *not* the reel; the string is *not* an umbilical cord; and if the little boy persuades himself otherwise then his belief, insofar as he clings to it, is a delusion. Neither is it true that his games of appearance and disappearance actually master his abandonment, or that life and death can be so easily controlled. "At the moment when he believes he is best able to master her appearance-disappearance, he is most slave to belief. Belief in himself and his power, of course, but also in her, since his link to her depends upon the belief that she is there, when she is not, that she is there more when she is not there (here), that she is where she isn't."[17]

But of course if he can believe that he can believe anything, believe in the teeth of the evidence, believe because it is impossible. What he cannot tolerate is doubt, open challenge to his beliefs, heresy. To preserve his beliefs, his mastery, he will go to any lengths, break more bodies, spill more blood, enact the violent history of christendom. And Irigaray emphasizes what has already become evident: "the most important *fort-da* – as you know, even, or especially when you refuse to believe it – refers, past the mother's presence, in the mother, beyond-veil, to the presence of God, beyond the sky, beyond the visual horizon."[18] The whole dwelling place of beliefs which men have built for themselves[19] may turn out not to be openness to the unconcealment of Being but self-constructed boundaries within which the meaning of Being must be contained at all costs, even if – especially if – the memory of the self-deception involved in this putative mastery is deeply repressed in forgetfulness.

It is as well to take a step back from Irigaray at this point and note the extent to which religion in modernity has been constructed in terms of beliefs. Creeds, affirmations of belief, have been important in christendom from very ancient times, of course. But in modernity they are not just important, they are actually deemed constitutive of what religion *is*: the world is divided up between "believers" and "unbelievers" as though this is what makes or unmakes ones religious stance. Whereas in late antiquity and medieval christendom much was made of, say, the beauty of holiness or the imitation of Christ or the wounds of love and the life of charity, these ways of thinking and expression have lost ground even among those who number themselves Christians, and have been supplanted by a relentless focus on beliefs.[20] Certainly English-speaking philosophy of religion has concentrated obsessively on beliefs and their justification, as though beliefs and beliefs alone matter. If Irigaray is anywhere near right, then part of what is required in rethinking religion and its genealogy in modernity is surely to probe what lies behind such a construction of religion, what sense of abandonment and control, at the expense of whose body and blood?

That, however, is not to suggest that secularism ("unbelief") is better: it may indeed be similarly constituted. By this I don't mean only that "unbelief" as much as "belief" takes belief's presence or absence as its defining characteristic. Far more important is the fact that in modernity rationality and knowledge have been constructed as from a "god's eye view."[21] Knowledge is held to be objective, neutral and dispassionate, having nothing to do with "distractions" like beauty or love or goodness. Whatever the value of such "attitudes," they must not be confused with facts, for which the paradigm is taken to be science and the practical consequence technology and the western mastery of nature and of the people of the earth. I am overstating the case, of course; but the caricature is all too recognizable. Religious belief and secular rationality, therefore, for all their supposed conflict, are very clearly epistemologically akin to one another in modernity. Though Irigaray does not address this epistemology directly, I believe that it, especially as mediated through Heidegger's "Question Concerning Technology"[22] is never far away from her considerations of belief and forgetting.

Moreover this obsession with beliefs and a *techné* of knowledge is, I suggest, interconnected with the preoccupation with death which is central to the masculinist symbolic of western modernity.[23] Irigaray sees the *fort-da* game, the belief game, as a way of trying to assert mastery over presence and absence, ultimately over birth and death. Death, in particular, must be brought under control. The favored way has been by assertion of immortality, whether, like the Greeks, through fame and songs of heroism, or like the Christians, in terms of heaven and hell, or in modernity through wealth passed down to legitimate sons. There can also be more subtle twists: whereas Plato saw death as the making of a true philosopher because it would free him of his body and its passions, the early Heidegger constructs authenticity upon death because it is reflection on death's facticity which frees him from "the they," the world of others' opinions and expectations.[24] Thus Plato looks to death to free him for true life beyond the grave whereas Heidegger looks to death to free him for true life on this side of it: the difference should not blind us to the similarity. Irigaray suggests that at the bottom of all these ways of thinking there is an attempt at mastery: mastery over the body, over thought, over society, and ultimately over death itself. Yet in each attempt at mastery, man "brings himself death, believing he thereby masters it in the form of eternity. And re-envelops himself in death in a variety of ways so as to protect himself from the permanence of becoming dead."[25]

All of this, she argues, is centered on man's refusal to deal with the one thing which he determinedly forgets: his birth, his mother, her body and her blood. With all the strength of his being this must be repressed.

> The ultimate in his power to be consists in this impossible reappropriation that marks out the horizon of his world. Never will he attain or revisit the move that constitutes it. Ever heading for this harbouring origin secreted away, he puts off forever the time of his death is due him, becoming immortal for never reaching this boundary. Dead always already and nevermore, from forgetting his own birth.[26]

Anything that would call to mind that which he so vigorously represses must likewise be kept under careful control: his own body and feelings, women, the earth . . . Thus the economy of mastery, which is the economy of death, is premised on the forgetting of birth, of sexual difference. It is based on the exclusion of women except in their service as mirror and receptacle and servant for men. Christendom has established the pattern of patriarchy and the celebration of death, but it is perpetuated in all the master discourses of secular modernity in a masculinist symbolic of violence and domination.

Now, if it is indeed the case that modernity thus reinscribes the death–dealing patriarchy of christendom, albeit in new forms, then although vigilance is required lest the oppressive god should return, it is obvious that secularism in itself is no defense. Indeed secularism precisely *is* this reinscription. The obsession with death returns in the compulsions of technology, commodification, and war-mongering, in the Mac-Donaldization of the world and the deforestation of the earth. Heidegger's romance with the Nazis can partly be understood (though in no way excused) as his deep revulsion to such commodification and to the utilitarian habitus of the west. But the Nazis were no answer. Can only a god save us now? Which god, if the gods are absent, if the gods themselves have died and abandoned the earth? From where shall new thinking arrive?

Both Heidegger and Irigaray consider that new thinking, a new imaginary, is crucial. The loss of the divine, the absence (or banishment) of the divine from the world, has involved other losses. First there is the loss of transcendence: with Cartesianism the human person was divided into body and soul, with the "soul-part" being god-like and immortal while the "body-part" could be accounted for in mechanistic terms. Dualism was then (rightly) rejected, and with it the soul; but since transcendence was defined as the opposite of immanence (rather than as the opposite of reductionism) transcendence also was dismissed, or at best retained in a vague, romantic way. Second, there is a loss of beauty: but what, then, will draw us outward and form us by its attraction? What will shape our desires when our longings are taught to revolve around commodities rather than being drawn to beauty? Third, interconnected, is the loss of "breath," of life with its constant possibilities of newness. Novelty, to be sure, is ubiquitous, whether in fashion, in technology, or in scientific and medical "advance"; but what about real newness, the birth of thought and creativity that can emerge only from thinking/being otherwise? Do we even know what that is anymore? From where – given that we can only think from where we are – shall a new imaginary arise?

Heidegger looks for a god to save us, a god whose traces of absence are followed by the intrepid poet-philosopher, the shepherd of Being. In the meantime, he finds one of his favorite heroic poets writing about the Angel, the one "who assures the recognition of a higher order of relation in the invisible."[27] The Angel is the one who holds disparate realms together in stillness, "recalling into the world's inner space" those willing to be "more daring by a breath," and thus releasing them from the rule of the merchant and the technocrat.[28]

> In the invisible of the world's inner space, as whose worldly oneness the Angel appears, the haleness of worldly beings becomes visible. Holiness can appear only within the widest orbit of the wholesome ... The holy binds the divine. The divine draws the god near.
> The more venturesome experience unshieldedness as holy. They bring to mortals the trace of the fugitive gods, the track into the dark of the world's night ...[29]

The messenger (*angellos*) of Being, the Angel, who turns out to be remarkably akin to the poet-philosopher, is again the solitary hero; and again the bleeding woman is nowhere to be seen. Does this Angel care about those who bleed in the world, the bleeding of the world? If not, will the appearance of the Angel really change anything, really enable thinking/being otherwise? Or will the Angel be another messenger of the same old death?

Irigaray points out that Angels have been "misunderstood, forgotten"[30] misrepresented by those who would want to see themselves as divine, or at least as messengers (*angelloi*) of the divine. But Irigaray remembers that the angel, in fact, "is sent, or comes, from heaven, on a mission, to do a job": a job which is an announcement to a bleeding woman, to a woman about her bleeding. "Sometimes a mediating angel or angels come to give us news about the place where the divine presence may be found, speaking of the word made flesh, returning, awaited."[31] But the angel cannot be captured, must not be domesticated in a dwelling, not even in one especially built, since such caging will turn the angel and its message of otherness "into parchments, skeletons, death masks."[32] We cannot keep an angel on a string: *Fort! Da!* "If we do not rethink and rebuild the whole scene of representation, the angels will never find a home, never stay anywhere. Guardians of a free passage, they cannot be captured, domesticated, even if our purpose is to see ourselves in them. They can light up our sight and all our senses but only if we note the moment when they pass by, hear their word and fulfil it . . . "[33]

But what, then, is this word? As Irigaray hears it, it is not an annunciation of Being but of word made flesh, becoming divine, becoming human. If the imaginary is to be transformed by heeding the angelic messenger it requires in the first place that we attend properly, notice what the angels are really saying and doing. And Irigaray remembers that in a crucial representation of angels, they are found in the most holy place, in the temple, on the mercy seat which covers the ark of the covenant. Moreover here there is not one angel but two, facing each other, holding the space of the divine presence of covenant and mercy.

> They turn toward one another, guarding and calling the divine presence between them. They do not go in one single direction . . . Face-to-face, they stand in almost timid contemplation, intent on something that is yet to come, yet to be situated, not yet inscribed, written, spoken . . . Coming from opposite directions, to meet one another, they halt the return from sameness to sameness, before any determination or opposition of presence or absence can be made . . . [34]

The angels are both similar and different, and in their difference hold open the space of thinking otherwise. Irigaray suggests that the crucial difference is sexual difference, although the tradition has denied and obscured this in its complex fear of bodies and sexuality. Angels in the tradition are sexless; ostensibly sexless, too, are the body and blood of the eucharist, even though each enactment is founded on further gendered violence and the absence of the bleeding woman. Irigaray holds that such sexlessness, such unmitigated sameness, would allow no scope for thinking otherwise, for the emergence of a new imaginary. If, however, there could be real face to face encounter by two beings who are similar but yet (sexually) different from one another, if there can be mutual openness to that difference without hasty amalgamation (let alone mastery of one over the other) then a space is opened for difference, for thinking and being differently. The two become, indeed, messengers of a new imaginary.

Irigaray considers further the refusal of sexual difference in the tradition of christendom, its fear of bodies and sexuality as symbolized by the sexlessness of angels. In the tradition, even Jesus' sexuality is minimized (except when it is used as an argument against women priests): the body and blood of the eucharist are not celebrated in relation to sexual difference. The son and the father, in an intermale society, "organise the world, bless the fruits of the earth, identify them with their body and blood, and in this way effect the communion between the units of the people that have been neutered, at least apparently."[35] The bleeding woman, the woman who represents sexual difference, is absent. The only women who may be present are women defined not in their own right as sexually different subjects but in relation to the men: as mothers, daughters, wives, and flower-arrangers they must be dutiful believers in the dogmas and rites which mark the boundaries of presence and absence constructed by the men in the name of the Father.

> But who is the Father if his will is that flesh be abolished? Is this the meaning of religion, as some would have us believe? Or are we dealing with the crypt of an order set up by one sex that claims to write the rules of truth at the price of life? . . . How are the spirit and mind to be woven of the threads of remoteness, belief, paralysis, denial, and negation of life?[36]

The very elements that are presented as the bread and wine of life are deeply invested in gendered death, written into the structures of belief, first of all in religion, but reinscribed, as I have discussed, in its secular variants.

But what if we return to the two angels facing one another across the mercy seat, the place designated as the place of divine presence in the open space above the law? And what if they, like that other angel who announced an incarnation, are there in order to announce between them the possibility of something new? "Neither like nor other, they guard and await the mystery of the divine presence that has yet to be made flesh,"[37] a becoming divine that is not the arrival of a strange god from outer space but of divine presence between them, enfleshed in them, as their difference opens the possibility of something new? Here there could be an imaginary based on alterity rather than sameness, on flourishing rather than mastery, on beauty and the longing which it generates rather than on desire premised upon a lack and fed by commodities. "Between them the flesh holds back and flows forth before any mastery can be exercised over it . . . the possibility of presence and of sharing in something divine that cannot be seen but can be felt, underlying all incarnation . . . "[38] Here we have a rethinking of religion that is not bounded by a dogma of a Father god whose absence constitutes modernity and whose death is mourned or celebrated. What we have instead is incarnation, divinity between us as the openness to difference changes the imaginary. The angels are not representatives of a heroic solitary poet on a quest for the traces of god. Rather, ordinary people, women and men, facing one another in openness to difference, become the messengers (*angelloi*) of word and flesh, of a new imaginary of becoming divine.[39]

But what, in the biblical story, is between the angels? They face one another, but they do not touch. Their presence to one another, the divine presence between them, is held in the space, the air, the openness that is not emptiness as they stand upon the covenant. Heidegger has written much about openness, about the clearing where Being can become manifest.[40] But whereas Irigaray, when she considers the space of openness between the angels, is aware of the air, the breath, the spirit between them, Heidegger writes of the openness as though it were empty, nothing: he passes over the element of air. Heidegger, in other words, has done exactly that for which he has berated western philosophy: he has forgotten the obvious. "The excess of air is both so immediately 'evident' and so little 'apparent' that he did not think of it";[41] he has forgotten the air. The air, however, is precisely the wind or breath, that which makes alive: *pneuma* can be translated either "wind" or "spirit." Heidegger therefore is forgetting or ignoring the very thing he professes to be seeking: the trace, the breath of the divine.

Now it is standard psychoanalytic teaching that if someone forgets or refuses to notice the obvious, there is an important reason for it, a pain or fear too deep to bring to light, but which the very vocabulary of the forgetting begins to indicate. Irigaray finds a clue in Heidegger's talk of "thrownness."

> To man, free air is first of all the advent of an absence that is too great: issuing from that surrounding into which he enters. He enters into the outside. He loses that living body of a home where he stayed before: there where she used to give herself to him, with no difference yet between his/her outside and his/her inside, between her and him, feeding him from the inside without demonstration . . . Free, out in the free air, he is – first of all – in a state of utmost "thrownness."[42]

The French for "thrownness," here, translation of Heidegger's *Geworfenheit*, is *dérélic-tion*: it is a word that also means abandonment or forsakenness, the utter loss of an infant separated from its mother. It is of course also the word used of Jesus' abandon-ment on the cross, the absence of god, the destitution of the world.

So what "man"/Heidegger has forgotten in forgetting the air is his birth, his mother, sexual difference, and the pain of separation and absence. We are back with the (absent) bleeding woman, the thought of whom must be repressed lest it remind him of this pain of separation. Thus creeds and rituals and boundaries are created: "once he has passed from inside her to outside, his boundaries will soon appear. He sets himself forth, and sets forth the whole, by surrounding himself, by surrounding it, with borders,"[43] dwelling places, temples, churches. It is at the expense of women. "Many, many years ago, in our tradition, the pick was driven into the earth-mother's womb in order to build the sacred enclosure of the tribe, the temple, finally the house."[44] But the efforts at containment do not work; the gods will not be caged. The divine has fled, leaving man master of his empty house. It has become a house of death.

Now, what would happen if, instead of going on an intrepid heroic quest looking for traces of the divine, we were to return to the mercy seat, to the space of divine presence, the breath/spirit which hovers between the angels? Perhaps it is not the divine that has absconded, but we ourselves who have forgotten the air, the spirit, and busied ourselves with merchandizing to fill the empty spaces of our temples and dwelling places? Irigaray's message is that central to a return must be the acceptance that the divine is to be found precisely in the space between, and thus in the recognition of sexual difference. It is only by acknowledging the loss of separation from the maternal, and coming to terms with that *déréliction* rather than repressing it, that it will become possible to go beyond the building of cages and doctrines and discourses of death, beyond the need of mastery and control. Only in that way can the sexes face and greet one another such that in their mutuality and difference the divine can be found between them. Only through such recognition of sexual difference, acknowledgment of otherness, can the word be made flesh, the incarnation take place. Only thus is there the opening toward becoming divine. It is "barely by a breath," by the spirit, the free air between the beings whose sexual difference is no longer forgotten.

In Irigaray's imaginary, sexual difference is construed literally, in heterosexual morphology: in "Belief Itself," for instance, she makes much of the "face to face" nature of the encounter in contrast to male homosexual encounter where "those who are alike tend to engage with each other from the back."[45] There has been much discussion of Irigaray's putative "essentialism";[46] and in my opinion she is not immune from the related charge of heterosexism. It is as though (hetero)sexual difference is the only difference that matters in changing the imaginary. But what about other differences, differences like race and sexuality and class and dis/ability which, like sexual difference, have been constructed into boundaries and divisions and the control of one by the other in an economy of domination?

Although I think that Irigaray passes over these other differences much too easily in her almost exclusive focus on heterosexual difference, it also seems to me that there is no need, in the scope of her imaginary, for her to do so. The angels facing one another can be imagined to be different in any number of ways: racially different, culturally different, different in age or class or ability or sexuality. The mutuality of respectful encounter with difference of *all* these sorts is the condition for the space and spirit of the divine between those thus willing to meet face to face.[47] Irigaray's use of sexual difference to explore the possibility of a new imaginary is not only enormously important in itself; it can also be extended to the many other forms of difference which have been treated as barriers rather than as spaces for the divine presence.

It is that recognition of the divine spirit, also, which overcomes the obsession with death and immortality that has preoccupied the western tradition. We will all die, certainly. But first we live; and in that life "we still feel a need to spend a little time on earth, in the sunshine, to open up to the joy of light and air."[48] This earth and our relationships upon it are to be savored and cared for, not belittled or destroyed in a focus on other worlds. I have developed some of what this means elsewhere, using the category of natality as a counterpoint to the category of mortality in which the western tradition has been saturated.[49] What I wish to do here is to show how Irigaray uses symbols drawn from medieval mystical writers, terms which Heidegger also uses, to open out what this life on earth might be if we were to remember the air, the breath, the spirit of the divine when we face one another in our differences with love.[50]

The first of these is the abyss. Heidegger writes of the abyss as the terrifying, awesome emptiness which the heroic poet cannot evade but must enter into, "the complete absence of the ground" when the gods have vanished. "The age for which the ground fails to come, hangs in the abyss . . . In the age of the world's night, the abyss of the world must be experienced and endured. But for this it is necessary that there are those who reach into the abyss."[51] As Hölderlin has described the abyss in his hymn "The Titans," on which Heidegger draws, it is only in the abyss that "the traces of the fugitive gods" can be found; but only the one who risks his life can venture in this quest.

Irigaray initially follows Heidegger in his insistence on the necessity and the risk of venturing the abyss. Thought (by which she here means the utilitarian rationality of modernity) has too often not touched the reality of its groundlessness, taking for granted breath, food, limitless resources, but forgetting being, forgetting the air. "As long as it does not touch upon that abyss, thought can still breathe . . . And the sublime, which thought consumes, is transformed into utilities . . . It shreds the air to coin it into values, trumpery values that no longer even shine with the mysterious light of being."[52] The poet, however, venturing the abyss, becomes aware of breath, aware of the air without which it is impossible to draw breath to sing the melody of the traces of the gods. The song is the song of venture, "a risk that risks life itself, going beyond it barely by a breath. A breath that, if it is held, saves through song, prophet of pure forces that call out and refuse shelter."[53]

But what is this abyss, this place of the trace of the divine? And why should Heidegger be so terrified of it? In Irigaray's imaginary, the abyss which has for Heidegger "a sort of horror"[54] is symbolically related precisely to that for which he has had to repress his desire, that which he has forgotten though it is obvious: the air, the womb, the bleeding woman. Really to remember, to venture this abyss, would "amount to recalling that his living body left the abyss by assimilating-appropriating to itself a female other who gave herself to him, first, in silence, first, in a non-solid form."[55] A genuine recall will therefore entail an acknowledgment of sexual difference, and therefore a reconfiguration of masculinity away from dominance and assimilation; a reconfiguration of femininity toward a female subject, so that mutuality can be risked. From *this* abyss, indeed, one might sing of traces of incarnation; for the abyss is the very space of the divine, held open by the angels facing one another.

Now, both Heidegger and Irigaray draw some of their imagery of the abyss from medieval mystical writers, for many of whom it was a significant trope. Meister Eckhart, for example, had made much of the idea of the abyss, the divine depth (Middle High German: *Grunt* or *Urgrunt*), an abyss from which all things come. Eckhart's teaching is that in the depths of the soul in which God gives it birth, "God's ground [*Grunt*/abyss] is my ground, and my ground is God's ground . . . Whoever has looked for an instant into this ground, to such a man, a thousand marks of red, minted gold are no more than a counterfeit penny."[56] No longer would thought "transform it into utilities" but rather find the resources for its own transformation.

In Eckhart, however, as in other mystical writers, the abyss is not a place of terror, but rather a place of awe and beauty and plenitude. Johannes Tauler, a disciple of Eckhart, wrote that those who truly meet God in spirit "draw all into their embrace in this same abyss, in this fire of love, as in a divine contemplation. Then they turn their gaze back to this loving abyss, to this fire of love, and there they rest; and after plunging into it, they descend to all who are in want until they return to the loving, dark, silent rest of the abyss."[57] The abyss, in Tauler's thinking, is not horrifying; rather it is the resource for every sort of appropriate engagement with the needs of the world. Similarly in Gertrude the Great of Helfta (from whom both Eckhart and Tauler may have drawn) the abyss is spoken of as "an abyss of divine counsel"; or again as "an abyss of mercy"; an "abyss of my [God's] love."[58] The abyss is like a deep well whose bottom cannot be plumbed, springing up with fresh and living water. No matter how much one draws, there is always more.

As Irigaray points out, however, from the beginning of western philosophy its practitioners have been prone so to forget things around them that, like Thales, they fall into the well. No wonder that Heidegger, forgetting the air, should be terrified that he might fall into the abyss; see the abyss as a place of danger and risk. So it would be if he were to fall, or even to try deliberately to clamber down into it. "Abstracted, abstract, ecstatic in his there, he tumbles into the well, which he does not see at his feet. Which sets the maidservants laughing."[59] There are, after all, more sensible ways of approaching the well, better uses for it than falling into it, as the maidservants with their buckets indicate. The well is there as a source of water, of life, from which once can draw ever and again without fear of exhaustion. If the abyss – the bleeding woman, sexual difference – is seen not as a place of horror but as a place of plenitude, there would be the potential for the renewal of the earth.

When Eckhart identifies the divine ground/abyss with his own ground, he immediately draws conclusions about how life should be lived, conclusions which both Heidegger and Irigaray echo. "Here [in my/God's *Grunt*/abyss] I live from what is my own, as God lives from what is his own . . . It is out of this inner ground that you should perform all your works without asking 'Why?' "[60] He goes on to explain what he means by giving examples. A rose blooms because it blooms: it is its nature [*Grunt*] to do so, and it does not have to ask "Why?" It is the same with life itself: it lives because it lives; it is its nature to live. "That is because life lives out of its own ground and springs from its own source, and so it lives without asking why it is itself living."[61] Similarly, he teaches that anyone living and thinking out of their own *Grunt* will live freely, without constant self-questioning, uncertainty, or paralyzing self-justification (*ohne warumba*).

Heidegger considers Eckhart's example of the rose in his fifth lecture in *The Principle of Reason*.[62] The French version is entitled "*La rose est sans pourquoi*"; and it is this upon which Irigaray comments. As she takes it up, it is not a matter of indifference that *la rose* is a noun marked feminine. She points out that, "mysteriously, the rose's bloom recalls something of blood and of the angel":[63] the bleeding woman, sexual difference, and the annunciation of the divine. "It is reborn ceaselessly, causelessly, because it must bloom, having no care for itself, no need to be seen, following in its own cycle and the cycle of the world."[64] It blooms "without why," finding plenitude in the earth and water and air, and giving joy to those who see. It lives out of its own ground, and thus gives "its gift beyond all reason, unless to give itself be reason. Its unpretentious blooming/unconcealment, its unadorned beauty."[65]

Such blossoming and flourishing, such living without a why, Irigaray presents as divine life. This is not a return of the old patriarchal gods and men whose body and blood are celebrated at the expense of bleeding women. It is the divinity that is found in a new imaginary, between those who meet face to face in mercy and respect. Thus be encountering difference, risking alterity, the divine, she holds, can come again between us, freeing us by its unlimited resources, for living without a why. Not forgetting the air, but using its spirit, its breath, to sing.

Notes

1   Martin Heidegger, "What are Poets For?" in his *Poetry, Language, Thought*, trans. Albert Hofstadter (New York: Harper and Row, 1971, p. 91.

2   Ibid.

3   Jacques Lacan, *Feminine Sexuality: Jacques Lacan and the École Freudienne*, ed. Juliet Mitchell and Jacqueline Rose (Basingstoke: Macmillan and New York: Pantheon Press, 1982), p. 140.

4   Melissa Raphael, *Theology and Embodiment: the Post-Patriarchal Reconstruction of Female Sacrality* (Sheffield: Sheffield Academic Press, 1996), p. 16.

5   Luce Irigaray, "Women, the Sacred, Money" in her *Sexes and Genealogies*, trans. Gillian C. Gill (New York: Columbia University Press, 1993), p. 75.

6   Luce Irigaray, "Belief Itself" in her *Sexes and Genealogies*.

7   Ibid., 25–6.

8   Especially by Tina Chanter in her *Ethics of Eros: Irigaray's Rewriting of the Philosophers* (New York and London: Routledge, 1995), ch. 4.

9   Although I have tried to be faithful to Irigaray's writing, it must be said that her poetic style allows for multiple interpretations, and I offer the following as *a*, not *the* reading of her work. See also my *Becoming Divine: Towards a Feminist Philosophy of Religion* (Manchester: Manchester University Press, 1998, and Bloomington, IN: Indiana, University Press, 1999).

10 "What are Poets For?", p. 94.

11 Ibid., p. 141.

12 " ... Poetically Man Dwells ... " in *Poetry, Language, Thought*, p. 213.

13 Cf. Rita Felski *The Gender of Modernity* (Cambridge, MA: Harvard University Press, 1995), pp. 1–5.

14 Luce Irigaray, *The Forgetting of Air in Martin Heidegger*, trans. Mary Beth Mader (Austin, TX: University of Texas Press, 1999), p. 154.

15 Sigmund Freud, *Beyond the Pleasure Principle*, trans. James Strachey (New York: Norton, 1961).

16 Irigaray, "Belief Itself," p. 31.

17 Ibid.

18 Ibid., p. 32.

19 Cf. Heidegger "Building Dwelling Thinking" in David Farrell Krell, ed. *Martin Heidegger: Basic Writings*, rev. edn. (London: Routledge, 1993).

20 I have explored this more fully in my *Becoming Divine*, ch. 4.

21 The phrase is from Donna Haraway, "Situated Knowledges: the Science Question in Feminism and the Privilege of Partial Perspective," in her *Simians, Cyborgs and Women: the Reinvention of Nature* (London: Free Association Press, 1991), p. 193.

22 In Krell, ed., *Martin Heidegger*.

23 Cf. my "Necrophilia and Natality: What does it mean to be Religious?" in *Scottish Journal of Religious Studies* 19/1 (Spring 1998).

24 Martin Heidegger *Being and Time*, trans. John MacQuarrie and Edward Robinson (Oxford: Blackwell, 1962), pp. 279f.

25 Irigaray, *The Forgetting of Air*, p. 100.

26 Ibid., pp. 100–1.

27 Rilke, quoted by Heidegger in "What are Poets For?", p. 134.

28 Ibid., p. 137.

29 Ibid., p. 141.

30   "Belief Itself," p. 35.
31   Ibid., p. 36.
32   Ibid., p. 42.
33   Ibid.
34   Ibid., p. 44.
35   Ibid., p. 46.
36   Ibid., p. 47.
37   Ibid., p. 45.
38   Ibid.
39   Cf. my *Becoming Divine*, ch. 11.
40   For example in "Building Dwelling Thinking."
41   Irigaray, *The Forgetting of Air*, p. 40.
42   Ibid., p. 41.
43   Ibid., p. 47.
44   "Belief Itself," p. 47.
45   Ibid., p. 44.
46   For example in Kathleen Lennon and Margaret Whitford, eds., *Knowing the Difference: Feminist Perspectives in Epistemology* (London and New York: Routledge, 1994).
47   Cf. Emmanuel Levinas *Totality and Infinity*, trans. A. Lingis (Pittsburgh: Duquesne University Press, 1969). For a discussion of Lévinas' impact on Irigaray, cf. Chanter.
48   "Belief Itself," p. 47.
49   In "Necrophilia and Natality: What does it mean to be Relgious?" in *Scottish Journal of Religious Studies* 19/2 (Spring 1998).
50   For want of space I shall discuss only two: the abyss, and "living without a why." There are, however, several more such symbols drawn from medieval mystics, notably "the dark night" and "*Gelasssenheit*" (detachment).
51   Heidegger, "What are Poets For?", p. 92.
52   Irigaray, "Belief Itself," p. 49.
53   Ibid., p. 50; cf. Heidegger "What are Poets For?" p. 131, discussing Rilke's poetry on the abyss and the singing poet.
54   Irigaray, "Forgetting of Air," p. 37.
55   Ibid.
56   *Meister Eckhart: The Essential Sermons, Commentaries, Treatieses and Defense*, trans. and intro by Edmund Colledge and Bernard McGinn. Classics of Western Spirituality (London: SPCK and New York: Paulist Press, 1981), p. 183; see also McGinn's "Introduction," p. 31.
57   *Johannes Tauler: Sermons*, trans. Maria Shrady. Classics of Western Spirituality (New York: Paulist Press, 1985), p. 90.
58   *Gertrude of Helfta: The Herald of Divine Love* trans. Margaret Winkworth. Classics of Western Spirituality (New York: Paulist Press, 1993), pp. 234, 191, 184.
59   Irigaray, "Forgetting of Air," p. 40.
60   Meister Eckhart, p. 183.
61   Ibid., p. 184.
62   Trans. Reginald Lilly (Bloomington: Indiana University Press, 1991).
63   "Belief Itself," p. 47.
64   Ibid.
65   *Forgetting of Air*, p. 148.

16

SECOND THOUGHTS ABOUT TRANSCENDENCE

Walter Lowe

It would be difficult to overstate the importance of "transcendence" for modern theology. Modern theology has characteristically been a mediating theology, seeking common ground between religion and secular culture; and mediation, i.e., the securing of some common ground, has often been sought via some notion of transcendence. In the face of doubt about the existence of a transcendent God, theologians could observe that the very fact that we raise such a question at all is evidence that humans do not exist the way a stone or tree does. Stones do not look about and ask, "Is this all there is?" Doing so is a distinctive mark of (human) transcendence. In the words of one theologian, "the vantage point from which man [sic] judges his insignificance is a rather significant vantage point."[1]

For a theology on the defensive, this argument is an attractive fallback position, a seemingly unassailable minimum. Further, it may then serve as the basis for a counterattack which might succeed in reclaiming the reality of God. The logic may be sketched in two theses. We may not know the capital-t Transcen*dent*, but (1) our very seeking is evidence of *some* sort of small-t transcend*ence*. That affirmation may seem minimal but its logic is compelling; and in a time when every certainty seems to be slipping away, that is not to be sneezed at. Moreover, the affirmation might have uses beyond the minimal. If transcendence can be linked to the Transcendent, then (2) transcendence becomes a sort of base camp from which to scale the heights, ascending, or transcending, toward the divine.

But how is one to justify the second move, the crucial step which puts theology back in business? Here the modern theologian often draws, explicitly or implicitly, upon a classic passage from Augustine. In the opening lines of his *Confessions* the author addresses his Creator, "[T]hou hast made us for thyself and restless is our heart until it rests in thee."[2] Put simply, God has placed in the created heart a "homing device," a penchant to return to the Divine. But Augustine was writing from within a context of belief. How can modern theology reinterpret the homing device in a manner credible to a culture which assumes no such Creator? How can theology reframe the restlessness? There is a solution which lies so close at hand that it seems more or less obvious: we are restless with all that is not God because that which is not God is *finite*. All the theologian has to do is introduce the language of finite and infinite, and the gap between thesis 1 and thesis 2 gratifyingly disappears. The first, virtually irrefutable thesis is that "(1) our very seeking is evidence of *some* sort of small-t transcend*ence*." Now the theologian can add that because of this transcendence we are unsatisfied by all that is finite, so that (2) by our very nature we are oriented toward God, i.e., the Infinite. We have an infinite longing which is a longing for the Infinite, our transcendence seeks the Transcendent. The homing device is restored.

The aim of the present essay is to question this rhetoric of infinite transcendence. I shall draw upon Plato, Augustine and even Descartes to help disengage the notion of transcendence from that of the infinite. As alternative, I do not propose that (human) transcendence must be conceived as simply, exhaustively finite. I do contend, how-ever, that a strong association between human transcendence and some notion of the infinite is not confined to theologians; it is something which affects us all. To borrow a term from Lacan and Irigaray, it is part of the Symbolic.[3] Evidence of this pervasive cultural dogma is the great difficulty we do in fact have in conceiving of a transcen-dence which is truly, and not just accidentally, finite. And that matters because, as I hope to show, the twofold association of transcendence with a rhetoric of the infinite and a rhetoric of ascent has an unacknowledged negative impact upon our under-standing of the finite, and of the human as well.

1   Distinguishing Transcendence

Plato's myth of ascent from the cave has been the ur-text for western reflection on transcendence. Prisoners who have seen only shadows realize that the shadows are not the truth when they turn to see the fire and objects which are source of the shadows. Struggling upward beyond the fire, they escape the cave altogether, to behold the vast world and the sun which illumines it. The imagery is ancient yet as contemporary as "consciousness raising." Even so brief a summary may allow us to distinguish three elements, the first of which is the simple *occurrence of* liberating insight. There is insight: it is something like this sheer event that Heidegger will eventually try to retrieve. For our purposes, we may note that this event is in principle distinct from two other elements which are immediately associated with it. The first is the notion of movement toward an appointed telos or goal. The second is a specification of movement and goal through imagery of ascent from darkness into light. The effect of these elements is to inscribe the insight event within a context which is (proto-) metaphysical.

But even at his most metaphysical Plato was no friend of the infinite. He was persuaded that reason operates by discerning the "shape" and character of things, cf., "de-finition." Some things are circular, some things are not; some actions are just, others are not. Absent that, there is no clarity; absent a measure of clarity, there is no thought. But the infinite is without shape or determinacy. Significantly, the infinite shares this characteristic with sheer matter (to anticipate the language of Aristotle). And as Plato knew that reason finds neither insight nor direction in sheer uncomprehended matter, so too he judged the notion of infinity to be void and barren. Thus at the ur-source of western reflection on transcendence, we are warned against eliding transcendence with the infinite.

If Plato was the reference point for interpreting transcendence in the classical period, Descartes played a corresponding role for modernity. He thematized human transcendence in a manner which is peculiarly modern. And he signalled, at least momentarily, a disengagement of transcendence from the metaphysics of ascent. The "*Cogito ergo sum*" of his *Meditations* responded to a doubt which was in part historical, due to the waning of the classical worldview under the impact of modern science; but in important part it was also a methodological doubt, the expression of a modern determination to demand in all things the same clarity and distinctness that one found in mathematics.[4] Pursuit of a math-like certainty inspired Descartes not to reduce doubt but to radicalize it. The effect of radicalized doubt, in turn, was a radicalized distinction, the distinguishing of human transcendence *per se*, as it were, from everything else. For the sheer event, the sheer occurrence of thought (or transcendence or reflection) was indeed – in its sheer "thatness," in the sheer givenness "that" it happened – an irreducible *certainty*. The Cartesian "Cogito," often maligned by theologians, is the historical basis for the first of the two moves we saw theology making in our introduction.[5]

Certainty came at a price, however. Put simply, the sheer "thatness" had certainty precisely because it had been distinguished or disengaged from any "whatness," i.e., from any (challengeable) thesis about what the Cogito is. But it is "whatness" or "essence" which bestows meaning. Certainty about the occurrence of the Cogito entails the loss of assurance regarding its meaning or significance! In this aspect of his thought, Descartes is the progenitor of the existentialists, for whom human existence precedes any specific essence. Alternatively, the problem may be stated in terms of *context*. Ascribing meaning to something entails placing it within some interpretive context. But it is in the nature of (human) transcendence to transcend any given context, e.g., by reflecting upon it or perhaps making an ironic comment about it.

That is one highly important aspect of Descartes, but it is not the only. Basic to modern science is the notion that space is uniform and extends on and on indefinitely. Alexandre Koyré's classic history of the rise of modern science bears the title *From Closed World to the Infinite Universe*.[6] Descartes' quest for certainty (prompted by this shift) produced a problem of meaning – and to that problem Descartes believed that the shift itself might provide an answer. For contrary to Plato, the shift was implicitly producing a positive assessment of the notion of "the infinite." Descartes, in his constructive philosophy, linked human reason to the Infinite (capital "I"), which he understood to be God. Whatever one thought of Descartes' logic, his association of human transcendence with the infinite was, for many who followed him, irresistible. For what a positive infinity did was to provide a context which is not a context. It promised meaning without confinement, a boundless significance seemingly free of metaphysics. And how flattering to the human!

Descartes deserves his fame. With him transcendence is disengaged decisively and peculiarly reengaged, distinguished and defined. In one moment, the limit idea of "transcendence per se" is glimpsed; in the next, it is obscured.[7]

2   The Cult of the Infinite

Infinity is the context which does not constrain, and thus the true "home" of humankind. This is the air that modernity breathes. Even the modern atheist is apt to say, in effect, "There is no infinite God out there, just time and space going on and on"; which is to say that time and space go on indefinitely. And while that which extends indefinitely is in principle distinct from the infinite, it serves the same function of providing a context which does not constrain. Such, then, is the conviction, at once inspiring and comforting, that stands behind modernity's firm association of (human) transcendence with the infinite.

Significantly, the Enlightenment still preserved something of the Platonic spirit in that it throve on de-finition. But the great Enlightenment endeavor to observe and reason out the underlying shape of things often declined to a wooden process of classification. In *Hard Times*, Dickens introduces the reader to Thomas Gradgrind, a man with "a rule and a pair of scales, and the multiplication table always in his pocket, sir, ready to weigh and measure any parcel of human nature, and tell you exactly what it comes to."[8] Against such aridity the human spirit protested in the prophetic visions of William Blake, and in Romanticism generally.[9] Byron's poetic play *Cain* places modernity's enthusiasm for the infinite at center stage. Cain is warned that, being finite, he cannot behold the deep mysteries of the universe without perishing. Unhesitatingly he responds, "And let me perish, so I see them!"[10] In its romantic aspect modernity is haunted by the infinite – as presence and as absence – whence an oscillating tonality of proclamation and lament.

Within postmodernism, one sometimes finds a facile tendency to identify modernity with the Enlightenment and the Enlightenment with the Newtonian worldview, all the while professing sensitivity to difference. It is hardly surprising that such postmodernism repeats the gestures of Romanticism in a variety of ways. It will tend, for example, to celebrate "transgression" in such a way as to cast boundaries in a largely negative light. But where boundaries are regarded as negative, is one likely to have a robust, positive understanding of the finite? Because it is chronologically close, Romanticism tends to be the lens through which we look, and which we do not see. Evidence is the fact that we do find it so difficult to dissociate (human) transcendence from the infinite.

Existentialism is and is not a critique of this association. On the one hand, we can say that existentialism took Descartes's brief glimpse of an enigmatic "transcendence per se" and made it the premise of a new philosophy. Human transcendence, translated as "existence," stood alone, detached from any meaning-bestowing context. Enigma became ambiguity, ambiguity became "the absurd." And in one important respect, there was a decisive disengagement of human transcendence from the infinite; for the fundamental absurdity was that human transcendence was a being-toward-death, irrevocably finite. Thus human finitude is acknowledged, even insisted upon, as fact – but it is regarded as absurd. In the early Sartre especially, finitude has no rightful claim on human freedom. It is rather a surd, a contradiction. Here existentialism becomes perhaps the most explicit demonstration of the West's inability to entertain a transcendence which is truly, positively finite.

3 Critique of Transcendence/Transcendence as Critique

With existentialism we conclude our highly selective historical survey. To clarify the issues raised, I take as text a line from Kierkegaard. On the opening page of *Sickness Unto Death*, Kierkegaard writes, "The self is a relation that relates itself to itself..."[11]

Let us examine this formula. It speaks of two relationships and three elements. The first relationship corresponds to the tension or duality by which observers, particularly in the West, have portrayed the human. Body vis-a-vis soul is classic; finitude vis-a-vis freedom evokes existentialism; brain vis-a-vis mind is current. Whatever the particulars, a distinction of this form constitutes what we may call the first-level relationship. It is at the heart of what Kierkegaard has to say, however, that there is not one relationship but two. For it is possible for us to say "the human being is a rational animal," and then to smile, perhaps a bit ironically. The least such gesture, a brief rolling of the eyes, signals a certain distance between the statement and oneself. It signals that we are not reducible to the first relationship (in this case, reason plus being an animal), because we can adopt one or another attitude toward that relationship. We can adopt a relationship to it. Formally speaking, that is the second level. (Of course we can adopt an attitude toward Kierkegaard's description. But it not at all clear whether in doing so we are exceeding or giving a further example of it. Such is the nature of human transcendence.)

Kierkegaard deploys this view of the human in ways that are fruitful but complex. A more straightforward use of Kierkegaard's basic insight may be found in the twentieth-century theologian Reinhold Niebuhr.[12] Niebuhr's use of the structure anticipates certain themes which later become prominent in deconstruction and in postmodernism at large. We may consider three points. First, Niebuhr observes that however the two elements of the first relationship may be portrayed, there is in practice a tendency to value one element more highly than the other. There is a tendency toward hierarchy. Secondly and crucially, there is a tendency *to identify oneself more closely with the "higher"* than with the "lower." Who wouldn't want to be on the side of the angels, as they say? But (thirdly) this natural tendency has a destructive effect on the very humanity one is seeking to honor. One will tend, for example, to deny one's finitude or view it negatively, and to overestimate the capacities of one's freedom.[13] The most telling effect, however, is the impact upon transcendence. For as one identifies oneself with the "higher" element, one will inevitably *associate or identify (one's) transcendence* with that element. There is in fact a chicken-and-egg relationship between this association and the almost unbreakable association we have observed between transcendence and ascent. We apply to transcendence the name of the "higher" element, e.g., freedom, because we assume transcending means moving upward. And because we value an upward movement, as in the inspirational use of the term "transcendence," we force the original distinction, e.g., finitude and freedom, into the form of a hierarchy.

This does indeed feel inspirational. But contrary to appearances, the effect is a *diminishment* of (human) transcendence. For the more closely transcendence is tied to the "higher" element, the less distance, detachment or perspective there is vis-a-vis that element. And this, to return to Kierkegaard's description, is a loss of that humanity which appears most clearly not in a definable relationship, but in an ability to relate oneself to any such relationship – e.g., to laugh at it. The common mark of self-righteousness, whether religious or secular, is that it takes itself too seriously. It lacks a certain humanity, it is not sufficiently "down to earth." The phrase suggests that being "down to earth," e.g., being able to laugh at oneself, would entail not less but more transcendence. It is a piece of folk wisdom that Kierkegaard knew well.

4   Sexual Difference

Two relations, three terms – Kierkegaard's minimal requirements for transcendence provide a touchstone for critique. It stands against any proposal in which an initial relation, almost certainly a hierarchy, defines transcendence. It holds that only a second relation, a relation to a relation, can constitute human transcendence. But for that there has to be a third term which really is a third and not just a disguised version or projection of the "higher" member of the initial relation. There has to be a third term which is genuinely "other."[14] It follows that *human transcendence is inherently, necessarily other* and that critical reflection must be vigilant in maintaining that otherness.

W. H. Auden writes of Sigmund Freud, "if often he was wrong, and, at times, absurd, / to us he is no more a person / now but a whole climate of opinion . . ."[15] It is possible to suggest that as physics and biology were to earlier epochs, so psychoanalysis is to ours. All of post-structuralism is evidence to this effect. In our terms, the significance of psychoanalysis is that it calls hierarchies into question; but also and perhaps less obviously, it is that with the unconscious psychoanalysis provides a third which is genuinely other. It calls hierarchy into question because it uncovers connections or correspondences between the culturally "higher" and the "lower." It shows how, unconsciously, the acceptable and the excluded substitute for one another. Art and feces converge; seemingly trivial elements in dreams connect with issues of life and death; one's very selfhood blurs with the image one has of a sexual organ. And with regard to all these matters, psychoanalysis looks to the affect. Recall our earlier observation that the least gesture, a flick of the eyebrow, can indicate how one relates to what one is saying. It is the job of the psychoanalyst to watch for the flick of the eyebrow, intonation of speech or lapse of memory – in order to get a clue, however momentary, to the *second* level relationship. Which is to say, in order to glimpse, however fleetingly, the workings of one's transcendence. Affect is the way to insight into *how one relates to* the original relationship, e.g., how one relates to one's embodiment, to the fact that one is both body and mind.

Here, I suggest, lies one of the lasting contributions of post-structuralism – the notion that psychoanalysis, or the peculiar mode of thought introduced by psychoanalysis, should be a sine qua non for the understanding of human transcendence. Examples abound but none is more pertinent to our concerns than the thought of the French psychoanalyst and philosopher, Luce Irigaray, who has reflected at length upon the crucial text of western transcendence, the myth of the cave.[16] Consider the imagery employed by Plato's narrative. There is an enclosed space, there is a laborious movement outward, there is emergence into a new life. Once one has read Irigaray the point is obvious – the cave is a womb! The longer one looks, the more details fit; the female passageway is implied but repressed, the hymenal membrane is hardened into a wall. As one reads, the first-relation hierarchies of mind and body, spirit and matter, the "ascent" of man and the abasement of woman begin to touch and meld.

And then there is the second relation, the relation to the relation, figured forth in affect or tone. Consider how the cave is portrayed – as an oppressive darkness, captivity. But if the cave is womb, that means that the womb, the very source of life, is depicted negatively! What madness is this? Things are sometimes said about the western tradition which are alarmist and overdrawn, but Irigaray's analysis has got to make one think that something is very, very wrong. The wrong is hidden because the rhetoric of transcendence does not speak against life; entirely to the contrary, it claims and depends upon the language of birth and emergence. But the rhetoric of ascent – as birthing upward – is an act of expropriation which bespeaks disdain of the birth of flesh.

> All oppositions that assume the *leap* from a worse to a better. An ascent, a displacement (?) upward, a progression along a line. Vertical. Phallic even? But what has been forgotten in all these oppositions, and with good reason, is how to pass through the passage, how to negotiate it – the forgotten transition. The corridor, the narrow pass, the neck.
>
> *Forgotten vagina.* The passage that is missing, left on the shelf, between the outside and the inside, between the plus and the minus. With the result that all divergencies will finally be proportions, functions, relations that can be referred back to *sameness*.[17]

The rhetoric "spiritualizes" what it wants and suppresses the rest. The result is an inhuman determination to be somehow "nobler than blood."[18]

In 1970, an inspirational fable entitled *Jonathan Livingston Seagull* captured the imagination of the American public.[19] The protagonist is presented as a bold non-conformist; but the tale itself, a paean to the myth of ascent, is an unthinking celebration of the western idée fixe. Jonathan is a bird obsessed with speed and altitude. We are told that by sheer will he transcends his very body, becoming "not bone and feather but a perfect idea of freedom and flight, *limited by nothing at all*."[20] One is reminded of Kant's cautionary reference to a dove who, sensing the resistance of the air against its wings, imagines it might fly more freely in a vacuum. Kant's common sense reminder retrieves our concrete humanity by thinking the positive, even liberating significance of limit.

Such wisdom is lost on Jonathan. We are variously instructed that "Heaven is being perfect," "perfection doesn't have limits" and indeed "[i]n heaven . . . there should be no limits."[21] Jonathan was the momentary poster child of docetic spirituality. We are asked to believe that his true home is the infinite; one might say that the meaning of his life is "inscribed in the infinite." *But is such an inscription possible?* Irigaray writes of the western myth of ascent, "This 'ascension,' which is not inscribed in place, makes a return to place possible only in the form of a downfall, a plunge into the abyss . . ."[22] A transcendence which is not "inscribed in a place" can experience a return to that place of origin only in negative terms, as a Fall.[23] For all its bravado, the flight is a fearful fleeing, an act of "inauthenticity." In tying transcendence to the "higher," this tradition annuls the true configuration of transcendence, viz. the otherness of the second relation. Promises of infinity come at the cost of mutilation. For this spirituality does not just ignore the lower – it actively "pushes off" against it. In so doing it creates a fissure such that, in Irigaray's words, "body and soul, sexuality and spirituality" can "neither mix, marry, nor form an alliance."[24]

Here Irigaray makes two points which are equally important. The first is a promise that to mix, marry and make alliances is the way toward an authentic "third."[25] The second is a caution, in effect a limit, that at present we have only a limited knowledge of what such a transcendence might be. It is not to be attained by a single romantic leap; if we imagine otherwise, we simply run along the established pathways of the Symbolic. A key example of both limit and promise is a theme to which Irigaray returns time and again, that of the "envelope" or the "container." Life itself (and if that is not transcendence, what is?) occurs within the unique container which is the womb. It occurs *in* the womb.

What then is the in-finite? The English prefix "in-" has a twofold resonance.[26] It can be privative, the equivalent of "non-", as in "inanimate" and "inconsistent." But it can also function in ways associated with the preposition "in", as in "inland" and "incarnate." The term "infinite" assumes the privative; it is defined as the not-finite, and that "not-" gesture is essential to it. But it follows, then, that the very meaning of the exalted infinite is linked necessarily, albeit negatively, to the finite – and is thus dependent upon it. It is inscribed within (an understanding of) the finite. It is in-(the)-finite.

5   The Differentness of God

Transcendence as ascent goes back at least as far as Plato and, no doubt, the mystery religions. With modern notions of freedom, something different came on the scene, what one might call a "lateral transcendence." The scientific revolution and the French Revolution variously demonstrated that humankind could transcend limitations *within* this world, by transforming it. Yet the lateral movement was simultaneously conceived as a movement upward, toward better things: the arc of progress. Even in the most secular accounts, the western Symbolic with its particular fantasy of ascent, held sway. In this context postmodernism can be understood as completing modernity's discovery by dissolving the vertical metaphysic so that lateral transcendence can be encountered and thought in its own right.

I believe that this development, while it has pitfalls of its own, is positively liberating for our understanding of God. As noted, Augustine's words "thou hast made us for thyself and restless is our heart until it comes to rest in thee" were voiced within a context of faith; the entirety of the *Confessions* is addressed to God. With modernity they began to function not within faith but as a "supplement" to faith. Not surprisingly, the "supplement" came to dominate as, under the pressure of skepticism from without and uncertainty within, theology allowed itself to be increasingly identified with apologetics. This was a loss, for it is the peculiar function of faith to remember to remember the *differentness* of God. (If God were not so fundamentally different, there would be no need for faith.) The purpose of transcendence as ascent is to establish some sort of pathway, some sort of line. But as the theologian Karl Barth shrewdly observes, "We suppose that we know what we are saying when we say 'God.' We assign to Him the highest place in our world; and in so doing we place Him fundamentally on one line with ourselves and with things."[27] Similarly, nothing is altered by calling God "infinite." For the infinite is still said to be the telos of a line or path which, in human transcendence, we can already partially discern.

The distortion is nowhere more apparent than in an antinomy which has haunted all of modern theology. In modernity God's differentness is rationalized, "represented" – in accordance with the underlying "*mathesis*" of "the era of the world picture" – as *distance*.[28] That God is transcendent is taken to mean that God is distant. God is far away. *Ipso facto*, the theological task becomes one of balancing that thesis with another which would make God near – a conception of "immanence." And how is this supposedly countervailing term, this balancing conception of the immanence of God conceived? Generally in terms of some form of (human) transcendence. It is said, for example, that (awareness of) the immanence of God brings peace of mind, enabling us to transcend or rise above the anxieties of daily life. There is undoubtedly an experiential truth to such a claim; religion can have this effect. But when we try to make of that the foundation for theology – then, so far from having risen above the dominant culture, we are in fact promoting the Symbolic shell-game whereby transcendence is the opposite of immanence, but immanence is a form of transcendence. The imaginary transcending of (modern) theology is the stock in trade of modern theology. And often enough "postmodern" theology repeats it.[29] Each instance is but further evidence that modern theology's most fundamental distinction, the north and south of its conceptual compass, occurs within the docile sameness of a domesticated transcendence.[30]

Already Heidegger affirmed that "Being itself is essentially finite."[31] Much of postmodernism derives from that insight, which is the death knell of the infinite as absolute. Derrida invokes a "finite infinite."[32] Irigaray's "sensible transcendental" performs a similar function.[33] And Jean-Luc Nancy has sought throughout his career to think "*une pensée finie*."[34] Now of course the notion of a ("merely") finite transcendence sounds like reductionism. That is the work of the Symbolic, to make it seem so. And of course it is difficult to open alternative spaces within the Symbolic. That is why Irigaray reflects that thinking sexual difference may be the task of an entire age.[35]

Irigaray has given perhaps the most concrete clue as to how to proceed.[36] If we say that one person is tall and another short, we affirm a difference. We affirm that they differ – but we do so according to single scale, e.g., the metric system. Though one is "greater" than the other, they are placed on a single line; their difference is understood within the encompassing sameness of one centimeter, then another centimeter, then another centimeter. What Irigaray is saying, in effect, is that there is no metric system for sexual difference. If there were, the difference could be contained within the Symbolic, as in the common stereotypes such as "men are more assertive, women are more caring." But no, it is not just that women differ; it is that they differ *differently*.

Seeking some "mathesis," some underlying coordinates of "more" and "less," seeking to lay things out upon a controllable cosmic graph, we reduced God's differentness to distance. That then generates the shell-game by which God's transcendence and God's immanence were are at one moment opposites, at the next, the same.

Only a theology open to God's differentness can escape the sterile alternation of antithesis and "synthesis," opposite and same. Our contemporary enslavement to the Symbolic is apparent in the fact that when we hear word of a God who is "Wholly Other," we imagine a God who is sheer Antithesis. By what logic is "otherness" a positive term when applied to other persons but negative when applied to God?

Surely we have the option of reading "God is Other" as "God is different," and "God is Wholly Other" as "God differs – differently." There would then be the conceptual space to conceive that "divine transcendence" might refer, perhaps, to God's *freedom*. Then transcendence would cease to be the opposite of immanence; for a God of freedom would not be isolated in some lofty place, but would be capable of being immanent precisely *because* of being transcendent, i.e., free. At that point, theology might begin to be more truly theological.

And within such a theology the treatment of humankind, of woman and of man, might well bear the title "Finitude Regained."

Notes

Or it may be the reverse: Plaskow. Some relative distinction between Plaskow and Irigaray.

1   Reinhold Niebuhr, *The Nature and Destiny of Man: A Christian Interpretation*, 2 vols., I. *Human Nature* (New York: Charles Scribner's Sons, 1941), p. 3.
2   Augustine, *Confessions and Enchiridion*, Library of Christian Classics, VII (Philadelphia: Westminster Press, 1955), p. 31.
3   For the purposes of this essay, emphasis is placed upon the constrictive aspect of the Symbolic.
4   See "Modern Science, Metaphysics and Mathematics" in Martin Heidegger, *Basic Writings from 'Being and Time' (1927) to 'The Task of Thinking' (1964)*, ed. David Farrell Krell (New York: Harper & Row, 1977), pp. 243–82, esp. 273–80.
5   In postmodern perspective one might judge that even the seemingly innocent "I" was something of an interpretation.
6   Alexandre Koyré, *From Closed World to the Infinite Universe* (Baltimore: Johns Hopkins Press, 1957).
7   Cf. Jean-Luc Marion's tracing of "a redoubled onto-tho-logy" in *On Descartes' Metaphysical Prism: The Constitution and the Limits of Onto-theo-logy in Cartesian Thought* (Chicago: University of Chicago Press, 1999), pp. 118–27, 346–52.
8   See Dickens, *Hard Times*, chapter 2, "Murdering the Innoncents."
9   See in particular Paul A. Cantor, *Creature and Creator: Myth-making and English Romanticism* (Cambridge: Cambridge University Press, 1984).
10 *Cain: A Mystery*, Act II, Scene 2, line 408 in George Gordon, Lord Byron, *The Poetical Works of Lord Byron* (New York: Oxford University Press, 1946), p. 537.
11 Soren Kierkegaard, *The Sickness Unto Death*. (Princeton University Press, 1980), p. 13.
12 Niebuhr, *The Nature and Destiny of Man*, My brief exposition of Niebuhr draws upon his work at large; one may refer to pp. 164, 178–79, 206–7.
13 In a highly influential essay published in 1960, Valerie Saiving argued that Niebuhr's emphasis upon pride fails to capture "the specifically feminine forms of sin" which are "better suggested by such terms as triviality, distractibility, and diffuseness; lack of an organizing center of focus, dependence upon others for one's self-definition...In short, underdevelopment or negation of the self." (Valerie Saiving Goldstein, "The Human

Situation: A Feminine View," *Journal of Religion* 40 (April 1960): 108–9). See also Judith Plaskow, *Sex, Sin and Grace: Women's Experience and the Theologies of Reinhold Niebuhr and Paul Tillich* (Lanham, NY: University Press of America, 1980).

14 Kierkegaard, *Sickness Unto Death*, p. 13.

15 W.H. Auden, "In Memory of Sigmund Freud," in *Collected Poems*, ed. Edward Mendelson (New York: Random House, 1976), p. 217.

16 Luce Irigaray, *Speculum of the Other Woman* (Ithaca: Cornell University Press, 1985), pp. 241–364.

17 Ibid., p. 273; emphases are Irigaray's.

18 Luce Irigaray, *An Ethics of Sexual Difference* (Ithaca: Cornell University Press, 1993), p. 101.

19 Richard Bach, *Jonathan Livingston Seagull* (New York: Macmillan, 1970). My comments on this minor episode in popular culture draw upon Philip Slater's insightful *Earthwalk* (Garden City, NY: Doubleday, 1974), pp. 94–7.

20 Ibid., p. 63, emphasis added.

21 Ibid., pp. 55, 55, 51.

22 Irigaray, *Ethics*, p. 39.

23 That Jonathan's flight is a fleeing is indicated by the insistence of his divebombing, which plays at returning to earth and then refuses to do so. It is noted in passing that the exercise nearly takes the life of a fellow gull.

24 Irigaray, *Ethics*, 15.

25 Ibid., p. 15, cf. p. 12.

26 See entries under "In-", *The Compact Edition of the Oxford English Dictionary*, Volume I (New York: Oxford University Press, 1971), p. 1396.

27 Karl Barth, *The Epistle to the Romans* (London: Oxford University Press, 1933), p. 44.

28 "Nature is now the realm of the uniform space–time context of motion, which is outlined in the axiomatic project and in which alone bodies can be bodies as a part of it and anchored in it" (Heidegger, "Modern Science, Metaphysics and Mathematics,") p. 268.

29 See Graham Ward's trenchant analysis in *The Postmodern God: A Theological Reader*, ed. Graham Ward (Oxford: Blackwell, 1997), xl–xliii.

30 ". . . love of sameness becomes that which permits the erection of space–time or space–times, as well as the constitution of a customarily autarchic discourse which opens up only toward a dialogue–monologue with God" (Irigaray, *Ethic*, 100).

31 "What is Metaphysics" in Heidegger, *Basic Writings*, op. cit., 110. See also Thomas A. Carlson, *Indiscretion: Finitude and the Naming of God* (Chicago: University of Chicago Press, 1998), 137–52 and *passim*.

32 Jacques Derrida, *Limited Inc* (Evanston: Northwestern University Press, 1988), p. 129 (referring to *Of Grammatology* and *Speech and Phenomena*.)

33 Irigaray, *Ethics*, pp. 115, 129, cf. 33.

34 Jean-Luc Nancy, *Une pensée finie* (Paris: Galilée, 1990). See also Jacques Taminiaux, *Dialectic and Difference: Finitude in Modern Thought* (New Jersey: Humanities, 1985), esp. p. 55–77.

35 Irigaray, *Ethics*, p. 5.

36 I share the reservations of Ellen Armour and others regarding Irigaray's suggestion that women project their own image onto the divine; see Ellen T. Armour, *Deconstruction, Feminist Theology, and the Problem of Difference: Subverting the Race–Gender Divide* (Chicago: University of Chicago Press, 1999), pp. 130–3.

17

MATERIALITY AND THEORETICAL REFLECTION

Charles E. Winquist

In her poignant novella *The Malady of Death*, Marguerite Duras writes, "You ask how loving can happen – the emotion of loving. She answers: perhaps a sudden lapse in the logic of the universe.... Never through an act of will.... It can come from anything, from the flight of a night bird, from a sleep, from a dream of sleep, from the approach of death, from a word, from a crime, of itself, from oneself, often without knowing how."[1] The complicated and intimate experience of love is not radically unlike what we mean by religion. Something happens. Our orientation to reality is shifted, slips or is transformed. This is not just an intellectual process that can be willed. It is more like the "flight of a night bird."

It is not just the flight of a night bird. This flight, this bird, has to be thought. That is, the materiality of the flight of the night bird has to be thought in the supplementary material textualization of discourse. The lapse in the logic of the universe is a lapse in the logic of discourse. There are multiple material contingencies. We are always in some place at some time. There is stuff wherever we are. There is usually consciousness wherever and whenever we are, even when it is a dream. In the discourses of love the lapses are epiphanies and in the discourses of religion the lapses are hierophanies. They are not always distinguishable from each other. We might think of the contingencies of our place and time as a gift. The world gives. It gives itself. And, unless there is a credible experience that suggests otherwise, we have to begin with Wittgenstein's assertion that "The world is all that is the case."[2] This claim does not challenge Charles Long's minimalist definition of religion as an orientation to reality in an ultimate sense.[3] The two concepts or words that are difficult in this definition are *ultimate* and *sense*. Is there a logic of sense? Is there a logic of *ultimate sense*? Do baskets make sense? Do trees make sense? Do crucified bodies make sense? Is "that than which nothing greater can be conceived" ultimate? Is the Tao ultimate? Is the brahman ultimate? These are all questions that deserve answers or at least further interrogation when it is no longer credible to think only in the missionary and colonial logics of the western ontotheological tradition. Indic spirituality, Taoism, Confucianism, Buddhism and many extra-literate traditions do not make sense in the sense of the Abrahamic traditions of the Mediterranean.

What I am outlining is a kind of peculiar monism or univocity of meaning in experience. There are baskets, stones and cities that are complex material networks and there is the materiality of supplementary textualities that is part of the experience of our thinking perceptions of the world of our place. Some materialities are visible and some are hidden.

Murphy Gell-Mann, an elementary particle physicist distinguishes between coarse and fined grained interrogations and analyses of experience in his book *The Quark and the Jaguar*.[4] There is a world of elementary particles that we do not see. And, there are Jaguars that we can see. One is not more real than the other. Elementary particles are relevant for understanding Jaguars but particle analysis alone does not allow us to understand Jaguars. There needs to be complementary analyses to grasp sense and especially if we are dealing with extreme formulations of ultimate sense. Sometimes there is a silence of the real that troubles us. It is not unlike those uncomfortable moments in an important conversation when you or a loved one cannot speak. The reality that is other is sometimes beside itself.

Naguib Mafouz, a secular Muslim Egyptian Nobel prize laureate, fashioned a short novella, *The Beggar*, in which Omar is a beggar for meaning. In the midst of Omar's dissolute nights he would regularly return to the pyramids of Giza and the Sphinx. "Omar's sphinx and pyramids taunt him and his community with their unrelenting silence."[5] The Secret of the Sphinx remains a secret. Victor Taylor in his book *ParaInquiry* writes that "the silence of the sphinx conjures up romantic expectations of receiving an answer to the ageless question 'why do we live?' "[6] He draws attention to a painting of Elihu Vedder from the 1863 "Question of the Sphinx" that depicts a man with his ear pressed up against the lips of the sphinx yearning to hear a sacred secret or answer; and, also to Mark Tansey's 1985 painting "Secret of the Sphinx (Homage to Elihu Vedder)" where a man kneels before the sphinx with recording device pressed against the lips of the sphinx. Technology now mediates the silence. The particular listening technology is a supplement that resolves nothing. Yet, Mafouz, Vedder, and Tansey are also mediators. Listening to the silence of the sphinx in a novella or in oil on canvas does say something about human experience. The sphinx is other than us which is part of our fantasy and it is other than itself which is part of its secret.

I don't think that there is any question that we have to account for the visible materialities and it would be naïve to privilege some expressions of material culture over others. As Mircea Eliade demonstrated so clearly, anything can be hierophanous. There is a this and a thatness to the empiricities that populate our world whose singularity is diminished by universalizing categories. What is tricky is that meta-analyses have their own material reality, but they are not the same as the matter under interrogation. We need to account for this multiplicity in our experience. There is no master system but there are instead networks where systems intersect each other, sometimes are imported into each other, complicating each other, and sometimes issuing forth in new systemization.

Idealisms or other poorly thought empiricisms and some empiricisms deny the material complexity of thinking. In contrast to poor thinking, I want to suggest that the rigorous empirico-idealism of Immanuel Kant's transcendental philosophy is both a problem and a paradigm for our contemporary interrogations of religion and culture.

Kant's transcendental method was rooted in David Hume's empiricism, albeit augmented by Cartesianism, Aristotlianism and Medieval Scholasticism. The *Critique of Pure Reason* opens with the claim that "All knowledge begins with experience." We have knowledge of objects, objective knowledge. We have the capacity to ask, we have the real experience of asking, "What are the conditions that makes this knowledge possible?" There is no assurance or guarantee of satisfactory answers.

Legend tells us that Kant never ventured beyond Königsburg. His sense of the material world of objects was the classical world of Newtonian physics. His transcendental aesthetic is a straight-forward rendering of the formal necessity for space as a condition for the presentation of any object and for time as a condition for the unity of apperception. The notion of necessity means that these are not *a posteriori* forms, forms that are not derived from experience but are instead conditions for experience. He learned from Hume that we have no experience of necessary connexion but that thinking causality is a subjective habit.

The problem is that to think the world is to phenomenalize it. We live with material objects but do not know them in themselves. Our thinking is an in-itself material supplement to what appears as phenomenal objects. There is no denial of reference but what is referred to in the world is re-presented so that it can be thought. Even thinking the reality of one's own thinking is representation and in this sense a substitution.

This is not just a technical exercise in philosophy. Kant thought that reason could over extend its competence and in paralogisms, antinomies and dialectical illusions falsify understanding. Existentially, to know the world is to be alienated from it. Kant seemed to be worried more about the arrogance of reason than guile and deceit. But, he opened a door by articulating a problematic that was later complicated by what Paul Ricoeur labeled the hermeneutics of suspicion of the nineteenth century, the work of Marx, Nietzsche and Freud. Guile, deceit, distortion and stereotyped symbolization entered the discussion of the conditions that make knowledge possible. The rigorous transcendental conditions were supplemented by quasi-transcendental conditions. The receptive matrix of thinking was more than the form of a transcendental aesthetic. It is less innocent. Theoretical reflection is not standing just in relationship to visible materialities but also to hidden materialities.

Karl Marx inverts Hegel and confronted the world of nineteenth century thinking with the hidden materialities of history. There are political and economic realities rooted in modes of production that create class consciousness and special interests with attendant ideologies. The task of thinking is not to disambiguate language but to understand the complexity of discourse through ideology critique. Material interests gets mixed in with the formality of representing the material world.

Nietzsche thinks the hidden materiality of language. Truth changes its meaning. He writes in *Truth and Lie in an Extramoral Sense* that "Truth is a mobile army of metaphors, metonyms, and anthropomorphisms."[7] These are tropes of substitution. Truth is a lie. Truth is textual and thereby text production. The word dog is not a dog, but to know a dog, a differential process, I have to name the animal, or let Adam name the animals and then borrow his dictionary. Truth is the simulacrum that is achieved by the relationality of differences. The traditional way of saying this is that the identity is in difference which means that it is not self-sameness. Your identity is always to some extent who you are not. We can understand Omar seeking out the sphinx because it is the other of himself. Because the sphinx is silent, the truth of the lie is our theoretical reflection. Can this supplementarity be a complementarity in experience and understanding?

The third hidden materiality associated with the hermeneutics of suspicion is Freud's understanding of the body. Bodies are visible. They have hides but the primary processes of the it (id) of the unconscious is not visible. Drives, sexual and aggressive, manifest themselves in disguise and distortion. Even if we don't accept psychoanalytical psychotherapy, Kant's epistemological problem is darkened and further complicated. This is particularly evident in the work of the French Freudians Jacques Lacan and Julia Kristeva.

Lacan makes a distinction between realms of the Real, the Imaginary and the Symbolic. The matter of things is most evidently expressed by the notion of the Real which is interestingly inaccessible to ordinary thinking. It is a figuration for a materiality that we don't know. The imaginary is the first access to the achievement of consciousness. There is a sensate experience of images. Within this realm the first embryonic possession of these images is referred to as the mirror stage. A child, usually between 12 and 18 months of age, identifies with their image in a mirror. This image is a substitution, a reversal, and a falsification. The image is a body without organs. The image of the "I" is not the reality of the "I" who thinks and feels; but, this image can be introduced into diverse semiotic systems that constitute the realm of the symbolic. The mirror stage is the semiotization of the child's body. It then makes sense to say as Lacan says that the unconscious is structured like a language. This restates the Freudian insight that the unconscious is never known as unconscious but only as it marks consciousness. We might say that the Real is a hermeneutic of disfiguration of symptoms in the symbolic realm.

Julia Kristeva in *Revolution and Poetic Language* nuances Lacan's three realms by referring to the Real as a *Chora*, a semiotic *chora*. She takes this term *chora* from Plato's *Timaeus* where it there functions as an aporetic marking for place or site. For Kristeva, it is not commensurate with the order of the symbolic. She attaches the adjective semiotic to this figuration of place to acknowledge that is does have an order, relational patterns, a complex sense. DNA is not English or Chinese, but it does have an order. Her understanding of the human subject as a subject in process/on trial is an understanding of multiple distributed processes that are temporally coincident. Some are visible and some are hidden. No single system of sense is whole or complete.

Although DNA is not English or Chinese, English and Chinese are systematicities that import themselves into the making of mind. Recently two Pandas came from Beijing to Zoo Atlanta. As simple as the Panda mind might be in its knowledge of Chinese it was obvious that essential words such as "sit" or "bamboo" had to be spoken in Chinese to accommodate these visitors from China. Place and system [the semiotic chora], New York, Beijing, London, New Orleans, the Internet constitute sense in parallel relationalities with bodies and histories.

What is the sense of place that is non-identical with the grammar, syntactical structures, and lexicon of English? We demand of graduate students that they learn multiple languages and that demand should be extended to learn the sense of multiple places. The problem is to access these multiple meanings of sense, multiple logics of sense. How does the symbolic realm acknowledge and consent to its incompleteness?

How do we surrender to the fantasy of a perfect dictionary? Can we accentuate the positivity and negativity of any symbolic system at the same time? This is Kristeva's revolution in poetic language. Poetic language is a negation that is transversally related to the Real or semiotic chora. It marks the trace of the other in and of language. It can be likened to the many extreme formulations in determinable traditional religions such as the Taoist legend that Lao Tsu's mother was impregnated by a shooting star. This is incommensurable with the sense of ordinary discourse. Its importance is that it is what ordinary discourse is not. It is an undecidability in the logic of the symbolic. The symbolic is unsettled by the other of the real.

In his recent writing, Jacques Derrida, without attribution to Kristeva, also uses Plato's *Khôra* to fathom a more profound and material sense of sense. Kristeva's semiotic chora tends to be biological and understood in relationship to the psychological symbolic. Derrida's *Khôra* resonates in a metaphysical or anti-metaphysical realm. It is almost as if he has become a theologian of a religion without religion, at least a traditional religion, although he uses the language and thematics of traditional religions in these recent works. His life long interest in the other in and of language was first marked by the re-inscription of the Kantian problematic by his aporetic nonconcept *différance* and now by his metaphysical aporetic nonconcept *Khôra*.

Khôra is a metaphysical place of what is epistemologically impossible. It marks something older and prior to what has taken place in visible symbolic elaborations. *Khôra* is a "a nameless name for the desert of différance."[8] The Kantian problematic is haunted by its metaphysical traces in the thought of Derrida. What was an epistemological problem is now the logic of the impossible. John Caputo describes the shift as finding expression in the prayers and tears of Derrida. Derrida, referring to his original name, Jackie, returns to the constitutional faith of his mother as he attends to her death. In this new thinking, there is a profound coherence with his earlier formulation of différance as a condition of the possibility of thinking. The *Khôra* is no more accessible than the nonconcept *différance* but it suggests in tonality the material matrix of the being of our thinking in the world. It is a place and not a procedure. The procedure is *différance*.

These hidden materialities bring us back to the importance of visible materialities. The philosopher is closely allied with the historian of religion and analyst of culture. The visible materialities give us something to think about, to interrogate. Fine grained analysis reinforces the importance of coarse grained analysis. Coarse grained analysis has to attend to fissures, gaps, and disfigurations in its own elaborations marked by the insights of fine grained analyses. It needs to be understood in the logic of sense that ultimacy drifts. It can express itself here and there, in the marketplace and in back alleys, in vociferous voices proclaiming a kerygma and in silence. The strategies for a complementary supplementarity are diverse and multiple. We are back to where we started–a lapse in the logic of the universe. Can we say yes to the flight of a nightbird, the jouisance in a smile, the silence of the sphinx.

My grandchildren's preschool in Boulder Co. is named *Make a Mess and Make Believe*. In context of this essay, we could restate the name as – *negate the pretension of the completeness of any thinking and enfranchise the pragmatics of theoretical reflection*. To make a mess and make believe is a strategy for accessing the possible *ultimate sense* in an orientation to reality that gives definition to religion. We make a mess to understand that the stuff of reality is complex and shows itself when carefully observed as a mess of heterogenous singularities. We make believe because of the incorrigible exigency of mind that makes sense of what we experience. The study of religion is most importantly an experiment in being human. We think the other to think ourselves.

Notes

1   Marguerite Duras, *The Malady of Death*, trans. Barbara Bray (New York: Grove Press, 1986), pp. 49–50.

2   Ludwig Wittgenstein, *Tractatus Logico-Philosophicus*, trans. D. F. Bears and B. F. McGuinness (London: Routledge and Kegan Paul, 1922, 1961), p. 7.

3   Charles H. Long, *Significations: Signs, Symbols, and Images in the Interpretation of Religion* (Aurora CO: The Davies Group Publishers, 1999), p. 7.

4   Murray Gell-Mann, *The Quark and the Jaguar: Adventures in the Simple and the Complex* (New York: W.H. Freeman and Company, 1994).

5   Victor E. Taylor, *Para/Inquiry: Postmodern Religion and Culture* (London and New York: Routledge, 2000), p. 33.

6   Ibid., p. 31.

7   *The Portable Nietzsche*, edited and translated by Walter Kaufmann (New York: The Viking Press, 1954, 1968), p. 46.

8   John D. Caputo, *The Prayers and Tears of Jacques Derrida: Religion Without Religion* (Bloomington and Indianapolis: Indiana University Press, 1997), p. 40.

18

DIVINE EXCESS: THE GOD WHO COMES AFTER

Merold Westphal

What, then, is the God I worship? . . . But what do I love, when I love my God?
Augustine, Confessions, *I,4 and X, 6*

The title of Cal Schrag's splendid little book, *The Self After Postmodernity*,[1] makes explicit his assumption that the postmodern assault on the self as conceived by major strands within the western philosophical tradition is not an abolition, not an annihilation without remainder. Schrag's work is inspired in large part by Paul Ricoeur's attempt, among the shards of the "shattered cogito" to develop a "hermeneutics of the self [that] is placed at an equal distance from the apology of the cogito and from its overthrow . . . at an equal distance from the cogito exalted by Descartes and from the cogito that Nietzsche proclaimed forfeit."[2] The "arduous detours" of this hermeneutics pass through a series of questions. "Who is speaking of what? Who does what? About whom and about what does one construct a narrative? Who is morally responsible for what? These are but so many different ways in which 'who?' is stated."[3] To answer these questions is to answer the question of a selfhood that survives the legitimate deconstruction of its illegitimate pretensions.

The same assumption is at work in another enticing title, *Who Comes After the Subject?*[4] The essays in this volume address "the critique of the deconstruction of subjectivity." But Jean-Luc Nancy tells us that with his question he wanted "to suggest a whole range – no doubt vast – in which such a critique or deconstruction has not simply obliterated its object (as those who groan or applaud before a supposed 'liquidation' of the subject would like to believe). That which obliterates is nihilism . . ."[5]

In the same spirit, John D. Caputo has posed the question, Who comes after the God of metaphysics, after the critique of onto-theology? In disseminating this question he doubtless joins Nancy in saying, "I did not send my question . . . to those who would find no validity in it, to those for whom it is on the contrary more important to denounce its presuppositions and to return, as though nothing had happened, to a style of thinking that we might simply call humanist . . ."[6] Or, in the present instance, metaphysical. Or onto-theological. Still, the assumption is that after the deluge we have the need, the desire, and the ability to speak of God. Somehow. But how, and of whom?

I shall reply to this question, but first it is necessary to be as clear as possible about the "after." We are to think and speak of God after... After what, precisely? For present purposes the critique that comes before is threefold: the critique of onto-theology in Heidegger, and the closely related critiques of ontology in Lévinas and Marion.

If one were to gather an understanding of Heidegger's critique of onto-theology second hand one might easily think that it is directed primarily at Augustine and Aquinas, Luther and Calvin, Pascal and Kierkegaard – against anyone who affirms a personal creator and redeemer. It is not always sufficiently noticed that his paradigms are Aristotle[7] and Hegel[8] and that the target of his analysis of "the onto-theo-logical constitution of metaphysics" is a tradition that stretches from Anaximander to Nietzsche,[9] which isn't quite the same as the tradition that stretches from Augustine to Kierkegaard.

Heidegger derives his term from the move by which Aristotle's metaphysics becomes theology. First philosophy starts out as ontology, as the theory of being qua being, but finds that in order to complete itself it needs to posit a highest being, the Unmoved Mover.[10] This ontology that becomes theology Heidegger calls onto-theology. Its fundamental assertion is that there is a Highest Being which is the key to the meaning of the whole of being.

But this affirmation is not obviously incoherent or self-refuting. If there is a critique here, if an overcoming of metaphysics in its onto-theological character is necessary, we shall have to ask what is wrong with this gesture, most overt and unambiguous in its Aristotelian form, but anticipated by Anaximander and reiterated by Hegel and Nietzsche.

Heidegger gives his answer to this question as the answer to another, "How does the deity enter into philosophy...?" – to which he replies that for metaphysics "the deity can come into philosophy only insofar as philosophy, of its own accord and by its own nature, requires and determines that and how the deity enters into it."[11]

In order to enter this discourse, God must first get an *imprimatur* or the Good Housekeeping Seal of Approval from philosophy. This scene, in which God makes a (not so) grand entry, suggests two others which can help us state why Heidegger thinks this move makes for bad philosophy and bad theology. The first scene occurs in the Preface to the Second Edition of the *Critique of Pure Reason*, where Kant is praising Galileo and others, who "learned that reason has insight only into that which it produces after a plan of its own, and that it must not allow itself to be kept, as it were, in nature's leading-strings, but must itself show the way... **constraining nature to give answer to questions of reason's own determining**."[12]

Heidegger lacks Kant's enthusiasm for this insistence on being in charge of the questioning. *What is Metaphysics?* (1929) contains a polemic against science and logic (philosophy's logos) because they are of no help in asking the truly metaphysical question about the nothing (which is the flip side of the question of being). In the Postscript to *What is Metaphysics?* (1943), "metaphysics" has become a dirty word and the task is now the overcoming of metaphysics; for posing the question of the nothing (and thus of being) is already to go beyond metaphysics as the truth (foundation?) of objectivising, calculating science. In the Introduction to *What is Metaphysics?* (1949), the metaphysics that needs to be overcome is set forth as onto-theology.

These three essays[13] make it clear why onto-theology is bad philosophy. It converts what might have been the question of being into the question of a being, albeit the Highest Being. In their focus on beings, science and metaphysics together, preoccupied with their own questions, are *Seinsvergessenheit*. When they compel beings to answer questions of their own determining, they desecrate being by depriving it of its mystery and become agents of that will to power that flourishes as modern technology. One needn't be as impressed with the ontological difference as Heidegger is to think there may be something to the charge that in various modes metaphysics has contributed to an arrogant humanism that has helped to create and sustain a very inhuman modern world.

But Heidegger thinks it obvious that when philosophy makes God a theme of discourse on its own terms, theology and not just philosophy is affected.[14] And not for the better. Here a second scene is evoked by Heidegger's analysis, this one from the book of Job. Job refuses to "curse God and die" (2:9–10), but he has a subpoena for God that he would deliver if only he could find him.

> Oh, that I knew where I might find him,
>   that I might come even to his dwelling!
> I would lay my case before him,
>   and fill my mouth with arguments.
> **I would learn what he would answer me**
>   and understand what he would say to me.

(23:3–5, emphasis added)

Job shouts, Where art Thou? and awaits the divine reply, *me voici*. Here it is not science compelling nature to answer questions of its own determining, but a man seeking to compel God to answer his questions. We know how the story ends. God shows up, but not to answer Job's questions. Rather, it is to insist on being the one who asks the questions.

> Gird up you loins like a man,
> I will question you, and you shall declare to me.

(38:3)

The remainder of chapters 38 and 39 is a barrage of questions addressed to Job, after which God says to Job

> Shall a fault finder contend with the Almighty?
> Anyone who argues with God must respond.

(40:2)

After Job admits that he does not know how to answer, God repeats the "Gird up your loins . . . I will question you . . . " admonition (40:7) and we get another divine barrage, including many more questions for Job, who finally acknowledges that he was without understanding and knowledge when he had said to God

> Hear, and I will speak;
> I will question you, and you declare to me.

(42:4)

The narrative makes it clear that for all his steadfast piety, Job is on the verge of blasphemy when he insists that God enter his discourse on his terms, that God's job is to answer Job's questions. This is what happens to theology when it allows itself to be seduced by metaphysics. It assumes that the purpose of God talk is to render the whole of being intelligible to human understanding, in short, to answer our questions.

For Heidegger it is the notion of God as *causa sui* that typifies this notion of God as Ultimate Explainer.[15] The problem is that when theology buys into this philosophical project, it renders the God of whom it speaks religiously useless. *Causa sui* is "the right name for the god of philosophy. Man can neither pray nor sacrifice to this god. Before the *causa sui*, man can neither fall to his knees in awe nor can he play music and dance before this god."[16]

Here Heidegger sounds less like Nietzsche celebrating the death of God than like Pascal contrasting the god of the philosophers with the God of Abraham, Isaac, and Jacob. This impression is strengthened when Heidegger challenges Christian theologians to consider whether their appropriation of Greek philosophy was "for better or for worse" with specific reference to the Pauline question, "Has not God the let wisdom of this world become foolishness?" (1 Corinthians 1:20), more specifically, the wisdom which "the Greeks seek" (1:22). "Will Christian theology one day resolve to take seriously the word of the apostle and thus also the conception of philosophy as foolishness?"[17] **We must think God as the mystery that exceeds the wisdom of the Greeks**.

Whereas for Heidegger "metaphysics" becomes the name of those features of the western philosophical tradition that must be overcome, that role is given to "ontology" by Lévinas, who reserves the name "metaphysics" for the ethical relation to which he gives priority over ontology.[18] So we have to stay on our terminological toes. Lévinas' definition of ontology has an epistemic flavor. It is "theory as comprehension of beings..." Thus *Being and Time* continues the western ontological tradition with its "one sole thesis: Being is inseparable from the comprehension of Being..."[19]

We should not read this anthropocentrically. It is being that gives itself to be understood. "Truth can consist only in the exposition of being to itself..." In the process by which being comes to consciousness by means of ideality and essence, "being thus carries on its affair of being." That we can think being means "that the appearing of being belongs to its very movement of being, that its phenomenality is essential, and that being cannot do without consciousness, to which manifestation is made... The thinking subject... is then, despite the activity of its searching... to be interpreted as a detour that being's essence takes to get arranged and thus to truly appear, to appear in truth. Intelligibility or signifyingness is part of the very exercise of being, of the *ipsum esse*. Everything is then on the same side, on the side of being."[20]

When everything is on the same side we have the totality against which *Totality and Infinity* is a protest. Ontology is that allergic reaction to alterity that is the reduction of the other to the same.[21] A very early (1951), very brief presentation of this critique of ontology is found in the essay, "Is Ontology Fundamental?" It states the theme whose many variations are the later writings, gives the exposition of a motif immediately taken up into the massive development section that completes Levinas' authorship. Perhaps we should speak of a first and second subject, of two contrasting themes or motifs. For first there is the presentation of ontology, then, as its critique, the presentation of an alternative, the "relation which is irreducible to comprehension."[22]

The essay begins in praise of Heidegger for his break with the intellectualist tradition of western philosophy. Recognizing the contingency and facticity at work in our thought, he points to the rootedness of thought in a comportment beyond theory and contemplation, to what might be called the priority of existence to our conscious intentions. But this radicality is immediately tamed, brought back into the ontological language game, when Heidegger interprets existence as comprehension, openness, understanding, and truth. Thus Heidegger sees the being of beings in their intelligibility.[23]

Since Plato comprehension and intelligibility have meant the subjection of the particular to the universal. For Heidegger, this occurs as the horizonal character of understanding. "The understanding of a being will thus consist in going beyond that being into the *openness* and in perceiving it *upon the horizon of being*. That is to say, comprehension, in Heidegger, rejoins the great tradition of Western philosophy: to comprehend the particular being is already to place oneself beyond the particular. To comprehend is to be related to the particular that only exists through knowledge, which is always knowledge of the universal."[24]

This is not merely a nominalist or an atomist protest. In Lévinas' view the purchase of intelligibility through universality or of comprehension through horizonal context is not innocent. Like the universal concept of the intellectualist tradition, the phenomenological horizon allows us to pigeonhole beings into a semantic totality which has a place for everything and correspondingly puts everything in its place. This is the "overcoming" of the object, and not merely in the sense that it is conceptually *mastered and grasped*, revealing as that language may be. Lévinas associates this overcoming with possession, consumption, power, property, assimilation, and violence. Possession, in particular, implies that since things belong to me and not to themselves, they are either to be used for or enjoyed by another. We encompass things within our conceptual horizons, thereby enabling us to incorporate them into our practical projects.[25]

Since ontology does this to every being, including other human beings, it is not surprising that Lévinas associates himself with Kantian ethics as a plea for respect.[26] But how does he make the transition from theory to practice, agreeing in effect with Heidegger that western philosophy culminates in the will to power? Why does he see ontological reason as "a ruse of the hunter who ensnares..."?[27] Lévinas' answer comes in a single sentence. "If things are only things, this is because the relation with them is established as comprehension."[28] In other words, it is the very nature of comprehension to treat its objects as one of a kind or as part of a whole in such a way as to deprive them of the respect, to speak with Kant, which forbids my reducing them to the ways I can use or enjoy them. Thus, in *Totality and Infinity*, just after he attributes to

Heidegger the thesis that "Being is inseparable from the comprehension of Being," Lévinas writes, "To affirm the priority of *Being* [as horizon] over *existents* is to already decide the essence of philosophy; it is to subordinate the relation with *someone*, who is an existent, (the ethical relation) to a relation with the *Being of existents*, which, *impersonal* [emphasis added], permits the apprehension, the domination of existents (a relation of knowing), subordinates justice to freedom."[29]

The fly in the ointment is the essentially impersonal character of comprehension, which reduces everything to only a thing. Its form is that of a subject seeing or intending an object. If there is to be room for something like Kantian respect, there will have to be a "relation which is irreducible to comprehension,"[30] one which involves more than subsuming a particular under a universal or apprehending some foreground against an horizonal background. Such a relation is impossible. "Unless it is the other (*Autrui*). Our relation with the other (*autrui*) certainly consists in wanting to comprehend him, but this relation overflows comprehension."[31]

Wherein consists this overflow? Quite simply, in speech, for the impersonal objects of comprehension are mute. Respect and justice, in short, the ethical relation becomes possible when sight is *aufgehoben* or teleologically suspended in speech.[32] Especially important are those speech acts which go beyond information sharing. If it is as interlocutor that the other overflows comprehension, it is especially by virtue of such speech acts as summoning, invocation, calling, greeting, and imploring, as in prayer.[33] Such acts, and not physiognomy as such, constitute the face of the other, the face which is at once the possibility and impossibility of murder. The voice/face of the other overflows comprehension by refusing to be captured without remainder by any horizon of understanding. It signifies itself, and it does so immediately.[34]

There is a link between Heidegger's critique of onto-theology and Lévinas' critique of ontology. Onto-theology, as Heidegger understands it, is the project of rendering the whole of being intelligible to human understanding. Since it has no room for that which overflows comprehension, it distorts our understanding of God (as well as of ourselves and the world of nature). Similarly, ontology, as Lévinas presents it, identifies being with its intelligibility to theory, to contemplation, to representation,[35] to intentionality.[36] Thereby it excludes the voice and the face of the other who is my neighbor and, *a fortiori*, the voice of the God who commands us to love our neighbor. **We must think God as the voice that exceeds vision so as to establish a relation irreducible to comprehension**

Lévinas insists that his critique is not an assault on reason but an attempt to go beyond reason as "a ruse of the hunter who ensnares . . . " to an "order of reason . . . where the resistance of beings qua beings is not broken but pacified."[37] Bad reason (ontology) is to be superseded (*aufgehoben*) by good reason (metaphysics). Similarly, Marion insists that his quest for "God without being" and thus a God beyond onto-theology and prior to ontology is the search for a "conceptual thought of God (conceptual, or rational, and not intuitive or "mystical" in the vulgar sense) . . . "[38]

Marion charges that onto-theology "imposes" its metaphysical names, such as *causa sui*, on God and in doing so hides "the mystery of God as such."[39] And he charges the ontological tradition which makes Being the first name of God with "chaining" God to Being, asking whether God is not better conceived in the first instance as charity, as *agape*, as the good, as gift.[40] When Marion speaks of "the failure of the metaphysical concept of God" and looks for a mode of God-talk that "allows the emergence of a God who is free from onto-theology...," it seems that the question concerns the priority of various categories or names in relation to others. But Marion has already just told us, "I am attempting to bring out the absolute freedom of God with regard to *all* determinations..."[41] If certain names are privileged over Being, it will be because they protect this freedom better.

This they accomplish by being icons rather than idols. Although he is interested in conceptual intelligibility, Marion turns (briefly) to sensible visibility for this analysis, retracing the path by which the tradition has modelled "seeing" intelligibles with the mind's eye on seeing sensibles with the body's eye. What distinguishes an icon from an idol is the how rather than the what of perception. In other words, a given visible can function as either idol or icon depending on the nature of the intentional act directed toward it.

It becomes an idol when the gaze that intends it is satisfied or (ful)filled with what it sees, when it stops, freezes, settles, or comes to rest at its visible object.[42] Marion seems to have in mind Husserl's account of adequation as fulfilled intention, the situation where what is given in experience corresponds exactly to what would otherwise have been an empty intention.[43] Since one didn't aim at more than is present, one can be satisfied with what is given, can be at rest with the results. When "every aim is exhausted," the gaze "admits no beyond," or, in this case, "allows no invisible."[44]

Idolatry means that the human gaze has become the measure of the divine being; God is now equated (hence adequation) with "what the human gaze has experienced of the divine." In this way the idol becomes an "invisible mirror," invisible because its role as mirror is not noticed.[45] But of what is it the mirror, the carbon copy, the exact duplicate? Not of the divine, unless God should just happen to fit, without remainder, into the confines of what is humanly visible. Rather the idol is the invisible mirror of the gaze, the human capacity by which it is experienced, and it is this which accounts for the perfect fit (adequation, correspondence, identity) between the aim of the gaze and the target on which it lands and at which it rests. Idolatry is this preestablished harmony.

The same visible becomes an icon when it is looked at differently, in the spirit, perhaps, of Andrea Del Sarto:[46]

> Ah, but a man's reach should exceed his grasp,
> Or what's a heaven for?

The gaze is not satisfied or fulfilled. It does not stop and rest. Instead it never ceases to "transpierce visible things" in an awareness of the essential invisibility of the divine. But this is only possible to a gaze that is always "transpiercing itself."[47] The iconic gaze looks beyond all visible things to the invisible because it refuses to make its own capacity the measure of what it intends. Knowing *itself* to be inadequate to that at which it aims, it does not equate what is given to sight with the God who gives sight.[48]

As the measure of the divine (which in turn becomes the mirror of its human measure), the idolatrous gaze "still remains in possession of the idol, its solitary master."[49] By contrast, the iconic gaze is not the director of the scene in which it plays a supporting role. Its double aim of transpiercing its object and itself to that which is beyond both is triggered by the discovery that it is aimed at. In iconic intention, "the gaze of the invisible, in person, aims at man . . . the icon opens in a face that gazes at our gazes" with the result that "the human gaze is engulfed . . . [and] does not cease, envisaged by the icon, there to watch the tide of the invisible come in . . . [The icon] offers an abyss that the eyes of men never finish probing."[50]

The ontological tradition is not embarrassed by the apeironic abyss of sensibility. Armed with the concept, it knows how to introduce some order into chaotic infinity, to dam up the engulfing ocean. Marion's critique of ontology is designed to rescue our God-talk from this move. So he applies that the very same idol/icon analysis to the concept that he has developed in relation to vision. When we assume the adequacy of our concepts to the divine reality, we make ourselves the measure and master of that reality and convert it into the invisible mirror of our intellectual capacities. It is not surprising that Marion mentions Feuerbach at this point.[51]

At the level of sense perception, the idolatrous aim is satisfied and thus at rest with the visible, while the iconic gaze transpierces it toward the invisible of which it is a trace. At the conceptual level, the invisible becomes the incomprehensible, that which we transpierce not only our images but also our concepts to aim at. Now idolatry is contentment with what the *mind's eye* can see, the assumption (or is it the demand?) that our concepts and the propositions in which we embed them can be equal to (*adequatio*) to divine being. As Gregory of Nyssa puts it, "Every concept, as it is produced according to an apprehension of the imagination in a conception that circumscribes and in an aim that pretends to attain the divine nature, models only an idol of God, without at all declaring God himself."[52]

We already know that Marion is interested in fleeing idolatry but not conceptuality, so we are not surprised to find him saying that "the icon also can proceed conceptually, provided at least that the concept renounce comprehending the incomprehensible, to attempt to conceive it, hence also to receive it, in its own excessiveness."[53] In other words, **we must think God as the gift of love who exceeds not merely the images and but also the concepts with which we aim at God**.

Like Lévinas, Marion points us toward a "relation which is irreducible to comprehension." But this is not just a call for epistemic humility, a kind *via analogica* following upon a *via negativa* and based on the "absolute freedom of God with regard to *all* determinations . . ."[54] As with Lévinas, it is a challenge to theory as the primary mode of God-talk. It isn't simply that we have a goal, adequation, which we cannot achieve. It is that we have a higher goal than making accurate assertions about God. This is why, in the final analysis, "predication must yield to praise – which, itself also, maintains a discourse." There is a silence appropriate to the God relation, not just because our language limps, but because God is love, and love "is not spoken, in the end, it is made. Only then can discourse be reborn, but as an enjoyment, a jubilation, a praise."[55] Marion follows Pseudo-Dionysius in following a "wise silence" with "songs of praise."[56] Praise is the language in which love welcomes the decentering presence of the Divine Other, recognizing the "of" in "gift of love" as at once an objective and subjective genitive.[57]

We must think God as the mystery that exceeds the wisdom of the Greeks.

We must think God as the voice that exceeds vision so as to establish a relation irreducible to comprehension.

We must think God as the gift of love who exceeds not merely the images but also the concepts with which we aim at God.

Who comes "after" the critiques that can be summarized in these three imperatives? What sort of God can withstand the scrutiny they encapsulate? Heidegger, Levinas, and Marion have replied to this question, which does not require only a single answer. I promise once again to give my own response, but only after reflecting briefly on the "must" of these commands. Whence this obligation? With what right (*quid juris*) does philosophy, or, more precisely, these philosophies (for these critiques make it clear that "philosophy" does not speak with a single voice, even when seeking to overcome onto-theological metaphysics) dictate how we shall think and speak of God? Is not the arrogance of onto-theology re-enacted when the critique thereof assumes the same hegemony? Are we not exchanging a Tsar for a Stalin, a Shah for an Ayatollah?

Under the heading of "Double Idolatry" Marion has raised this very question in relation to Heidegger.[58] It is a legitimate question, and, given the substantial over-lapping consensus among our three critiques and the sternness with which we are told how we "must" think about God, we cannot restrict the question to Heidegger.

One or more of these commandments can come to have normative force for us in one of two ways. They can be philosophically persuasive without any (apparent) theological assumptions, in other words, independently (it would seem) of how we think, affirmatively or negatively, about God. Or they can be philosophically persuasive in significant part precisely because they highlight, or reinforce, or make explicit what we already think about God.

In either case we are dealing with cognitive dissonance and reflective equilibrium. Even if with our trio we deny primacy to theory in the God relation, we want our philosophical theorizing about God-talk to be at peace with our pre-and-post reflective, everyday thinking about God. So we seek reflective equilibrium.

If we do not achieve it at first, we experience cognitive dissonance. One side or the other (or perhaps both) needs revision. We have learned in other contexts that there is no single, self-evident solution to the problem. Faced with an anomaly, we can revise our theory or question either our data or our intuitions.

I suggest two principles, or better, warnings for dealing with situations of cognitive dissonance between our philosophical and theological persuasions (meaning by the latter our God-talk habits, whether academically formed or not and whether they are affirmative or negative). I believe, though I shall not try to show, that one can find support for them in all three of our thinkers.

The first of these I shall call the Warning Against Philosophical Arrogance. This warning is implicit in the *quid juris* questions just posed and in Marion's "Double Idolatry" charge. It is the reminder that the days of Absolute Monarchy are over in philosophy, that no philosophy is Absolute Knowledge or possesses Absolute Author-ity, that no theology should be expected automatically and a priori to bow the knee before philosophy's correction.[59] If cognitive dissonance arises, it may be my philos-ophical theory that needs to be revised to accommodate my theology.

The second is like unto the first and is called the Warning Against Theological Arrogance. It is the reminder that my theology does not cease to be human, all too human, just because it purports to be about God. In a variety of ways, both formal and substantive, it can be more idolatrous than iconic.[60] The days of Absolute Monarchy, Absolute Knowledge, and Absolute Authority are over in theology too, and in the search for reflective equilibrium, it may be my theology that needs revision in the light of a philosophical critique. All the more so if that critique has it roots, consciously or unconsciously, in a theological horizon in which I also stand. The suspicion of idolatry originates in prophetic belief (e.g., Kierkegaard) as well as in skeptical unbelief (e.g., Nietzsche).[61]

So, then, who comes "after" the overcoming of onto-theologically constituted metaphysics? I shall not try to say how we "must" think, for while I take the triple Thou Shalt developed above very seriously, I also think there are many ways to think and talk about God which remain within the parameters they specify. So I shall speak of how we "may" think and talk about God.

I began this essay by posing its question in words taken from Augustine's *Confessions*. Now I want to answer that question quite simply and directly. The God who comes after onto-theology, who would be overcome by metaphysics (in Heidegger's sense) and who thus is the overcoming of metaphysics can be the God of Augustine. I believe the reader can confirm at each stage of its development that nothing in the triple critique presented above precludes the affirmation of a personal creator and redeemer, though each critique precludes certain ways of understanding such God-talk, in particular certain epistemic meta-claims about it. Without trying to defend everything Augustine says about God, I will try to show how his God, especially as presented in the *Confessions*, not only can withstand the scrutiny encapsulated in the threefold "must" we've been exploring, but even can be seen as part of its prehistory, an origin (by no means absolute) from which these critiques might emerge. Postmodernism just might help us to rediscover and rethink things premodern.[62] Heidegger has affirmed what Lévinas and Marion have enacted, namely that faith requires and thus can motivate the critique of onto-theology. That critique is not the monopoly of secular postmodernism, and, *a fortiori*, not of cynical nihilism.

Augustine begins his *Confessions* with two citations from the Psalms. "*Can any praise be worthy of the Lord's majesty? How magnificent his strength!. Now inscrutable his wisdom*" (I:1).[63] Already he is "lost in wonder, love, and praise."[64] Especially praise. Having read his Marion, he remembers that "predication must yield to praise" − so he immediately reminds himself that any predications implicit in the psalmist's questions have their telos in praise. "Man is one of your creatures, Lord, and his instinct is to praise you . . . he is part of your creation, he wishes to praise you. The thought of you stirs him so deeply that he cannot be content unless he praises you, because you made us for yourself and our hearts find no peace until they rest in you" (I:1).

Three times in this brief passage Augustine affirms God as creator, and this will be a constantly recurring theme in what is to follow. It would not be difficult to show that his creator is an uncaused cause, a *causa sui*, if you please. But this is conspicuously not the *causa sui* Heidegger has in mind, before whom there is no prayer or sacrifice, no awe, music, or dance. The *Confessions* are indeed one long prayer, addressed continuously to God. We see how ontology is teleologically suspended in prayer when

Augustine writes, "In you are the first causes of all things not eternal, the unchangeable origins of all things that suffer change, the everlasting reason of all things that are subject to the passage of time and have no reason in themselves. Have pity, then, on me, O God, for it is pity that I need" (I:6).

Augustine opens Book VIII with the words of the psalmist, "*You have broken the chains that bound me; I will sacrifice in your honour*," and he opens Book IX by linking sacrifice to praise as appropriate responses to God's grace. Nor are prayer and sacrifice unaccompanied by awe, as we see, for example, when he describes his encounter with the Uncreated Light that "was above me because it was itself that Light that made me, and I was below because I was made by it." (N.B. Here again we have the affirmation of God as creator, as *causa sui*.) "I gazed on you with eyes too weak to resist the dazzle of your splendour. Your light shone upon me in its brilliance, and I thrilled with love and dread alike. I realized that I was far away from you. It was as though I were in a land where all is different from your own . . . " (VII:10).

A few pages later, we find Augustine looking for the immutable source (an un-originated origin) of his own changeable reason, which somehow knows "the immutable itself. For unless, by some means, it had know the immutable, it could not possibly have been certain that it was preferable to the mutable. And so, in an instant of awe, my mind attained to the sight of the God who IS. Then, at last, *I caught sight of your invisible nature, as it is known through your creatures*" (VII:17).

Unlike the *causa sui* of onto-theology, "who" is religiously otiose, Augustine's Creator evokes prayer, sacrifice, and awe. What about singing and dance? I must confess (a good thing to do when writing on the *Confessions*) that I have not found Augustine dancing. But he sings, and thereby hangs a tale. As he recounts in Book X how far he has come and how far he still has to go in the life of faith, he writes, "Let my brothers draw their breath in joy for the one and sigh with grief for the other. Let hymns of thanksgiving and cries of sorrow rise together from their hearts, as though they were vessels burning with incense before you" (X:4)[65] This does not come as easily to Augustine as it might to others. "Without committing myself to an irrevoc-able opinion, I am inclined to approve of the custom of singing in church, in order that by indulging the ears weaker spirits may be inspired with feelings of devotion." His hesitancy stems from the fear of finding "the singing itself more moving than the truth which it conveys" (X:33).[66] Yet in the very next chapter we find him saying, "But O my God, my Glory, for these things too I offer you a hymn of thanksgiving. I make a sacrifice of praise to him who sanctifies me" (X:34). And he complains that the books of the Platonists "make no mention of tears of confession or of *the sacrifice that you will never disdain* . . . In them no one sings" (VII:21).

Although he affirms a Highest Being who is the clue to the meaning of the whole of being, it is clear (and will become clearer) that Augustine is not an onto-theologian in Heidegger's sense. Yet he, and the whole theistic tradition of which he is a major representative, are widely thought to be paradigms of that heresy. One reason for that, no doubt, is an incomplete reading of Heidegger. But that is not the whole story. Insofar as there is a great deal of Platonism in Augustine, there surely are onto-theological themes and possibilities. His preoccupation with immutable truth and the role of the vision metaphor in his account of knowledge are but two conspicuous examples. It is regularly acknowledged that there is a continuous

Aufhebung or recontextualizing of Augustine's Platonism in his Christianity. We need to see this as his continuous resistance to the temptations of onto-theology.

When we hear Augustine panting, "Truth! Truth! How the very marrow of my soul within me yearned for it" (III:6), we might think him engaged in the "metaphysical" project of rendering the whole of reality intelligible to human understanding. But a closer look reveals something quite different. In the first place, inspired by Cicero's *Hortensius*, his heart "began to throb with a bewildering passion for the *wisdom* of eternal truth" (III:4, emphasis added), and he never forgets the essential linkage, already present in Cicero and the Platonists, between wisdom and truth.

In the second place, he subordinates propositional truth to its ultimate object, the source of all wisdom and knowledge. He complains of the Manichees, "Much of what they say about the created world is true, but they do not search with piety for the Truth, its Creator" (V:3). This is why Augustine can say to God "you are Truth itself" (III:61) and can speak of the "Word made flesh" as "Truth in person" (VII:19).

Finally, just because truth is not ultimately our mastery of the world's form but the personal God on whom we are dependent for the whole of our life, including its knowledge, it is God's agenda that has priority; and God's highest priority is love. When we encounter Truth itself in person we find, not the answer to all our questions or a possession that gives us power but the command to transcend ourselves in love for the Other (I:5). Thus, "Blessed are those who love you, O God, and love their friends in you and their enemies for your sake" (IV:9). In the final analysis, knowledge is *aufgehoben* in its proper telos, love of God (of which praise is a part) and neighbor (both friend and enemy). Although there is a good deal of Platonic eros in this – the "blessed" above signifies a eudaemonism Augustine shares with Plato – Augustine insists that charity is not one of the things to be learned from the Platonist books (VII:20).[67] Christian *caritas* is more than Platonic *eros*. No doubt part of the reason lies in the personal character of that for which the heavenly eros longs and in an ethic that goes beyond justice within the polis to love of enemy, commanded by "Truth itself" and modelled for us by "Truth in person."

The vision metaphor is central to Platonism and to the metaphysics of presence that constitutes so many of the footnotes to Plato. It suggests an immediate, intuitive presence to the world's essential intelligibility. Augustine is anything but skittish about the vision metaphor, and his illumination theory of knowledge mirrors Plato's account of the subject, the object, and the light which enables the subject to "see" the object, whether it be a sensible or intelligible object. Of course, the light is a personal God and not an impersonal Good or One. But what is to keep this God from being reduced to the means by which philosophy carries out its onto-theological project of bringing everything to the presence of direct insight in which the totality of being becomes the transcendental signified, a mirror, a resting place that idolatrously calls forth no transpiercing?

The first thing to notice is that vision is not the only sense to play a metaphorical role in Augustine. For example, just after telling us in a passage already cited how he caught sight of the God who IS, he describes his inability to maintain that moment by saying he "had sensed the fragrance of the fare but was not yet able to eat it" (VII:17). Thus he prays, "Let us scent your fragrance and taste your sweetness" (VII:4). In the famous passage in which he describes the mystical ascent he shared with his mother, Monica, he tells us that "for one fleeting instant we reached out and touched it" (IX:10). And in an astonishing passage, he includes all five senses. "You called me; you cried aloud to me; you broke my barrier of deafness. You shone upon me; your radiance enveloped me; you put my blindness to flight. You shed your fragrance about me; I drew breath and now I gasp for your sweet odour. I tasted you, and now I hunger and thirst for you. You touched me, and I am inflamed with love of your peace" (X:27).

It might be argued that all the senses signify immediate presence. But while there was already for Augustine a long tradition of interpreting conceptual knowledge as a kind of seeing, neither for him nor for us is there that kind of linkage between intelligibility and smell, taste, or touch. To which it might be argued that these are the senses of mystical, trans-conceptual immediacy and that mysticism is just another version of the metaphysics of presence.[68]

Two responses seem to me in order. First, mysticism, of which there is plenty in Augustine, may well be a version of the metaphysics of presence, but it is not the onto-theological version. Mysticism, so far from being the demand that the whole of reality be intelligible to representational, calculative thinking is the conscious, even insistent realization that it cannot be.[69]

Second, and more important, in the all-five-senses passage just cited, hearing relates not merely to sound but to speech. "You called me." The continuous *aufhebung* of vision in the voice is utterly central to Augustine's understanding of God. It is made possible by the personal character of his Highest Being and First Cause such that he constantly addresses God as "you". But this you is not just someone to whom Augustine speaks, but someone who speaks to Augustine. The God of Augustine is the Highest Voice and the First Interlocutor.

A few examples. In the midst of confessing his hunger for "Truth! Truth!" upon reading the *Hortensius*, Augustine not only says to God "you are Truth itself" but also "you have spoken to me" (III:6). If and as we find truth we find that it has already found us and has addressed us. In a striking description of the incarnation, Augustine writes, "Our Life himself came down into this world and took away our death. He slew it with his own abounding life, and with thunder in his voice he called us from this world to return to him in heaven . . . He did not linger on his way but ran, calling us to return to him, calling us by his words and deeds, by his life and death, by his descent into hell and his ascension into heaven" (IV:12). The passage where Augustine thrills "with love and dread alike" and realizes how far he is from God continues, and "I heard your voice calling from on high, saying 'I am the food of full-grown men. Grow and you shall feed on me'" (VII:10).

It is clear from these examples that the voice of God is not just the claim of a propositional content upon our capacity for assent. It is a voice of law and of grace, a voice that decenters the would be autonomous self both by demanding our love and by giving itself in and as love. That which is visible but mute cannot do this. In my encounter with God I am never the spectator but always the one addressed.[70] No doubt that is why, having spoken of sacrificing and singing before God, Augustine says with reference to the Platonists' books, "In them no one listens to the voice which says, *Come to me all you that labour*" (VII:21). It is also why, in spite of Augustine's desire to gain understanding for what he has believed, faith is never the opinion (*pistis, doxa*) of Plato's divided line, a purely cognitive act of an inferior sort.

We see this in the dramatic culmination of his conversion. In Book VII his intellectual problems have been resolved to his satisfaction. He believes, but he has not come to faith. It is in Book VIII that "I heard the sing-song voice of a child in a nearby house. Whether it was the voice of a boy or a girl I cannot say, but again and again it repeated the refrain 'Take it and read, take it and read' ... I stemmed my flood of tears and stood up, telling myself that this could only be a divine command to open my book of Scripture and read ... " Only then, when he had heard God speaking to him through the voice of a child and through Scripture and had obeyed was he able to say, "You converted me to yourself" (VIII:12).[71]

We have seen that for Augustine predication yields to praise, truth is in the service of love, and vision is *aufgehoben* in the voice that precedes and superecedes all our intentional acts (in both senses, cognitive and volitional). It would appear that Augustine has flunked Metaphysics 101. For metaphysics, in its onto-theological constitution, "the deity can come into philosophy only insofar as philosophy, of its own accord and by its own nature, requires and determines that and how the deity enters into it."[72] But the tradition of which Aristotle and Hegel are paradigms is not about praise, or commanded love, or the decentering voice; it has other work for God to do, namely to make the whole of reality intelligible to human understanding. If Augustine is a canonical figure in relation to this tradition, it is not by providing sacred texts for its scriptures but by being a howitzer aimed at its central assumptions.

We can see this in one final way by noting that God remains for Augustine an ultimately ineffable mystery. He is not shy about predication when it comes to God. He regularly affirms that God is creator, unchangeable, and omnipresent. In response to the question, "What, then, is the God I worship?" he writes, "You, my God, are supreme, utmost in goodness, mightiest and all-powerful, most merciful and most just." But this is not a catechetical Q and A on the attributes of God. For he immediately continues, "You are the most hidden from us and yet the most present amongst us, the most beautiful and yet the most strong, ever enduring and yet we cannot comprehend you ... For even those who are most gifted with speech cannot find words to describe you" (I:4).

This question, the epigraph for this essay, is repeated twice, in slightly altered form, in Book X: "What do I love when I love my God?" (X:6–7). Given the intensely personal character of Augustine's God, it may seem strange that three times, once at the beginning and twice at the end of his story, he acknowledges the divine mystery with a What question. To be sure, the third time he follows it up with a Who question: "Who is this Being who is so far above my soul?" (X:7), but he seems to prefer the What form. Perhaps the reason is simply this. Through intense conversation over a long period of years, Augustine has a fairly good idea Who God is, although that question has not been satisfied and silenced. But in terms of the essence of this Interlocutor, he remains more deeply puzzled. The *Wesensschau* that philosophy requires is, for Augustine (as for Aquinas), precisely what he does not have.[73]

Be that as it may, Augustine points to two reasons why none of the many answers he can give to the What? or the Who? question is adequate to the question. First, there is the temporary limitation of his earthly condition. "This much I know, although *at present I am looking at a confused reflection in a mirror*, not yet *face to face*, and therefore, as long as I am away from you, during my pilgrimage, I am more aware of myself than of you." This will continue "until I see you face to face and *my dusk is noonday*" (X:5). The illumination of which Augustine is currently capable, compared to what it will be in the life to come, is as dusk to noonday. Augustine, bishop and theologian nonpareil, is still in the cave.

Perhaps, however, this limitation is permanent, as we learn from a passage that at first sounds like a Platonic reflection on God as *ipsum esse* and *causa sui*. "'We exist,' [heaven and earth] tell us, 'because we were made' . . . It was you, then, O Lord, who made them, you who are beautiful, for they too are beautiful, you who are good, for they too are good; you who ARE, for they too are. But they are not beautiful and good as you are beautiful and good, nor do they have their being as you, their Creator, have your being. In comparison with you they have neither beauty nor goodness nor being at all. This we know, and thanks be to you for this knowledge." Up to this point we have classic onto-theology. God earns a living by gathering all things into an intelligible whole and by making it possible for us to understand this totality.

Everything is turned topsy-turvy, however, by the brief sentence with which the chapter ends. "But our knowledge, compared with yours, is ignorance" (XI:4). The deficiency of our knowledge, *vis-à-vis* God's, is not quantitative but qualitative. Like everything about us, it is participatory, not originary, dependent on a Light which we ourselves are not and therefore cannot supply.[74] It is far from evident that this deficiency will be eradicated even when, according to Augustine's confident hope, we see God face to face in the life to come. Because the soul is created, it is not divine. Even when it is lifted out of the cave into the immediate presence of the Uncreated Light, its knowledge will remain human and not divine.[75]

But if the Highest Being, who is the clue to the meaning of the whole of being, remains a mystery that continues to elude our cognitive grasp, the whole of being, no matter how many facts we can learn about it, remains mysterious. If philosophy begins in wonder for the Greeks, it ends in wonder for Augustine. And love. And praise.

We might say that Augustine has carefully read his Heidegger, his Lévinas, and his Marion and has learned that

We must think God as the mystery that exceeds the wisdom of the Greeks, that

We must think God as the voice that exceeds vision so as to establish a relation irreducible to comprehension, and that

We must think God as the gift of love who exceeds not merely the images but also the concepts with which we aim at God.

Notes

1   Calvin O. Schrag, *The Self After Postmodernity* (New Haven: Yale University Press, 1997).
2   Paul Ricoeur, *Oneself as Another*, trans. Kathleen Blamey (Chicago: University of Chicago Press, 1992), pp. 11, 4, 23.
3   Ricoeur, *Oneself*, p. 19.
4   *Who Comes After the Subject?*, ed. Eduardo Cadava, Peter Connor, Jean-Luc Nancy (New York: Routledge, 1991).
5   *Who Comes*, p. 4.

6   *Who Comes*, p. 3.
7   In the 1949 Introduction to *What is Metaphysics* entitled "The Way Back into the Ground of Metaphysics," in *Pathmarks*, ed. William McNeill (New York: Cambridge University Press, 1998).
8   In "The Onto-theo-logical Constitution of Metaphysics" in *Identity and Difference*, trans. Joan Stambaugh (New York: Harper & Row, 1969).
9   McNeill, *Pathmarks*, p. 280.
10 Assuming that we can speak here in the singular. In Hegel's version, we begin with a logic that is an ontology and end with an account of Absolute Spirit as the Highest (because, in this case, the all inclusive) Being which is the key to the whole of being.
11 *Identity and Difference*, pp. 55–6.
12 B xiii. Emphasis added.
13 Along with *Identity and Difference*, of course. All three components of *What is Metaphysics?* are to be found in McNeill, *Pathmarks*. They also appear in *Existentialism from Dostoevsky to Sartre*, ed. Walter Kaufmann (revised edition; New York: New American Library, 1975).
14 *Identity and Difference*, p. 56.
15 See the extended analysis in *The Principle of Reason*, trans. Reginald Lilly (Bloomington: Indiana University Press, 1991).
16 *Identity and Difference*, p. 72.
17 McNeill, *Pathmarks*, p. 288. Kierkegaard obviously joins Pascal in the background of Heidegger's critique here.
18 *Totality and Infinity*, trans. Alphonso Lingis (Pittsburgh: Duquesne University Press, 1969), pp. 42–8. Henceforth TI. Cf. "Is Ontology Fundamental," in Emmanuel Lévinas, *Basic Philosophical Writings*, ed. Adriaan T. Peperzak, Simon Critchley, and Robert Bernasconi (Bloomington: Indiana University Press, 1996). Henceforth IOF
19 TI, 42, 45.
20 *Otherwise then Being or Beyond Essence*, trans. Alphonso Lingis (Boston: Kluwer, 1991), pp. 61, 99, 131, 134. These statements come at the beginning of chapters III, IV, and V. In *Of God Who Comes to Mind*, trans. Bettina Bergo (Stanford: Standford University Press, 1998), this activity of being is translated being's "gesture". Thus, "The intelligibility of being, which is also its 'gesture of being' [*la geste d'être*] . . . ," p. 36. Cf. pp. 45, 112. In the latter passage, this gesture is the "ess*a*nce" or the "insist*a*nce" of being, terms designed to highlight the verbal character of being, its fundamental self-assertion.
21 TI, 47, 42.
22 IOF, 5, 7–8.
23 IOF, 3–5. In TI, 28, 65, 67, 71, 75, Lévinas will make this latter point in terms of Heidegger's account of disclosure. "The Thinking of Being and the Question of the Other," in *Of God Who Comes to Mind*, has essentially the same dyadic structure as IOF, but there the critique is extended to the Derrida of *Speech and Phenomena*.
24 IOF, 5.
25 IOF, 7–9. Cf. Heidegger's linkage of metaphysics with modern technology.
26 IOF, 8, 10. Needless to say, Lévinas does not associate himself with Kant's attempt to preserve autonomy in ethics.
27 IOF, 8.
28 IOF, 9.
29 TI, 45.
30 See note 22 above.
31 IOF, 6.
32 Thus, in TI, 33–35, desire for the transcendent other is desire for the invisible, and "The face speaks. The manifestation of the face is already discourse" (66; cf. 39, 51). The

transcendent "cuts across the vision of forms and can be stated neither in terms of contemplation nor in terms of practice. It is the face; its revelation is speech" (193).

33   IOF, 6–8. Here the other is the one to whom I speak. In later writings, in order to emphasize the asymmetry of the relation, the focus is more on the fact that the other speaks to me. There is an important and largely unexplored relation to Habermas in this notion that we fundamentally related to each other as performers of speech acts.

34   IOF, 9–10. In TI, 23, 51–52, 65, 67, 74, and 77, Levinas will develop this non-horizonal immediacy as the claim that the face is *"signification without a context,"* that it expresses itself καθ' αὐτό. I have discussed this theme in "Levinas and the Immediacy of the Face," *Faith and Philosophy*, 9:4 (October, 1993), 486–502.

35   See "The Ruin of Representation," in *Discovering Existence with Husserl*, trans. Richard A. Cohen and Michael B. Smith (Evanston: Northwestern University Press, 1998).

36   See "Intentionality and Metaphysics" and "Intentionality and Sensation" in *Discovering Existence with Husserl*; "Hermeneutics and Beyond" and "Nonintentional Consciousness" in *Entre Nous: On Thinking-of-the-Other*, trans. Michael B. Smith and Barbara Harshav (New York: Columbia University Press, 1998); and "Beyond Intentionality" in *Philosophy in France Today*, ed. Alan Montefiore (New York: Cambridge University Press, 1983).

37   IOF, 5, 8.

38   *God without Being*, trans. Thomas A. Carlson (Chicago: Chicago University Press, 1991), p. xxiv. Henceforth GWB.

39   GWB, xxi. Marion follows Heidegger rather than Levinas in the use of the term "metaphysics". In "Metaphysics and Phenomenology: A Relief for Theology," *Critical Inquiry* 20 (Summer 1994), 572–91, he explicitly adopts and provides historical validation for Heidegger's onto-theological concept of metaphysics. For him phenomenology is the philosophical alternative to metaphysics. Hence the importance of *Reduction and Givenness*, trans. Thomas A. Carlson (Evanston: Northwestern University Press, 1998), in which he distinguishes his phenomenology from that of Husserl and Heidegger.

40   GWB, xx–xxiv.

41   GWB, xx–xxi. Emphasis added.

42   GWB, 10–15.

43   See especially the Fifth and Sixth Investigations of Husserl's *Logical Investigations* (2 vols.), trans. J. N. Findlay (London: Routledge & Keegan Paul, 1970).

44   GWB, 13.

45   GWB, 13–16.

46   In the poem by Robert Browning that bears his name.

47   GWB, 11, 17.

48   Like Lévinas, Marion alludes to Descartes' discussion of the idea of the infinite as the idea which exceeds our capacity to think it as an instance of iconic thought. GWB, 23, 202.

49   GWB, 24.

50   GWB, 19–21. There are two Lévinasian motifs here: the passive "intentionality" of our awareness of the infinite and the notion "that only the icon gives us a face (in other words, that every face is given as an icon)." In "L'Interloqué," in *Who Comes After the Subject*, Marion develops the linguistic thesis, that we are addressed (not as Dasein, which "appeals only to itself" but as *der Angesprochene*), that the one who says I is the one who has already been claimed as me. This essay is chapter 9 of this volume.

51   GWB, 16. Cf. 29–31. For a phenomenology of that which exceeds adequation, see Marion's "The Saturated Phenomenon," *Philosophy Today* 40/1 (Spring, 1996).

52   Quoted at GBW, 203. See Gregory of Nyssa, *The Life of Moses*, trans. Abraham J. Malherbe and Everett Ferguson (New York: Paulist Press, 1978), pp. 95–6 for context and a different translation.

53 GWB, 22–23.

54 See notes 22 and 41 above.

55 GWB, 106–107.

56 *Pseudo-Dionysius: The Complete Works*, trans. Colm Luibheid (New York: Paulist Press, 1987), pp. 50–51. Cf. GWB, 76–77 where the theme of praise is linked to the priority of goodness to being as the name of God in Pseudo-Dionysius. I have discussed this theme in Dionysius and Cyril of Jerusalem in "Overcoming Onto-Theology," in *God, the Gift, and Postmodernism*, ed. John D. Caputo and Michael J. Scanlon (Bloomington: Indiana University Press, 1999).

57 The absence of a personal other who could be respected, loved, welcomed, even praised, is what sets Heidegger off from Levinas and Marion. See John D. Caputo, *Demythologizing Heidegger* (Bloomington: Indiana University Press, 1993), ch. 2–3. and Norman Wirzba, "Love's Reason: From Heideggerian Care to Christian Charity," in *Postmodern Philosophy and Christian Faith*, ed. Merold Westphal (Bloomington: Indiana University Press, 1999).

58 GWB, ch. 2. I have tried to sort out the issues raised by his critique in "Overcoming Onto-Theology."

59 Marion takes offense especially at Heidegger's essay, "Phenomenology and Theology," in *The Piety of Thinking*, trans. James G. Hart and John C. Maraldo (Bloomington: Indiana University Press, 1976), in which phenomenology is repeatedly assigned the task of "correcting" theology.

60 Substantive idolatry would occur when my God is the invisible mirror, not of my cognitive capacities, but of my (our) unholy interests.

61 In *Suspicion and Faith: The Religious Uses of Modern Atheism* (New York: Fordham University Press, 1998), I have accused Marx, Nietzsche, and Freud of plagiarizing the Bible, suggesting that their hermeneutics of suspicion has its true origin in prophetic biblical faith.

62 Recent scholarship has reminded us of the Christian texts that belong to the prehistory of Heidegger's thinking. See especially John Van Buren, *The Young Heidegger: Rumor of the Hidden King* (Bloomington: Indiana University Press, 1994) and Theodore Kisiel, *The Genesis of Heidegger's Being and Time* (Berkeley: University of California Press, 1993). Levinas is not the least bashful about the "more ancient volcano" of Hebraic "prophetic speech" and "messianic eschatology" from which his thought emerges (as described by Derrida in "Violence and Metaphysics," in *Writing and Difference*, trans. Alan Bass (Chicago: University of Chicago Press, 1978), pp. 82–3.

63 Quotations from the *Confessions* will be from the Pine-Coffin translation (Baltimore: Penguin Books, 1961) by book and chapter number. I follow his practice of placing biblical phrases in italics.

64 The phrase comes from Charles Wesley's hymn, "Love Divine, All Loves Excelling."

65 Like the psalms of Israel, Christian liturgies regularly include both hymns of praise and prayers of confession. Incense is a psalmic image of the offering of these to God.

66 One can appreciate the nature of Augustine's concern by comparing meditative, devotional settings of the *Stabat Mater* by Palestrina, Vivaldi, or Pärt with the operatic versions by Verdi and Rossini. No doubt Augustine would classify the Pergolesi with the latter, though I would place it with the former.

67 This is also why Augustine speaks of "the Light that charity knows" (VII:10) rather than the Light which the soul detached from the body knows.

68 Derrida speaks of "a certain complicity" between rationalism and mysticism. *Of Grammatology*, trans. Gayatri Chakravorty Spivak (Baltimore: Johns Hopkins University Press, 1976), p. 80. Hegel's philosophy is often called a rationalized mysticism.

69   This is why Derrida is right to recognize the affinity as well as the discontinuity between negative theology and deconstruction. See "Différance" in Jacques Derrida, *Margins of Philosophy*, trans. Alan Bass (Chicago: University of Chicago Press, 1982); *Derrida and Negative Theology*, ed. Harold Coward and Toby Foshay (Albany: SUNY Press, 1992); "Sauf le nom (Post-Scriptum)," in Jacques Derrida, *On the Name*, ed. Thomas Dutoit (Stanford: Stanford University Press, 1995); and the very helpful discussion by John D. Caputo in *The Prayers and Tears of Jacques Derrida* (Bloomington: Indiana University Press, 1997).

70   A similar *aufhebung* takes place in Levinas. I encounter the Other as a visible, as a face, but never merely as a visible. "The face speaks," even if empirically it is mute. See note 32 above. Cf. Sylviane Agacinski, "Another Experience of the Question, or Experiencing the Question Other-Wise," in *Who Comes After the Subject*.

71   In his book, *Divine Discourse: Philosophical reflections on the claim that God speaks* (New York: Cambridge University Press, 1995), Nicholas Wolterstorff brilliantly illuminates the significance of this phenomenon of indirect or double discourse, where one speaker speaks through the utterances or inscriptions of another. I have suggested that because he assumes that God speaks and analyses some of the ways in which this might be understood, Wolterstorff is "engaged in the very Heideggerian task of overcoming metaphysics in its ontotheological sense." See "Theology as Talking About a God Who Talks," *Modern Theology* 13/4 (October, 1997), p. 526.

72   See note 11 above.

73   For Aquinas' consistent denial that we can grasp the essence of God, see John F. Wippel, "Quidditative Knowledge of God," in *Metaphysical* (sic) *Themes in Thomas Aquinas* (Washington: Catholic University of America Press, 1984).

74   It is in an Augustinian tone of voice that Gabriel Marcel says "that the more I actually participate in being, the less I am capable of knowing or saying in what it is that I participate..." *Creative Fidelity*, trans. Robert Rosthal (New York: Farrar, Straus and Giroux, 1964), p. 56.

75   Speaking of mystical union with God, *The Cloud of Unknowing* promises "a real knowledge and experience of God as he is. Not as he is in himself, of course, for that is impossible to any save God" (New York: Penguin Books, 1978), ch. 14. Following the same logic, Gregory Palamas teaches that our knowledge does not transcend its finitude even in heaven. See *The Triads*, trans. Nicholas Gendle (New York: Paulist Press, 1983), pp. 32–9 and 123 n. 45.

19

DARKNESS AND SILENCE: EVIL AND THE WESTERN LEGACY

John Milbank

I

Traditionally, in Greek, Christian and Jewish thought evil has been denied any positive foothold in being. It has not been seen as a real force, or quality, but as the absence of force and quality, and as the privation of being itself. It has not been regarded as glamorous, but as sterile; never as more, always as less. For many recent philosophers, however (e.g. Jacob Rogozinski, Slavoj Žižek, J.-L. Nancy), this view appears inadequate in the face of what they consider to be the unprecedented evil of the twentieth century: the mass organization of totalitarian control and terror, systematic genocide, and the enslavement of people who are deliberately worked to the point of enfeeblement and then slaughtered.[1] Such evil, they argue, cannot be regarded as privative, because this view claims that evil arises only from the deliberate pursuit of a lesser good. Power directed towards extermination suggests, rather, destruction and annihilation pursued perversely for its own sake, as an alternative end in itself. Such a motive towards the pure negation of being, as towards the cold infliction of suffering – that may not even be enjoyed by its perpetrators – suggests that the will to destroy is a positive and surd attribute of being itself and no mere inhibition of being in its plenitude.

This supposed positive evil for its own sake is often dubbed "radical evil," following a term used by Immauel Kant in his book *Religion Within the Bounds of Mere Reason.*[2] With some plausibility, Kant's account of evil is seen as encouraging a break with the traditional privation view focused upon being in general in favour of a view focused purely upon the finite human will. This new view comprehends evil as a positively willed denial of the good and so as a pure act of perversity without ground. The development of such a position is traced from Kant, through Schelling, to Heidegger.

In this way, a specifically modern *theory* of evil is held to be adequate to account for a specifically modern extremism of evil *practice* – which the theory, nonetheless, predates. Despite this predating – which might suggest some causal link – the modern practical extremity of evil is held to be, at least in part, the outcome of a far older western tradition of metaphysical reflection on evil which trivializes it and underrates it. So not only is evil as privation refuted by Auschwitz, it is also indicted by it as responsible for such an outcome. Evil denied as mere denial leaves us unvigilant against its real positivity.

This position, then, traces no lineage to the Holocaust from the specifically German and modern accounts of radical evil, yet asserts, perhaps all too vaguely, a lineage from the age-old western metaphysical understanding of evil as privation. Here, however, the advocates of "radical evil" (or "postmodern Kantians," as I will henceforth describe them), have to face the diametrically opposite alignment of theoretical and practical evil proposed by Heidegger's pupil, Hannah Arendt – and arguably against her former teacher.[3] For Arendt, famously, the mass murderer Albert Eichmann, on trial in Jerusalem, discloses not a pre-Satanic will to evil, nor a lust for horror, but instead "the banality of evil," an incremental and pathetic inadequacy of motive which escalated imperceptibly into complicity with unimaginable wickedness. It has now been shown, against those (for various reasons) prone to doubt this, that Arendt's account of evil as "banal," is most certainly linked with her Augustinian predilections, and support for Augustine's account of evil as negative.[4] Thus the horror of Auschwitz, for Arendt, is not the revelation of evil perpetrated for its own sake, but rather a demonstration that even the most seemingly absolute evil tends to be carried out by people who imagine, albeit reluctantly, that they are fulfilling the goods of order, obedience, political stability and social peace.

In this fashion, Arendt implicitly sees the western metaphysical account of evil as privation as confirmed, not denied, by the holocaust. *A fortiori*, therefore, this trad-itional theory of evil is not for her complicit with the modern practical excess of evil. In addition, Arendt established very astutely certain links between a debased Kantian-ism, and the cooperation of many of the German people with the implementing of the final solution.[5] To this degree she also raised the question of a link between the modern theory of evil and the modern excessive practice of evil. And where she did, in her political theory, deploy Kant favorably, she adverted to social convergence in judgment, which is linked, by Kant, with the beautiful, and not to the common experience of the natural sublime that for Kant has profoundly to do both with respect for the formal law *and* with radical evil.[6]

Despite this opening of the issue concerning the relation between modern theory of evil and modern evil as practiced, Arendt veered well away from any indictment of Kant as such. *Debased* Kantianism is culpable, not the real Kantian philosophical legacy. Thus while, in relation to the Holocaust, the ancient view of evil is confirmed and therefore exonerated, the modern, positive view of evil is not accused of a certain responsibility. And yet this intellectual lineage would seem to be, at least *prima facie*, more plausible in terms of time, locality and proximity than the supposed genealogy which traces back to western onto-theology. It would also allow some significance to the predating of the modern practice of evil by the modern theory of evil. After all, the opponents of the privation theory have already contended for the profound alignment of radical evil with the Holocaust, since this theory alone is held adequately to interpret it. Supposing, instead, that privation theory can interpret the holocaust, then this alignment would appear very differently: not as the retrospective match of event to detached theory, but as the prior perverse attempt to enact a false theory. Instead of the view that the negation of evil as merely negative permits its positivity to erupt, one would have the view that the false assertion of evil as positive leads to an impossible quest to enact such positivity, which can in reality only unleash a bad infinite of further and further privation, since being will not *permit* any final solution, any finished or perfected evil.

One can see immediately, from this formulation however, why Arendt could not have traced the genealogy it expresses, quite apart from her residual respect for Kant. To ascribe causality to the pursuit of the Satanic illusion, the illusion of the pursuit of evil for its own sake, appears clean contrary to the invocation of the banality of evil behavior. It may be significant here that Arendt, as many have pointed out, had all too little to say about the psychology of the *instigators* of the final solution, rather than those of people who must be judged its mere executives, albeit paramount ones, like Eichmann. All the same, this is not to say that a privation theory, nor even aspects of a banality theory, cannot apply also to the instigators. Hitler and his henchmen were not exactly Satanists and their articulation of their motives were not like that of the Californian Charles Manson or the English "Moors murderer" Ian Brady, a close student of de Sade and decadent literature. In these extreme cases one has something like the illusion of the belief that evil is being performed for its own sake – although privation theory is able to discern amidst this vaunted Satanic glory the pathetic desire for control of those whose high self-esteem has been in no way socially confirmed.[7] Something of that may, indeed, have been operative amongst the Nazi cohorts, but they still articulated their defective desires more positively, in terms of the promotion of the racial health and excellence of humanity: indeed in their paganism or atheism they remained all too humanist, and Hitler sought avowedly to produce a human being worthy of worship.[8] Likewise, the suppression and finally liquidation of the Jews was not articulated in nihilistic terms, but could be viewed as "rational," given that one's objective was to secure a German power absolutely untainted by socialism and the influence of international commerce, and a German identity based on cultural uniformity and demotion of the Christian and Biblical legacy in favour of a Nordic one.

The Nazis did not, therefore, like Charles Manson, avowedly elect radical evil, saying "Be Thou my Good." Such Satanism discovers itself to be an illusion at the point where it finds it can establish no stable positive kingdom of evil, nor encompass absolute destruction of being, but instead can only unleash an ever-escalating slide of deprivation which will usually cease with self-destruction. Clearly, the theory of radical evil is not implicated in the Holocaust in this extreme Satanic fashion. However, in a much more subtle fashion, it may after all, be implicated. Here one can claim first of all (as I will later demonstrate), that Nazi concepts of universal power and legality were much more compatible with, and even derived from, the Kantian categorical imperative, than Arendt allowed. In the second place, one can claim that if the Nazis still affirmed a Kantian free will as their good, then they also inherited the *aporias* of this free will, as half-admitted by Kant in *Reason Within the Bounds of Mere Reason*. For these *aporias*, there is no clear way of distinguishing between the will which genuinely wills freedom, and the will which wills against itself, restraining freedom – this self-opposition for Kant characterizes the evil will.[9] As we shall see, these *aporias* arise because of the lack, in Kant, at this highest level, of any teleology which can discriminate the good substance of what is willed, from a deficient instance of such substance. Here, instead, the only thing willed is the law of free-willing itself, which defines legality as untrammeled autonomy – and it might seem that the free-will to bind oneself equally instantiates such autonomy. At the very least one can ask, exactly how is one to discriminate between the will binding itself to be free, and the will binding itself in unfreedom, if there is no desirable content here to prove the goodness of the genuine good will to freedom?

But if this is really the case with Kant, then one must face up to something which seems at first highly unlikely: namely that political totalitarianism and terror really could, with a certain plausibility, pose as the fulfilling of the categorical imperative, just as much as the most stringent code of personal self-denial. Later we shall see more clearly how these opposites can converge and mutually reinforce each other. In effect, the promotion of formal freedom can become akin to the systematic promotion of the inhibition of freedom by an imperceptible slide. And such self-deceiving espousal of evil would in practice be very like the setting up of a Satanic organisation. Here also, no stable realm of evil would result, but instead the pace of privation of being would be horrendously quickened.

In what follows I shall offer, in the first place, a further defence and exposition of the view of evil as privation and banality. I shall therefore argue that it can apply also to modern extreme evil, and is in no sense responsible for this evil. However, in the second place, beyond Arendt, I shall argue that the modern, positive theory of evil *is* in a measure responsible for the modern actuality of evil.

II

To begin with, however, I must offer a much fuller exposition of the modern theory, of evil as positive and "radical".

Contemporary proponents of this view start with the proposition that totalitarian phenomena of the twentieth century and in particular the holocaust, exhibit something uniquely evil. (These phenomena include, of course, state terror enacted in the name of socialism. I do not doubt that the Soviet state, like the Nazi one, was intrinsically criminal; however I would claim that this criminality flowed from Lenin's nihilism, from the exacerbation of modern state sovereignty, and certainly also from Marxist productivism and anti-agrarianism, but not from socialism as such. Indeed the presence of genuine socialist ideals allowed the Soviet state later somewhat to reform itself, whereas the more unadulterated nihilism of the Nazis led shortly to self-destruction.) And this is, indeed, more than arguable. For in these instances, not just executive forces became poisoned, but sovereign law itself consented to criminal principles and dedicated the resources of the state to mass murder on a legal, organized and bureau-cratic basis. In particular, sections of the population deemed difficult or surplus to requirement, were not simply oppressed or incarcerated, but were literally worked to death and discarded. So whereas previous slave economies still preserved some sense of the human status of the slaves, here this was denied in the context of a new hierarchical humanism which restricted full humanity to certain racial, physical and mental ideals.[10]

For the postmodern Kantians, this new degree of malevolence suggests in effect a will towards evil for its own sake – not merely evil as a lack of reality, or a lack of power, but evil as an alternative and viable exercise of power, whereby some human beings can devote themselves primarily to the destruction of others. This is now revealed as a possibility: it worked; scarcely any Jews now inhabit Germany. And if evil is now revealed as having equal potency with the good – an equal potency which proceeds to an equal actuality, then it is also shown as proceeding entirely from the rational will. It would surely be unthinkable to proffer any excuses for the Holocaust, or to lay out a set of mitigating circumstances. Yet the postmodern Kantians suggest that privation theory unfolds precisely by offering mitigating circumstances for all evil, so allowing radical evil to slip through its theoretical net. What it amounts to, they argue, is a kind of justification of being, an ontodicy (by analogy with theodicy), which also exonerates all creatures who exist, including human beings. For privation theory, all being as being is good, and since all power to be effective manifests the actuality of being, all power, as power, is good, and evil not only is impotent but can even be defined, at least in one valid way, as weakness and impotence (this is underscored most heavily by Dionysius the Areopagite).[11] It follows that, since the will is a potency, it is only actual and effective when it wills the good – hence for both Dionysius and Augustine, it is not exactly the case that evil can be willed; rather there is evil precisely to the degree that there is an absence of willing. No one, as willing, wills anything but the good, and evil only affects the will to the extent that a deficient good is being willed.[12]

This exoneration of the will as such, suggests, to the postmodern Kantians, that thereby the will is excused, and evil displaced from human origin. Instead of a primary referral of evil to potency and will, privation theory seems to imply a root of evil prior to power and will, in impersonal ontological circumstances, or rather in meontological circumstances.[13] For according to Jewish and Christian tradition, at least up to Maimonides and Aquinas, Being in its pure self-origination is infinite, and if Being as such is good, then, also, the infinite as such is good, indefeasibly good, beyond the possibility of swerving. Hence it would seem that goodness is a property of non-limitation, and not a derivative of personal election. Conversely, if evil is only possible for finite creatures, then finitude can always be proffered as something of an excuse: the will falls into evil by choosing the lesser good (since to will at all it must will *some* good), but here it is a victim of its finite partiality of perspective, and its finite lack of power to affirm. Indeed, even St. Paul appears entirely to exonerate the will: lamenting that he does what he hates, the opposite of what he wants to do (Romans 7: 15, 18; Gal. 5: 17). Thereby he blames the incapacity of his flesh, but not exactly the purity of his intentions. For where the will has failed to will what it should, then, for this traditional metaphysical perspective, it has failed to will in some measure, and the will is held captive by something prior to will: either, for the ancient Greeks, materiality as such; or else for Jews and Christian, certain perverse habits that hold our materiality and psychic passions in their grip.[14] Thus while it might seem that privation theory, by defining evil as lack of being, prevents any rooting of evil in the ontological, in fact it does affirm such rooting. For since evil is grounded in finitude, and the finite is caused by the infinite, the infinite is the real ultimate source of lack – the ontological of the meontological. And because the infinite is essentially impersonal, freedom as the origin of evil is here subordinated to ontological *cause* as the origin of evil. In this way, it is argued by the postmodern Kantians, human evil is mystified, and blame shifted to a metaphysical scenario. Yet at the same time, their apparently more humanist account involves also an *alternative* metaphysical scenario. They wish to regard the alternative good/evil in pre-ontological terms as entirely prior to the distinction between infinite and finite. This means, for them, that the finite will as such, in willing the good of the other, can manifest the extreme of goodness – an infinite good, if you like.[15] But conversely, as they concede, following Schelling, this must also mean that the infinite can manifest the extreme of evil.[16] Thus for Schelling, the good will of God is the result of a radical decision within the dark indifferent ground of the infinite – and this alone ensures that God *really* is good, according to any fashion of goodness that we can understand. God's goodness also is a loving decision; it is an offer, a free-gift, not an inevitability. Were it the latter, how could we be grateful, how could we feel infinitely loved? (Schelling has a certain point here, even though I shall later dissent.)

III

In articulating their post-Holocaust alternative to privation theory, the postmodern Kantians draw primarily upon Kant's account of radical evil, which they see as explicitly or implicitly developed by Schelling and Heidegger.

In Kant's account, evil is not really referred to finitude and so not primarily to any sort of lack or deficiency. He produces instead a theory of the pure "self-binding" of the will, which is sometimes seen as his qualification of the enlightenment, and retrieval, or even purer expression of, a Biblical, Pauline and Augustinian thematic.[17] But this is a mistake; radical evil is *not* original sin (even though Kant sees it as the rational re-thinking of the latter), and it *is* an enlightenment substitute for original sin, in a fashion that I shall demonstrate. First of all, one should recall my invocation of St. Paul. In his understanding of will, he still assumes a Biblical and Hellenic teleology: human beings are created to will the love of God as their final end and beatitude. As created they have a certain foretaste of the vision of God, and sufficient power to pursue this vision as they ought. When the will does pursue this vision, it is free from perverse, unnatural restrictions of its appointed nature, which thereby inhibit its free-dom as such – for the inner reality of creaturely freedom is just this passing beyond given finite nature in diverse ways towards the infinite. Will is nothing other, as Augustine makes clear in *De Libero Arbitrio*, than the site of the *dynamism* of the participation of the finite in the infinite, in the case of rational creatures (angels and humans).[18] Thus "will" arises where an as-not-yet-fully accessible rational vision lures forward through our desire (under grace) our finite potency. It follows that will as such cannot fail of the choice of its final end without in some measure slipping away from its freedom. And this slipping away *cannot* – either for St. Paul or Augustine – be accomplished by a surd choice of will alone, since will is nothing but the impact of omnipotent infinite reason upon finite rational power. Instead, the slipping must involve either or both an unnatural restriction of intellectual reason and of forceful capacity. St. Paul dwells upon the latter, Augustine on both: for Augustine we cannot will what we will to will, because the inherited sin of Adam has impaired both our vision and our potency. If there was any pure "sin of the will" (unknown to the Greeks), then this was the original sin of Adam himself, who, enjoying perfect vision and perfect capacity and so perfect freedom, nonetheless freely and without ground willed these things away.[19] This act, for Augustine, is strictly baffling and incomprehensible. It is not at all *explained* by free will, because free will in its natural created state knows only the willing of the good, under the compulsion of the vision of the good, and no choice between good and evil at all. To the contrary, the very, as it were, "fictional" notion that there is such a choice, was invented by Adam at the fall (or by Satan in the angelic fall). The problem of the fall is the sheer apparent impossibility of this invention – the imagining of a false simulacrum within the repleteness of reality. This imagining alone erects an illusory autonomy, or self-governance of the will, since it is precisely the will of a creature to hold sway over himself, in disregard of his appointed substantive end. That is to say, it is the will to prefer the identical repetition of emptiness of rule for no purpose, but rather for its own sake, over submission to the natural superiority of the infinite which must be perceived in ever-renewed, non-identical repetition. Indeed, finitude alone renders this delusion possible – yet finitude here is not really, as critics of privation theory imagine, invoked as an excuse, since the entire life of the finite, as created out of nothing, resides in its orientation to the infinite. Thus to assert the pure self-governing of the finite entity over-against the infinite – which, as boundless, *cannot* be self-governing in this fashion – is also to deny that which sustains its bounds and specific substance, in favour of an emptiness – an *infinite* emptiness – which alone belongs to it solely.

Since Adam's choice was for the illusion of a finite autonomy of the will (that is to say, for the idea of a groundless free choice between good and evil as expressing the very essence of freedom), it is not at all true to say that, for Christian theology, the descendants of Adam inherit a tendency to evil which is primarily a tendency of *the will*. To the contrary, this would be to perpetuate Adam's fantasy. Instead the *reality* of Adam's election is revealed first and foremost as loss of the vision of God and as physical death and incapacity of the body. As a result of this twin impairment will as desire lacks both vision and capacity, and degenerates into concupiscence: the original sin of Adam which through ignorance and weakness we tend to *repeat*.

But then how, it might be asked, if the will is so inhibited, does St. Paul think he can even will the good, although not carry it out? The answer is provided by Augustine in *De Libero Arbitrio*. Matching the aberrant leading role taken by the will at the fall, is the aberrant leading role taken by the will under grace. The miracle of grace consists *precisely* in our capacity to desire truth beyond our intellectual and forceful inhibitions.[20] To be sure, for Augustine following Plato, all human knowing is an interplay between always already knowing something and not yet knowing it, which amounts to the thesis that for us (ontologically and so even for Adam), fully knowing something is *always* in some measure the desire to know it. In this way, it has to be understood that, in Augustine, the vision which "governs" the will, is nonetheless a vision only secured to a degree *through* right will. Moreover, since effective will must be enacted, a true and unimpaired potency is also essential for the enjoyment of vision (in the much later *De Trinitate*, such "trinitarian" equality of power, understanding and will is much more emphatically expressed). And yet a loss primarily of vision and impulsion (rather than will/desire) after the fall, implies the cessation or at least inhibition of the interplay between the already and the not yet of cognition. Just as, before the fall, the lure of true vision pulled desire towards itself, so, now, after the fall, the loss of vision weakens drastically the impulse of desire (while the loss of power equally impairs its capacity to express itself). Yet God does not restore our plight by proffering us primarily true vision and power once more; rather his new accommodation remains appropriately true to our finitely necessary interplay of already and not yet, by now *accentuating* the role of desire upon which such interplay depends. Hence what God, by grace, restores to us, in the face of the loss of the magnetic poles of the already of power and the not yet of fully attained knowledge (it should be realized that power and knowledge are finally, in God, transcendentally co-extensive), is precisely the "middle" of interplay between them, the middle of desire which reintegrates their magnetism.

It will be seen from the above that it is not at all the case for Augustine, as in post-Reformation misreadings of his work, that after the fall, human beings are left with a will to the good and to salvation which they cannot enact, thereby becoming aware of original sin, and an impotence that is only cured after the Incarnation.[21] To the contrary, Augustine affirms that the original justification assured to humans by divine grace before the fall is seamlessly continued as the offer of redeeming grace through Christ which becomes immediately available by typological anticipation after the fall.[22] In consequence, for Augustine (and he never retracted this) *no one*, after the fall, is guilty *as an individual* (rather than member of Adam) on account of original sin; people are only guilty if they refuse the offer of grace and remain content with their deficient inheritance.[23] And this grace arrives precisely *as* our immediately renewed capacity for a free-willing of submission to God. Thus if we experience original sin as the frustration of our will, then this is only because this will to fulfill the law is itself grace, and therefore, as James Alison has argued, original sin is only disclosed in the light of our salvation in Christ.[24] It is clear that in no way are grace and free-will here set against each other in a Lutheran fashion. Instead, the gift of grace consists in a miraculously restored desire for God, despite the loss of original vision and capacity.

But if will operating properly as will is guided, for Augustine, by a true vision, how is it able to take the lead in our restoration? How can purification of vision and capacity first of all be induced by a true desiring? To understand this, we have to comprehend the complex double hierarchy of will and virtue, which Augustine explains in the *De Libero Arbitrio*. He declares there that possessed intellectual and moral virtues lie hierarchically above the will, since virtue *as* virtue can only be good, while the will can be good or bad (meaning that the will can perversely inhibit itself). Nevertheless, he also asserts that the will wills a good *beyond* the good of virtue (beyond, therefore, one can note, the pagan conception of the good).[25] What is this good beyond virtue? Augustine describes "a virtue" as the possession of an individual, which *as* virtue he cannot lose, since virtue lost is vice. By contrast, the will desires, beyond virtue, an inaccessible divine good, which can never belong to an individual, and can only be enjoyed in common. This superabundant good is shared between us, and never possessed – just like sunlight, says Augustine, which is more truly precious than gold, even though gold can be held through private ownership. This good, since it is infinite and above us, and held securely by God, *can* be lost by us, unlike virtue as virtue. Nevertheless, insecure will, which should be guided by secure virtue, still takes the lead over virtue, because virtue is less fundamentally a possession than it is a sharing in the common good. Such sharing in what surpasses us, is only ever to be attained by desire, even if a true desire, for Augustine, involves a kind of true, but inchoate, envisaging.

Moreover, if desire exceeds virtue in the direction of the more common and universal, then it also, according to *De Libero Arbitrio*, exceeds virtue in the direction of the more individual and particular. For the will is linked not just to discrimination of right from wrong, and the following of truth rather than falsehood, but also with idiosyncratic, but equally valid, moral and aesthetic preferences. Thus, Augustine says, some in a landscape will admire more the "height of a mountain," others the "verdure of a forest," others "the pulsing tranquility of the sea"; and in like fashion the cleaving of desire to the good refracts it according to our specific local affinities.[26] In this way, the will for Augustine at once directs us beyond private virtue to the common good, and yet at the same time does so through a desire necessarily more individuated than virtues like patience, taken in the abstract, which though privately possessed, like gold, show, also like gold, the same identical quality in all instances. This is why "will," in Augustine, names the drastic participatory tension between the infinitely general and the finitely particular. And it is clear that this tension has for him also a political dimension, since it implies the equipoise of the "aristocracy" of virtue, with the "democracy" of will and varied affinity. Thus towards the end of Book One of *De Libero Arbitrio*, Augustine affirms clearly that theology requires a politics economically adapted to times and places: Monarchy or Aristocracy should be the norm where few are virtuous, and therefore the Good is not much refracted; but Democracy should be the norm where the Good is widely (and we can infer, variously) distributed. This same tension indicates also an "economic" dimension in every sense: enjoyment in common does not inhibit individual expression – rather each is the precondition of the other.

In this light one can see that Adam's error was to deny this ontological tension which at once validates individual expressiveness and collective sharing, in favour of a confinement to "virtue," or to merely *private* possession of the nonetheless *abstractly general* (whose abstraction travesties the real superabundant infinite varied specificity of the true divine universal – described in other terms by Maximus the Confessor as the identity of the infinitely various *Logoi* with the one *Logos*: see *Ambiguum* 7). His error was, by an act of will, to deny the aspect in which will is hierarchically superior to virtue, and instead to affirm only the one-sided hierarchy of virtue over the will, or desire. This is tantamount to denying the participatory aspect of virtue, and imagining that one can entirely possess, with absolute security, one's own virtue. However, where the security of virtue depends upon oneself, this is simply because one wills virtue, entirely out of one's own volition, with a will poised, like the post-Kantian will, equally between good and evil. Self-possession of virtue, which ranks above will, since it can only be good, nonetheless entirely depends upon the self-possession of the will. Adam's error was to imagine that he could possess his own will. And the legacy of this error is that human beings think of the highest good, in stoic fashion, as that which can be self-possessed, and is not subject to external erosion. The good is now thought of as the exercise of the most autonomous, which is free will.

By contrast, for Augustine, free will is only returned to us as the arrival from outside of grace, and as the restoration of a good that we can only enjoy in common, and yet must receive according to our own unique affinities. To will, here, means to be moved beyond oneself towards a sharing and ontological distribution (according to real requirement, not formal equality), of the inexhaustible common good. It is through this moving that desire attracts once more to itself true vision, and draws along with it new resources of power for self-realization.

IV

Turning back now, to Kant, one finds instead an entirely different picture. He is not concerned with a lack of power to do good, since for him this would be contradictory; "ought implies can." Nor is he concerned with a lack of guiding vision, since he has defined the good *as* a good will, or more precisely as the law which freedom gives itself, and which secures freedom. Since the good is primarily in this fashion law, it first of all concerns the form or manner in which things are done, and is indifferent as to content. To introduce some substantive good or aim towards such good into one's *primary* understanding of what is "right" is, for Kant, actually to subvert morality.[27] ("Ends" are only admissible for Kant as a secondary consideration, and they concern, first of all our willing of our perfect submission to the *formality* of duty, and second, our willing of the happiness of others, where "happiness" means a mere empirical state, and *not* something inherently consequent upon virtue.)[28] It is true that, owing to the conditions of our understanding, we cannot fully grasp the noumenally formal in itself as unmediated by the phenomenally substantive; but this ensures that freedom and its law remain for us an ineffable idea. Thus, both as formal and as ineffable, the Kantian "right" which orientates the good, entirely exceeds all envisaging. And in no sense could radical evil for him connote loss of vision of the infinite, since the bounds between the finite and the infinite are permanently fixed and permit of no participatory mediation. For Kant, we will, adequately, as finite creatures, with reference only to our finitude; at the same time, we do invoke a noumenal infinitude in which our spirits are truly at home, yet this infinitude only impinges on the finite as the empty and incomprehensible formality of freedom which is inexplicably able to interrupt the fatedness of phenomenal causality.

Therefore Kant does not regard the will as bound by incapacity or blindness in the intellectualist and historicist fashion of St. Paul and Augustine – which is as Biblical as it is Greek. To the contrary, he regards the will as self-bound, as mysteriously unable to will will, or as willing against itself, pathologically. He is not concerned with a Pauline acting contrary to what one wills, but with an innate failure of the will itself to will freedom. This failure has, for Kant, two aspects. First of all, we tend to adopt non-moral maxims instead of moral ones: this means that where one's actions should embody in their most immediate meaning and palpability a maxim that we could will to turn into a universal law – for example the imperative to tell the truth – they tend, instead, to be contaminated by a pragmatic and egoistic concern for individual or collective material survival and well-being – hence we usually succumb to the temptation to lie.[29] Now it might seem that here Kant does, indeed, see freedom as trammeled by the flesh in the manner of St. Paul. However, this is not the case, because, in the Pauline instance, as developed by Augustine, there is a certain continuity between the lower passions and the higher desire for God (were it not so, for St. Paul, then sexual union with a prostitute would not be able to contaminate our collective bodily union with Christ). Correctly orientated and disciplined, the lower passions should encourage and give way to the higher desire, and indeed this mediation is essential, such that, given corrupt passions, given corrupt *flesh*, no person can truly love God – and St. Paul spilt much ink denying such a self-deluding illusion. However, for Kant, there is no such sphere of participatory mediation between the physical and the psychic. For him it is rather a given that the sensory is neither moral nor immoral, but instead amoral, and so naturally orientated towards self-preservation and self-enjoyment. In consequence morality is not for him primarily a matter of the reorientation of the feelings, or the passions: rather a necessary "moral feeling" is the paradoxical feeling of "the sublime" which is the feeling of a break with feeling, or the counter-attractive attraction of self-sacrifice.[30] This sublimity also mediates, by rupture and not by participation, between the sensory with its natural egotism and the noumenal or spiritual with its equally natural and inevitable upholding of the freedom of self along with the freedom of others. Given that we are free as noumenal, and that this freedom is both intellectually and competently sufficient unto itself (as not for St. Paul and Augustine), there is, in principle, absolutely no reason for it to be externally contaminated. Thus in no way, as for the Greeks, the Church fathers and high scholastics, might sensory passions inevitably pull downwards the good will in Kant, unless entirely of its own perverse volition this will elects to substitute contingent for categorical ends.

In this way, Kantian "Radical Evil" is a far more unsoundable mystery than Augustinian "original sin." And a second aspect to our failure to will freedom, redoubles the mystery. Here we do not adopt non-moral maxims, but rather dilute our adoption of moral ones.[31] Kant avers that the dilution is always present, and even that the degree of such dilution is radically undecidable. This situation arises from the necessary role of "moral feeling" in his account of morality. For, given that morality is the law of the noumenal, outside the bounds of our understanding which is confined to the phenomenal practical reason requires to be sensorily "schematized" (or "pictured" with an intrinsic appropriateness) and yet, unlike the categories of theoretical understanding, which are *orientated* to the phenomenal, it cannot, as Reason, which is concerned with what lies beyond the phenomenal, be schematized in any truly legitimate sense.[32] Normally, Kant declares, it is improperly "symbolized" according to a mere formal analogy, and schematised only at the curious point where we register, negatively, a break with the phenomenal when it becomes sublimely infinitized. Such a break, Kant associates with heroism and self-sacrifice. Now in so far as these human phenomena belong with the natural sublime, they are not in any way for Kant necessarily moral: to the contrary, they concern our pride in, and awe at, a natural resistance to, and transcending of, nature. By contrast, Kant declares that the moral law in itself has nothing to do with sacrifice and admiration for sacrifice, which we tend to associate with the superogatory. Instead, the moral law commands only duty, and no-one deserves admiration for fulfilling the minimum of duty; only disdain if they fail to do so.[33] And yet, according to Kant, we have *no* immediate access to this stringency and purity of duty – because for us the law of freedom is an essentially unknown idea, which, indeed, we can only affirm through "rational faith"; we are assured of freedom at the point where we feel the attraction of giving up phenomenal well being, or are led to admire such renunciation. Hence the moral law is registered improperly as moral feeling, or the strange attraction of sacrifice. (Even in the case where a sensory inclination *happens* to coincide with duty, we only exercise virtue, according to Kant, when we are motivated purely by duty – so here also the sensory inclination must be sacrificed.)

However, this state of affairs also drives the entire Kantian theory of ethics into irresolvable *aporias*, as he half-concedes. We are supposed to know the moral law *a priori*, without recourse (as with theoretical reason) to the application of categories to sensible intuition. And yet, if the moral law is only registered through the schematisation of the natural sublime, then Kant is forced to supplement his case for the *a priori* status of the moral law, as he does in the *Critique of Judgment*, through illegitimate appeal to the admiration of all men in all ages for the heroism of sacrifice, as an inchoate registering of the categorical imperative (the problem here being, why has something the most humanly vital and so democratically knowable by all, even the most theoretically stupid, namely the categorical imperative, only just been discovered – by Kant?).[34]

But then of course, the problem ensues, how is one ever to know that sacrificial motives are pure? How is one sure that even a Thomas More died for the moral law, and not out of self-pride or the love of admiration?[35] And how is one to discriminate within oneself, if only a feeling of love of self-sacrifice registers the law, and yet *even this feeling* contaminates the purity of duty and is only valid insofar as this feeling constantly negates itself, sacrificing even the love of sacrifice? If this sacrifice even of sacrifice is still, nevertheless sacrifice, how to distinguish a diminution of love of sacrifice, and denial of self, from a subtle increase of love of sacrifice and affirmation of self?

This is the aporetic situation more or less admitted by Kant in *Religion Within the Bounds of Mere Reason*. Here it is notable that some of the empirical instances he gives of "radical evil," namely horrific slaughter in wars conducted for their own sakes, lie all too close to the instances of heroism practised for its own sake which he had earlier seen as evidence for the universal but inchoate registering of the categorical imperative.[36] However, the case, in Kantian terms, for regarding "radical evil" as *a priori*, appears stronger than the case for the categorical imperative, since the *a priori* character of radical evil resides in the very undecidable uncertainty regarding human motivation as just described. If radical evil is more clearly *a priori* than the categorical imperative, then this implies, beyond Kant, that the reality of freedom itself, and its law, must remain uncertain (within the terms of a Kantian perspective).

As the self-binding of will, radical evil is a given fact precisely in the sense of an *a priori*. It is not, for Kant, like original sin, a biologically or socially inherited reality, because for him nothing in the causal order can affect the order of freedom. Nor, like original sin, is it a contingent event which distorts the created order (and one can note here that original sin, by remaining with narrative and an endless regress, is really *less* hypostatized and ahistorical than radical evil). Instead, radical evil is co-given along with freedom as an inherent possibility of freedom. This makes sense, because if what defines freedom is not its willing of an infinite goal which allows the flourishing of the free creature, but rather the willing of freedom as such, then freedom can only be free if it might will against itself. For this reason, radical evil is *implied by* enlightenment autonomy and does not qualify it – though only Kant was clever enough to see this. Pure freedom is as free in self-denial as in its self-affirmation. And we have further seen that actually, under these conditions, self-denial becomes indistinguishable from self-affirmation.

In point of fact, though, Kant does not admit the pure positivity of the evil will. He retains a minimal attachment to privation theory, by distinguishing *Wille* from *Willkür* – however much the latter acting will may elect the unfree, it can never entirely pervert the pure faculty of will which is orientated to its own freedom and not to its own destruction.[37] Nevertheless, this Kantian distinction appears unstable, precisely because Kant regards evil as an original possibility constitutive of freedom as such. For Christian tradition, this was not the case: to the contrary, it regarded evil as the very *invention* of counter-possibility – of possibility in the drastic sense of an alternative to the actual. Therefore, by making such counter-possibility a surd dimension of the will, Kant lodges possibility within being as co-equal with actuality. In order for freedom to be actual, the capacity for self-destruction must lurk; in consequence, freedom appears more original than either actuality or possibility, indeed prior to being and nonbeing. It was this implication of radical evil which was developed by Schelling, and we can now see that the problem with his de-ontologization and de-infinitization of the good, is that thereby it inherits the Kantian problem of an undecidability between good and evil.[38] If God decides to share a neutral infinite with us, what renders this a gift, rather than a kind of establishing of empire via a grant of being? How might the gift of being not be perhaps disguised domination, unless the infinite we are granted to share in is in itself unshakable, as infinite peace and harmony according to a substantive aesthetic measure? Since peace and harmony and affinity only make sense as subjectively experienced and judged, there is really no danger that the ineluctable infinite good might be merely impersonal.

After Schelling, the God-beyond-God of a ground of freedom prior to good and evil is transmuted by Heidegger into the ontological identical with nothing and indifferent to the resolute ontic decision for actuality.[39] Indeed, the ground for the authentic autonomy of this decision which fully admits its contingency, remains a preserving of the sense of the equal validity of cancelling such a decision: this preserving constitutes our necessary "guilt" in the face of Being. Jean-Luc Nancy rightly worries that both this ontic humanist affirmation and its reverse face of resignation to the indifference of fate – whereby the ontological can only manifest itself in occluding itself (as apologetically resorted to by the later Heidegger, at the end of the Nazi era) – are both complicit with the Holocaust.[40] And yet Heidegger is logical within the terms of the legacy of radical evil: to desire, like Nancy, that the will to affirmation have ontological priority, is, in effect, to reassert the vision of good as ontological and evil as privative. If Nancy were able to admit this, then he would also be able to admit that it is perverse to suggest that the extremity of modern evil reveals the co-primacy of evil in power and in being. For this renders all being and all power superior either to good or to evil, and therefore ensures that any act of power is legitimate and "good" as undecidably good or evil. (Or to put it in another fashion: where good is not identical with being as such, willed good has only an "ironic" fictional status – and in the end no one acts in the name of a fiction. This is one crucial reason why there *cannot* really be a secular privation theory: secularity will not see being as such as good and so will have to identify the good in terms other than the full presence of the actual. The nearest one gets to such a secular theory is Spinoza – and later Nietzsche – but Spinoza still has an immanent God, and being and power remain convertible with goodness. Nonetheless, his immanentism means that evil in the cosmos, which is deficient weakness, is fated and inevitable, and in this way it would seem that evil *does* get lodged in being and privation is compromised, unless the perspectives of becoming have no true reality. One can conclude, therefore, that privation theory does require transcendence and creation *ex nihilo*.)

Where being is rendered as indifferent to good and evil, Auschwitz is falsely accorded the status of a revelation; in this way taking evil seriously by granting it positive status passes over into resignation to the sway of evil itself. In this way Hitler enjoys a ghostly theoretical victory.

V

It will be recalled that the main objection of the postmodern Kantians to privation theory was that it provides an ontological excuse for evil which diminishes the responsibility of freedom. Now, however, it can be seen that this charge should be thrown back at them. For on their view, the decision for evil is referred to a prior possibility for such freedom – to a freedom prior to freedom and indifferent to good and evil, which alone establishes freedom as freedom. The demonic breaking in of such a radical pre-personal freedom which is *prior* to decision (Schelling's "dark ground"), surely cannot be blamed on the person so possessed? This is really an ontological excuse. Moreover, worse still, where one starts by asserting that the good has its ground in freedom *rather than* being, one inevitably winds up by saying that Being, as neither good nor evil, itself trumps freedom. Even if at first it allows it, it must in the end obliterate it, since without participatory mediation between a partially good finite, and an absolutely good infinite, the finite good Will only arises through a concealment of Being with which it is essentially in conflict.

By contrast, the privation theory avoids all excuses, by denying that evil is lodged in any reality, power or being whatsoever. Somehow, it is impossibly instigated by will alone. If it is true, as we have seen, that it is not really *caused* by freedom, since freedom, as free, causes only the good, then this shows that the bad will cannot *even* blame a possibility lodged within the order of causality (within which freedom, for the tradition, as not for Kant, itself lies). And as for the idea that privation theory offers finitude as an excuse, this may apply to the ancient Greeks, but not to Augustine and Dionysius. For them there is nothing defective in finitude as such, rather what is defective is the disallowing of finite things from reaching their own proper finite share of perfection. (For Dionysius, it should be noted, privation is more the removal of the Good than the removal of Being, since the Good for him lies beyond Being; however this detail does not really affect the present argument.)[41]

Thus evil for the Christian tradition was radically without cause – indeed it was not even self-caused, but rather the (impossible) refusal of cause. In this way privation theory offers not an "explanation" of evil, but instead rigorously remains with its inexplicability, for explanation can pertain only to existences, and here evil is not seen as sometimes in existence. Indeed it is regarded for this reason as not even explicable *in principle*, not even explicable for God. Since evil is in this way *so* problematic that it falls outside the range of *problema*, there has never been for theologians any "problem of evil." The idea that there is such a problem, has only arisen since, roughly, the time of Leibniz. As inherited evil was held to have already impaired our finitude, there was, indeed, *in us* a causal bias to evil; yet since grace renews our will, our evil decision to refuse grace is as groundless and causeless as Adam's original sin. For this reason, according to Augustine, the origin of evil must be passed over as "darkness and silence," as if there were a dreadful *apophasis* of evil that parodied the *apophasis* of the Divine.[42] Because evil is uncaused, there is indeed a sense in which it possesses us like an anti-cause proceeding from a Satanic black hole (as J.-L. Marion argues – the non-existence of the Devil *is* the existence of the Devil).[43] But when it possesses us, not only are we responsible for this possession, it is also the case that this possession delivers the very phenomenon of autonomous responsibility. Evil is just that for which alone we are solely responsible. Evil is self-governing autonomy – evil *is* the Kantian good, the modern good.

Since evil is for privation theory so radically uncaused, it does not require to be justified by an ontodicy. Indeed, the rise of theodicy, and so of ontodicy, is much more correlated with a post-Scotist univocity of Being, and a sense that, if the finite equally *is*, as much as the infinite, then even the lacking within finitude that is evil equally *is* along with the good – in consequence the presence of evil must be "justified" in terms of providential design.[44] (It is true that that this has some germs within the Church fathers, but they confined it to a correct insistence that certain local pains and sufferings can, indeed – like thirst that will be quenched – contribute to the overall good.)[45]

VI

From such theodicy and ontodicy, the theory of radical evil is in fact by no means immune. If, for Kant, human good will is only evidenced in resistance to suffering, then certainly non-moral evil in nature plays for him a providential role. But in addition, the most "signal" virtue is for Kant displayed in our resistance to other human beings. Here moral evil, also, is a providential training ground for virtue, because Kant explicitly states that only the exercise of heroism in warfare (which, it will be recalled, is a sublime schema of the moral law), could have gradually trained up the strength of the will, such that it is finally able to resist its own self-denial, and to arrive at the moral preconditions for the establishing of "perpetual peace" amongst the nations. The passage to moral virtue via the sublime also traverses the exercise of radical evil, just as the path to civilized peace lies dialetically through warfare.

However, we have already seen how this theodicy and ontodicy come unstuck: the purportedly moral self-overcoming will might still be the natural heroic will – at once sublime and radically evil, or one might well say, Miltonically Satanic. How is one to decide? As Jacques Lacan pointed out, the Sadean sadistic will also wills only its own freedom, and is also prepared to sacrifice comfort, security and survival for the sake of its own exercise.[46]

But Kant was near to conceding this problem. How did he try to cope with it? The answer is that he sought to supplement morality with grace. Supposedly, Kant brings religion within the bounds of reason by reducing it to morality, but we have already seen how practical reason problematically transgresses the bounds established by theoretical reason, since it claims knowledge of noumenal freedom. And we have also seen how, when moral knowledge is brought back within the schematic bounds of the phenomenal, our claim to know the noumenal as moral is rendered uncertain. Thus practical reason, if it is to be saved, must, on the grounds of its own rational demand, be *supplemented* by religious faith. *Religion within the Bounds of Mere Reason* should really be entitled "reason outside its own bounds in the sphere of religion." For it turns out that ethics, the essence of religion, cannot after all dispense with the mere *parerga* or "inessentials" of religion which exceed, for Kant, the ethical. Thus it cannot dispense with unmerited grace, with the Sacraments, with the organized Church.[47] Grace must be invoked, because we can only distinguish the will to freedom from radical evil, if we have faith that our aspiration to a good will is graciously taken by God as equivalent to his infinite and ineluctably holy will (here Kant clearly has not gone as far as Schelling). And to have this faith is also to have faith in an eschatological discrimination, when the good wills are finally divided from the bad wills, and the mere empirical pursuit of egoistic happiness is finally subordinated to freedom, since the virtuous are rewarded with happiness and the vicious with unhappiness. Moreover, this faith cannot merely be entertained by individuals, because radical evil arises for Kant (here influenced by Rousseau), only from cultural association which gives rise to envy and greed and so forth, and contaminates a supposed "private" exercise of moral autonomy.[48] (One can contrast Augustine here, for whom, as we have seen, the good will is enjoyment, according to a specific refraction that is not in rivalry with other specific refractions, of an essentially common good.) The only way, according to Kant, to combat this corruption of the inward by the social, is to set up, not merely a state founded on a social contract and directed by a general will, but also a Church which seeks really to overcome and not merely to inhibit the inner desires of egotism. A Church is supposed, for Kant, to engender a kind of "general moral will". And its Sacraments, although arbitrary signs, are necessary reminders of the hope of the eschaton, without which morality remains uncertain.[49]

In this fashion, the theory of radical evil, which is supposed to locate evil within human limits, must after all, as Kant admits (though not his contemporary heirs), in order to avoid antinomianism, invoke divine grace. However, Kantian free will is not, like Augustinian free will, identified with grace as the gift par excellence of grace. Instead, for Kant, freedom is no gift, but an inert *given*, and equally given along with it, is radical evil: so if it is a gift, it is a poisoned one. And as for Luther, free will as such cannot aspire to God; this Lutheran legacy is part of what leads Kant to conclude that finite will simply in itself is "bound."[50] Thus, bizarrely enough, Kantian grace is *far more* positivistically and pietistically irruptive than Augustinian or Thomist grace. For it does not give free will, but juristically supplements its (ontologically) *given* deficiency, since here the will to the good has reduced to the mere will to have a good will in the hope that God, by grace, will *impute* to us a good will.

If the Kantian account of grace and free will as it were parodies the Augustinian one, then so also does his account of the Church. For the Augustinian, as for the Pauline vision, the *ecclesia* aspires to, and partially realizes, a real harmony of differentiated persons by blending together a diversity of characters and roles according to a beautiful and analogical affinity that is rooted in the Church's manifestation of the incarnate *logos*. Kant seems almost to come near to this, and yet the diverse persons in his Church are only united under the abstract formal resemblance of their wills, and only aspire to be "one body" according to a just matching of happiness to freedom. It is not that here the specific happiness which is also the specific freedom of one person (according to a teleological flourishing), is concretely blended with the specific free happiness of another, within the advent of affinity under grace, as for the Pauline view which Augustine elaborated. (Not seeing this distinction, Arendt, like many others, overrates the anti-liberal potential of "beautiful" reflexive judgment in the third critique.)[51]

And in this way it becomes apparent that radical evil does *not* offer a secular view of evil, but only an alternative theology, which is an alternative account both of theological reason and of divine revelation to the traditional account provided by Christian privation theory. Now, then, we can attempt a theological discrimination between the two. And what is apparent is that, paradoxically, only privation theory (plus original sin and Satanic possession), allow for a *human* discrimination of good and evil in the here and now, and so the possibility of a substantively just social order. By contrast, the theology of radical evil is also a theology of radical eschatological postponement of a guaranteed good and a guaranteed justice. And this theology cannot really allow any *anticipation* of the eschaton.

VII

It is finally the political implications of the Kantian legacy which I wish to explore. I have already defended at length the view of evil as privation which undergirds the view of evil as banal. The two views are not, however, identical: it is possible for negativity to take a sublime quasi-heroic form. Nevertheless, one can extend Arendt's theory of banality by arguing that this quasi-Satanism of the perpetrators of state horror is usually prepared by an incremental pilling up of small deficient preferences which gradually and "accidentally" (as Aquinas argued), produce the monstrous. (Aquinas after Dionysius speaks of "accidental" causing of evil [ST I Q 49 a1; *De malo* Q1 a.3; Dionysius DN V 32] where Augustine seems to speak of no causing at all. However, by this they mean that pursuit of a too limited good "accidentally" causes the lack of good that should ensue. This is an odd sort of accidentality, since it really brings nothing about, and involves not merely a non-intended consequence, but also an overlooked one.)

In the case of the Holocaust, the Satanism of the final solution was the outcome of a long drift of deficient science, deficient philosophy, deficient politics, deficient religion and deficient sociality. To take the converse view, and to imagine that Hitler was a deliberate Satanist, or even that a Manson can attain a fully Satanic perspective, is to lend credence to that saddest of all the errors of evil (and of Satan) whereby it always imagines that it is yet more evil than it really is. For evil to be at all, it must still deploy and invoke some good, yet it would like to forget this: evil as positive is evil's own fondest illusion.

Insisting in this way upon the pathos of evil and upon its creeping and incremental character by no means, as many fear, involves a taking away from the responsibility of individual wills. On the contrary, this insistence points to the gravity of even the smallest responsibilities and the dangers of apparently good intentions (which it does *not* quite deem to be tragically unavoidable); also it does not excuse or regard as inevitable the long-encouraged emergence of "monstrous" wills. Nor does this insistence tend to deny the unprecedented character of the Holocaust: all that it denies is the notion of a metaphysical revelation of an unexpected ontological status for evil. By contrast it points to the Holocaust's real disclosure of the terrible capacities of an ancient depravity whose character, nonetheless, retains all too tediously its perennial nature. (Even if it be pointed out that many minor implementers of the "logic" of the final solution indulged their own sadism, one should see that even sadism has its pathos and pathetic pursuit of displaced goods. Berhard Schlink's – in many ways problematic – novel *The Reader* illustrates this point. Here the sadism of a female camp official is inseparable from the fact of her illiteracy, which has led her to select this job as one of the few where it can be successfully disguised.)

But if the final solution was the outcome of a long incremental drift, then we must finally ask, was the Kantian legacy itself part of this process?

Hannah Arendt in part considered this to be the case. Albert Eichmann did, as she noted, have a self-admitted Kantian habit of mind insofar as he thought sovereign law must be obeyed; must be obeyed without exception, and must be obeyed beyond the call of duty in the spirit of the letter.[52] For Arendt, it is this popularized Kantianism which explains how the utterly inefficient Nazis were nonetheless able to co-opt the internalized efficiency of the German people.

However, Arendt took Eichmann's Kantian habit as to be a parody of Kantian nobility – and indeed it appears that Eichmann himself had thought so. Thus she says that, for the ineffability of the sovereign law of free will as such, Eichmann had substituted the sovereign will of the Führer. This is not to be confused with the command of the categorical imperative. But is it not? And was Eichmann merely parodying?

Politics, for Kant, though rooted in the moral law, had to deal mainly with the contingent, empirical imperatives of material well-being. However, we have seen how the categorical imperative has to be schematized and symbolized in terms of these lesser imperatives. And the Kantian account of the just polity suggests indeed that the self-governing state symbolizes the self-governing moral individual according to a formal analogy ("symbol" for Kant, always denotes a mere common ratio, which is also how he understands "analogy"). This analogy involves nothing more nor less than *the division of powers*. At the center of the state should stand an unchanging sovereign power, whose issuing of laws without enacting them renders it akin to the transcendent law of freedom in the individual. Kant himself makes this analogy when, in *Religion*

Within the Bounds of Mere Reason he compares God the Father who is the ultimate source of the moral law, to a political sovereign.[53] God the Son is then compared to a political executive, and also to the individual will which is incited by moral feeling, to obey the ineffable law. Thus we see that, for Kant, the political executive is akin to individual moral activity, inspired by moral feeling. Finally, God the Holy Spirit is at once like the political judiciary and the individual judgment. These two are akin, because they both seek to apply the law to particular circumstances, and to match freedom to happiness – according to extrinsic desert, not intrinsic co-belonging. In this way Kant, according to his logic of essential inessentials (*parerga*), reveals that his hierarchy of cold duty over warm feeling is grounded in a heterodox and Arian Trinity. At the same time he reveals how the same Trinity secures a political sovereignty which can be taken as absolute and persisting, over and above what is enacted and judged in its name.

To be absolutely fair to Kant here, he is clear that tyranny results when the powers are confused with each other and especially when the executive usurps the sovereignty.[54] By this measure Hitler would surely have been deemed a tyrant. Kant allows for the popular overthrow of a corrupt executive and judiciary, and this was the basis for his qualified support for the French revolution. Nevertheless, in his famous footnote on regicide in the *Metaphysics of Morals*, Kant ferociously disallows overthrow of the sovereign power as utterly contradictory.[55] So where sovereign and executive have coalesced, albeit through usurpation (as in the Nazi case), what Kantian basis remains to support resistance and non-obedience, even if the original usurpation was denounced, since the *de jure* basis of sovereignty in Kant seems to reduce to the *de facto*? For Kant, sovereign political authority *is* the point where moral and political rule, categorical and contingent imperative, actually come together. Since the sovereign power embodies the collective general will, and is the absolute source of all legality, to will against the sovereign power in person is to will against political legality. This cannot be universally willed, under the maxim "I will to destroy a corrupt sovereign power," because it removes the very basis of legality, just as lying for Kant destroys the possibility of trust and thus of all free association. Hence regicide *does* fall foul of the categorical imperative and to oppose the political sovereign *is* to oppose the moral sovereign. This conclusion really results because the ground of legitimacy in Kant is entirely one of immanent consent and procedural emission from a consensually established center: thus he cannot allow that a substantive natural law would remain, even in the absence of sovereign power. To the contrary, the only political law of nature for Kant is that there must be an earthly sovereign center if there is to be collective justice. Here the closed bounds of human reason which disallow a mediation of the infinite, also absolutize established human authority. This absolutization is very extreme in Kant, since he describes regicide as the *supreme* instance of radical evil and of sublime horror, almost displacing the crucifixion of the Son of God in this respect. Here the only thing that prevents regicide as an act of freedom from being seen as an act of moral liberation is the identification of the sovereign idea of freedom we must respect with a *given*, established, specific exercise of freedom by a political ruler. But then how else, short of the eschaton, *are* we now, in Kantian terms, to discriminate a good will from a bad one? Even though Kant never drew this conclusion, it seems to follow, if one thinks through his *aporias* to their ends. Kantian morality, deconstructed, says, you know your will is good when you obey the law of the State without exception and beyond the call of duty. Eichmann had it more right than he knew.

If this analysis is correct, then the Nazi episode casts suspicion not just upon Fichte or Müller or Nietzsche or Heidegger, but on the main lines of the Germanic philosophical legacy to which the second half of the twentieth century has remained in some ways too dangerously subservient. This is not, however, to indict an entire culture, because Kant's most decisive and insightful opponents – Jacobi, Hamann, Herder – were also German and also strongly informed a later Germanic tradition. Moreover, in relation to the Nazis, many other currents are equally culpable, including an originally British evolutionism in some of its manifestations.[56] But the ambiguity of the Kantian legacy does raise specifically the question which must still haunt us, of the collusion between liberalism and totalitarianism. Moral liberalism tends to engender an uneasy oscillation between absolute promotion of one's own freedom for any goal whatsoever, and absolute sacrifice to the freedom of the other, again without any conditions as to the goals that others should pursue. Writ large at the level of the state, this produces a giant scale oscillation between a present collective identity as an end in itself, and the endless self-sacrifice of individuals for the sake of a better future. Thus political liberalism itself engenders today an increasingly joyless and puritanical world in which we work harder and harder towards obscure ends, while "surplus" populations of the young, the old, the cultural misfits, and the poor, are increasingly marginalized, disciplined, put to degrading work, or indeed simply destroyed. The liberal state already exhibits a certain totalitarian drift and may always become really totalitarian at the point where its empty heart is besieged by an irrational cult of race, class, science, style or belief.

This slide of liberalism toward totality confirms that where free will as such is identified with the good, the promotion of self-respect and autonomy will be simultaneously and indistinguishably the promotion of self-inhibition and radical evil. But for privation theory it is this very promotion of abstract free autonomy that itself enshrines what is evil, and radically deficient.

Notes

1   See Joan Copjec, ed., *Radical Evil* (London: Verso, 1996); Jean-Luc Nancy, *The Experience of Freedom*, trans. Bridget McDonald (Stanford: Stanford University Press, 1993); Slavoj Žižek, *For They Know Not What They Do: Enjoyment as a Political Factor* (London: Verso, 1991). See also, to some extent, Jacques Derrida, "Faith and Knowledge: The Two Sources of 'Religion' at the Limits of Reason Alone," in *Religion*, ed. J. Derrida and G. Vattimo (Cambridge: Polity, 1988), pp. 1–79.

2   Immanuel Kant, "Religion Within the Bounds of Mere Reason," trans. George di Giovanni, in Immanuel Kant, *Religion and Rational Theology*, trans. and ed. Allen W. Wood and George di Giovanni (Cambridge: Cambridge University Press, 1996), 57–213.

3   Hannah Arendt, *Eichmann in Jerusalem: A Report on the Banality of Evil* (London: Penguin, 1992).

4   See Hannah Arendt, *Love and Saint Augustine* (Chicago: Chicago University Press, 1996) and the introduction by J. V. Scott and J. C. Stark, "Rediscovering Hannah Arendt."

5   Arendt, *Eichmann*, 137.

6   See Michael Halberstramm, *Totalitarianism and the Modern Conception of Politics* (New Haven: Yale, 1999).

7   For a good account of this, see Roy F. Baumeister, *Evil: Inside Human Cruelty and Violence* (New York: W. H. Freeman, 1997), esp. pp. 375–88.

8   See Jacob Rogozinski, "Hell on Earth: Hannah Arendt in the Face of Hitler," in *Philosophy Today* 37, 3/4 (Fall 1993), pp. 257–74, esp. p. 267.

9   Kant, "Religion Within the Bounds of Mere Reason," 6:20–6:53, pp. 69–97.

10 See Richard L. Rubinstein's classic text, *The Cunning of Reason: Mass Death and the American Future* (New York: Harper and Row, 1975).

11 Dionysius the Areopagite, *The Divine Names*, Book 4, 19–35, 716D–736B, esp. 31: "it is not principles and powers which produce evil, but impotence and weakness."

12 Dionysius, *The Divine Names*, Book 4, 20: "Abolish the good and you will abolish being, life, desire, movement, everything"; Augustine, *City of Good*, XIV, II: "The choice of the will . . . is genuinely free, only when it is not subservient to faults and sins."

13 See Slavoj Žižek, "Selfhood as Such is Spirit" in Copjec, ed., *Radical Evil*, pp. 1–30. In the same volume, see Jacob Rogozinski, "It makes us wrong: Kant and Radical Evil," pp. 30–45. See also Jean-Luc Nancy, *The Experience of Freedom*, chapter 12, "Evil: Decision," pp. 121–41.

14 Both Paul Ricoeur and Pierre Watté interpret Kant as offering the finest interpretation of a Pauline "Self-Inhibition," in a fashion that "frees" the theme of liberty from cosmology, and discovers the seed of evil to be purely in the will taken as a *positive* assertion of self. The whole of this present essay is designed in part to demonstrate that such a view is historically false, pseudo-profound, and profoundly dangerous. Ricoeur also sees such positivity of evil as anticipated in primitive "symbolisation" of evil as visible taint or disorder. However, this aspect of aesthetic disharmony was rightly viewed by Dionysius as also privative: nothing that *appears* to us lacks beauty – rather what offends the eye is a deficiency of appropriate, requisite order that should pertain variously in any given instance. Thus evil for him, while negative, is also "an inharmonious mingling of discordances": *Divine Names*, 4, 31. The invocation of an aesthetic aspect to privation does, nonetheless, serve to emphasize that evil as privation is not purely and simply nothing: as "substance" it may be nothing, but in its effect of removal and deficiency it engenders a distorted positive act, even though, as positive, this act is not distorted. See Pierre Watté, *Structures Philosophiques du Péché Originel: S. Augustin, S. Thomas, Kant* (Gembloux: J. Duclot S. A. 1974) and the preface by Paul Ricoeur, esp. p. 8 and Paul Ricoeur, *The Symbolism of Evil*, trans. Emerson Buchanan (Boston: Beacon, 1967), pp. 70–100.

15 At this point these thinkers are incorporating a Levinasian thematic.

16 See Žižek, "Selfhood as Such is Spirit." And F. W. J. Schelling, "Philosophical Investigations into the Essence of Human Freedom and Related Matters," in *Philosophy of German Idealism*, ed. Ernest Behler (New York: Continuum, 1987); *Of Human Freedom*, trans. J. Gutman (Chicago: Open Court, 1936).

17 See Watté, *Structures Philosophiques*, 128–215.

18 Augustine, *On Free Choice of the Will*, trans. Thomas Williams (Indianapolis: Hackett, 1993), Book One, 1, 4, 12, 13; 25; Book Two, 14, 16, 13, p. 57: "this is our freedom: when we are subject to the [infinite] truth."

19 Augustine, *City of God*, XIV, 13; *On Free Choice of the Will*, Book I, 8.

20 Augustine, *On the Free Choice of the Will*, Book One, 11: once "inordinate desire" has gripped the mind after Adam, it takes "false things" for true, and becomes a prey to "fear" and "anxiety." See further Book Three, 3, 4, 18, p. 106: " . . . as it is [since the fall] they [humans] are not good, and it is not in their power to be good, either because they do not

see how they ought to be, or because they lack the power to be what they see they ought to be"; "because of our ignorance we lack the free choice or the will to choose to act rightly"; "or . . . even when we do see what is right and will to do it, we cannot do it because of the resistance of carnal habit" Here Augustine is commenting on Romans 7:18: "To will the good is present to me, but I find no way to do it" and Galatians 5:17, "You do not do what you will, as flesh and spirit lust against each other." Augustine continues, "thus we who knew what was right but did not do it, lost the knowledge of what is right, and we who had the power but not the will to act rightly lost the power even when we have the will." He then has to face the objection that if our free will is so inhibited by loss of vision and incapacity, then we are not to blame for failure to will the good. But he answers (p. 107), "Perhaps their complaint would be justified if there were no victor over error and inordinate desire. But in fact there is one who is present everywhere and speaks in many ways through the creation that serves him as Lord. He calls out to those who have turned their backs on him, and instructs them who believe in him." Desires of the good remains possible through grace, and so our lack of vision and incapacity is exceeded and potentially overcome (since the Pauline impotence, recognized *after* grace, is not really seen by Paul as an absolute check). See also Book Two, 16, where it is made clear that the discernment of truth by will/desire is also the kenotic descent of divine wisdom towards us. At section 52 of *On the Spirit and the Letter* Augustine stresses that free will itself is the supreme gift of grace, while in *De Gratia et Libero Arbitrio* at 4:8, citing Mathew 19:10–11, he notes that while marriage as sexual union is supremely what we *will*, marriage is also the sacramental *gift* of God. Here then again, what is given to us by God is to will.

21   See Martin Luther, "The Bondage of the Will" in *Martin Luther's Basic Theological Writings*, ed. Timothy F. Lull (Minneapolis: Fortress, 1989), pp. 178–82 and 206.

22   See note 20, above and the passage quoted from *On the Free Choice of the Will*, Book Three, 18, p. 107.

23   *On the Free Choice of the Will*, Book Three, 18, p. 107: "You are not to blame for your unwilling ignorance [the legacy of Adam's sin], but because you fail to ask about what you do not know. You are not blamed because you do not bind up your own wounds [the post-Adamic incapacity], but because you spurn the one who wants to heal you, for no one is prevented from leaving behind the disadvantage of ignorance and seeking the advantage of knowledge, or from humbly confessing his weakness, so that God, whose help is effortless and unerring, will come to his assistance. When someone acts wrongly out of ignorance, or cannot do what he rightly wills to do, his actions are called sins because they have their origin in that first sin, which was committed by free will. The later sins are the just result of that first sin." This shows that Augustine's account of original sin is objective, collective, historical and realist, and involves no contorted doctrines about an inevitable willing of the bad for which we are to blame. These rather descend to us from Luther and Kant.

24   James Alison, *The Joy of Being Wrong* (New York: Crossroad, 1998).

25   *On the Free Choice of the Will*, Book Two, 19.

26   *On the Free Choice of the Will*, Book Two, 9, p. 49. Augustine associates the common true/ good with light, enjoyed by all sight at once, unlike a touchable object, which we can only touch one at a time, in turn. However, it seems to me implicit in Augustine that in the Eucharist "sight" and "touch" are fused, since here the most intimate touching that is eating is a simultaneous and collective eating of a body not "used up," and not enjoyed exclusively "one at a time" by eating. So here a body is like light, and in this fashion the Eucharist supremely combines the most common and the most intimate. Therefore the Eucharist most exemplifies true willing or desiring and restored participation. Augustine in this dialogue also figures the dialectic of common and particular with the co-belonging of

"wisdom" with "number." Here he is not always easy to follow, but roughly it seems that "number" is at times associated with the eternal divine ideas, and at other times with the diversity of the creation: as in God numbering sparrows and the hairs on our head. By contrast, wisdom is associated with the kenotic "reach" of omnipotence to the ends of the earth, as with the figure of personified wisdom rushing to meet us, which Augustine alludes to. In this way the eternal numbers reach to the created numbers, and Augustine indicates that the diversity of instance and preference is not alien to the common, universal, eternal and measured.

27 Immanuel Kant, *The Metaphysics of Morals*, trans. Mary Gregor (Cambridge: Cambridge University Press, 1991), p. 183 [378], p. 193 [389]; *Critique of Practical Reason*, trans. L. W. Beck (Upper Saddle River, NJ: Prentice Hall, 1993), Part I, Book I, Chap. I, II, pp. 65–8; "Religion within the Bounds of Mere Reason," 6:22, p. 72 and footnote; 6:24–6:31, pp. 73–8.

28 This is why the "revisionist" attempt to read Kant as a virtue ethicist cannot be rendered plausible.

29 "Religion within the Bounds of Mere Reason," 6:29, p. 77; *Groundwork of the Metaphysics of Morals*, trans. H. J. Paton (New York: Harper and Row, 1964), Preface vi–viii, p. 57 [389–90].

30 *Metaphysics of Morals*, pp. 201–2 [400]; *Groundwork of the Metaphysics of Morals*, pp. 128–9 [460], *Critique of Judgment*, trans. J. C. Meredith (Oxford: Oxford University Press, 1989), Part I, §;4, pp. 46–48 §6, p. 51; §;26, p. 103; §29, p. 120.

31 "Religion Within the Bounds of Mere Reason," 6:30, p. 77.

32 *Groundwork*, pp. 128–9 [460]; *Critique of Practical Reason*, Part I, Book I, Chapter I, pp. 32 3, 43–52; Chapter II, pp. 70–74; *Critique of Judgment*, Part I §29, p. 121; §30, p. 134; §59, p. 221–5.

33 *Groundwork*, p. 128 [460];

34 *Critique of Judgment*, Part I, §29, pp. 112–13.

35 *Critique of Practical Reason*, Part II, pp. 161–3.

36 "Religion Within the Bounds," 6:33, p. 80.

37 "Religion Within the Bounds," 6: 36, p. 82.

38 Schelling, *Of Human Freedom*.

39 See J.-L. Nancy, *The Experience of Freedom*, §4, "The Space Left free by Heidegger," pp. 33–43.

40 Nancy, *Experience of Freedom*, and "Evil: Decision," pp. 121–41. Nancy also gives analyses of freedom highly compatible with Augustinianism, which describe it as that which "surprises" us, rather than as something we control, and as primordially "sharing," since every free expression must "give" something of oneself to others. See §3 "Impossibility of the Question of Freedom," pp. 21–32.

41 For example, Dionysius, *The Divine Names*, Book 4, 26: "there is no evil nature – rather evil lies in the inability of things to reach their *acme* of perfection."

42 Augustine, *City of God*, X11, 7: "To try to discover the causes of such defection . . . is like trying to see darkness or to hear silence."

43 Jean-Luc Marion, "Le Mal en Personne" in *Protégomenes à la Charité* (Paris: La Différance, 1986), pp. 11–43.

44 For Scotus and after, see Catherine Pickstock, *After Writing* (Oxford: Blackwell, 1999), 121–67. Privation theory plays little role within Leibniz's *Theodicy*. See G. W. Leibniz, *Theodicy*, ed. Austin Farrer (La Salle, IL: Open Court, 1985).

45 See, for example, Augustine, *On the Free Choice of the Will*, Book 3, 15, pp. 100–1.

46 Jacques Lacan, "Kant with Sade," trans. James Swenson, *October 51* (Winter, 1989); Slavoj Žižek, "Why is Sade the Truth of Kant?" in *For They Know Not What They Do*, pp. 229–41.

47 "Religion Within the Bounds of Mere Reason," Parts III and IV, pp. 129–215.

48 "Religion within the Bounds of Mere Reason," 6: 94–5, pp. 129–30.

49 "Religion within the Bounds of Mere Reason," Part four, 6:151–6:202, pp. 175–215 esp. 6:153, p. 176.

50 Luther, "The Bondage of the Will."

51 See Halberstramm's discussion of Arendt's use of the *Critique of Judgment* in *Totalitarianism* (see note 6 above)

52 Arendt, *Eichmann in Jerusalem*, 1.

53 "Religion Within the Bounds of Mere Reason," 6:139–43, pp. 165–8.

54 Immanuel Kant, *Metaphysics of Morals*, Part II, Section I, §44–§48, pp. 123–8.

55 *Metaphysics of Morals*, Part II, Section I, §49, pp. 129–33, and Immanuel Kant, "Perpetual Peace," in *Kant: Political Writings*, trans. A. B. Nisbet (Cambridge: Cambridge University Press, 1991), p. 124.

56 See the magnificent book by David Depew and Bruce H. Weber, *Darwinism Evolving: Systems Dynamics and the Genealogy of Natural Selection* (Cambridge, MA: MIT Press, 1997).

20

RETURN TO LAUGHTER

Sharon Welch

What are we doing when we do theology? What types of claims are we making about "beings-beyond being"?[1] What "symbolic of desire" is manifest in our concepts and our definitions of religious truth?[2] What realities are we invoking, what behaviors, what states of mind do we conjure in our prayers, rituals and theological and philosophical explorations of the sacred and the profane?

We often like to think that there was a time when it was easy to know what we were doing when we spoke of gods or "convened the ritual cosmos"[3]: we responded to the unambiguous demand of divine revelation: we witnessed to the transformative power of religious experience: we participated in communal rituals that sustained the world.

While I doubt that religious experience and activity within fundamentalisms of the present or in premodern religious communities was as simple as it appears to us who live in a postmodern world, we can be certain of one thing – it is not simple now, and it is not simple for us. After deconstruction, each term of our discourse, each gesture of our rituals, each movement of desire is seen as contested, indeterminate, and socially constructed. And, not only are our concepts, gestures and desires constructed, and indeterminate, but they are implicated in master narratives that help sustain oppression, domination, violence and exclusion.[4]

The work of philosophers of religion and of theologians now highlights these dual concerns. The god of metaphysics and the methods and claims of onto-theology are discredited as much for their legitimization of oppression as for their conceptual idolatry. Where does this leave us theologically? What are our options in the present moment?

In this essay I could take up the deconstructive task as described by Grace Jantzen, a critique and an alternative that is a therapeutic intervention in a dangerous symbolic of desire.[5] Placing my work in the camp of feminist theology, I could take up Irigaray's "becoming divine," and with Jantzen construe a symbolic of desire based on natality rather than death.[6] In short, I could propose another symbolic that is more fitting to the epistemic challenges of postmodernity, and more suited to the imperative of establishing justice. In contrast to all of these philosophers, I could argue that each is still implicated in logics of oppression that elide the power of finitude and ambiguity, and provide a more adequate symbolics of natality and finitude, one informed by an African, African-American and American Indian symbolics of balance and beauty.

I could play the dualistic game of point-counterpoint, but I will not. I will not repeat the cut, the division into legitimate/illegitimate, natality/death, faith/religion for a simple reason. To take refuge in such a divide (or even in the possibility of such a divide) is to miss the power and peril of the religious and of all religious discourse. "In itself" (a loaded phrase to be sure) religious experience is profoundly meaningful, central to a community's and an individual's sense of identity, and, at the same time, intrinsically amoral.

I once claimed that the cause of justice was better served if, rather than focus on God as the source of "right relations" we saw divinity as being "right relations," thus construing divinity as a quality of relations, an adverb rather than a noun.[7] At that time I limited divinity to "*right*" relations, a move similar to that of other liberal and liberation theologians who describe God as the force of creativity and justice. Now I see creativity and intense relatedness as themselves amoral, and the task of giving them moral expression is socially and culturally mediated, perilous and haphazard.

In describing what this means for a positive, although intrinsically ambiguous appreciation of spirituality, I emphasize an ironic spirituality that holds the paradox of being founded by that which is also amoral, contingent and malleable.

I speak for those who find the Barthian and Derridean escape untenable: your encounter with the divine is religious and a projection and we have received a revelation which has shattered even the pretensions of our Protestant religion and natural theology (Barth) or, your vision of justice is an idolatrous concrete messianism while ours, in its radical openness, in its "*universal* longing and restlessness" is free from the projections that create religious violence, coercion and fanaticism."[8] In much (all?) western philosophies of religion and theology we find an odd logic indeed, so sensitive to the potential and actual harm of other religious symbolics, so certain that we have found the key that can help us escape the same dynamic (the Protestant principle, Derrida's messianic affirmation which is not a concrete messianism).

Just as there is no *universal* longing for a total surprise, there is no definitive escape from injustice and error. I will describe a symbolic of the "fully now" (not the *tout autre*), a desire for the plenitude of presence that can also evoke justice, freedom and respect. Yet this form of religious discourse stands *alongside*, not over-against, Marion's construals of a God beyond Being and the symbolic of the gift, alongside Jantzen's and Irigaray's "becoming divine," alongside Derrida's *tout autre* and Lévinas' God whose name is the call for justice.[9] Although this construal differs in its placement of error and injustice, (acknowledging the amorality at the core of the religious), *it is not, for that reason, more likely, nor less likely than any other construal to lead to justice or injustice.* Here I draw on Nietzshe's notion of the longest lie — the belief that "outside the haphazard and perilous experiments we perform there lies something (God, Science, Knowledge, Rationality, or Truth) which will, if only we perform the correct rituals, step in to save us."[10]

It is important to realize that not one of these variants of religious experience (*ours included*), not one of these construals of the divine or divinities or spiritualities, inevitably and reliably leads to ethical action. The construal of divinity as wholly other, as the excess of possibility, the not–yet that destabilizes all concrete messianism, can be found in prophetic denunciations of social injustice as well as in the cultured despair of the middle and upper classes and our withdrawal from political engagement. There is nothing that inevitably and irrevocably grounds our desire for justice. Justice, in all its forms, is our work, our creation, our unfinished task.

I. Alchemy

How exquisitely human was the wish for permanent happiness, and how thin human imagination became trying to achieve it.[11]

Toni Morrison, Paradise

How is it possible that all "manifestations" of the religious are amoral, if morality, if the demand for justice, is intrinsic to our names for the religious? For Lévinas, the name of God is a call for justice; for Derrida, the *"tout autre"* challenges the violence and fanaticism of any concrete messianism; for Irigaray and Jantzen, the imperative of the religious is to "become divine," which in itself is an act of justice, the open–ended participation in human flourishing.

I am not saying the religious is *immoral*, and thus, such names are, by definition, unwarranted. Rather, the language of freedom and openness to others, the language of love and justice, coheres with the ecstasy and claim of the religious as easily, but *no more easily*, than the language of exclusion and self–righteousness.

Another form of construing the sacred, found in feminist theology, process theology and some African–American theologies is also instructive. Here the sacred is perceived as creativity itself.[12] Let us think, though, about creativity. Creativity itself is as easily expressed in the operations of global capitalism, in the production of music videos and web sites, in the design and use of deadly weapons as it is in works of justice.[13] And, what feeds creativity? powerful connections with available human and natural resources. The work of scientists in Los Alamos constructing the first atomic weapons, for example, was a vivid manifestation of the power of human connection and creativity. The connections of the scientists at Los Alamos were, of course, partial. If they had been equally connected to the value of the people of Hiroshima and Nagasaki, if equally connected to the natural order, no such destructive weapons would have been built or used. And yet, could it be that the relative weakness of pacifist and prophetic movements in the face of military expansion and global capitalism is that *we are not as creative* as are they, because we, from our vantage point in the ideal, are not as connected as are they to the actual human and natural resources of the world around us? If we ground our prophetic social critique in the *"tout autre,"* do we then lack the creativity that comes from working with the resources that are here now? Injustice flourishes because those who love justice are singularly lacking in creativity, content to denounce the structures we see causing harm, inept in producing other forms of art, other economic structures, other political systems.

The experience of creativity, of intense forms of connection is simply this – the crucial synthesis of energies of people from the past, within the present, and even in the future. We may be energized, but that does not meant that our theological and political analyses are true, that our ethics and political strategies are just. It is disconcerting to acknowledge that our ecstasy in connection, whether political or conceptual, is simply the energy of connection, an energy that may be used in amoral, immoral or moral ways. We so want the energy we experience in connection, the affirmation we encounter in "being-seen" or "being-loved" to be an affirmation of the rightness of our choices, our actions, beliefs, and desires. While these may be affirmations of our being, they are not affirmations of how we frame and express that being.

What shape can imagination take, where is its thickness, its vitality, if we are no longer constituted by the desire for perfection? What happens if we are no longer propelled by the goal of perfection and the sanction of a moral divine? What, then, is the symbolics of desire, the symbolics of justice and creativity?

I'll describe a journey, one that beings with a recognition of the ambiguity of our actions and then moves to an imagination that encompasses the amorality of the religious.

Theophus Smith describes the power of conjure in African-American religion. Conjure is the eliciting of spiritual power which transforms internalized oppression, and evokes and sustains acts of political transformation through a complex interaction of religious symbol systems, ritual performances and political action.[14] By definition, conjure escapes the dualistic oppositions of good and evil, sacred and profane. Working with Derrida's notion of the *pharmokos*, Smith claims that that which can heal can also harm.[15]

In some African religions and in the African-American religion of Vodou, Anthony Pinn claims that we find not only a recognition of the ambiguity of our own sacral activities but a recognition of the ambiguity of the divine. In his description of Orisha service in the United States, the orishas are seen as "neutral energy forces affecting our lives," energy that "can be used for good or ill."[16] It is startling, to the western eye, to see a clear recognition of the amorality of the divine: " . . . [i]ndeed, there is no force in heaven which dictates a morality."[17]

If the forces that create and sustain us and the universe are amoral, what is the source of any particular moral vision? For there is a strong moral sense in orisha service, a morality that seeks to create and sustain a "proper relationship with the service, ancestors, other humans, and the earth."[18] We learn how to be moral not from God, not from a "being beyond-being," but from the experiences, teachings and guidance conveyed to us by other human beings.[19]

What differentiates communal responses to constitutive energies? Our perception of these energies is socially constructed – the creation, and legacy, of our ancestors. Our mobilization of these energies is the creation of the interpretive communities in which we are formed. This energy can be used, and is used, for moral and political purposes: justifying our superiority and control of others, or, conversely, eliciting greater respect for and openness to others.

In her novels, Toni Morrison expresses this sensibility. In *Sula*, for example, she describes a nondualistic view of good and evil, and a clearly humanly-based rejection by African-Americans of violence and domination. The time frame of the novel is 1919–65, a time of violent and systemic racism: lynching, mob violence and harassment; legalized job discrimination and segregation.

What was taken by outsiders to be slackness, slovenliness or even generosity was in fact a full recognition of the legitimacy of forces other than good ones... They did not believe Nature was ever askew – only inconvenient. Plague and drought were as "natural" as springtime. If milk could curdle, God knows robins could fall. The purpose of evil was to survive it and they determined (without ever knowing they had made up their minds to do it) to survive floods, white people, tuberculosis, famine and ignorance. They knew anger well but not despair, and they didn't stone sinners for the same reason they didn't commit suicide – it was beneath them.[20]

Despair and violence were "beneath them": this is the gift of a communal legacy of resilience and respect, expressed as well by Patrick Chamoiseau in *Texaco*. Chamoiseau writes of those who knew "through which vices to rifle in order to stumble on virtue."[21] And, in so doing, we receive, we express a humanity of solicitude, tenderness, and dreams:

> I was surrounded by that solicitude which Quarters breed. I was given reinvigorating teas, hardy soups, bay rum rubs. I received nets of tenderness, cast seines full of dreams in which hands were held together... Each one of them tried to bring life back to my eyes.[22]

And, in return for this gift of solicitude, the protagonist of *Texaco*, Marie-Sophie, is able to give life to others:

> I had become something like the center of this resistance against the unrelenting beke. He took note of me himself. He came to me every day on errands of hate. The women handed me their swaddled misfortunes which I was unable to undo and which terrified me. All I had to do was look all-knowing, not wide-eyed before their fateful nonsense. And the little I would say to them would be enough to bring them back (for yet another moment) to the courage of living. That attitude gave the grave face and intense eyes men run away from.[23]

What brings us back "to the courage of living"? This is a matter of alchemy and desire. I see the religious not in terms of right beliefs and sure foundations, but as responses to amoral powers that can be given self-critically moral purposes. There are alchemical processes that have turned the bare bones of onto-theology into fierce, compassionate and sustained movements for justice, and we can do the same.

II.   An a-theology of wonder, suffering, memory, and desire

Lives don't make sense in reality, they come and go and often, like tsunamis, with the same crash, and they sweep away the dregs stagnating in your head like they were relics, which are treasures to you but don't stand still.[24]

Chamboiseau, Texaco

I write as one of the masses, immersed fully in the wonder, pain, joy, fears and hopes of the everyday. What is the religious symbolic, the poetics of desire that evokes meaning, that compels our work for justice without desire for the transcendent, without desire for the "*tout autre*," without desire for "becoming divine"? I am an atheist, not just in the sense of the binary opposition of belief/unbelief, but in the sense of the symbolics of desire.[25] I write as one of those who does not desire God. We do not desire to become divine, but rather, we work to be human, "spirit and dust," and our prayers are venues opening us to our embeddedness in nature, in history, with all their peril and promise.[26] The horizon of our being is not "becoming divine," but being human, "vibrantly imperfect," attuned to the shifting forms of reciprocity between us and "all our relations."[27] At times we respond to the needs of vulnerable others, at times others respond to our vulnerablity and our needs in an exchange that nourishes and sustains us, but cannot be calculated, predicted nor controlled (does anyone give more than infants and children? what love, delight and awe they unleash in the worlds of those who respect them).[28]

I am dependent on the theological and political work of other feminists and womanists in a dual sense. Grounded in this work, I find untenable declarations of the impossibility of female subjectivity and agency.[29] We turn to the work and lives of the oppressed for a dual reason. Here there is not only an indictment of structures of bias, exclusion and oppression, the legitimacy of religious traditions and social and political institutions challenged by lives shattered and voices broken, but construals of subjectivity, community and agency that are partial *and* are powerful.[30] Womanist theologians and ethicists, for example, celebrate and analyze the life and work of all those, who though oppressed, have "made a way out of no way."[31]

There are two realities in the writings of many African-American and American Indian peoples: an indictment of the dominating alchemy given my cultures most precious and constitutive ideals, and, visions of subjectivity, agency, freedom and community that resonate with the construction of self, desire and world that I know. Patricia Williams, a critical legal theorist, uses the analogy of "alchemy" to describe the centuries-long process of giving political form to the ideals of equal rights, freedom and justice.

> To say that blacks never fully believed in rights is true. Yet it is also true that blacks believed in them so much and so hard that we gave them life where there was none before ... This was the resurrection of life from ashes four hundred years old. The making of something out of nothing took immense alchemical fire-the fusion of a whole nation and the kindling of several generations ...[32]

The language of rights, the logic of divine justice, can be mobilized for justice, and can also be part of an alchemy of distance, isolation and domination.[33]

Such a plethora of foundational "experiences" or encounters: a "god" who evokes love and justice, Schleiermacher's absolute dependence, Kierkegardian and Pauline "fear and trembling," Carol Christ's "great matrix of love," Tillichian "acceptance," Buber's "I and Thou," Derrida's "*tout autre*," Jantzen and Irigary's "becoming divine." How odd, how human, the impulse to reduce them to one, or to rank them, "ours" as the revelation, "theirs" as natural theology or mere human projection. What if the matter of the religious is far more complex, and far more diverse than can be reduced to any monism or any dualism of authentic/inauthentic, liberating/oppressive, freeing/reifying?[34] What all of these construals of the religious have in common is not any specific content, but their power, a power that is intrinsically ambiguous, the power of conjure, the power to heal and to harm.

Wonder

Say what you will, do what you will, life is not to be measured by the ell of its sorrows. For that reason, I, Marie-Sophie Laborieux, despite the river my eyes have shed, have always looked at the world in a good light. But how many wretched ones around me have choked the life out of their bodies?

. . .

But I never had these bad thoughts. With so many rags to launder in misery's rivers, I've never had time for melancholy. What's more, in the few moments life has left me, I learned to let my heart gallop on the saddle of intense feelings, to live life, as they say, to let her be. And note if you please that neither laughter nor smiles have ever tired the skin of my lips.

Chamboiseau, Texaco

Many long for the wholly other, yet we revel in the fully now. Our desire is the present in its abundance and wonder; our desire for justice a way of honoring the integrity of that which is, our political work an exuberant "virtuosity in the face of adversity."[35] This is not the religion of the "healthy-minded" criticized by William James, an unabashed embrace of life's pleasures and a resolute denial of life's horrors.[36] No, this is a passion, not for perfection, but for the "vibrantly imperfect" possible. It is not a passion for transgression, but a passion for the excess, the depth, the wonder, and the possibilities of the every day. We work for justice with the tools of the present, and because of our love and respect for the present texture of lives. Not all is just, not all is honored, but that which *is valued* serves as the fulcrum from which to challenge all that devalues life. To us, it is the passion for the impossible that seems bereft, isolated from the beauty and vibrant connections that evoke respect and can be mobilized to work for justice.

As the quote from Chamboiseau makes clear, here we have a full awareness that life does destroy many people: injustice destroys lives and drives people mad. And yet, to again quote Chamboiseau: "To be part of it [City], I chose to act. And like the local youths say about politics around here: I chose battle over tears."[37]

Our passion is one of connection, open-eyed, and aware of the fragility of the matrix in which we live. Brock and Thistlethewaite describe a meditation on breath that can lead us to know the significance of these connections.

When we are trapped in the musings of our minds, wandering the temporal spheres of memory and future, . . . we are not fully in the present. When our whole being is fully attuned to the present, . . . enormous energy and life are unleashed. The discipline of learning to breathe in such restorative ways comes in community with others who breathe . . . In this breathing together we can inspire each other with grace and compassion to conspire for change.[38]

Being in the present can bring stasis and closure. Being in the present may also open us, connect us, and empower us with dynamic fullness. As Chamboiseau states, "draw in excess from those you love."[39]

What we draw "from those we love" can be described, but not trapped in definitive formulations, in truths that can be reflected in the logic of belief/unbelief. Leslie Marmon Silko, for example, describes the truths that are communal, the legacy of the people of the Laguna Pueblo, truths whose meaning is intrinsically open and multifaceted:

> Communal storytelling was a self-correcting process in which listeners were encouraged to speak up if they noted an important fact or detail omitted. The people were happy to listen to two or three different versions of the same event . . . The ancient Pueblo people sought a communal truth, not an absolute. For them this truth lived somewhere within the web of differing versions, disputes over minor points, outright contradictions tangling with old feuds and village rivalries.[40]

This "living truth" is a truth of engagement and desire, a way of being in a world we can never fully understand, not a metaphysics of how things really are.[41]

This is not a story with an end, although it is a story with many meanings. It is an engagement with life, and a passion for its wealth. It is not hope for an end, for a lasting resolution: it is not a longing for the totally new nor is it the expectation of the repetition of the same, the endless return of the known and the expected. Morrison writes of our desire for, our solace in, the rhythms of the present, their openness and their resonance:

> In ocean hush a woman black as firewood is singing. Next to her is a younger woman whose head rests on the singing woman's lap.
>
> . . . .
>
> There is nothing to beat this solace which is what Piedade's song is about, although the words evoke memories neither one has ever had: of reaching age in the company of the other; of speech shared and divided bread smoking from the fire; the unambivalent bliss of going home to be at home – the ease of coming back to love begun. When the oceans heave sending rhythms of water ashore, Piedade looks to see what has come. Another ship, perhaps, but different, heading to port, crew and passengers, lost and saved, atremble, for they have been disconsolate for some time. Now they will rest before shouldering the endless work they were created to do down here in Paradise.[42]

Memory / Generations

Write The Word? *No. But tie the knot with life again, yes.*[43]

Chamboiseau, Texaco

Ours is not the desire of becoming divine. It is the passion of "shouldering the endless work" in "Paradise," of tying the knot with life again. We "tie the knot" not because of master narratives of destiny and promise, of resolution won, but we live out of the threads of connection, the threads of recognition within which we come to life. Chamboiseau recounts a tale of persistent work in face of defeat:

> I wanted to show strength, and so never, . . . would I stand round taking pity on my fate like I so often felt like doing . . . Under the dull eyes of the others, I lifted my poles back up, straightened my partitions, spread my oilcloths . . . And my tears drowned in my sweat. The others looked at me for a long time, then, one by one, the women went back to their own wreckage.[44]

How do we gain the will to continue, to let "our tears drown in our sweat"? This persistent affirmation of life does not emerge from an exercise of will; it is not the result of our reason, it is, rather, the gift, the legacy, of generations.

Brock and Thistlethewaite point to the fragility of "truth" and the need of a social movement to hold the "truths" of compassion and commitment.[45] This "holding" is communal and generational, a form of power expressed through its fragility and not in spite of it. This power of generations is described well by Kasimu and Karen Baker-Fletcher. In their systematic theology, they add another category to the well-known list of eschatology, ecclesiology, christology, anthropology and doctrine of God. They speak of generations: the collective matrix of our being; the past which engendered us, the present and future we engender. They cite the cosmological community principle *muntu*, of the Bantu peoples of Southeastern Africa: "I am because We are; and We are because I am."[46]

> On a plantation, on a slave ship, on a farm, in the city, in the suburbs, in the church, in a mosque, in the wilderness – we have found and must continue to find ways to carve our sacred time and space to pass on tools of wisdom and survival to our children, our children's children, and one another.[47]

Karen and Kasimu Baker-Fletcher also remind us that "generations must not be romanticized": "[w]hen we idealize the elders we learn far less of what life has taught them or can teach us than if we learn from their strenths and their weaknesses."[48]

This legacy of virtuosity, of living fully in the "vibrantly imperfect" possible, is described as well by Leslie Marmon Silko. She sees this as the gift of Laguna story-telling, an oral tradition that recounts even "disturbing or provocative" events.

> The effect of these inter-family or inter-clan exchanges is the reassurance of each person that she or he will never be separated or apart from the clan . . . Neither the worst blunders or disasters nor the greatest financial prosperity and joy will ever be permitted to isolate anyone from the rest of the group . . . You are never the first to suffer a grave loss or profound humiliation. You are never the first, and you understand that you will probably not be the last to commit or be victimized by a repugnant act.[49]

We are not the first to suffer and fail, and we will not be the last. We are not the first to also embody a measure of justice, and we will not be the last.

To see the world through the lenses of compassion and empathy, to create our world with this passion for life-affirming justice, is not a duty, a demand, an obligation or a sacrifice. It is, rather, a blessing and a gift. This life of seeking justice does have costs, but the ability to respect others enough to have a passion for justice, the ability to mourn and rage our own suffering and that of others, is not an onerous task, but a rich legacy. Its source is not our own achievement, but the gift of the generations who shaped us, the ancestors who gave ethical and aesthetic form to the energy of life.[50]

This symbolic of religion has, at its core, horror and rage at injustice and a fierce longing for justice, for personal and individual institutions that embody respect.

What do we mean by justice? What is the criteria for our work? respect for the other. Patricia Williams claims that if we respect each other, we "give to all of society's objects and untouchables the rights of privacy, integrity, and self-assertion; [we] give them distance and respect."[51] Carol Lee Sanchez describes the respect at the core of the traditions of people of the Laguna Pueblo, recognizing the integrity of "all my relations," human, natural, animal, and the dynamic balance that can exist between all of us.[52] This is not the vulnerable face of Lévinas, but the compelling "you" of Buber's I–You relationship.[53] Lévinas describes a way some people see otherness, as threat, as vulnerable, as demand, and he tries to limit the violence against that other.[54] Within the work of feminist, womanist, and liberation theologians, we see, however, a basically different reception of otherness.[55] At its core, there is reciprocity. This reciprocity is expressed in Chamboiseau's description of building the Quarters:

> I was piling up all these things by my hutch, waiting for a hand.
>
> If someone gives you a hand, you have to stand ready with at least one canari of vegetables, with a piece of cod, a gallon of rum, glasses and madou. Once I was ready, I rang out the call . . . Then things went very fast. My hutch attracted other hutches . . . The very people on the slope lent a helping hand, gave advice, helped, shouldered each other.[56]

This is not caring for the vulnerable other. Nor is this reciprocity calculated, or constrained. It is, rather, the exuberant expression of mutuality.

Many of us cannot see the other, the face, the way Lévinas does. Our alternative seeing, one of curiosity and respect, is not a choice, but the gift of the ancestors. We see as we were seen; we love as we were loved.

What would it mean for our political organizing if we began with the premise that our passion for justice is not our achievement, but a gift? What if we realized that caring about injustice is not the result of our astute socio-political analyses, our compassion, our courage, and our will, but the result of being loved, recognized, and seen by others? Longing for justice, mourning and raging in the face of injustice is the gift of the ancestors; it is the gift of "all our relations." What would it mean if we focused on the blessing of respect? I do not know, but I want to find out.[57]

I know that this recognition does call us away from prophetic denunciation of the hard-heartedness and close-mindedness of others. It calls us from any satisfaction in merely denouncing structures and peoples who exploit or ignore others. When we acknowledge the strength and dignity of others, when we empathize with the suffering of others, when we cast our lot in acts of creating justice, our selves are enlarged by the blessing of openness, the blessings of an open heart, and the blessing of an enlivened imagination.

Conclusion

What then, is the religious? This is the name we give to those encounters, those energies, which are constitutive, but amoral; those encounters, those energies, which are vivid, compelling and meaningful, but fragile. This symbolic of desire is not better than other construals of the religious, for it has its own peril and promise.[58] It does lead to justice and it can also sustain structures of isolation and domination. I am not as aware of the fundamental, constitutive dangers of this logic as I would I like to be, but I can identify four. One of the greatest dangers is complacency: if we are relatively safe and comfortable, removed from the immediate costs of oppression, it is easy to relish the beauty of life and leave the work of building justice to those who are suffering direct injustice.

Another constitutive danger is settling for too little. If one foregoes the illusion of utopia, and chooses instead "connections that are real and hopes that are realizable," we may settle for reforms that are less far-reaching than is actually possible.[59] There is an element of madness, folly and excess in any work for justice – an exuberant overreaching of the limits of the present. Embedded as we are in complex networks of other actors, with other hopes and desires, we cannot tell the difference between what we can change and what we cannot. We cannot tell in advance of the struggle if we will succeed or fail; we cannot predict the ramifications of our actions in the present or the future. Our wager is more audacious: what improbable task, with which unfathomable and unpredictable results shall we undertake today?

Another constitutive risk, one true of any construal of the religious that valorizes religious ecstasy, and the intensity of religious experience, is that this mysticism, or this intense connection to other people, separates us from life and leads us to have disdain for "ordinary" life and "ordinary" people, who supposedly, do not know this ecstatic connection. The dangers are twofold: it is often difficult to translate the ecstasy of mystical experiences into the possibilities and demands of daily life. Rather than mysticism being a way of "illumining the everyday," it can be an escape from the everyday, or construed as more than the material, more valuable than the daily tasks of life.[60] These intense experiences and connections can also lead to disdain for other people. If this sense of connection and energy seems new to us, and our prior life seems meaningless or shallow in contrast to what we now know, we may project our prior meaninglessness onto others, assuming, to quote the camp song, that we know a love, a peace, a joy "that the world does not know."

In her novel *Paradise*, Morrison recounts the tragedy of a town that in escaping slavery and exclusion, defined itself as exclusive, and violently so, a town that in trying to give its youth safety, denied their vitality and creativity. *Even the energy of generations is amoral*: it can be used to stifle and bind, rather than to frame and nourish.

> How exquisitely human was the wish for permanent happiness, and how thin human imagination became trying to achieve it. Soon Ruby will be like any other country town: the young thinking of elsewhere; the old full of regret. The sermons will be eloquent but fewer and fewer will pay attention or connect them to everyday life. How can they hold

it together, he wondered, this hard-won heaven defined only by the absence of the unsaved, the unworthy and the strange? Who will protect them from their leaders?[61]

How can we acknowledge that there is no fundamental divide of us, the righteous, us the vanguard, us the enlightened, and the "unsaved, the unworthy and the strange?" We can "return to laughter," learning from the stranger within and the stranger outside, blessed with the legacy of seeing all as worthy of dignity, privacy and respect.[62] We can return to laughter, the generous laughter that relishes the irony of knowing that that which funds our morality is itself amoral, and morality, far from being the demand or gift of the divine, is the perilous and at times beautiful human response to the energy and wonder of life.

Notes

Return to Laughter is an anthropological novel written by Laura Bohannen under the pseudonym of Elenore Smith Bowen, and first published in 1954. Bohannen, an American anthropologist, describes her attempts to "objectively" study tribal peoples in Nigeria. Bohannen describes the breakdown of her conviction of cultural superiority, from her initial arrogant impatience with education into the names of different plants, to her discovery of a communal social logic of rage, laughter, forgiveness and intensity that proved more resilient in the face of social crisis than her own dualistic moral vocabulary of good and evil, friend and foe. Elenore Smith Bowen, *Return to Laughter: An Anthropological Novel* (New York: Anchor Books, 1964).

1 Jean-Luc Marion, *God Without Being* (Chicago: The University of Chicago Press, 1991).
2 Grace Jantzen provides a philosophy of religion from a feminist perspective. Building on the work of Luce Irigaray, she develops a new imaginary of religion, a feminist symbolic of natality and flourishing to replace a masculinist symbolic of death. In so doing, her focus is on a symbolics of desire and not the justification of belief: "What might happen, then, if we were to relinquish the preoccupation with the rational justification of beliefs and the evaluation of truth-claims and try to follow the path of desire to/for the divine?" (p. 65)
    In this essay I follow Grace Jantzen and the recasting of the philosophy of religion in terms of the "opening of desire" and not the insistence on belief, and hence, the "centrality of evidence argument, counter-argument and so on." "But once we note that this is the case for either pole of the binary, then a gap opens up, a possibility of thinking differently, and asking whether, instead of this insistence upon belief, we might focus on other possibilities – love, for example, or longing, or desire...what if instead we were to explore...the opening of desire that interrupts this emphasis on belief with longing for the divine horizon?" p. 65 and chapter 4. Grace Jantzen, *Becoming Divine: Towards a Feminist Philosophy of Religion* (Bloomington: Indiana University Press, 1999).
3 Thee Smith, "W/Riting Black Theology," *Forum* 5: 4 (December 1980), pp. 50–1.
4 For a representative critique of the claims of metaphysical theology and the methods of onto-theology, see, Grace Jantzen, *Becoming Divine*; Philippa Berry and Andrew Wernick, *Shadow of Spirit: Postmodernism and Religion* (London and New York: Routledge, 1992) Paul Lakeland, *Postmodernity: Christian Identity in a Fragmented Age* (Minneapolis: Fortress Press, 1997).
5 Jantzen, *Becoming Divine*, p. 97.
6 "Religion marks the place of the absolute *for us*, its path, the hope of its fulfillment. All too often that fulfillment has been postponed or transferred to some transcendental time and

place. It has not been interpreted as the infinite that resides within us and among us, the god in us, the Other for us, becoming with and in us . . . This God, are we capable of imagining it as a woman? Can we dimly see it as the perfection of our subjectivity?" Luce Irigaray, *Sexes and Genealogies*, trans. Gillian C. Gill (New York: Columbia University Press, 1993), p. 63.

7   Sharon D. Welch, *A Feminist Ethic of Risk* (Minneapolis: Fortress Press, 1990).

8   Karl Barth, "the Question of Natural Theology," pp. 49–86, *in Church Dogmatics: A Selection*, selected and with an Introduction by Helmut Gollwitzer, translated and edited by G. W. Bromiley (New York: Harper, 1962). See, also, Derrida's contrast between legitimate and illegitimate forms of messianic expectation: "Now, if there is a spirit of Marxism which I will never be ready to renounce, it is not only the critical idea or the questioning stance (a consistent deconstruction must insist on them even as it also learns that this is not the last or first word). It is even more a certain emancipatory and *messianic* affirmation, a certain experience of the promise that one can try to liberate from any dogmatics and even from any metaphysico-religious determination, from any *messianism*. And a promise must promise to be kept, that is, not to remain "spiritual" or "abstract," but to produce events, new effective forms of action, practice, organization, and so forth" (p. 89). *Specters of Marx: The State of the Debt, the Work of Mourning, and the New International*, trans. Peggy Kamuf (New York: Routledge, 1994). See also John D. Caputo's thorough discussion of the critique of concrete messianism, religious violence and coercion in *The Prayers and Tears of Jacques Derrida: Religion Without Religion* (Bloomington: Indiana University Press, 1997), introduction, chapter 3, and conclusion.

9   Jacques Derrida, *The Gift of Death*, trans. David Willis (Chicago: University of Chicago Press). See also Caputo's exploration of the theological and philosophical significance of Derrida's thought, *The Prayers and Tears of Jacques Derrida*; Emmanuel Lévinas, *Basic Philosophical Writings*, ed. Adriaan T. Peperzak, Simon Critchley, and Robert Bernasconi (Bloomington: Indiana University Press, 1996), p. 29.

10 Nietzsche, *Twilight of the Idols, or, How One Philosophizes With a Hammer*, trans. Richard Polt (Indianapolis, Indiana: Hackett, 1997).

11 Toni Morrison, *Paradise* (New York: Alfred A. Knopf, 1998), p. 306.

12 Karen Baker-Fletcher and Garth Kasimu Baker-Fletcher, *My Sister, My Brother: Womanist and Xodus God-Talk* (Maryknoll, New York: Orbis, 1997), p. 180; see also Birch and Cobb's discussion of trusting "life as the creative good" (p. 180). Charles Birch and John B. Cobb, Jr. *The Liberation of Life: From the Cell to the Community* (Cambridge: Cambridge University Press, 1981).

13 Rosabeth Moss Kanter extols the creativity of global capitalism, and argues that it is fed by the skills and worldviews of "cosmopolitans": "Cosmopolitans are rich in three intangible assets . . . that translate into preeminence and power in a global economy: concepts – the best and latest knowledge and ideas; competence – the ability to operate at the highest standards of any place anywhere; and connections – the best relationships, which provide access to the resources of other people and organizations around the world." Rosabeth Moss Kanter, *World Class: Thriving Locally in the Global Economy* (New York: Simon and Schuster, 1995), p. 23.

14 Theophus Smith, *Conjuring Culture: Biblical Formations of Black America* (Oxford: Oxford University Press, 1994), pp. 3–12, 18. Smith's understanding of "conjure" is different in emphasis from that of Derrida in *Specters of Marx*. Derrida also refers to "conjuration" as "the appeal that causes to come forth . . . what *is not there* at the present moment of the appeal" (p. 41). Yet his focus is on conjure as exorcism, the "destruction" and "disavowal" of a "malignant, demonized, diabolized force" (48). Smith's "conjure" is performative and creative: the evocation of freedom, of particular forms of life, and not primarily "certifying death" (Derrida, p. 48).

15   Smith, *Conjuring Culture*, pp. 31, 43. Jacques Derrida, "Plato's Pharmacy," in *Dissemination*, trans. Barbara Johnson (Chicago: University of Chicago Press, 1981).

16   Anthony B. Pinn, *Varieties of African American Religious Experience* (Minneapolis: Fortress Press, 1998), p. 101.

17   Ibid., p. 102.

18   Ibid., p. 72. See also the work of Karen McCarthy Brown for a thorough exploration of the moral sense of Haitian Vodou: Karen McCarthy Brown, "Alourdes: A Case Study of Moral Leadership in Haitian Vodou," in *Saints and Virtues*, ed. John Hawley (Berkeley: University of California Press, 1987); Karen McCarthy Brown, *Mama Lola: A Vodou Priestess in Brooklyn* (Berkeley: University of California Press, 1991).

19   Pinn, *Varieties of African American Religious Experience*, p. 102. See also Charles Long's discussion of the role of interpretive communities in *Significations*.

20   Toni Morrison, *Sula* (New York: Bantam, 1973), p. 90.

21   In *Texaco*, the winner of the Prix Goncourt, Patrick Chamoiseau traces one hundred and fifty years of post-slavery Caribbean history, told from the perspective of Marie-Sophie Labor-ieux, the daughter of a slave, who leads in the establishment of a shantytown on the outskirts of a Caribbean city. Patrick Chamoiseau, *Texaco*, translated from the French and Creole by Rose-Myriam Rejouis and Val Vinokurov (New York: Pantheon Books, 1997), p. 119.

22   Ibid., pp. 263–4.

23   Ibid., p. 341.

24   Ibid., p. 310.

25   Jantzen argues that "it would be more accurate to see atheism/theism not as itself the relevantly significant binary, but as one *pole* of a binary, the repressed other being every-thing else which is unacknowledged in the centrality of this pair" (p. 65). Jantzen claims that "the repressed other" is the "opening of desire that interrupts this emphasis on belief" (p. 65). Following Irigaray, she looks for a "new morning of the world," "developing a feminist philosophy of religion whose founding gesture is not the justification of beliefs which separates the "true" from the "false", but rather an imaginative longing for the divine in a reduplication of desire not content with the old gods but seeking the horizon and the foundation needed to progress between past and future" (Irigaray). Jantzen, *Becoming Divine*, p. 99.

26   This is an atheistic version of the theistic symbolic of "spirit and dust" developed by Karen Baker-Fletcher in *Sisters of Dust, Sisters of Spirit: Womanist Wordings on God and Creation* (Minneapolis: Fortress Press, 1998). The "atheism" highlights our acceptance of finitude and imperfection. I agree with Jantzen's symbolic of natality, but think the force of our full affirmation of finitude is clearer if we relinquish Irigaray's symbolic of perfection and Jantzen's symbolic of becoming divine. It is important to note however, that for Jantzen, "becoming divine" does not mean that finitude is devalued: "A symbolic of natality is not in any sense a denial of death or a pretense that death does not matter" (p. 152). "The acceptance of life is an acceptance of limits, which, after all, enable as much as they constrain: the boundless is beyond capacity. The obligation to become divine is not an obligation to become limitless; the quest for infinity would be a renunciation, not a fulfillment, of our gendered, embodied selves" (p. 154). "Rather than squander our energy in a futile struggle against finitude, we can rejoice in the (limited) life we have as natals and act for love of the world" (p. 155).

27   In our affirmation of the present and the everyday, we address the critique voiced by Rieder: "For some time now, the cultural left has been going around in a funk, deconstructing everything in sight, wavering between scolding a culture that seems hostile to liberation and conducting a promiscuous search for signs of resistance to that culture's dominating symbols. But in all this rage for representation, the left has often committed

soul murder too, projecting disappointment onto the objects of its gaze, representing itself rather than the complex reality of a vibrantly imperfect culture." Jonathan Rieder, *New York Times Book Review*, December 26, 1998, p. 15.

28   Cynthia Willett, for example, contrasts a patriarchal (and elitist) symbolic of self and desire with resources for self, community, freedom, and desire seen in African American experience and in the mother–child interaction. She describes the sensually mediated logic of intersubjectivity found in the writing of Frederick Douglass, who evoked the power of the touch of his mother and grandmother to create a self correlated with community and openness (pp. 8, 170). She also turns to Daniel Stern and the analysis of the activity of the infant in relationship to the mother to show the limits of views that see this experience as inchoate and passive, as either one-sided or amorphous and prior to meaning, meaning occurring only through the phallic intervention of language (pp. 24, 43, 47). Cynthia Willett, *Maternal Ethics and Other Slave Moralities* (New York: Routledge, 1995).

29   Irigaray claims that "[t]he (male) ideal other has been imposed upon women by men. Man is supposedly woman's more perfect other, her model, her essence. The most human and the most divine goal woman can conceive is to become *man*. If she is to become woman, if she is to accomplish her female subjectivity, woman needs a god who is a figure for the perfection of *her* subjectivity. *Sexes and Genealogies*, p. 64.

30   Iris Marion Young describes five faces of oppression and their constraints on agency and subjectivity in *Justice and the Politics of Difference* (Princeton: Princeton University Press, 1990).

31   Central to the work of womanist theologians and ethicists is the recognition that these limits have not completely shaped the agency and subjectivity of people of color. D. Soyini Madison, for example, begins her collection of writings by women of color, by explaining the significance of this saying: "I remember my mother standing, in 'colored woman' style, her arms akimbo and her head tilted to the side, speaking quietly but forcefully in a tone that could scare a bull. She would willfully declare: 'Being the woman that I am I will make a way out of no way.' These were *mother's* words, but they are also the words and the will of *all* women of color who assert who they are, who create sound out of silence, and who build worlds out of remnants. . . . *The Woman That I Am* is a proclamation of the 'I' in each individual woman's identity, but it is also a testament to the collective power of women of color," p. 1. *The Woman That I Am: The Literature and Culture of Contemporary Women of Color* (New York: St. Martin's Press, 1994).

As an example of womanist theology and ethics, see also the works of Karen Baker-Fletcher; Emilie M. Townes, *In A Blaze of Glory: Womanist Spirituality As Social Witness* (Nashville: Abingdon Press, 1995); Emilie M. Townes, ed., *Embracing the Spirit: Womanist Perspectives on Hope, Salvation and Transformation* (Maryknoll, New York: Orbis Books, 1997); Katie G. Cannon, *Black Womanist Ethics* (Atlanta: Scholars Press, (1988); Delores Williams, *Sisters in the Wilderness: The Challenge of Womanist God-Talk* (Maryknoll, New York: Orbis, 1993).

32   Patricia J. Williams, *The Alchemy of Race and Rights: Diary of Law Professor* (Cambridge, MA: Harvard University Press, 1991), p. 163.

33   Philip Arnold describes the way the language of "utopia" justified the "complete annihilation of indigenous people": "the hope of a technological utopian dream was expressed at the 1892 Columbian Exposition in Chicago. At this World's Fair and those that followed, Lakota people specifically, and indigenous people from around the world more generally, were presented as the clear and identifiable impediments to a modern view of progress" (p. 94) In the writing of L. Frank Baum (later the author of *The Wizard of Oz*), there was the explicit claim that "the realization of this utopian dream . . . required the complete annihilation of indigenous people, . . . in order to protect our civilization" (p. 88), Philip

Arnold, "Black Elk and Book Culture," *Journal of the American Academy of Religion* 67/1 (March 1999).

34   For an alternative examination of the significance of the diversity of religious experience, see Laurel C. Schneider, *Re-Imaging the Divine: Confronting the Backlash against Feminist Theology* (Cleveland: Pilgrim Press, 1998). Schneider argues for a monistic polytheism that "lends authority and legitimacy to revelatory religious experience in all of its diversity" (p. 175). Where I differ, fundamentally, from Schneider's thought-provoking proposal is her use of metaphors of divine certainty, finality, power and goodness.

35   Chamboiseau, *Texaco*, p. 33.

36   Eric Lott uses this metaphor to describe the artistic power of the jazz musician Charlie Parker: "Jazz was a struggle which pitted mind against the perversity of circumstance, and . . . in this struggle blinding virtuosity was the best weapon." "Double V, Double-Time: Bebop's Politics of Style," in *Jazz Among the Discourses*, ed. Krin Gabbard (Durham: Duke University Press, 1995), p. 243.

37   William James, *The Varieties of Religious Experience* (Cambridge, MA: Harvard University Press, 1985). James' critique of "healthy-mindedness" is found in lectures four and five. These lectures were delivered as the Gifford Lectures on Natural Religion at Edinburgh University in 1901 and 1902.

38   Chamboiseau, *Texaco*, p. 34.

39   Rita Nakashima Brock and Susan Brooks Thistlethewaite, *Casting Stones: Prostitution and Liberation in Asia and the United States* (Minneapolis: Fortress Press, 1996), p. 279.

40   Leslie Marmon Silko, "Landscape, History and the Pueblo Imagination," in *The Woman that I Am*, ed. D. Soyini Madison, p. 502.

41   Ibid., p. 499.

42   Morrison, *Paradise*, p. 318.

43   Chamboiseau, *Texaco*, p. 294.

44   Ibid., p. 340.

45   Brock and Thistlethewaite, *Casting Stones*, p. 279.

46   Karen and Kasimu Baker-Fletcher, *My Sister, My Brother*, pp. 203–4.

47   Ibid., p. 178.

48   Ibid., pp. 178, 184.

49   Silko, "Landscape, History and the Pueblo Imagination," p. 506.

50   Pinn, *Varieties of African American Religious Experience*, pp. 10–102.

51   Patricia Williams, *The Alchemy of Race and Rights*, p. 165.

52   Carol Lee Sanchez is a native New Mexican of Laguna Pueblo, Lakota, and Lebanese heritage. She states that "the most fundamental meaning of the word *Sacred* for Native Americans is 'entitled to reverence and respect' . . . American Indians believe the universe and everything in it is 'entitled to reverence and respect' . . . Thus the Tribal Principle of Relationship, that we are all related, is a natural extension of this belief. The Tribes teach that when we are disrespectful, irreverent, or abusive to the inhabitants of our environment, they will abandon us" (p. 224). Attention to "all our relations," human, animal, plant, and mineral, is the ground of living a good life, or "walking in Beauty." If we pay attention to "all our relations," we see where we are abusive and out of balance, and we gain insight in how harmony and balance may be restored (p. 211). "Animal, Vegetable, and Mineral," in *Ecofeminism and the Sacred*, ed. Carol J. Adams, (New York: Continuum, 1994), pp. 207–28.

53   Martin Buber, *I and Thou*, (New York: Charles' Scribner's Son 1970).

54   See Jantzen's thorough critique of Lévinas' reification of the "vulnerable" face: "what sort of symbolic does it bespeak and reinforce if the most insistent thing that comes to mind in being face to face with the Other is the desire to kill? Even granting that this is what

Lévinas sees as the violent logic of western ontology, in which mastery is the founding gesture and killing is its logical conclusion, to speak of this in terms of individual desire and temptation is shocking. ... Why the impulse to kill? Why not, say, an impulse to smile, or feed, or kiss, or converse? Why the assumed hostility, what Lévinas later writes of as 'the face of the neighbor in its persecuting hatred'? .... Could he say what he does if the face which confronts him is the face of an infant? a mother? one natal greeting another?" (p. 239). See also pages 237–53, Jantzen, *Becoming Divine*.

55   For feminist and womanist explorations of mutuality and reciprocity, see, for example, Rosemary Radford Ruether, *Women and Redemption: A Theological History*, (Minneapolis: Fortress Press, 1998); Rosemary Radford Ruether, *Gaia and God: An Ecofeminist Theology of Earth Healing* (San Francisco: HarperSanFrancisco, 1992); Carter Heyward, *Touching Our Strength: The Erotic as Power and the Love of God* (San Francisco: Harper and Row, 1989); Catherine Keller, *From a Broken Web: Separation, Sexism and Self* (Boston: Beacon, 1986); Chung Hyun Kyung, *Struggle to be the Sun Again: Introducing Asian Women's Theology* (Maryknoll, NY: Orbis, 1990); Ada Mariá Isási-Diáz, *Mujerista Theology* (Maryknoll, NY: Orbis, 1997); Rebecca Chopp. *The Power to Speak: Feminism, Language, God* (New York: Crossroad, 1989); Mary Daly, *Gyn/Ecology: the Metaethics of Radical Feminism* (Boston: Beacon Press, 1985); Paula Cooey, *Religious Imagination and the Body: A Feminist Analysis* (New York: Oxford University Press, 1994); Rita Nakashima Brock, *Journeys by Heart: A Christology of Erotic Power* (New York: Crossroad, 1991); Sallie McFague, *The Body of God: An Ecological Theology* (Minneapolis: Fortress Press, 1993).

56   Chamboiseau, *Texaco*, p. 300.

57   I have been an activist in left and feminist politics all of my adult life. This is not the attitude that fueled our protests, our demands for social justice and our denunciations of oppressive institutions and individuals.

58   I have followed here the example set by Roger S. Gottlieb in "The Transcendence of Justice and the Justice of Transcendence: Mysticism, Deep Ecology and Political Life," *Journal of the American Academy of Religion*, 67/1 (March 1999), pp. 149–66. Gottlieb disavows any metaphysical grounding for his vision of mysticism, describes the mysticism of "deep ecology" clearly, and yet describes what he sees as four intrinsic dangers of this form of mysticism.

59   Pinn, p. 184.

60   Gottlieb, "The vision of mysticism offered here will not satisfy everyone. It is a particularly non-metaphysical view in which ultimate reality is pretty much exhausted by 'ordinary' reality. Of course, when illuminated by the sparks of mystical experience, 'ordinary' reality can shine quite brightly – as in the old Zen story that identifies true enlightenment with simply seeing 'a mountain as a mountain and a river as a river,'" p. 164

61   Morrison, *Paradise*, p. 306. For another discussion of the importance of generational connections, and yet a recognition of the oppressive potential and actuality of those connections, see Isási-Diáz, *Mujerista Theology*, pp. 137–44.

62   "They knew how to live at close quarters with tragedy, how to live with their own failure and yet laugh. They knew the terror of a broken society, where brother's hand is raised against brother in hate and fear; they knew how to come back, brother to brother, and create life anew... these people... who all know they may themselves be faithless and crippled, and who all know that they build on shifting sand, have yet the courage to build what they know will fall... It is the laughter of people who value love and friendship and plenty, who have lived with terror and death and hate." Bowen, *Return to Laughter*, p. 297.

INDEX